Oracle Backup & Recovery:
Expert Secrets for Using RMAN and Data Pump

Oracle In-Focus Series

Kamran Agayev Agamehdi
Aman Sharma

First of all, I would like to thank God, the Almighty, for giving me the knowledge, vision, and ability to proceed and for making everything possible by giving me strength and courage to do this work. It is only through His grace that achievement can truly be accomplished

I would also like to thank to my best Oracle friend and the co-author of this book, Aman Sharma, for his contribution. He is an impressive DBA with a deep understanding of Oracle and this book would not be complete without his help.

Finally, I would like to thank all my family members, especially my father. All the support he has provided me over the years was the greatest gift anyone has ever given me. It is through him that I first grasped the importance of learning.

I dedicate this book to my beloved country Azerbaijan, to my lovely family and especially to my father for his unconditional love and support throughout my life and my career.

Kamran Agayev Agamehdi

Oracle Backup and Recovery:
Expert Secrets for Using RMAN and Data Pump

By Kamran Agayev Agamehdi & Aman Sharma

Copyright © 2011 by Rampant TechPress. All rights reserved.
Printed in the United States of America.
Published in Kittrell, North Carolina, USA.
Oracle In-focus Series: Book 42
Series Editor: Donald K. Burleson
Production Manager: Robin Rademacher and Jennifer Stanley
Production Editor: Valerre Aquitaine
Cover Design: Janet Burleson
Printing History: June 2011 for First Edition

Oracle, Oracle7, Oracle8, Oracle8i, Oracle9i, Oracle10g and Oracle 11g are trademarks of Oracle Corporation.

Many of the designations used by computer vendors to distinguish their products are claimed as Trademarks. All names known by Rampant TechPress to be trademark names appear in this text as initial caps.

The information provided by the authors of this work is believed to be accurate and reliable. However, because of the possibility of human error by our authors and staff, Rampant TechPress cannot guarantee the accuracy or completeness of any information included in this work and is not responsible for any errors, omissions, or inaccurate results obtained from the use of information or scripts in this work.

ISBN 10: 0-9844282-3-2
ISBN 13: 978-0-9844282-3-6-0-9823061-69-12
Library of Congress Control Number: 2011925691

Table of Contents

Chapter 4: Restoring and Recovering the Database Using RMAN 115

Using the Online Code Depot

Purchase of this book provides complete access to the online code depot that contains sample code scripts. Any code depot scripts in this book are located at the following URL in zip format and ready to load and use:

rampant.cc/backup_recovery.htm

If technical assistance is needed with downloading or accessing the scripts, please contact Rampant TechPress at rtp@rampant.cc.

Conventions Used in this Book

It is critical for any technical publication to follow rigorous standards and employ consistent punctuation conventions to make the text easy to read. However, this is not an easy task. Within database terminology, there are many types of notation that can confuse a reader. For example, some Oracle utilities such as STATSPACK and TKPROF are always spelled in CAPITAL letters, while Oracle parameters and procedures have varying naming conventions in the database documentation. It is also important to remember that many database commands are case sensitive, are always left in their original executable form and never altered with italics or capitalization. Hence, all Rampant TechPress books follow these conventions:

- Parameters: All database parameters will be lowercase italics. Exceptions to this rule are parameter arguments that are commonly capitalized (KEEP pool, TKPROF); these will be left in ALL CAPS.

- Variables: All procedural language (e.g. PL/SQL) program variables and arguments will also remain in lowercase italics (*dbms_job, dbms_utility*).

- Tables & dictionary objects: All data dictionary objects are referenced in lowercase italics (*dba_indexes, v$sql*). This includes all *v$* and *x$* views (*x$kcbcbh, v$parameter*) and dictionary views (*dba_tables, user_indexes*).

- SQL: All SQL is formatted for easy use in the code depot, and all SQL is displayed in lowercase. The main SQL terms (select, from, where, group by, order by, having) will always appear on a separate line.

- Programs & Products: All products and programs that are known to the author are capitalized according to the vendor specifications (CentOS, VMware, Oracle, etc.). All names known by Rampant TechPress to be trademark names appear in this text as initial caps. References to UNIX are always made in uppercase.

Acknowledgements

This type of highly technical reference book requires the dedicated efforts of many people. Even though we are the authors, our work ends when we deliver the content. After each chapter is delivered, several Oracle DBAs carefully review and correct the technical content. After the technical review, experienced copy editors polish the grammar and syntax. The finished work is then reviewed as page proofs and turned over to the production manager, who arranges the creation of the online code depot and manages the cover art, printing distribution, and warehousing.

We really appreciate the great job done by Sabdar Syed and Hemant K. Chitale in the technical review they have made. A lot of professional effort and thought went into the book by these two experts. Not only were they friendly and extremely helpful, but they also passed on valuable ideas and tips on every chapter of the book. Thank you for you business guys!

Realistically, the authors play a small role in the development of this book, and we need to thank and acknowledge everyone who helped bring this book to fruition:

- **Robin Rademacher and Jennifer Stanley** for the production management including the coordination of the cover art, page proofing, printing, and distribution.

- **Valerre Q Aquitaine** for help in the production of the page proofs.

- **Janet Burleson** for exceptional cover design and graphics.

- **John Lavender** for assistance with the web site, and for creating the code depot and the online shopping cart for this book.

- **Don Burleson** for the opportunity given to write the book, for his support and belief.

With our sincerest thanks,

Kamran Agayev Agamehdi and Aman Sharma

Backup and Recovery Overview

Introduction to Backup and Recovery

The Oracle database presents a lot of powerful techniques for protecting the data and recovering it from any type of failure. Administering a database without having enough information about these techniques is very risky and by doing so, some part of the data or the whole database may be lost. A DBA's responsiblility is to know and practice all these techniques successfully so that they are ready in case the database becomes corrupted.

This book will first cover key backup and recovery principles and their importance to the DBA. Next, types of failures will be shown which are likely to occur in every system as well as the best way to address them. Since Oracle has a powerful mechanism to protect the database, it can be recovered in any situation by taking correct measures. The chapter concerning types of backups and recoveries made by RMAN will introduce the main types of backup and recovery made by the RMAN utility. These are explained briefly with real life scenarios in order to offer a better understanding of how and what happens.

The main concepts on backup and recovery of the database by using the RMAN utility are presented later in this book. RMAN is used to perform backup, restore and recover operations of an Oracle database. As a DBA, it is important to understand the main concepts such as channel allocation, type of RMAN backup files, backup retention policy and more in terms of making a backup of the database. Also shown will be the advanced recovery features of RMAN such as creating a duplicate database, creating a standby database and making a Block Media Recovery with simple commands and step-by-step video tutorials.

DBA Duties

Each DBA is responsible for the database which he/she maintains. This is the main duty of the DBA. As a DBA, there is a need to have a backup strategy for each database that exists. Moreover, an experienced DBA should be proactive with regard to problems likely to occur in the databases and use all Oracle suggested opportunities to prevent them, create a backup strategy in the best manner, and solve the problems promptly with the correct action.

It is common knowledge that database systems of huge companies are running 24/7. Even the lack of a database for a minute could lead to the dissatisfaction of clients and the loss of millions of dollars. Imagine being employed in a large bank, airline, big shopping network or a government office as a DBA and all of a sudden all the data is lost because of media failure (hard drive corruption). If there is not a backup of the database, it means that it cannot be recovered.

Loss of database for any company can result in bankruptcy. According to statistics of the National Archives & Records Administration in Washington, 60% of companies that lose their data will shut down within six months of the disaster. 93% of companies that lost their data center for 10 days or more due to a disaster filed for bankruptcy within one year of the disaster. 50% of businesses that found themselves without data management for this same time period filed for bankruptcy immediately. However, if the database is protected as recommended by Oracle, the database can be recovered in almost any situation.

There are two types of backup in the Oracle database: physical backup and logical backup. Physical backup is for backing up the physical operating system files that build up the database. This concept is examined further in the Chapter 3. Since transaction logging, i.e. redo logs, are based on physical changes, a physical backup can be used to restore and roll forward a database to any point in time.

Logical backup means backing up the logical structure of the database. By using the Data Pump utility, a backup of the logical structure of the database can be taken such as schemas, tables, views and such. This concept is highlighted in more detail in Chapter 14.

Many DBAs confuse the term restore with the term recover, but there is a clear difference between them. Restore is an operation in which a backup is extracted and made accessible to Oracle and recover is a process of applying archived redo log files to the restored backup of the database. For this, the database needs to run in archivelog mode. Below are examples provided for better understanding.

Scenario 1

On January 1, Bob came to work and took a backup of the database. Until January 10th, a huge amount of data is inserted into the database. To be able to recover the database, Bob runs the database in archivelog mode. However, he does not take any backup of the database during these 10 days. Being in archivelog mode, a lot of archived redo log files were created and Bob takes their backups as well. On January 10th, hard drives where all datafiles of the database resided crashed. Bob immediately restored the backup of the database which was taken on January 1 and recovered it by applying archived redo log files created after full backup. Then he opened the database and got all his data back.

This process can be viewed more thoroughly in the following figure:

Oracle Backup and Recovery

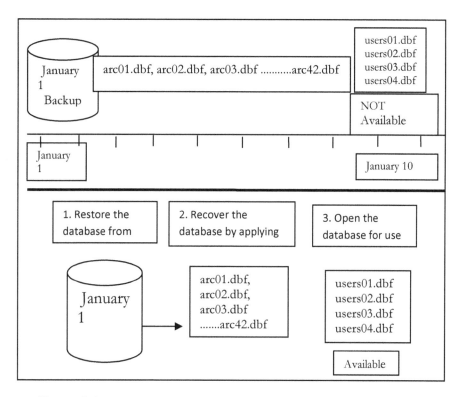

Figure 1.1: *Recovering Database by Applying Archived Redo Log Files*

The DBA must ensure that every transaction committed in Oracle will not be lost.

🔔 Data can be lost due to media failure or user error.

Errors and Failures Requiring Recovery

While using the Oracle database, some failures may be encountered. It is one of the basic functions of a DBA to prevent these failures, or if they occur, to define and solve them on time with correct techniques in place. Below, the main types of failures, the way they occur and key solutions are described.

1. Statement failure: This type of failure may occur when any SQL statement does not finish successfully for some reason. When this failure occurs, Oracle automatically detects it and rolls back the transaction. This type of failure may occur in one of the following events:

   - When a user wants to access an object which he/she has no authority to do so

   - When a user attempts to insert data in a column with incompatible data type

   - Due to huge amount of data, quota of user exceeds or no space can be found in database

   - During some logical errors

   - Insufficient privileges

If a user does not have access to a table, then he will get an error:

```
usr2@ORCL>insert into usr1.table1 values(1);
insert into usr1.table1 values(1)
                *

ERROR at line 1:
ORA-01031: insufficient privileges
usr2@ORCL>
```

From the example above, it appears that user usr2 does not have the *insert* privilege on the table of user usr1, so he gets an error. Imagine running a procedure consisting of hundreds of lines and at the end prior to the *commit* statement, this error occurs. It means that the procedure is rolled back and no changes are made to the database objects.

2. Invalid data: This error may occur in any operation which causes a constraint violation or while inserting data to a column with a different data type. The application/system should be designed to prevent such errors arising and being presented to users.

```
sys@ORCL>create table invalid_data (id number);

Table created.

sys@ORCL>alter table invalid_data add constraint unq_invalid_data unique
(id);

Table altered.

sys@ORCL>insert into invalid_data values(1);
```

Oracle Backup and Recovery

```
1 row created.

sys@ORCL>insert into invalid_data values(1);
insert into invalid_data values(1)
*

ERROR at line 1:
ORA-00001: unique constraint (sys.unq_invalid_data) violated
ssys@ORCL>
```

In the above example, data was not inserted due to constraint violation. The following is another example from the invalid data failure type:

```
sys@ORCL>insert into invalid_data values('hello');
insert into invalid_data values('hello')
                                  *

ERROR at line 1:
ORA-01722: invalid number
sys@ORCL>
```

If a user attempts to insert data with string type to a column with number type, she will get an error. This problem also should be solved in the application level and the datatype should be checked before being sent to the database.

3. Running out of space: When a user makes a change to a database and the user's quota or tablespace gets filled, the user gets an error and the statement is rolled back. The following example illustrates this type of situation:

```
sys@ORCL>create tablespace tbs_new datafile '/u01/oradata/br/tbs_new' SIZE
100K;
Tablespace created.

sys@ORCL>create table tab1 (id number) tablespace tbs_new;

Table created.

sys@ORCL>begin
  2   for i in 1..100000 loop
  3   insert into tab1 values(i);
  4   end loop;
  5   end;
  6   /
begin
*

error at line 1:
ORA-01653: unable to extend table SYS.TAB1 by 8 in tablespace tbs_new
ORA-06512: at line 3
sys@ORCL>
```

Errors and Failures Requiring Recovery

9

It should be clear from this example that if the tablespace's size is small, then any user may face this type of failure at any time. Say a nightly job is run which updates billing information of subscribers and suddenly the script stops running because of a space problem. If there are some *commit* statements in the code, then part of the data will be committed.

However, another part of the data, after having no space to continue script, will be uncommitted. This situation is unacceptable and the database needs to be recovered. If there are no *commit* statements except one at the end, then all the data will be rolled back and the job will fail. To avoid such failure, either control the size of the tablespace in the database or quota of the user or use the Resumable Space Allocation feature. Using this feature, the script is suspended, information about it is written in the *alert.log* file, and it is not interrupted and rolled back. Once the problem is resolved, the operations automatically resume.

4. Process failure: A connected user disconnects in an unusual way from the database. The reason may be the application that user employs or abnormal termination of the user's computer. In this situation, the background process PMON finds disconnected sessions, rolls them back and releases their locks. As DBAs, there is no need to intervene. Oracle discovers this failure automatically and solves it by using the PMON process.

5. User error failure: Dropping a table by accident, updating a table which consists of millions of rows without putting the WHERE clause and committing the statement could be examples of such failures. This problem can be solved only with the assistance of the DBA. As a DBA, when encountering such failures, use Oracle flashback technology immediately and solve this problem without issuing any recovery or disruption in the database. This concept is covered in further detail in Chapter 11 and all necessary steps to solve such user failures are shown.

   Sometimes it is not possible to use flashback technology for some reason. In this situation, use the TSPITR technique and recover the database to a time before this error occurred. Read about this concept in Chapter 4 for more details.

6. Instance failure: This type of error occurs on the server where the Oracle database is installed. The main reason for this failure is an unexpected power outage or shutting down of any vital background processes such as

DBW, LGWR or CKPT. Shutting down of the server is the same as the shutdown abort mode. After the problem is resolved, on the subsequent startup Oracle rolls back uncommitted transactions, rolls forward committed transactions to datafiles and opens the database. This is done by the background process SMON automatically and no DBA interference is needed.

7. Network failure: This type of failure occurs when the network card of the server fails or the listener overloads and crashes, and users are unable to connect to the database. To solve this problem, configure both network cards of the server and one listener to each network card. At the same time, configure connect time failover and load balancing features in the listener. By configuring load balancing, the connection is distributed among the number of listeners. Connect time failover directs clients to connect to another listener if the connection to the first listener fails.

8. Media failure: This type of failure could happen when an administrator accidentally deletes physical files of the database or when these files get corrupted due to media failure such as hard drive failure. By getting media failure, immediately choose the right recovery strategy and recover the database using backups.

To prevent media failure from occurring is not something that depends on the DBA. The crash of the hard drive or corruption of some datafiles in the hard drive cannot be prevented. However, what does depend on the DBA is implementing the correct backup steps to overcome this problem and making the database available as soon as possible. Somehow, there are some prerequisites to protect the main physical files against corruption and the database from abnormally terminating because of media failure. More details on this are found in Chapter 4.

Oracle Backup and Recovery Techniques and Solutions

As stated before, the Oracle database mainly consists of two structures: the physical and logical structure. Each structure has its own backup techniques. Below is shown the main physical structure of the database and the backup methods.

The main files which build up the base physical structure of the Oracle database include datafiles, control files and redo log files. As far as physical backup of the database is concerned, this means the backup of the above-mentioned files. It is important to emphasize that taking backup of redo log files is not permitted. Instead, take a backup of the archived redo log files. Now see the importance of these files for the database.

Datafiles

Datafiles keep all object structures and data. Logically, each datafile belongs to a tablespace. Each time a user (schema) and object are created, such as tables, views, and procedures, and data inserted in the tables, all changes at the end are written (after checkpoint) to datafiles. Where the database backup is concerned, this mainly means a backup of datafiles which keep all the data. To get information about the datafiles of the database, query the *v$datafile* view:

```
SQL>
select
 name
from
 v$datafile;

NAME
----------------------------------------------------
C:\ORACLE\PRODUCT\10.2.0\ORADATA\ORCL\SYSTEM01.DBF
C:\ORACLE\PRODUCT\10.2.0\ORADATA\ORCL\UNDOTBS01.DBF
C:\ORACLE\PRODUCT\10.2.0\ORADATA\ORCL\SYSAUX01.DBF
C:\ORACLE\PRODUCT\10.2.0\ORADATA\ORCL\USERS01.DBF
SQL>
```

Control Files

Each database has at least one control file. This file is a small binary file which keeps the main structure of the database. The control file records the locations of datafiles and redo log files, log sequence number, name and creation time of the database. Without this file, the database cannot be opened because in startup mount mode, Oracle tries to open control files. Each time structural changes are made on the database, these changes are written to control files as well. Backing up the control file is vitally important.

Redo Log Files

These files hold all changes made to database objects. Changes made to the database are kept in redo log files in the form of redo records. These redo records are made of change vectors. These change vectors hold information about changes made to data blocks of the database. Redo log files are vital for the database recovery process. When datafiles are backed up and restored in case of a database crash, the DBA comes back to the time when the backup was taken. By applying archived redo log files, the database can be brought to the time before the crash happened.

There are mainly three methods for backing up physical files of the database: RMAN (Recovery Manager); user-managed; and using Enterprise Manager which invokes RMAN commands in the background. RMAN originally was introduced in Oracle 8 and since then, many functions have been added. By employing this tool, a backup of the database can be taken according to any criteria. Oracle recommends that the database be backed up using RMAN. RMAN, is mainly used through the command line interface; however, in Oracle 10g, a backup of the database can easily be taken through the Enterprise Manager.

The user-managed type of backup and recovery means taking backup of the database and recovering it using a combination of SQL*Plus and OS/3rd party utility commands. Additionally, Oracle provides flashback technologies for the recovery process. When using flashback commands, the data, such as a dropped table or huge amount of rows changed incorrectly, can be obtained by using simple commands instead of restoring datafiles and recovering it through adding all archived redo log files which consume a lot of time. See Chapter 11 for more information.

⚏ User ID = book, password = reader

First of all, it is important to know that if recovery is mentioned, it means that there should be archived redo log files or incremental backup. By adding archived redo log files to the last backup taken, recovery does occur. For that, Oracle strongly recommends the database be run in archivelog mode. As is well known, when the current online redo log file is filled, LGWR begins to write to the next redo log file. Without running the database in archivelog mode, the filled redo log file is not archived and is rewritten by LGWR on further log switches in a circular fashion. Therefore, there will not be any changed information on the database except those that were in datafiles and the data will be lost.

This can be seen from Bob's example illustrated in Figure 1.1. According to the figure, if Bob had been running the database in noarchivelog mode, then he would not have archived redo log files which keep information from January 1 until January 10. In the event of a database crash, he would be able to restore the database from the January 1 backup but would not be able to recover it.

After understanding the importance of backup, see what type of backups should be taken by Oracle's backup and recovery utility: RMAN. Generally, RMAN has the following types of backup methods:

- Consistent and inconsistent backups (open and closed)

- Whole and partial backups

- Full and incremental backups

Consistent and Inconsistent Backups

The simplest way to back up an Oracle database is by doing a consistent or closed backup. It is enough to shut down the database and get a copy of all its physical files, i.e. datafiles, redo log files and control files, to have a cold backup. The main advantage of this backup type is that there is no need to recover after restoring it in case of a database crash. All files are consistent. But the main disadvantage of this backup type is that the database needs to be closed to get a copy of the files. For large companies, it is impossible to shut down the database and to make it unavailable even for a minute. For that reason, the closed backup is not an appropriate way to backup 24/7 systems.

The required backup in most production systems is the backup where the database does not need to be shut down. It is called an inconsistent, open or online backup. When taking an inconsistent backup, although the DBA may be faced with performance degradation, users are able to make changes to the database. It is recommended that an inconsistent backup should be done during the off-peak hours.

To understand these two backup types in depth, look at how Oracle writes data to the files and synchronizes them. Each time a *commit* statement is issued, an automatic incremented value called SCN increments and is inserted with a change made to an object or to a redo log file. When a redo log file is filled, log switches occur and it triggers a checkpoint process. The CKPT process writes all dirty blocks to data files from the database buffer cache and updates datafiles and control file headers with the last SCN number.

Next time the database opens according to the *SCN value* of each file, Oracle defines whether the database needs recovery or not. During an inconsistent backup, as changes are made to the database, file headers of datafiles and control files are not synchronized and become inconsistent. To make them consistent, they need to be recovered by applying archived redo log files or redo log files.

Whole and Partial Backups

In most cases, the backup consists of all physical files that comprise the database with the exception of redo log files. This type of backup is called a whole backup. By taking a whole backup, a backup of the entire database is made. Online redo log files should never be backed up because during recovery, if that file is replaced with a current redo log file (with the older log files), transactions may be lost and the database may be corrupted. In some cases, according to business requirements, some part of the database, such as a datafile or a tablespace, could be backed up. This backup type is called a partial backup. This concept is examined in greater detail in Chapter 3.

Full and Incremental Backups

These types of backups can only be taken by using RMAN. Full backup means backing up all used blocks of a data file. While taking full backup, RMAN does not take unused data blocks, thereby reducing the size of the backup file. The main advantage of RMAN over the user-managed backup is taking incremental backups. By taking incremental backups, only those data blocks that changed before the last incremental backup are backed up. As a default, RMAN uses incremental backups rather than archived redo log files because it is faster.

Crash Recovery

If the server where the database resides shuts down abnormally because of a power outage, the database shuts down in abort mode and files are not synchronized. This state of database is called instance crash, and it needs to be recovered. When the database opens, instance recovery occurs without DBA interaction. The background process called SMON starts, checks headers of datafiles, redo log files and control files and determines the inconsistency between them. Because all changes made to the database were in the database buffer cache and it was cleared with an abnormal termination of the server, no changes were added to data files. As all changes are kept in redo log files, SMON applies all committed and uncommitted changes from redo log files to datafiles. This process is called rolling forward. Then, SMON rolls back all uncommitted changes in the datafiles by using the undo tablespace. This process is called rolling back. Again, all these operations are made by the background process SMON without DBA interaction.

Media Recovery

When the hard drive where datafiles reside crashes or some physical files are deleted from OS by mistake, media recovery is needed. It should be emphasized that the recovery process made by RMAN is simplified and fully automated. If a backup is taken in a proper manner, then it is very easy to recover. Recovery is required when one of the datafiles or all control files are inaccessible. This concept will be covered in details in Chapter 4.

Complete and Incomplete Recovery

When the database crashes and needs a media recovery, the complete recovery is performed. It means that all transactions are applied from archived redo log files or incremental backups to the datafiles. But what if a user drops a table or makes some changes to the database which he/she should not have done and may need to recover the database through a specific time and then stop the recovery process? This type of recovery is called incomplete recovery. It means that all transactions are not applied from archived redo log files to the database.

Incomplete recovery consists of three types:

- Time-based recovery (identified by a specific point in time)

- SCN-based recovery (identified by a specific SCN)
- Cancel-based recovery (identified by the last log sequence applied)

Time-based recovery is used for getting back all changes made to the database up to a specific point in time. By defining the exact time, all transactions until that specific time are applied and the recovery is stopped.

SCN-based recovery is used the same as time-based recovery except the definition. Here, the SCN number is defined in the recovery process and by applying changes until the specified SCN number is reached, the recovery process stops.

In cancel-based recovery, the user is prompted to specify archived redo logs that should be applied. Whenever required, by typing the *cancel* command, the user can stop the recovery process and open the database. It is done when the archived redo log files are missed.

Block Media Recovery

One of the key advantages of RMAN is its capability of making recovery at the data block level. By having corrupted blocks, the whole datafile should not be restored and recovered. Instead, Block Media Recovery is conducted which restores and recovers only corrupted blocks, thus reducing recovery time. This concept is covered in detail in Chapter 4.

Flashback Technologies used for Database Recovery

The easiest way of taking the database to the appropriate time is to use flashback technologies. By using techniques provided by this technology, data from user errors can be recovered without issuing an incomplete recovery. This concept is highlighted in Chapter 11. Here are the main features of flashback technologies in nutshell.

NOTE: Some flashback technologies require additional configuration and cannot be assumed to work "out of the box". For example, a database cannot be flashed back unless there is a previously configured flash recovery area and flashback logs.

- Flashback database was firstly introduced in Oracle 10g. By using flashback logs, which are created by the RVWR background process and are kept before the image of the data block, this feature helps to flash the database back to a specific time. It is much quicker than performing an incomplete recovery because archived redo log files or incremental backups are not added to datafiles. Changes are only made to necessary data blocks using information from flashback log files.

- Flashback table is used to recover the table changed by an incorrect *update* statement. By using information written in the undo tablespace, the table can be flashed back to a specific time.

- Flashback drop is used to recover a table accidently dropped by a user from the recycle bin.

- Flashback query is used to view the database as it was at a point in the past by using undo segments.

- Flashback versions query is used for getting all versions of changes made to a table specifying the time interval by using information from the undo tablespace. Moreover, by getting a transaction identifier of committed transactions, all undo information, even undo SQL which can be used to undo specific committed transactions, can be taken from undo segments by using flashback transaction query.

- Flashback transaction query is used to get all undo information about a statement as mentioned above.

- Flashback transactions history is a new feature in Oracle 11g and is used to roll back all dependent transactions.

- Flashback data archive is a new feature in Oracle 11g which helps to maintain compressed and partitioned archives for any table for a long time period.

RMAN Backup Concepts

As far as Oracle database backup techniques are concerned, the main tool that is suggested by Oracle is RMAN. Before using RMAN, become familiar with its key definitions.

RMAN is a client application used for backup, restore and recovery operations of an Oracle database. No extra effort is needed to configure or install RMAN;

it is installed automatically when the Oracle software is installed and more importantly, it is a free utility with no extra license required to use it. By running commands in the command line interface of RMAN, backup and recovery processes of the database can be easily controlled. When backup of the database is taken by using RMAN, it can be mainly in two formats: backup set; or image copy.

Backup Set

Backup set, which is a default format, is made up of one or more backup pieces. Each time a backup is taken, RMAN automatically takes a backup of the datafiles and puts it in its specific backup type: a backup set which consists of one or more backup pieces. Actually, each backup piece is a physical file. At the same time, RMAN automatically takes a backup of the controlfile and parameter file to another backup piece. If backing up archived redo log files is defined, RMAN creates another backup piece to store them as well. All these backup pieces are created in one backup set. In fact, backup set is a logical definition.

Backup Piece

The backup piece consists of data blocks. It is a special RMAN format which can be created and restored only by RMAN. It stores data blocks in a specially compressed format.

Taking a backup using RMAN is very simple and involves just running the *backup database* command. This will be studied further in Chapter 2. With this introduction to the backup set and backup piece, take a backup and have a look at the following example to further make clear these concepts.

```
1.  RMAN> backup database;

2.  Starting backup at 20-JUL-09

3.  using target database control file instead of recovery catalog
       allocated channel: ORA_DISK_1

4.  channel ORA_DISK_1: sid=147 devtype=DISK

5.  channel ORA_DISK_1: starting full datafile backupset

6.  channel ORA_DISK_1: specifying datafile(s) in backupset
```

```
7.  input datafile fno=00001
    name=C:\ORACLE\PRODUCT\10.2.0\ORADATA\ORCL\SYSTEM01.DBF

8.  input datafile fno=00003
    name=C:\ORACLE\PRODUCT\10.2.0\ORADATA\ORCL\SYSAUX01.DBF

9.  input datafile fno=00002
    name=C:\ORACLE\PRODUCT\10.2.0\ORADATA\ORCL\UNDOTBS01.DBF

10. input datafile fno=00004
    name=C:\ORACLE\PRODUCT\10.2.0\ORADATA\ORCL\USERS01.DBF

11. channel ORA_DISK_1: starting piece 1 at 20-JUL-09

12. channel ORA_DISK_1: finished piece 1 at 20-JUL-09

13. piece handle=-------\O1_MF_NNNDF_TAG20090720T112958_5683Q7CQ_.BKP
    tag=TAG20090720T112958 comment=NONE

14. channel ORA_DISK_1: backup set complete, elapsed time: 00:00:45

15. channel ORA_DISK_1: starting full datafile backupset

16. channel ORA_DISK_1: specifying datafile(s) in backupset

17. including current control file in backupset

18. including current SPFILE in backupset

19. channel ORA_DISK_1: starting piece 1 at 20-JUL-09

20. channel ORA_DISK_1: finished piece 1 at 20-JUL-09

21. piece handle=-------\O1_MF_NCSNF_TAG20090720T112958_5683RP00_.BKP
    tag=TAG20090720T112958 comment=NONE

22. channel ORA_DISK_1: backup set complete, elapsed time: 00:00:02

23. Finished backup at 20-JUL-09

24. RMAN>
```

In line 1, *backup database* command is issued to take a full backup of the database. In line 5, the logical backup set is created to keep all datafiles. From line 6 to line 10, the datafiles that make up this backup set are defined.

In line 13, destination of the backup piece is provided. In lines 17 and 18, information is given about a new backup piece created to hold control files and the parameter file. By default, automatic backup of the control file configuration is OFF, so these files are created in the same backup set. In line 21, directory of the backup piece is shown and the backup process ends.

If the newly created backup pieces from the OS level are viewed, the following results come up:

```
C:\oracle------->dir
O1_MF_NCSNF_TAG20090720T112958_5683RP00_.BKP
O1_MF_NNNDF_TAG20090720T112958_5683Q7CQ_.BKP
```

This example shows that taking a backup with default parameters, RMAN creates two backup pieces (physical file) within one logical backup set. One backup piece contains information on data blocks for data files and the second one contains the control file and parameter file.

Image Copies

Another type of backup created by RMAN is the image copy. Image copies are the same as datafiles. Any image copy of the datafile taken by RMAN is similar to the copy made by the OS command. The main advantage of an image copy over an OS level backup is that by taking an image copy backup, RMAN checks the content of the datafile for corruption. Image copies can be used to quickly switch to a datafile copy without having to actually restore the copy to the expected location of a datafile. While restoring a datafile from the backup piece, the structure of a datafile is created from the start and it consumes some time. With regard to an image copy, as it has the structure of a datafile, there is no need to create it. However, the disadvantage of image copy backup mode is that it occupies a considerable amount of space and does not skip unused data blocks. Moreover, an image copy can be written only to disk.

Channel Allocation

RMAN uses channels to make a connection with the database. A channel is a connection between RMAN and the target database. It creates a new session in the server where a database resides and this session manages all database backup and recovery processes. The RMAN channel can be configured in two ways: automatically and manually.

By using the *configure* command, the default channel allocation option in RMAN configuration is defined. RMAN uses this configuration when one of the commands such as *backup*, *restore* or *delete* is issued. By using the *allocate channel* command, manual channels can be allocated directly from the command line. Even though it is configured to use the automatic channel, this can be overridden using the manual channel allocation by allocating it directly inside the RMAN block.

By allocating channels, additional parameters can be used to make the channel more functional. When a channel is allocated, the backup can be saved either to disk or to tape. Default value is disk. The following list includes other parameters with a short description:

- *connect*: Defines the connection method. Has three parameters: *target*; *catalog;* and *auxiliary*. Default connection type is the target database. While cloning a database, the *auxiliary* connection type is used as in the following example:

```
allocate auxiliary channel ch device type disk;
```

- *format*: Defines the filesystem path and name of the backup piece. Using this option, a unique name can be created for each backup making it easy to define the correct backup file to be used in the restore and recovery process. When the *format* option is not defined, the default *%U* format is used. It has more than 20 different formats which can be taken from documentation. Below is shown an example of this option:

```
RMAN> configure channel device type disk format 'backup_%d_%T_%I.bkp';
using target database control file instead of recovery catalog
new RMAN configuration parameters:
configure channel device type disk format  'backup_%d_%T_%I.bkp';
new RMAN configuration parameters are successfully stored

RMAN>backup database;

piece handle=C-----\BACKUP_ORCL_20090728_2174767164.BKP
tag=TAG20090728T122930 comment=NONE
piece handle=-----\CTL_C-2174767164-20090728-00
```

In this example, the format was changed to *backup_%d_%T_%I.bkp* and RMAN created the file named *backup_orcl_20090728_2174767164.bkp*. Here, *%d* is the name of the database, *%T* the current date and *%I* the DBID of the database. Standard format of the control file is *%F*. This tag translates into dbid+day+month+year+sequence in hexadecimal number.

- *maxopenfiles*: Defines the number of files which can be read using one channel at the same time. Default value is eight. To change the default value, try this command:

```
allocate channel ch device type disk maxopenfiles 4;
```

- *maxpiecesize*: Defines maximum size of the backup piece created using the channel. Its syntax is as follows:

```
configure channel ch device type disk maxpiecesize 100m;
```

Sometimes, there may be some hard drive limitations for backup size or the DBA may be asked to split the backup into parts during the backup operation. In this situation, a maximum size value for the channel can be set using the *maxpiecesize* parameter. This results in the backup file being split into pieces. Below is an example:

```
RMAN> configure channel device type disk maxpiecesize 100M;

RMAN> backup database;
RMAN> configure channel device type disk clear;

RMAN> backup database;

-----\>dir

104 857 600 O1_MF_NNNDF_TAG20090729T164526_570FLPPG_.BKP
104 857 600 O1_MF_NNNDF_TAG20090729T164526_570FM5QG_.BKP
104 857 600 O1_MF_NNNDF_TAG20090729T164526_570FMNVT_.BKP
104 857 600 O1_MF_NNNDF_TAG20090729T164526_570FN42X_.BKP
104 857 600 O1_MF_NNNDF_TAG20090729T164526_570FNM7B_.BKP
12 009 472 O1_MF_NNNDF_TAG20090729T164526_570FNTG5_.BKP
536 141 824 O1_MF_NNNDF_TAG20090729T165000_570FV94D_.BKP
```

From this example, the value of the *maxpiecesize* parameter changes to 100M, so RMAN creates a backup of the database by splitting the file into 100M per piece. Next, by using the *clear* option, reset its default value and make another backup. Consequently, the size of the last backup is 536M.

- *rate*: Defines and limits I/O bandwidth of the channel. While getting a backup, RMAN uses maximum I/O bandwidth. To decrease bandwidth and define a specific value, the *rate* option should be used:

```
configure channel ch device type disk rate 1M;
```

- *send*: Sends vendor specific commands to all channels

Any RMAN configuration can be easily restored by using the *clear* option:

```
RMAN> configure device type disk parallelism 3;
new RMAN configuration parameters:
configure device type disk parallelism 3 backup type to backupset;

new RMAN configuration parameters are successfully stored

RMAN> show all;
RMAN configuration parameters are:
configure device type disk parallelism 3 backup type to backupset;

RMAN> configure device type disk clear;
old RMAN configuration parameters:
configure device type disk parallelism 3 backup type to backupset;

RMAN configuration parameters are successfully reset to default value

RMAN> show all;
RMAN configuration parameters are:
configure device type disk parallelism 1 backup type to backupset; #

default
RMAN>
```

In this example, the parallelism configuration is changed to three. Then the *configure..clear* command is used restore the default value of this setting.

Autobackups

RMAN can be configured so that the control file's backup is taken automatically; however, it is important to remember that the default value the control file automatic backup is OFF. When a backup is taken of the database, a backup of the control file and spfile is created automatically in the same backup set.

If a control file is set for *autobackup* ON, an automatic backup of the control file will be taken each time a structural change is made to the database by allocating the default automatic disk channel. In the event of all database files (datafiles, controlfiles and spfile) are lost, the spfile can be easily restored from autobackup. By starting an instance with the restored spfile, the control file can be restored from autobackup as well. By mounting the instance and using information about RMAN backups in the control file, datafiles can be restored. This scenario will be covered in Chapter 4.

From the following example, the automatic control file backup process made by RMAN after structural change has been made to the database can be seen:

1. First, connect to RMAN and make it so the control file is backed up automatically:

```
configure controlfile autobackup on;
```

2. Take a backup of the database:

```
backup database;
```

3. Check the AUTOBACKUP folder in the flash recovery area. This shows a backup of the control file and spfile made by RMAN automatically.

```
C:\----------------\2009_07_26>dir
26.07.2009  19:02         7 143 424 O1_MF_S_693255723_56RRGW8S_.BKP
```

4. Now connect to the database and add a new datafile to the users tablespace. By adding this datafile, a structural change is made to the database and the control file is updated. Once the *controlfile autobackup* is set to ON, the automatic backup of the control file and spfile will be created.

```
SQL> alter tablespace users add datafile 'c:\users02.dbf' SIZE 10m;

Tablespace altered.
SQL>
```

Check the same directory and see a new backup file that is created automatically.

```
C:\------\AUTOBACKUP\2009_07_26>dir
26.07.2009  19:02         7 143 424 O1_MF_S_693255723_56RRGW8S_.BKP
26.07.2009  19:09         7 143 424 O1_MF_S_693256181_56RRX6PY_.BKP
```

RMAN Recovery Concepts

For the purpose of simplicity and wide functionality, RMAN is mainly used on backup and recovery processes. While restoring the backup taken by RMAN, it automatically finds the last backup taken and restores it. Then by running the *recover* command, it applies either incremental backups or archived redo log files and makes the database run.

RMAN has a lot of advantages over the user-managed backup and recovery. Some of the advantages are as follows:

- It selects the most appropriate backup for database recovery and renders it very easily through use of simple commands.

- Using RMAN, the database can be automatically be backed up to tape.

- Using RMAN Block Media Recovery, the database can be recovered in the data block level. If some data blocks of huge datafiles are corrupted, there is no need to restore and recover the whole datafile. In this case, by using Block Media Recovery, only corrupted data blocks are recovered.

- Most production databases are big in size and change frequently. It is not the right option to backup the whole database each time (every day). By using the incremental backup functionality, only a backup of changed data blocks are taken, thereby reducing time of backup and future recover process.

- Using compression, binary compressed backup sets can be readily created. Although more CPU is used while taking such backups, the backup pieces are smaller, reducing the requirement for disk/tape space to hold the backups.

- Using the Encryption feature, encrypted backup sets which make this backup more secure can be created. By using the correct key, these backup sets is decrypted automatically during restore and recovery operations.

- Using the cross platform tablespace conversion functionality, the tablespace which was created in one OS can be converted to another.

- Because RMAN does not take a backup of the temporary tablespace, during recovery it is created automatically by RMAN. It makes the DBAs work easier.

- Using RMAN, the database can be cloned to the remote host by using the *duplicate* command provided by RMAN. When this command is used, RMAN backs up the primary database and restores it on the remote host. To open the clone database by using the *resetlogs* option for creating new redo log files, RMAN performs an incomplete recovery and assigns it a new DBID.

- Moreover, databases can be cloned to any point in time. For example, if it is assumed that a huge amount of data has been inserted into the primary database within a specific time, it would be best not have this in the clone database. For this, incomplete recovery is used by running the *set until* command in duplicate process.

- Using RMAN, a physical standby database can be created just by following simple steps. This concept is examined in Chapter 5. RMAN automatically restores the standby control file and datafiles from the backup taken in the primary database. Subsequently, by recovering datafiles, RMAN makes the standby database functional. Furthermore, datafiles of the standby database can be used as a backup for the primary database and should be replaced any time in case of media failure in the primary database.

In this book, the intent is to show all the above-mentioned functionalities of RMAN with plenty of examples.

Summary

This chapter focused on the basics of backup and recovery techniques of the Oracle database. By providing information about the basics, the main failures that might occur in the database were covered. The Oracle tool RMAN was introduced as the primary tool used for backup and recovery processes.

This chapter also showed the main concepts of RMAN backup and recovery and many examples and configurations of RMAN were given. The difference between RMAN and user-managed backup and recovery techniques by learning main RMAN advantages was explained. Also, the main features of RMAN recovery such as creating clone and standby databases were given.

Chapter 2 will delve into the steps involved in configuring RMAN including how to use the recovery catalog and connecting to the database.

Configuring RMAN and Connecting to the Database

RMAN basics were covered in Chapter 1. This chapter will continue to delve into the RMAN repository as well as some important configurations that can help in running RMAN smoothly and efficiently. Also, the configuration and usage of the flashback recovery area will be implemented in taking our first backup which will be helpful in doing our first ever recovery.

Using the Recovery Catalog

RMAN captures information about the target database to which it connects. This information is vital for RMAN to work since when the information is needed to use the backup, it is picked up from this metadata only. As demonstrated in the last chapter, this information is stored in the target database's control file in the default manner. In general this approach is fine, but it can fail at certain points.

The control file has two sections which are used to store the information. One is called the reusable section. These entries would be recycled after the time period of the *control_file_record_keep_time* parameter is over (defaults to seven days). The other section is the non-reusable section, which is not overwritten. In general, it is proposed that the time period of retention should be adjusted depending on the requirement of the business as well as for how long the backup related information should be kept in it.

This might look like the ideal way out, but it still leaves some questions unanswered. For example, what if having a centralized repository of 10 databases that are in the organization is desired? What if only the information in the target database's control file is stored and somehow, that control file is lost? What if the backup information needs to be kept for more than the default retention period of seven days, like 30 days or 60 days, and the target database size is huge? All these and many more questions do not necessarily yield a positive result when only the control file is used for the repository information.

The recover catalog provides a very good solution of the above mentioned stated and unstated questions. The recovery catalog is easy to create and easier to use as a centralized repository for storing the RMAN's metadata. It gives many more options as compared to the default control file, such as the use of the stored scripts, making use of the backups taken via O/S through the *catalog* command and so on. In Chapter 7, *Managing the Recovery Catalog*, the creation, registration and management of the recovery catalog will be shown in greater detail.

Setting Persistent RMAN Configurations

RMAN is preset with default values for a couple of options. Most of the time the default settings may not serve the DBA well, so these need to be changed according to certain requirements. All the settings are changed by the RMAN *configure* command which makes the settings persistent across shutdown of the database. The *configure* command can be used both in single as well as parallel (RAC) database instances.

To see the preset configuration settings of RMAN, use the *show all* command on the RMAN prompt.

```
RMAN> show all;

RMAN configuration parameters are:
configure retention policy to redundancy 2;
configure backup optimization on;
configure default device type to disk; # default
configure controlfile autobackup off; # default
configure controlfile autobackup format for device type disk to '%f'; #
default
configure device type disk parallelism 6 backup type to backupset;
configure datafile backup copies for device type disk to 1; # default
configure archivelog backup copies for device type disk to 1; # default
configure maxsetsize to unlimited; # default
configure encryption for database off; # default
configure encryption algorithm 'aes128'; # default
configure archivelog deletion policy to none; # default
configure snapshot controlfile name to
'E:\ORACLE\product\10.2.0\db_1\database\sncforcl.ora'; # default
```

There is the comment *default* mentioned at the end of each setting giving an indication that all the settings are at their preset defaults at the time the *show all* was executed. The following section will demonstrate what these settings mean and how to change them from their default presets.

Retention Policy

It is always important to have backups of the database. In the same manner, it is also important to delete those backups no longer required for the recovery. RMAN makes the identification of these backups very easy using *retention policy*, which governs which backups are safe to be deleted. Using *retention policy*, backups are marked as obsolete, which means not required anymore. There are two possible settings for *retention policy*:

- Redundancy
- Recovery window

Redundancy stands for the number of copies that must be available. Once the chosen number of backup copies has been collected, any older backups are marked as obsolete. This does not put any sort of restriction on how long the backups can be kept. This kind of setting works best for environments where, depending on the SLA (service level agreement), some specified number of backup copies must be kept. By default, this is the setting on which RMAN works, using only the most current backup copy. Depending on the requirement, the number of copies can be changed using the *configure* command as shown:

```
RMAN> configure retention policy to redundancy 2;
```

In the above example, the redundancy has been set to two. This means that if two backups of the database are taken now, the oldest copy of the backup would be marked as obsolete.

The other setting, recovery window, is not based on the number of backup copies, but on the number of days for which the backup needs to be kept. This does not put any condition on the number of backup copies that can be retained; there can be *n* number of copies within the specified period of the recovery window. Any backup that is older than the recovery window is marked as obsolete.

In the recovery window, Oracle checks the current backup and looks for its relevance backwards in time. This is a default set to seven days which means that the backup must be kept for exactly seven days, ensuring that it can be used for the recovery within any point of time for this time period. Any file which does not come in this range of *n* days would require a backup to be done for it and the same would be reported from RMAN as well. To illustrate the above, look at a hypothetical situation where the backup is done after every week and the recovery window is also set for seven days, its default value.

The backup is taken every seventh day. Now, assume that the DBA started on July 1st and has taken or planned backups on the 8th, 15th, 22nd and 29th of July. Assuming the current date is the 25th of July, according to the recovery window of seven days, the point of recoverability goes back seven days to the 18th of July. This means that to ensure the recoverability, the backup taken on the 15th will be kept by Oracle so that it can be recovered up to that point.

Remember: To be able to recover to the 18th with a database backup of the 15th, subsequent archived redo logs from the 15th to the 18th are required.

One interesting part of this type of retention policy setting is that it is not mandatory for RMAN to keep the backup only for the mentioned number of days. If the last level 0 backup has been taken and the time period of that exceeds the recovery window timing, Oracle would have to ensure that it is not marked as obsolete because just using the level 1 backup will not guarantee the complete recovery.

The default retention policy is set to a redundancy of 1. This can be changed from its default value by using the *configure* command. Note that both redundancy and recovery window retention policies are mutually exclusive. Now check what retention policy the database is set to. The *show retention policy* command can be used for this:

```
RMAN> show retention policy;

RMAN configuration parameters are:
configure retention policy to redundancy 1;
```

So the retention policy is now set to redundancy 1. Change it to the recovery window of seven days:

```
RMAN> configure retention policy to recovery window of 7 days;

old RMAN configuration parameters:
configure retention policy to redundancy 1;
new RMAN configuration parameters:
configure retention policy to recovery window of 7 days;
```

```
new RMAN configuration parameters are successfully stored
```

Now the retention policy is set to seven days of the recovery window. In case the retention policy needs to be disabled for some reason, this can also be done. Here is how:

```
configure retention policy to none;
```

This would disable the retention policy settings. However, doing so would stop the *report obsolete* and *delete obsolete* commands from marking any of the previous backups as obsolete.

Backup Optimization

Server space is very costly and competent DBAs do everything possible to use it efficiently. It is always good to have multiple copies of the backups, but that is only necessary when the next copy actually contains something new, such as some changes which were not there in the last backup. If nothing has changed and multiple backup copies of the said file(s) are still being created, precious space is actually being wasted in the storage.

Fortunately, RMAN has an backup optimization technique, using the logic that duplicate copies of backups will not be created if nothing in the original file has changed since the last backup. Backup optimization by default is not on. This means copies will continue to be created over the same location even if there are no changes to the source database/datafile. The current setting of the backup optimization can be seen from the *show optimization* command:

```
RMAN> show backup optimization;

RMAN configuration parameters are:
configure backup optimization OFF;
```

The setting can be changed using the *configure* command as follows:

```
RMAN> configure backup optimization ON;
```

Now the backup optimization is on, which stops the creation of duplicate copies of those files which are unchanged.

Backup optimization does not work with all the commands. The following three commands are the only ones which provide the backup optimization.

Oracle Backup and Recovery

- *backup database*

- *backup archivelog* with the *all* or *like* option

- *backup backupset all*

If any other command except these three is going to be used, optimization does not come into the picture and Oracle keeps on taking the backups even though there are no changes recorded in the source file. Here is what it looks like when RMAN skips the file which is already backed up.

```
RMAN> backup archivelog all;

<....output trimmed .....>
input archive log thread=1 sequence=149 recid=104 stamp=694215000
<....output trimmed .....>

RMAN> backup archivelog all;

<....output trimmed .....>
skipping archive log file E:\-------\01_MF_1_149_57OZJ098_.ARC; already
backed up 1 time(s)
input archive log thread=1 sequence=150 recid=105 stamp=694215007

RMAN> backup archivelog all;

<....output trimmed .....>
skipping archive log file
E:\ORACLE\product\10.2.0\flash_recovery_area\orcl\archivelog\2009_08_06\01_M
F_1_149_57OZJ098_.ARC; already backed up 1 time(s)
skipping archive log file
E:\ORACLE\product\10.2.0\flash_recovery_area\orcl\archivelog\2009_08_06\01_M
F_1_150_57OZJ74D_.ARC; already backed up 1 time(s)
input archive log thread=1 sequence=151 recid=106 stamp=694215018
<....output trimmed .....>
```

This shows that the archive log file was skipped by the backup the second time when the command was issued. But the same does not apply if some other command is used; for example, *backup as copy*. This would not use optimization and would keep on creating backup copies.

The algorithm that works in the backend for the optimization takes care of different files with different conditions. For datafiles, they must have the same DBID, checkpoint SCN and resetlogs SCN. For the archivelogs, the previous and current archivelog files must match in their DBID, thread number and log sequence number. For the backup sets, the same record ID and timestamp must be there.

Determining the Device Type

When planning to take a backup, there must be a destination as well where that backup should go. RMAN is capable of taking backups both on disk and tape media. By default, RMAN is configured to take a backup over the disk where the default destination is set to the flash recovery area, an automatically maintained destination by Oracle specifically set for the backups. The flash recovery area will be examined in a later section. Other than that, RMAN is also capable of including tape drives for its backup operations. The configuration of the tape drive can be done either using the Media Management Library (MML) or Oracle Secure Backup which comes with a built-in MML.

The default device type can be changed for the backup by using the *configure* command:

```
configure default device type to disk
configure default device type to sbt
```

Setting up Automatic Backups of the Control File

With the information that has been gathered already from the first chapter about control files, DBAs must be assured now that they are very important and play a key part in the working of the database. Anything happening to the control file can put the database into a very critical situation because without it, the database will not be able to even get mounted. RMAN takes this into account and takes the backup of the control file each time when the system tablespace is copied, either by the backup set or by backup copy.

But if any other file is used, the same operation does not work, and it is necessary to take a manual backup. Automatic backup of the control file can be switched so that it not only gets backed up with the system datafile, but also with any datafile or backup option. This can be done by enabling automatic backup of the control file. Now see it in action:

```
RMAN> configure controlfile autobackup ON;
RMAN> backup datafile 2;

<....output trimmed ....>
input datafile fno=00002 name=E:\-----\UNDOTBS01.DBF
piece handle=E:\-------\O1_MF_NNNDF_TAG20090808T015734_57S3KQ7B_.BKP
tag=TAG20090808T015734 comment=NONE
```

```
Starting Control File and SPFILE Autobackup at 08-AUG-09
piece handle=E:\----\O1_MF_S_694317458_57S3KV6T_.BKP comment=NONE
Finished Control File and SPFILE Autobackup at 08-AUG-09
RMAN>
```

The backup of the system datafile was not taken, but the second datafile which is the *undo* datafile in the backup was included. Even though the system datafile is not in the picture, the control file and spfile are still included in the backup. This ensures that the control file's backup is never missed. This option becomes very important when there is an OLTP system where things are changing faster than can be imagined. At that time, losing the control file without backup would just be suicide. The *autobackup* control file saves the user from issues like this.

Backup Naming Format

There are various formats that can be used to give a proper naming convention to the backups. RMAN comes up with many conventions which are listed in the table below:

Format	Explanation
%a	Indicates activation ID of database
%c	Indicates copy number of the backup piece within a set of duplexed backup pieces. If a backup was not duplexed, then this variable is 1 for backup sets and 0 for proxy copies. If one of these commands is enabled, then the variable shows the copy number. Maximum value for %c is 256.
%d	Indicates name of database
%D	Specifies the current day of the month from the Gregorian calender in format DD
%e	Indicates archived log sequence number
%f	Indicates the absolute file number
%F	Combines the DBID, day, month, year, and sequence into a unique and repeatable generated name. This variable renders into c-IIIIIIIIII-YYYYMMDD-QQ, where: IIIIIIIIII stands for the DBID. The DBID is printed in decimal, so it can be readily associated with target database. YYYYMMDD is a time stamp in the Gregorian calendar of the day the backup is generated. QQ is the sequence in hexadecimal number that starts with 00 and has a maximum of FF (256).
%h	Indicates archived redo log thread number
%I	Indicates DBID

Setting Persistent RMAN Configurations

%M	Indicates the month in the Gregorian calendar in format MM
%N	Indicates tablespace name
%n	Indicates name of database, padded on the right with x characters to a total length of eight characters. For example, if prod1 is the database name, then the padded name is prod1xxx.
%p	Indicates piece number within the backup set. This value starts at 1 for each backup set and is incremented by 1 as each backup piece is created.
%s	Indicates backup set number. This number is a counter in the control file that is incremented for each backup set. The counter value starts at 1 and is unique for the lifetime of the control file. If a backup control file is restored, then duplicate values can result. Also, created control file initializes the counter back to 1.
%t	Indicates the backup set time stamp, which is a 4-byte value stemming from the number of seconds elapsed since a fixed reference time. The combination of %s and %t can be used to form a unique name for the backup set.
%T	Indicates the year, month and day in the Gregorian calendar in this format: YYYYMMDD
%u	Indicates an 8-character name comprised of compressed representations of the backup set or image copy number and the time the backup set or image copy was created.
%U	Indicates a system-generated unique filename (default). The meaning of %U is different for image copies and backup pieces.
%Y	Indicates the year in the format YYYY

Table 2.1: *List of Naming Formats*

If a format is not specified when making a backup, then RMAN uses *%U* by default.

For an image copy of a datafile, *%U* means the following:

```
data-D-%d_id-%I_TS-%N_FNO-%f_%u
```

For an image copy of an archived redo log, *%U* means the following:

```
arch-D_%d-id-%I_S-%e_T-%h_A-%a_%u
```

For an image copy of a control file, *%U* means the following:

```
cf-D_%d-id-%I_%u
```

Configuring Parallelism

RMAN works with the database via channels which are actual sessions that do all the work of backup, restore and recovery. These channels play a huge part in the working of RMAN to make it function better and much faster. The channels can be configured to do the work either on disk or on the tape. RMAN comes with a default channel configured to take a backup on the disk device in the flashback recovery area. The number of channels can be increased if there is a larger set of datafiles that should be worked on. The preset channels can be changed with the *configure* command.

```
RMAN> configure device type disk parallelism 4;
```

There can be two channels linked with the type of devices on which a backup can be taken, disk and tape (SBT). The channel for the device it is configured for would take the backup on that device only. There is a default channel for the device type disk which is already configured, thereby allowing work with RMAN to begin immediately over the disk drive.

The channel allocation can be manual or automatic. Normally, it is better to let the allocation be automatic only, but at times, it may need to get changed. For example, it may happen that a backup is being taken of a single data file only and for that, there is no need to allocate all the *n* channels that have been allocated. At that time, manual channel allocation can come in handy. Please note that any manual allocation would override the automatic configuration for the duration of the backup session. The *configure channel* command allocates an automatic channel allocation. To allocate a manual channel, use the *allocate channel* command which is a batch command and can only run within the run block.

Configuring Datafile and Archivelog File Copies

RMAN is configured by default to create a single backup copy of both the datafile and archivelog file. But with a single copy, there is a chance of losing it and thus, losing the option to recover the loss would also be affected, so it is always better to configure multiple copies of the backup files for both. This should surely not be set to very many copies as the more copies get created, the more resource the backup job would consume, and the system performance could be affected for no good reasn.

The number of copies done for the files can be changed by the *configure* command like following:

```
RMAN> configure datafile backup copies for device type disk to 2;
```

Configuring the Backup Set Size

RMAN takes the backup in the form of a backup piece and sets, where set is the logical configuration and piece is the actual backup file which gets created over the device. It is important to decide a proper size of the backup set matching with the device over which it would be placed. Normally, the backups are pushed over to the tape drives so it is important that the backup set size match with the tape volume. It is possible to configure the backup set to span over multiple tape volumes, but this would just increase the possibility of losing the entire backup even when only one tape would get corrupted or become unavailable for any reason. When the size of the backup set is set by the *configure* command, the entire backup set must fit over one tape only.

The default size is set to unlimited. The size of the backup set is set using:

```
RMAN> configure maxsetsize to 100M;
#To clear the configuration use:
RMAN> configure maxsetsize clear;
```

Here, the maximum set size has been changed to 100 M from its default value.

It is very important to ensure that the *maxsetsize* be at least as large as the largest datafile. A datafile cannot span multiple backup sets. So if the *maxsetsize* is smaller than the datafile size, a backup of the datafile would fail with the error "RMAN-06183: datafile or datafile copy larger than *maxsetsize*". Another way to limit the size of backup pieces is to configure *maxpiecesize* for the channel. For example,

```
configure channel device type disk maxpiecesize 100m;
backup database;
```

will result in the backup set(s) consisting of multiple pieces, i.e. files, of 100MB each.

Setting Up Encryption and Encryption Algorithm for the Backup

Security is one of the most important aspects in the database and the same is true for the backups as well. Normally, there are enormous amounts of security options for the database and the applications accessing it, but often backups are taken for granted. What can possibly go wrong with the backups, who would steal them? Right? Wrong!

Backups are nothing but the complete image of the database itself and by stealing them, someone can very easily recreate the database. Taking this huge security loophole into consideration, from 10g onwards, Oracle backups created by RMAN can be encrypted as well. This encryption consists of three types:

- Password protected

- Transparent encryption (encryption with Oracle wallet)

- Both

By default the encryption is off, which means there are no restrictions on the backups created and they can be used without any checks. If the encryption is set to ON, the backups can be password protected where a valid password is required before the backup can be restored. There is no need to supply the password before the backup is done, thus impacting nothing on all the existing backup scripts that are present. But the restoration of the backup, without the right password, would fail.

Backups can also be encrypted using the security certificate stored in the wallet. The wallet is password protected. This is called the transparent encryption of the backups and is the default mode. This mode works the best for day-to-day jobs provided the wallet is open and accessible. It is really important to have the backup of the wallet because if it is lost, there is no way to use the backups protected by it.

The last mode combines both the options where the backups have encryption set for them using the wallet and also contains a password. This option is the best for those sites where the backups are done and used on the same server where they are created and protected by the wallet stored on the server itself.

However, they are also sent offsite where the wallet is not available and the password protection would be helpful in safeguarding them.

There are three possible values for the algorithm used for encryption, AES128, AES192 and AES256, out of which AES128 is the default. This can be changed at any time as well. Note that to use the encryption feature, the database *compatibility* parameter must be set to 10.2.0. The backup encryption is described in detail in Chapter 3.

To enable RMAN encrypted backups, use the *configure* and *set* commands where *configure* makes a persistent setting for the backups either for the whole database or a single tablespace or datafile(s). The *set* command is used to either override the previously completed setting or to supply the password before restoring a backup that is password protected.

Configuring Archivelog Deletion Policy

Archivelogs are not just used for the recovery of the primary database, they are also often used with the standby environments. Over these environments, it is important to keep the archivelogs as long as they are not shipped to the standby server, making it synchronized with the primary server.

Using the *configure* command, set the deletion policies for the archivelogs to say when they should get deleted. There are three possible options for this: *applied on standby*, *none* and *clear*. *applied on standby* gets the archivelogs deleted only after they are applied over the standby database as well. *none* lets the archivelogs be deleted once they exceed the retention policy that has been set for them. *clear* would revert back the configured settings to the default one, *none*.

Configuring the Snapshot Control File

The snapshot control file is a temporary file that is created at a certain location specified over the operating system. This file is used by RMAN to synchronize the information with the current control file. This file, except for synchronizing the information with the current control file, does not do anything else and hence, is not included in the recovery catalog. It does not contain any information about the current backup that has been taken, though it does know about the last backups that were done and are not marked yet as obsolete. So this file can be used to recover a scenario where everything has been lost and also the catalog was not being used. The last backup information recorded in this file can be used and the database can be recovered with that backup.

The location of this file depends on the platform and also uses a default naming convention as well. Interestingly, irrespective of the flash recovery area being configured, the snapshot control file does not use it and is set for the location, normally to the *ORACLE_HOME*/*database* or *ORACLE_HOME*/*dbs* location with the name *sncf<sid>.ora*.

The current name and location of the file can be seen by the *show* command.

```
RMAN> show snapshot controlfile name;
```

RMAN configuration parameters are:

```
configure snapshot controlfile name to
'E:\ORACLE\product\10.2.0\db_1\database\sncforcl.ora'; # default
```

In this case, it is set to the default location. It can be changed using the *configure* command.

Configuring and Using the Flashback Recovery Area

Out of the most important aspects of a robust backup strategy, one is configuring a destination where the backup would be actually stored. The choice of the right destination with proper configuration plays a huge part in making the entire backup strategy complete. In using RMAN for the same, it is very important that the location chosen will help maintain the backups in the most flexible yet beneficial manner.

There are a couple of places where backups can be placed, be it a disk or tape, but they all come with their own pros and cons. For example, using a disk location is the easier approach and that is why it is the default mode as well, but this requires checking the location constantly to make sure it is not full. Also, the backups which are placed over there should be checked constantly and when they become obsolete, they should be deleted. No one likes to get a page at 2:00 AM stating that the backup job failed because the space got exhausted! Surely a space warning page should be received way before it is actually going to cause harm. Using a disk location would not do all of this.

Last, but certainly not least, what if the disk goes away where the backups are kept?

Tape drives can certainly be used for the storage of the backups. Tape drives will not report that the tape drive size is not sufficient for the backups and so on but still, they are used worldwide because the backups can be pushed over them and they can be stored somewhere far from the data centers. If there is a disaster and the database is lost, the backups are still saved safely on tape which can be used to recreate everything.

However, using tape drives is certainly not as easy as using a disk drive and this has been a topic of discussion for many years among DBAs. Fortunately, Oracle has come up with Oracle Secure Backup (OSB) which has made the task really easy. This will be covered in much more detail in Chapter 10.

Yet despite using OSB, the complexities of using tape drives for backups are certainly not something to be overlooked, making the disk backups as the favorite among many DBAs. To make sure that the disk backups work in the best possible manner, Oracle from 10g onwards introduced a special designated area over the disk which can be solely used for the backup operations.

This area is called the flashback recovery area and once configured, is the default location for all backups and related files. It does solve many of those earlier challenges that DBAs used to face. Though it is a location on the disk, it is not like any dumb mount point or directory which is just lying there. It is an intelligent area, managed by Oracle's own background process, the Manageability Monitor (MMON).

Oracle uses MMON to monitor the area constantly for any space related issues and when there is a drop in the space, the alert interface from 10g onwards is capable of sending an alert both on the Enterprise Manager (OEM) and through emails. This area is checked by MMON every night for any backups which can be deleted in accordance with the retention policies set by the DBA, making them obsolete, and thus releasing space for the new backups. To make things really simple, this is configurable by just a single parameter which is dynamically modifiable. This area can be set by using:

```
alter system set db_recovery_file_dest=<our preferred destination>
```

By default, this area is set to 2 GB in size. This size can be changed to a larger limit if needed by using:

```
alter system set db_recovery_file_dest_size=<our preferred size>
```

The flashback recovery area location can be set to a directory, a completely different file system or even an ASM disk group. The flashback recovery area cannot be on a tape drive. The flashback recovery area will be used for all of the backups in this and other chapters as well.

Connecting to RMAN

RMAN is an O/S level tool and is available at the *$ORACLE_HOME/bin* folder. If Oracle Home is not set, then give a complete path for the binary to fire it up. Otherwise, it can just be started by simply typing over the command prompt (terminal prompt over Linux) as:

```
E:\>rman
```

This brings the DBA to the RMAN prompt. From there they can connect to the target database both by using or not using the recovery catalog. Note that just typing RMAN would not actually get the DBA connected and an explicit connect command needs to be given before RMAN can be used.

Connecting to RMAN Without Using Recovery Catalog

If the recovery catalog has not been created yet, RMAN can still be used without any issues. To connect to RMAN without using the catalog, all is needed is to pass on the target database's sys user name and its password with the correct network alias if RMAN is being fired up while sitting at another machine other than the actual server. All the following commands assume that the DBA is on the same machine where the database is installed that should be backed up.

```
E:\> set ORACLE_SID=ORCL
E:\>rman target / catalog=rcat/rcat@<catalog database>

connected to target database: ORCL (DBID=1214859607)
using target database control file instead of recovery catalog
RMAN>
```

This shows that RMAN has stated that the recovery catalog is not being used; instead, it is using the target database's control file. The switch *nocatalog* is the default option and can be skipped if the intention is not to use the catalog. If this would have been a client machine, the connection string can be used along with the sys user and its password to get connected like below:

```
E:\>rman target sys/oracle@orcl

connected to target database: ORCL (DBID=1214859607)
using target database control file instead of recovery catalog
RMAN>
```

One thing which must be apparent to anyone reading this closely is that the above command displays the password wide open for any one which surely is not a good idea. This can be changed by just typing the user name sys and entering the password in the next line without it being displayed to anyone.

```
E:\>rman target sys@orcl
target database Password:

connected to target database: ORCL (DBID=1214859607)
RMAN>
```

Connecting to RMAN Using a Recovery Catalog

If RMAN is to be used with the recovery catalog, there is nothing much that needs to be done except to use one switch with the user name and password of the catalog user. This user should be created in the catalog database.

```
E:\>rman target / catalog=rcat/rcat

connected to target database: ORCL (DBID=1214859607)
connected to recovery catalog database
RMAN>
```

This time the catalog is being used, not the control file of the target database. This topic is explained in detail in Chapter 7, *Managing the Recovery Catalog*.

A log file can also be used for future reference to see all the commands and their outputs which were entered. By default, the entire output is printed on the screen of the RMAN prompt itself, which would be lost once the session is closed. Using the log file helps preserve that output for any kind of reference or debugging that could be done. The file can be written in the append mode as well so that the previously written content will not get erased.

Here is how the log file can be used. Note how nothing is printed on the RMAN's prompt but gets logged into the log file.

```
E:\>rman target / catalog=rcat/rcat LOG=E:\RMAN.LOG
RMAN> report schema;
RMAN> exit

E:\>more RMAN.log

connected to target database: ORCL (DBID=1214859607)
connected to recovery catalog database
RMAN>
starting full resync of recovery catalog
full resync complete
Report of database schema

List of Permanent Datafiles
===========================
File Size(MB) Tablespace              RB segs Datafile Name
---- -------- -------------------- ------- ------------------------
1    500      SYSTEM                  YES
E:\ORACLE\PRODUCT\10.2.0\ORADATA\ORCL\SYSTEM01.DBF
2    30       UNDOTBS1                YES
E:\ORACLE\PRODUCT\10.2.0\ORADATA\ORCL\UNDOTBS01.DBF
```

If some specific command needs to be run while connecting to the RMAN prompt, this can be done by using the switch *cmdfile* parameter which is similar to running a SQL file while connecting to the SQL prompt. This does require a RMAN script file to be available which can be created using any chosen editor. The file should be usable by the user who is running the RMAN with proper permissions and correct syntax. Here is a simple script that shows how it can be used while firing up RMAN.

```
E:\>copy con samplefile
report schema;

        1 file(s) copied.

E:\> set ORACLE_SID=ORCL
E:\>rman target / catalog=rcat/rcat@<catalog database>
cmdfile='e:\samplefile'

connected to target database: ORCL (DBID=1214859607)
connected to recovery catalog database

RMAN> report schema;

<.....output trimmed .....>
# The output is the same as in the above command. RMAN will automatically
run the command from 'e:\sampefile' file
```

If a duplicate database is going to be created, the auxilary mode of the RMAN connection can be used. By doing this, a connection can be made to the auxiliary instance, which is required to create a duplicate database. This can be done like this:

```
E:\ rman AUXILIARY SYS/aux@remote
```

This type of connection is described further in Chapter 5.

Switching to Archivelog Mode

The Oracle database stores all the changes that are done in the redo log files. These files are used in the cyclical manner and the background process LGWR (log writer) keeps on writing to them again and again. Whenever LGWR switches over from one file and jumps onto another one, the previous log group is set to be checkpointed. LGWR would then, in the next cycle, overwrite the redo log file only if the checkpoint has been completed. By default, no copy of the checkpointed data is made elsewhere except putting it into the corresponding datafile, thereby opening up a serious loophole for the time when recovery of this data would be needed. Following is a hypothetical situation to describe this.

Assume a situation where a whole database backup was taken last Sunday. The type of the database used is OLTP, which means that since that backup, there is a quite a bit of activity that has happened. Assume the current day is Friday and there is a crash. A backup was taken on Sunday which has data up to that day. Since then, there has been a lot of activity and the redo log files have been constantly checkpointed to store those changes, remembering that they are circular. Therefore, if the backup that was taken last Sunday is to be restored, the DBA is thrown back to that stage. Since all the changes which happened since that time are overwritten, thanks to the circular nature of the redo logs, the database cannot be recovered. Even though there was a cold backup, the data for the one week is still lost, which is surely not acceptable. Think about that happening with the bank in which someone has their account!

The solution for the above problem is that somehow, before the redo logs are to be overwritten, they should be saved somewhere. If they cannot, something like their copy at least should be or in other words, the redo logs should be archived. Oracle gives exactly the same solution for this issue with the concept of archived redo log files which are created at every log switch and protect the changes recorded in the redo logs before they can be reused.

Once the ARCH process finishes creating the archived redo log of the current redo log file, the LGWR process is able to continue. The file is associated with the current log sequence of the redo log file that has the same contents. This file is used by Oracle to recover the database without losing a single byte.

Besides using archived logs for the recovery, they are also used in the high availability environments in synching the standby database. Using archived logs, there can be a complete disaster recovery solution ready which would help in getting up a standby database in no time when some unfortunate disaster stops the primary database. Also for some reason, like point-in-time recovery, there is a need at times to peek into the database. This can be done using the archivelog files when what is desired is not the current information but some statement fired up last week.

Setting Up the Archivelog Mode

By default, the Oracle database is not configured to work in the archivelog mode. This means that there is no archivelog file created. To see whether the database is in the archivelog mode or not, use the command *archive log list* like below:

```
SQL>
archive log list

Database log mode              Archive Mode
Automatic archival             Enabled
Archive destination            USE_DB_RECOVERY_FILE_DEST
Oldest online log sequence     164
Next log sequence to archive   166
Current log sequence           166
SQL>
```

So looking at the above command and results, the database is indeed in the archivelog mode and automatic archivelog creation is enabled. Also, the destination where the archived log files go is set to the flashback recovery area which is the default location if no destination is set. The next three numbers are the log sequences which were generated by the database and will be archived.

The default destination of the archiving is the flashback recovery area from 10g onwards. In addition to this, there can be nine other destinations that can be set for archiving which can be either to the local database or to some remote database primarily used for standby configurations. To do this, set the parameter *log_archive_dest_n* where *n* stands for 1 to 10. In 10g, the 10th destination is set to the flashback recovery area by default which can be changed also if so desired. Archiving is done by a dedicated background process, the archiver (ARCH), which is by default started as a single process and the number can be changed to 10 if there are any issues or contentions. This can be done with the parameter *log_archive_max_processes* which can be changed when the database is running as well.

Just like there are 10 destinations, there can be states of them as well which can be set that tell the archive process to use or discard those destinations. This is done through the *log_archive_dest_state_n* parameter which can be set to three values: *enable*, *defer* and *alternate*, out of which *enable* is the default value designating that the state can be used for archiving the redo log files. *defer* is used when the destination is not working for some reason and the archive logs should be stopped from being created over there. *alternate* reflects that the specific destination is not enabled by default but is usable if some other destination becomes unavailable.

All the archivelog files use a formatting for the naming convention which is controlled by the *log_archive_format* parameter. The default value for this parameter is dependent on the database version and the operating system. For example, from 10g onwards, this parameter uses *%r* as one of the formatting strings where *r* represents the reset log number used where the archivelogs of the previous incarnation number of the database can be incorporated as well without needing to throw them away.

So with all the parameters' information in hand, put the database in the archivelog mode. This involves a clean shutdown of the database and the database must be in the mount stage. So do this:

```
SQL>
shut immediate
SQL>
startup mount
SQL>
alter
 database archivelog;

Database altered.

SQL> alter
 database open;

Database altered.
```

```
SQL>
```

The status of the database that is in the archivelog mode can be verified or not by using the *archivelog list* command. Now the database is in archivelog mode which opens the door to all the options available for backup and recoveries. If the database is highly OLTP, it can be an enormous space that archivelogs take up, so it is essential to delete those archivelogs which are not needed any more and for this, setting up proper retention policy for them would be beneficial.

Taking the First Backup and Performing the First Recovery

Now it is nearly time to take the first backup and perform the first ever recovery. To keep things simple, take the backup of the non-system tablespace users and perform a recover of it as well. For doing both, use RMAN. Start first by checking whether there is any backup of the tablespace users or not.

```
RMAN> list backup of tablespace users;

using target database control file instead of recovery catalog

RMAN> backup tablespace users;

input datafile fno=00004
name=E:\ORACLE\product\10.2.0\oradata\orcl\users01.dbf
Finished backup at 16-AUG-09

Starting Control File and spfile Autobackup at 16-AUG-09
piece
handle=E:\ORACLE\product\10.2.0\flash_recovery_area\orcl\autobackup\2009_08_
16\O1_MF_S_695070559_58J30800_.BKP comment=NONE
Finished Control File and SPFILE Autobackup at 16-AUG-09
RMAN>
```

Remember that multiple channels were configured as well as the control file's autobackup, so those are being obtained with the tablespace backup. The backup has gone to the flashback recovery area only. Try to list the backup now:

```
RMAN> list backup of tablespace users;

List of Backup Sets
===================

BS Key  Type LV Size       Device Type Elapsed Time Completion Time
------- ---- -- ---------- ----------- ------------ ---------------
168     Full    8.19M      DISK        00:00:01     16-AUG-09
        BP Key: 168   Status: AVAILABLE  Compressed: NO  Tag:
TAG20090816T190917
```

```
     Piece Name:
E:\ORACLE\product\10.2.0\flash_recovery_area\orcl\backupset\2009_08_16\O1_mf
_nnndf_tag20090816t190917_58j3065v_.bkp
  List of Datafiles in backup set 168
  File LV Type Ckp SCN    Ckp Time   Name
  ---- -- ---- ---------- --------- ----
   4       Full 4691653    16-AUG-09
E:\ORACLE\PRODUCT\10.2.0\ORADATA\ORCL\USERS01.DBF
RMAN>
```

Nice! So now there is a backup with the status *available* which means it can be used to perform the recovery. For this, the original file of the tablespace has been removed.

When using Windows, just shut the instance down and move the datafile of the users tablespace. Do not try this on the production database!

Next, drop this datafile and try to start up the database.

```
E:\oracle\product\10.2.0\oradata\orcl>sqlplus / as sysdba

Connected to an idle instance.

SQL>
startup

ORACLE instance started.
Total System Global Area  167772160 bytes
Fixed Size                  1247900 bytes
Variable Size              71304548 bytes
Database Buffers           92274688 bytes
Redo Buffers                2945024 bytes
Database mounted.
ORA-01157: cannot identify/lock data file 4 - see DBWR trace file
ORA-01110: data file 4: 'E:\ORACLE\product\10.2.0\oradata\orcl\users01.dbf'
```

As expected, the database cannot be started since the datafile is not found by Oracle. Check what the issue is with the file.

```
SQL>
select * from
 V$recover_file;

FILE# ONLINE  ONLINE_STATUS    ERROR        CHANGE#      TIME
----  ------- ---------------- ------       -------      ----
 4    ONLINE  ONLINE           FILE NOT FOUND      0
```

This shows that the file is not found. This is expected as the file has been removed by the DBA. The file is still online, so as a good practice, make it offline before attempting recovery of it.

```
SQL>
alter
 database datafile 4 offline;
```

Now restore and recover the datafile with the backup that has already been taken.

```
RMAN> restore datafile 4;

restoring datafile 00004 to
E:\ORACLE\product\10.2.0\oradata\orcl\users01.dbf
channel ORA_DISK_1: reading from backup piece
E:\ORACLE\product\10.2.0\flash_recovery_area\orcl\backupset\2009_08_16\O1_mf
_nnndf_tag20090816t190917_58J3065V_.bkp
channel ORA_DISK_1: restored backup piece 1
piece
handle=E:\ORACLE\product\10.2.0\flash_recovery_area\orcl\backupset\2009_08_1
6\o1_mf_nnndf_tag20090816t190917_58j3065v_.bkp tag=tag20090816t190917
channel ORA_DISK_1: restore complete, elapsed time: 00:00:02
Finished restore at 16-AUG-09

RMAN> recover datafile 4;
```

As per RMAN, the file is recovered. Now verify it.

```
SQL>
select * from
 v$recover_file;

no rows selected
```
So there is no output from the view which indeed means that the file has finally been recovered.

To recover other files, a similar technique is used. It may happen for some files, not necessarily the same way that would be picked up due to the nature of the files, but in general, only these two steps are being used: restoring of the damaged file(s) or the entire database and then recovering it. Easy, yes?

Checking RMAN Syntax Using *checksyntax*

As RMAN is a very feature-rich tool, there are many options which come with it. It is not possible to remember all the commands with their numerous options. To check the commands issued at the command line or the commands within the scripts of RMAN, there is a syntax-check mode that RMAN offers. It can be fired up using:

```
C:\rman checksyntax
RMAN> run { backup as database; }
```

```
RMAN-00571: ===========================================================
RMAN-00569: =============== ERROR MESSAGE STACK FOLLOWS ===============
RMAN-00571: ===========================================================
RMAN-00558: error encountered while parsing input commands
RMAN-01009: syntax error: found "database": expecting one of: "backupset,
copy, compressed"
RMAN-01007: at line 1 column 17 file: standard input
```

The output shows that the command is wrong, and the actual command should contain either a *copy* or *backup set* option. Try putting one in:

```
RMAN> run { backup as copy database; }

The command has no syntax errors
```

So it is indeed correct and RMAN says so as well. This *checksyntax* can come in very handy when the RMAN documentation cannot be accessed quickly, either offline or online. With this, within minutes the option can be checked.

There is one more way to check the RMAN commands for the remaining parts if they cannot be recalled. Try typing in the *backup* command and see what can be used with it:

```
RMAN> backup
2>
3>

RMAN-00571: ===========================================================
RMAN-00569: =============== ERROR MESSAGE STACK FOLLOWS ===============
RMAN-00571: ===========================================================
RMAN-00558: error encountered while parsing input commands
RMAN-01009: syntax error: found "end-of-file": expecting one of:
"archivelog, as, backup, backupset, blocks, channel, check, copy, copies,
controlfilecopy, cumulative, current, database, datafile, datafilecopy,
device, diskratio, db_recovery_file_dest, db_file_name_convert, duration,
filesperset, for, format, full, force, incremental, keep, (, maxsetsize,
nochecksum, noexclude, nokeep, not, proxy, pool, reuse, recovery, skip,
spfile, setsize, tablespace, tag, to, validate"
RMAN-01007: at line 3 column 1 file: standard input
```

This reveals that after three lines, all the options of the *backup* command are presented. Surely this is not a very clean way, but can be useful at times when the DBA is trying to form a command and has forgotten what to put and where.

Conclusion

In this chapter, how to configure the environment for RMAN using the *configure* command was detailed. Also shown was how connections to RMAN can be established with or without using a recovery catalog. Additionally, the database was converted to archivelog mode, enabling maximum availability for all the backup and recovery options.

Next, how to check the syntax of RMAN commands using *checksyntax* was illustrated. After that, the first backup of a single tablespace was accomplished and how it can be recovered using that backup was revealed.

Chapter 3 will give a much more detailed view of how to do backups using RMAN and several techniques will be covered including incremental and physical backups as well as an in-depth look into compression and encryption.

Backing Up the
Database Using RMAN

Introduction

This chapter covers almost all aspects of RMAN database backup techniques. The first section of this chapter will cover backup of all physical files of the database such as the control file, datafile, spfile and archived redo log files and test all procedures with real examples.

In addition to physical file backup techniques, one of RMAN's key features will be shown: incremental backups. Using this technique, RMAN makes a backup of only the changed data blocks, thereby saving time and space. In this chapter, the reader will first become familiar with the different types of incremental backups and then examine each one in depth.

The second section of this chapter will cover other RMAN features such as compression and encryption. In order to securely back up datafiles, RMAN can encrypt them using different encryption algorithms so that a backup file cannot be restored unless the password is known. By using the RMAN compression feature, the backup of the database can be compressed using different compression algorithms which will inevitably reduce disk space.

Two commands used to get detailed information from the database about backup will be reviewed at the end of the chapter: the *list* and *report* commands. Using these commands allows broad information about the backups to be obtained. They also can be used to get information about obsolete backups that are not needed and should be deleted, and information about the files which need to be backed up. Those will be explored in scenarios in this chapter as follows:

- Backing up the whole database

- Backing up the database in noarchivelog mode

- Backing up the control file

- Backing up the server parameter file

- Backing up datafiles

- Backing up archived redo log files

- Backing up tablespaces

- Backing up backup sets

- Taking incremental backups

- Block change tracking overview

- Creating compressed and encrypted backups

It is time to explore the backup world of Oracle and look at backup techniques and solutions with detailed step-by-step explanations.

The examples in this chapter assume that a Flash Recovery Area (FRA) has been configured in the database instance. This is done by setting the *db_recovery_file_dest_size* and *db_recovery_file_dest* instance parameters. In this case, the *db_recovery_file_dest* instance parameter is *C:\oracle\product\10.2.0\flash_recovery_area*. Oracle automatically uses the name of the database for the subdirectory that actually holds the backups. For more information on the flashback recovery area, please refer to Chapter 2.

Backing Up the Whole Database

Whole database backup means backing up all datafiles and control files. This type of backup is performed in two cases:

- When the database is open and users can insert data to the database

- When the database is closed

RMAN can backup the database while it is in use and open for users. In this situation, all changes made by users are written to redo log files. If the backup process takes a long time and users make a lot of changes to the database, the redo log files are switched and archived during backup. All these archived redo log files have to be backed up as well. Also, verify that the current redo log file at the end of the database backup is also archived and backed up.

If backup does not take a long time and there are no log switches, then all changes made to the database are in the current redo log file. This file is then archived and backed up during the database backup process for further recovery operation capability. When backup is restored, RMAN uses archived redo log files to apply all changes made during backup.

To implement the whole database backup process, follow these steps:

```
RMAN> backup database;
RMAN> SQL
'alter system switch logfile'';
RMAN> exit

C:\oracle\------>dir
06.08.2009  19:10              7 143 424
o1_mf_ncsnf_tag20090806t190942_57os2p4w_.bkp
06.08.2009  19:10          539 058 176
o1_mf_nnndf_tag20090806t190942_57os17f5_.bkp

c:\oracle\-------->dir
06.08.2009  19:11          24 986 112 o1_mf_1_2_57os3mnz_.arc
```

In the example above, it can be seen how simple it is to create a backup of the database using RMAN. Using the above commands, RMAN created two backup files:

1. One for controlfile and spfile:

    ```
    O1_mf_ncsnf_tag20090806t190942_57os2p4w_.bkp
    ```

2. One for datafiles:

    ```
    O1_mf_nnndf_tag20090806t190942_57os17f5_.bkp
    ```

Then, the current online redo log file is switched and archived in the archivelog folder:

```
O1_mf_1_2_57os3mnz_.arc
```

RMAN performs the backup process while the database is running and redo logs filled with changes are made to the database. When the backup process finishes, changes are made in the current redo log file, so archive those and keep them in the backup of the database. To see this more clearly, look at the following scenario.

In this scenario, some changes are made to the database during RMAN backup and the database is restored by not applying archived redo log files generated during backup. Do not try this scenario in real life; if done, the data will be lost!

Open three connections as follows:

- In the first session, get the SCN number of the database.

- In the second session, back up the database using RMAN.

- In the third session, insert data into the database while performing the RMAN backup.

In the first session, get the SCN number of the database:

```
SQL>
select
 current_scn
from
v$database;

CURRENT_SCN
-----------
     547409
SQL>
```

In the second session, create a table.

```
SQL>
Create
table tbl_test_rman (id NUMBER);

Table created.
SQL>
```

In the third session, take a backup of the database using RMAN.

```
RMAN> backup database;
```

While RMAN creates the backup of the database, switch to the second session and insert a row in a table and commit it.

```
SQL> insert into
tbl_test_rman values(1);
SQL>
commit;
```

When the backup finishes, switch to the first session and get the last SCN value of the database:

```
SQL>
select
current_scn
from
v$database;

CURRENT_SCN
-----------
    547507
SQL>
```

Now, check the SCN value of the row which was inserted during RMAN backup:

```
SQL>
select
ora_rowscn, id
from
 tbl_test_rman;

ORA_ROWSCN          ID
----------  ----------
    547445           1
SQL>
```

The SCN code result values are as follows:

```
Before Backup scn    547409
Row Insert scn       547445
After backup scn     547507
```

Now close the database, take it to the mount mode and restore the backup:

```
RMAN> shutdown immediate
RMAN> startup mount
RMAN> restore database;
```

Exit from RMAN and connect to SQL*Plus. Then perform a user-managed recovery with the *until cancel* option to not apply any archived redo log files:

```
SQL>
recover database until cancel;

ORA-00279: change 547436 generated at 08/06/2009 20:12:42 needed for thread
1
ORA-00289: suggestion :
C:\ORACLE\product\10.2.0\flash_recovery_area\orcl\archivelog\2009_08_06\O1_m
f_1_2_%u_.arc
ORA-00280: change 547436 for thread 1 is in sequence #2

Specify log: {<RET>=suggested | filename | auto | cancel}
cancel

Media recovery cancelled.
```

```
SQL>
alter database open resetlogs;

Database altered.

SQL>
select * from
tbl_test_rman;

no rows selected
SQL>
```

The changes made to the database were in the redo log file and not applied to the datafile during recovery. This is because an incomplete recovery was performed, although still to a consistent point for all the datafiles in the database, and the redo log file was reset, thereby overwriting the contents of the last active, i.e., current as of the time of the backup, redo log. If the datafiles were not consistent, Oracle would not allow opening the database, even with a *resetlogs* command.

Had the database been opened in the normal way, then the SMON process would see the last SCN number (547507) in the control file and a different value in the headers of the datafile (547409 because it was restored from backup) and would have automatically applied changes from the current redo log file. Therefore, it would have added the row of the table which relates to the 547445 SCN number from the redo log file to the datafile. By opening the database, the user can see the row that was added during backup. In fact, this is not a row coming from backup of the datafile; it is the one added automatically from the redo log when the database opens.

The main purpose of the above scenario was to show the importance of backing up the current online redo log file after the RMAN backup in order to be able to recover the database and not lose the data. This should be pointed out again: do not try the above-mentioned scenario in the production database, or the data will be lost!

Backing Up a Database Running in noarchivelog Mode

Although Oracle strongly recommends running the production database in archivelog mode, there will likely be some circumstances where the database needs to be run in noarchivelog mode. The obvious case is that when running the data warehouse system, archived redo logs should not have to be created for each of the running batch jobs. By running the database in noarchivelog mode, any recovery process is automatically refused because there will not be any archived redo logs to apply to the restored datafiles.

The only option is reverting the database to the last full backup and with that, all changes made after the full backup will be lost. This type of backup is called cold backup. If archived redo log files being generated is not desired and the data to the database that was changed after the last full backup can be easily loaded, then running the noarchivelog database may be an option.

To create a cold backup of the database running in noarchivelog mode using RMAN, the database should be mounted but not opened. If the database is backed up in the open state, the following error appears:

```
RMAN> backup database;

<....... output trimmed .......>
<....... output trimmed .......>
RMAN-00571: ===========================================================
RMAN-00569: =============== error message stack follows ===============
RMAN-00571: ===========================================================
RMAN-03009: failure of backup command on ORA_DISK_1 channel at 03/09/2010
02:01:14
ORA-19602: cannot backup or copy active file in noarchivelog mode
```

The following script shuts down the database and starts it in mount mode, and then creates a backup of the database:

```
RMAN> run
2> {
3> shutdown immediate
4> startup mount
5> backup database;
6> }
```

 Please note that Oracle does not recommend running the database in noarchivelog mode!

Backing Up the Control File

The control file is of great importance to the Oracle database. If the control file is lost, the database will not run. Therefore, control files need to be protected from any failure and backed up correctly. A backup of the control file can be created using RMAN as follows:

```
RMAN> backup current controlfile;
```

Using the above command, a new backup set is created and the control file is backed up.

If a backup of control files needs to be created each time a backup of the database is done, use the *include current controlfile* command. In this example, datafile 4 is backed up and the current control file together using one command:

```
RMAN> backup datafile 4 include current controlfile;
```

When the *system01.dbf* file is backed up, the control file and the spfile are automatically backed up. This is shown in the following example:

```
C:\oracle\---------->dir
              0 File(s)              0 bytes
RMAN> backup device type disk datafile 1;
C:\oracle\--------->dir
O1_mf_ncsnf_tag20090808t002639_57s00o1y_.bkp
o1_mf_nnndf_tag20090808t002639_57rzzhg5_.bkp
```

From the above example, it is obvious that even though the control file and the spfile were not individually backed up, by backing up the *system01.dbf* file, those files have been backed up automatically.

If the autobackup feature in RMAN configuration is enabled, then each time a structural change is made to the database, an automatic backup of the control file is performed. This concept was described in detail in Chapter 1 under the section on autobackup.

To create an image copy of the control file, use the following command:

```
RMAN> backup as copy current controlfile format `c:\bkp_controlfile.ctl';
```

Using this command, *c:\bkp_controlfile.ctl* is created. This file will be a binary copy of the current control file. This type of file may be used directly without RMAN restoration when all control files are lost. In the scenario below, an image copy of the control file is created and the database is recovered using this file from loss of all control files:

```
C:\>rman target \
RMAN> backup as copy current controlfile format 'c:\control.ctl';

#We take image copy of current control file
<....... output omitted .......>
output filename=C:\control.ctl tag=tag20090819t134500 recid=1
stamp=695310300
RMAN> exit
Recovery Manager complete.

C:\>sqlplus "/ as sysdba"
SQL>
shutdown immediate
SQL>
host

C:\>cd c:\oracle\product\10.2.0\oradata\test
#Below, after shutting down the database, we delete all control files and
copy newly created image copy of control file to original destination
C:\oracle\product\10.2.0\oradata\test>del *.ctl
C:\>copy control.ctl c:\oracle\product\10.2.0\oradata\test
        1 file(s) copied.
C:\>exit

SQL>
startup nomount
SQL>
alter
system set control_files='c:\oracle\product\10.2.0\oradata\test\control.ctl'
scope=spfile;

System altered.
#Above, in startup nomount mode, we change control_files parameter in spfile
and indicate newly create image copy of control file. Then shutdown the
database and bring it to mount mode.

SQL>
Shutdown immediate
SQL>
startup mount
SQL>
alter
database open;
alter database open
*

Error at line 1:
ORA-01589: must use resetlogs or noresetlogs option for database open
```

```
#Now, we do not need to open database in resetlogs mode, or we lose data in
redo log files. So we connect to RMAN and recover the database. RMAN
automatically finds proper redo log file and apply all changes to datafiles

SQL>
exit
C:\>rman target /

RMAN> recover database;

<....... output omitted .......>
archive log thread 1 sequence 2 is already on disk as file
C:\oracle\product\10.2.0\oradata\test\redo01.log
archive log filename=C:\oracle\product\10.2.0\oradata\test\redo01.log
thread=1 sequence=2
media recovery complete, elapsed time: 00:00:01
Finished recover at 19-AUG-09

#Now, we can easily open the database using resetlogs option

RMAN> alter database open resetlogs;
database opened
RMAN>
```

> 🔔 Note: The *resetlogs* operation, performed after having
> applied the online redo log file in recovery, is done because
> the control file used is a backup control file and the
> resetlogs operation synchronizes datafile and redo log
> headers to the control file.

An RMAN backup set can be made from the control file created above. To
do that, use the *backup controlfilecopy* command as shown below:

```
RMAN> backup as copy current controlfile format 'c:\control.ctl';
RMAN> backup controlfilecopy 'c:\control.ctl';

channel ora_disk_1: starting full datafile backupset
input control file copy name=C:\control.ctl
RMAN>
```

Multiplexing Control Files

DBAs need to protect control files from any type of loss, and to help with
that, Oracle recommends multiplexing control files and locating them at
different hard drive partitions. Use the following steps where the control files
are multiplexed to a different hard drive:

Backing Up the Control File

```
SQL>
shutdown immediate

startup
nomount

alter
system set
control_files='C:\oracle\product\10.2.0\oradata\test\control01.ctl',
'd:\control01.ctl' scope=spfile;
SQL>
shutdown immediate
```

Now copy the *control01.ctl* file to the second location and start the database.

```
SQL>
startup

select
name
from
v$control file;

Name
-----------------------------
C:\oracle\product\10.2.0\oradata\test\control01.ctl
d:\control01.ctl
SQL>
```

Oracle now uses both images of the control file, i.e. it is effectively duplexed.

Backing Up the Server Parameter File

If the spfile is used as recommended, then a backup can easily be created using RMAN as follows:

```
RMAN> backup spfile;
```

If the database is run by using the text parameter file (not the spfile), it cannot be backed up and an error occurs. In that case, create a spfile and take its backup as follows:

```
RMAN> backup spfile;

RMAN-06062: can not backup spfile because the instance was not started with
spfile
#Connect from sqlplus and create spfile. Shutdown the server and startup it
using spfile. Then try to take backup using RMAN

SQL>
create
```

```
spfile from pfile;

File created.

SQL>
shutdown immediate
startup

RMAN> backup spfile;
```

Once a spfile has been created, Oracle uses it at the next startup. Please note that if the control file has been configured to autobackup mode, a backup of the spfile is also created automatically.

Backing Up Datafiles

Using RMAN, a backup of datafiles can be created when the database is running. To perform this type of backup, indicate the datafile number which can be obtained from the *v$datafile* data dictionary view.

 Note: In these examples, the backups are not written to the Flash Recovery Area, but instead are written to a custom location specified by the format clause.

```
SQL>
select
 file#, name
from
 v$datafile;

 FILE#            NAME
 -------          -----------------------------------------------
      1           C:\oracle\product\10.2.0\oradata\test\system01.dbf
      2           c:\oracle\product\10.2.0\oradata\test\undotbs01.dbf
      3           c:\oracle\product\10.2.0\oradata\test\sysaux01.dbf
      4           c:\oracle\product\10.2.0\oradata\test\users01.dbf
```

To back up *users01.dbf*, use this command:

```
RMAN> backup datafile 4 format 'c:\users01.bkp';

input datafile fno=00004
name=C:\oracle\product\10.2.0\oradata\test\users01.dbf
piece handle=C:\users01.bkp tag=TAG20090808T132957 comment=none
```

To back up more than one datafile, indicate the number of datafiles:

```
RMAN> backup datafile 2, 4 format ='c:\datafiles_2_4.bkp';

input datafile fno=00002
name=C:\oracle\product\10.2.0\oradata\test\undotbs01.dbf
input datafile fno=00004
name=C:\oracle\product\10.2.0\oradata\test\users01.dbf
piece handle=C:\datafiles_2_4.bkp tag=TAG20090808T133405 comment=none
```

A datafile can be backed up by using its location as shown below:

```
RMAN> backup datafile 'c:\oracle\product\10.2.0\oradata\test\users01.dbf'
FORMAT='c:\user01.bkp';

input datafile fno=00004
name=C:\oracle\product\10.2.0\oradata\test\users01.dbf
piece handle=C:\user01.bkp tag=tag20090808t133052 comment=none
```

To automatically add *ORACLE_HOME* and *ORACLE_SID*, use the ? and @ characters. For example, to backup datafile number 4 (which is *users01.dbf*) to the *C:\oracle\product\10.2.0\db_1\oradata\test* directory, use the following syntax:

```
RMAN> backup datafile 4 format='?/oradata/@/users01.bkp';

input datafile fno=00004
name=C:\oracle\product\10.2.0\oradata\test\users01.dbf
piece handle=c:\oracle\product\10.2.0\db_1\oradata\test\users01.bkp
```

To create an image copy of a datafile, use the following command:

```
RMAN> backup as copy datafile 4 format 'c:\users01_ascopy.dbf';

input datafile fno=00004
name=c:\oracle\product\10.2.0\oradata\test\users01.dbf
output filename=c:\users01_ascopy.dbf tag=tag20090808t133123 recid=4
stamp=694359084
```

To backup an image copy of the datafile, use the *backup datafilecopy* command:

```
RMAN> backup datafilecopy 'c:\users01_ascopy.dbf' format
='c:\users01_image_backup.bkp';
```

It should be noted that image copy backup of datafiles is the same as the datafiles themselves block by block. But the main advantage of image copy over OS copy is that while creating an image copy of the datafile, RMAN checks the content of the datafile for corruption, and it can also be restored by RMAN.

Optimizing UNDO in Oracle 11g

Undo tablespace contains both committed and uncommitted data. On the versions prior to Oracle 11g, RMAN was backing up the undo data completely. But starting with Oracle 11g, RMAN backs up only uncommitted transactions that are written to the undo datafile. That is because when backing up the database, RMAN backs up the original datafile which already contains committed data, so there is no need to backup the committed data written in the undo datafile once again. The undo optimization feature is enabled by default.

Taking Multisection Backups

Starting with Oracle 11g, large datafiles can be backed up in a parallel mode in sections. More than one channel can be allocated and a backup of a single huge datafile, for example, with one terabyte (TB) in size, can be taken in sections using all allocated channels. This type of backup method is called multisectional backup. As a result, each backup piece has a section which contains contiguous blocks of a datafile. To take a multisection backup, use the *section size* command.

In the following example, the datafile is backed up with 1 GB in size by dividing it into three sections and backup in parallel mode over three channels:

```
RMAN> run
2> {    allocate channel ch1 device type disk;
3>      allocate channel ch2 device type disk;
4>      allocate channel ch3 device type disk;
5>      backup section size 400m datafile 4;
6> }
```

And here is the output:

```
allocated channel: ch1
allocated channel: ch2
allocated channel: ch3

channel ch1: starting full datafile backup set
backing up blocks 1 through 51200
<....output trimmed .....>

channel ch2: specifying datafile(s) in backup set
backing up blocks 51201 through 102400
<....output trimmed .....>

channel ch3: starting full datafile backup set
```

```
backing up blocks 102401 through 137432
<....output trimmed .....>
```

RMAN divided the datafile into three different sections identifying the block range for each section and created backup files through three parallel channels.

Backing Up Archived Redo Log Files

Archived redo log files are used during the recovery process. They contain all the changes made to a database after backup, so backing up archived redo log files is of vital importance. If more than one archive destination is declared, RMAN will refer to only one of them and create backup from that location. If one of the archived redo log files is corrupted at that location, then RMAN will copy that archived redo log file from the second location. To backup all archived redo log files in the database, use this command:

```
RMAN> backup archivelog all;
```

Additionally, backup of archived redo log files may be done after every backup command. To backup archived redo log files as an addition to another backup, add the *plus archivelog* command. When using the *plus archivelog* command, RMAN:

- Archives current redo log file

- Archives all archived redo log files

- Backs up the files which were indicated at the first part of the command

- Archives current redo log file again

- Backs up all archived redo log files that were generated during backup

In the following example, a backup of the user's tablespace and all archived redo logs is taken. Before this backup process, have a look at the list of archived redo log files which were already created:

```
SQL>
select
recid, stamp, sequence#, name
from
v$archived_log;

RECID       STAMP         SEQUENCE#   NAME
----------  ----------    ----------  --------------------------------
1           695127182     3
            C:\ORACLE\PRODUCT\10.2.0\FLASH_RECOVERY_AREA\ORCL\ARCHIVELOG\2009_08_17\O1_MF_1_3_58KW1XWS_.ARC
2           695127183     2
            C:\ORACLE\PRODUCT\10.2.0\FLASH_RECOVERY_AREA\ORCL\ARCHIVELOG\2009_08_17\O1_MF_1_2_58KW1XQX_.ARC
```

Now create a backup of the user's tablespace and all archived redo log files:

```
RMAN> backup tablespace users plus archivelog;

Starting backup at 17-AUG-09
current log archived
#As we see, firstly RMAN archived current online redo log file
<....... output omitted .......>
#Below it defines archived redo log files which will backed up and archives
them as well
input archive log thread=1 sequence=2 recid=2 stamp=695127183
input archive log thread=1 sequence=3 recid=1 stamp=695127182
input archive log thread=1 sequence=4 recid=3 stamp=695127443
piece
handle=C:\oracle\product\10.2.0\flash_recovery_area\orcl\backupset\2009_08_1
7\o1_mf_annnn_tag20090817t105724_58kwb6k2_.bkp tag=TAG20090817T105724
comment=NONE
channel ORA_DISK_1: backup set complete, elapsed time: 00:00:04
Finished backup at 17-AUG-09

Starting backup at 17-AUG-09
using channel ORA_DISK_1
channel ORA_DISK_1: starting full datafile backupset
channel ORA_DISK_1: specifying datafile(s) in backupset
#Backups datafile users01.dbf
input datafile fno=00004
name=C:\oracle\product\10.2.0\oradata\orcl\users01.dbf
channel ORA_DISK_1: starting piece 1 at 17-AUG-09
channel ORA_DISK_1: finished piece 1 at 17-AUG-09
piece
handle=C:\ORACLE\product\10.2.0\flash_recovery_area\orcl\backupset\2009_08_1
7\o1_mf_nnndf_tag20090817t105729_58kwbb5v_.bkp tag=TAG20090817T105729
comment=NONE
channel ORA_DISK_1: backup set complete, elapsed time: 00:00:01
Finished backup at 17-AUG-09

Starting backup at 17-AUG-09
current log archived
#Archives current online redo log file and backups all archived redo log
files which were created when backup of users tablespace started
using channel ORA_DISK_1
channel ORA_DISK_1: starting archive log backupset
channel ORA_DISK_1: specifying archive log(s) in backup set
input archive log thread=1 sequence=5 recid=4 stamp=695127451
channel ORA_DISK_1: starting piece 1 at 17-AUG-09
channel ORA_DISK_1: finished piece 1 at 17-AUG-09
piece
handle=C:\oracle\product\10.2.0\flash_recovery_area\orcl\backupset\2009_08_1
7\o1_mf_annnn_tag20090817t105731_58kwbdws_.bkp tag=TAG20090817T105731
comment=none
channel ORA_DISK_1: backup set complete, elapsed time: 00:00:02
Finished backup at 17-AUG-09

SQL>
select
recid, stamp, sequence#, name
from
v$archived_log;
```

```
RECID    STAMP       SEQUENCE#     NAME
-----    --------    ------        ----------------------------
  1      695127182      3          ..\o1_mf_1_3_58kw1xws_.arc
  2      695127183      2          ..\o1_mf_1_2_58kw1xqx_.arc
  3      695127443      4          ..\o1_mf_1_4_58kwb3wb_.arc
  4      695127451      5          ..\o1_mf_1_5_58kwbck2_.arc
SQL>
```

As this shows, before this backup process there were two archived redo log files. After backup, two more archived redo log files have been created. Those resulted from the action where RMAN archives the current online redo log files before and after tablespace backup. If tablespace backup takes longer and additional archived redo log files are created during backup, then RMAN archives the current online redo log file and backs up all archived redo log files created after tablespace backup.

Backup of archived redo logs can be limited according to the SCN number, time and the log sequence number. To get the SCN sequence number and timestamp of the archived redo log file, query the *v$archived_log* view. Then, using the *from*, *until* and *between* commands with the *scn*, *sequence* and *time* clauses, the archived redo log files can be backed up based on the requirements selected. The use of these commands is shown in the following example.

To back up the archived redo log file based on log sequence number, use the following command:

```
RMAN> backup archivelog sequence between 2 and 5;
```

Then, to get all archivelogs up to sequence number 5, use:

```
RMAN> backup archivelog until sequence 5;
```

Next, to get archive log file with sequence number 3, use:

```
RMAN> backup archivelog sequence 3;
```

Then to get all archive redo log files starting from sequence number 6 until the end, use:

```
RMAN> backup archivelog from sequence 6;
```

If the archived redo logs need to be backed up based on SCN number, use the same syntax as shown next:

```
RMAN> backup archivelog from scn 552234;
```

The archived redo log file can be backed up based on the timestamp of the first change in the file. To perform this backup, use the TIME clause. In this example, by getting a list of the archived redo log files, all archived redo log files which have been accessed during the previous hour can be backed up:

```
SQL>
select
 to_char(first_time,'ddmmyyyy hh24:mi:ss')
first_time,to_char(next_time,'ddmmyyyy hh24:mi:ss') next_time, sequence#,
stamp from v$archived_log;

FIRST_TIME          NEXT_TIME          SEQUENCE#      STAMP
----------------    ----------------   ----------    ----------
17082009 15:07:55 17082009 15:10:27           14    695142627
17082009 15:10:27 17082009 15:21:18           15    695143278
17082009 15:21:18 17082009 15:22:32           16    695143352
17082009 15:22:32 17082009 15:37:39           17    695144260
17082009 15:37:39 17082009 16:42:24           18    695148144
17082009 16:42:24 17082009 16:42:38           19    695148158
17082009 16:42:38 17082009 16:42:42           20    695148162
17082009 16:42:42 17082009 16:42:43           21    695148163
20 rows selected.
SQL>

RMAN> backup archivelog from time 'sysdate-(1/24)';
```

Delete Input

It is not necessary to keep archived redo log files after backup. They can be easily delete, but they may be deleted by RMAN automatically after backup. To do this, use the *delete input* command. As noted above, when RMAN backs up the archived redo log files, it refers only to one log destination even though there may be more than one. The same holds true with the *delete input* command. Using this command, RMAN deletes the archived redo log files from only one destination. If the *delete all input* command is used, all archived redo log files from all destinations will be deleted. The following example explains this process in more detail.

Here there are two log archive destinations, arc_1 and arc_2, which reside in directory C:\. They have two archived redo log files whose sequence numbers arc 6 and 7, accordingly.

```
C:\>dir arc_1, arc_2

 Directory of C:\arc_1
17.08.2009  17:35              10 752 arc00006_0695149148.001
```

```
17.08.2009  17:35               1 024 arc00007_0695149148.001
              2 File(s)          11 776 bytes

 Directory of C:\arc_2
17.08.2009  17:35              10 752 arc00006_0695149148.001
17.08.2009  17:35               1 024 arc00007_0695149148.001
              2 File(s)          11 776 bytes
```

First, back up archived log 6 and use the *delete input* command to delete it, but only from one log destination:

```
RMAN> backup archivelog sequence 6 delete input;
```

With that command, after backing up that archived redo log file, RMAN deletes it from only one destination. See both destinations as follows:

```
C:\>dir arc_1, arc_2

 Directory of C:\arc_1
17.08.2009  17:35              10 752 arc00006_0695149148.001
17.08.2009  17:35               1 024 arc00007_0695149148.001
              2 File(s)          11 776 bytes

 Directory of C:\arc_2
17.08.2009  17:35               1 024 arc00007_0695149148.001
              1 File(s)           1 024 bytes
```

The archived redo log file from the arc_2 folder has been deleted. Now, back up archived redo log file 7 and use the *delete all input* command to delete that file from all log destinations.

```
RMAN> backup archivelog sequence 7 delete all input;

C:\>dir arc_1, arc_2
 Directory of C:\arc_1
17.08.2009  17:35              10 752 arc00006_0695149148.001
              1 File(s)          10 752 bytes

 Directory of C:\arc_2
              0 File(s)               0 bytes
```

All archived redo log files with sequence number 7 have been deleted from both directories.

Back Up Tablespaces

To back up a tablespace, use the *backup tablespace* command. Using this command, RMAN automatically creates a backup of all datafiles in the tablespace.

```
RMAN> backup tablespace users, system;

input datafile fno=00001
name=c:\oracle\product\10.2.0\oradata\test\system01.dbf
input datafile fno=00004
name=c:\oracle\product\10.2.0\oradata\test\users01.dbf
```

To create a backup file with a specific format, add the *format* keyword:

```
RMAN> backup tablespace users format 'C:\users_tbs.bkp';
```

Moreover, image copy of datafiles in a tablespace may be backed up. In this example, the size of the two datafiles is obtained from the OS.

```
C:\oracle\product\10.2.0\oradata\test1>dir sysaux01.dbf, users01.dbf
09.08.2009  01:00       251 666 432 sysaux01.dbf
09.08.2009  00:58         5 251 072 users01.dbf
```

Then back up these datafiles at the tablespace level and compare the two results:

```
RMAN> backup as copy tablespace users, sysaux format
'c:\backup_tbs_%t_4.bkp';

c:\>dir *.bkp
09.08.2009  00:58       251 666 432 backup_tbs_694400269_4.bkp
09.08.2009  00:58         5 251 072 backup_tbs_694400284_4.bkp
```

The size of the image copy and the datafile are the same. Those files are restored with RMAN if the database crashes. RMAN does not back up temporary tablespace. Those can be viewed in the list of files shown in the RMAN backup output. If RMAN is not able to create temporary tablespaces for some reason, then the message is recorded to the *alert.log* file and the database opens successfully. If backing up the temporary tablespace is attempted, an error message like this appears:

```
RMAN> backup tablespace temp;

Starting backup at 15-AUG-09
using target database control file instead of recovery catalog
allocated channel: ORA_DISK_1
channel ORA_DISK_1: sid=143 devtype=DISK
RMAN-00571: ===========================================================
RMAN-00569: =============== error message stack follows ===============
RMAN-00571: ===========================================================
RMAN-03002: failure of backup command at 08/15/2009 11:34:05
RMAN-20202: tablespace not found in the recovery catalog
RMAN-06019: could not translate tablespace name "TEMP"
```

Backing Up Archived Redo Log Files

73

Because RMAN does not back up the temporary tablespace, during the recovery process it creates the temporary tablespace automatically. In this example, the database is restored at 11:43, and all datafiles are restored except tempfile. At 11:44, when the database is recovered, the temporary tablespace is created automatically as follows:

```
C:\oracle\product\10.2.0\oradata\orcl>dir /tc /od *.dbf
15.08.2009  11:43       503 324 672 system01.dbf
15.08.2009  11:43       251 666 432 sysaux01.dbf
15.08.2009  11:43        26 222 592 undotbs01.dbf
15.08.2009  11:43         5 251 072 users01.dbf
15.08.2009  11:44        20 979 712 temp01.dbf
              5 File(s)     807 444 480 bytes
              0 Dir(s)   14 827 810 816 bytes free
C:\oracle\product\10.2.0\oradata\orcl>
```

Creating Archival Backups

To take backup out of retention policy and make it exempt, use the *keep* option with the *backup* command. In Oracle 10g, the *logs* or *nologs* options can be used to specify that RMAN will, or will not, keep archived redo log files that are necessary for the recovery. However, starting with Oracle 11g, RMAN does not let the DBA keep all the archived redo log files generated after backup is taken. The only archived redo log files backed up are those files which are needed to take the backup to its routine status. The backup can be kept until a specific time or forever.

In the following example, the database is backed up and is taken out of retention policy after 10 days:

```
RMAN>       backup database
2>    keep until time 'sysdate+10'
3>    format 'c:\tmp\test_db%u'
4>    tag testdb_backup;

current log archived
backup will be obsolete on date 05-JUN-10
archived logs required to recover from this backup will be backed up
```

To change the parameter of the *keep* option, use the *change* command. In the following example, the obsolete time of the backup named *testdb_backup* is changed to 20 days:

```
RMAN> change backup
2>    tag testdb_backup
3>    keep until time 'sysdate+20';
```

```
using channel ORA_DISK_1
keep attributes for the backup are changed
backup will be obsolete on date 15-JUN-10
backup set key=21 recid=21 stamp=720028138
RMAN>
```

Creating Compressed Backups

Before Oracle 10gR2, RMAN was not backing up data blocks that had never been used. But if it found a data block that was used once, it was backing it up even if it was empty. That is called NULL compression. Starting from 10gR2, RMAN skips the data blocks that are empty and do not contain any data. This is called unused block compression. The last type of compression is called binary compression where RMAN applies a binary compression algorithm as it writes data blocks to the backup pieces.

Although RMAN uses more CPU space during compression, ultimately compressed backups show up with a smaller size. To use this feature, add the phrase *as compressed backupset* after the *backup* command. To follow the compression process and its difference from backup which is taken without compression, see the following example. Here, a normal, non-compressed backup of the SYSAUX datafile is taken. Then a compressed backup is created and their size is compared:

```
RMAN>backup datafile 3 format 'c:\uncompressed_sysaux.bkp';

rman>backup as compressed backupset datafile 3 format

'c:\compressed_sysaux.bkp';

c:\>dir *.bkp
 09.08.2009  02:20        11 419 648 copmressed_sysaux.bkp
 09.08.2009  02:20       151 863 296 uncompressed_sysaux.bkp
```

As shown, the compressed backup is smaller in size than the uncompressed backup. To identify which files were compressed, query *v$backup_files* as follows:

```
SQL>
select
fname, compressed
from
v$backup_files;

FNAME                     COMPRESSED
-----------               -----------
C:\uncompressed_sysaux.bkp NO
C:\copmressed_sysaux.bkp   YES
```

It is possible to compress archived redo log and incremental backups as follows:

```
RMAN> backup as compressed backupset archivelog all;
RMAN> backup as compressed backupset incremental level 0 database;
RMAN> backup as compressed backupset incremental level 1 database;
RMAN> backup as compressed backupset incremental level 1 cumulative
database;
```

For more information on creating incremental backups, see the *Making Incremental Backups* section later in this chapter.

To set all backups to be compressed as the default mode, make changes in the RMAN configuration parameter as follows:

```
RMAN> configure device type disk backup type to compressed backupset;

using target database control file instead of recovery catalog
new RMAN configuration parameters:
configure device type disk backup type to compressed backupset parallelism
1;
new RMAN configuration parameters are successfully stored

RMAN> show all;
configure device type disk backup type to compressed backupset parallelism
1;
```

By changing this parameter, all backups will be compressed. To return to the default non-compressed configuration, clear the configuration to make future backups be non-compressed:

```
RMAN> configure device type disk clear;
old RMAN configuration parameters:
configure device type disk backup type to compressed backupset parallelism
1;

RMAN configuration parameters are successfully reset to default value

RMAN> show all;
configure device type disk parallelism 1 backup type to backupset;

 # default
```

There is a new compression algorithm that comes with Oracle 11g: ZLIB. This compression algorithm does not use as much CPU as BZIP2, but it produces a backup larger in size than what BZIP2 does. In the following example, three different backups are created: non-compressed; default BZIP2 compressed; and ZLIB compressed. The difference can be seen by checking their sizes.

Backup of the database without using any compression algorithm is created:

```
RMAN> backup database;

piece handle=o1_mf_nnndf_tag20100525t114933_5zpwqy2x_.bkp
tag=TAG20100525T114933 comment=none
```

Now compress the backup using the default BZIP2 compression algorithm:

```
RMAN> show compression algorithm;
RMAN configuration parameters for database with db_unique_name ORCL are:
configure compression algorithm 'BZIP2';

 # default

RMAN> backup as compressed backupset database;

piece handle=o1_mf_nnndf_tag20100525t115237_5zpwxotc_.bkp
tag=TAG20100525T115237 comment=none
```

Next change the configuration of the compression algorithm to create a ZLIB backup:

```
RMAN> configure compression algorithm "ZLIB";
new RMAN configuration parameters:
configure compression algorithm 'ZLIB';

new RMAN configuration parameters are successfully stored

RMAN> backup as compressed backupset database;

piece handle=o1_mf_nnndf_tag20100525t115451_5zpx1w6t_.bkp
tag=tag20100525t115451 comment=none
RMAN>
```

Now check the sizes of all the backup sets and see the difference:

```
1,027,399,680        NO        O1_mf_nnndf_tag20100525t114933_5zpwqy2x_.bkp
186,687,488          bzip2     o1_mf_nnndf_tag20100525t115237_5zpwxotc_.bkp
202,997,760          ZLIB      O1_mf_nnndf_tag20100525t115451_5zpx1w6t_.bkp
```

ZLIB compression requires the Oracle Advanced Compression option and is available in Oracle 11g. Although the output of the backup set size is bigger than backup set compressed with BZIP2 algorithm, ZLIB consumes less CPU space.

Creating Encrypted Backups

It is very simple to restore the database created by RMAN using simple commands. If someone has stolen the backup of the database, they can easily restore it and steal all the data, too. To prevent that from happening, encrypt the backup that has been made. By querying the *v$rman_encryption_algorithms* view, a list of RMAN encryption algorithms can be obtained:

```
SQL>
select
algorithm_id, algorithm_name, algorithm_description, is_default
from
v$rman_encryption_algorithms;

ALGORITHM_ID ALGORITHM_NAME        ALGORITHM_DESCRIPTION IS_DEFAULT
------------ --------------        -------------------------- ---
1            AES128                AES 128-bit key       YES
2            AES192                AES 192-bit key       NO
3            AES256                AES 256-bit key       NO
SQL>
```

There are three forms of encryption in Oracle 10g: transparent, password and dual mode.

- To use transparent mode encryption, Oracle Encryption Wallet should be used.

- To use password mode, a password should be provide by the DBA which will be used in encryption.

- By using dual mode encryption, boh above mentioned modes will be used.

The following example shows how to use password mode to encrypt the backup. Use the *set encryption on* command and the password using the *identified by* command, and encrypt the backup that is taken in this session. Use the *only* keyword at the end to use only password encryption. If the keyword *only* is missed, RMAN uses dual mode encryption and demands the presence of Oracle Encryption Wallet, too.

```
RMAN> set encryption on identified by 'test' only;
```

Backup the users tablespace:

```
RMAN> backup tablespace users;
```

Now try to restore it:

```
RMAN> restore tablespace users;

ORA-19913: unable to decrypt backup
ORA-28365: wallet is not open
```

It is impossible to restore already encrypted backup without using the password. In this situation, if someone has stolen the backup, they will not be able to restore it and steal the data, too, without providing the correct password. Now provide the password and restore the backup:

```
RMAN> set decryption identified by 'test';
RMAN> restore tablespace users;
```

Using the password, tablespace is restored successfully. If a wrong password is provided, it will not restore the backup:

```
RMAN> set decryption identified by 'wrong';

 #wrong password

RMAN> restore tablespace users;

ORA-19913: unable to decrypt backup
ORA-28365: wallet is not open
RMAN>
```

By default, RMAN uses the AES 128-bit key algorithm for encryption. The algorithm can be easily changed using the *configure encryption algorithm* command as follows:

```
RMAN> show encryption algorithm;
RMAN configuration parameters are:
configure encryption algorithm 'AES128';

#default

RMAN> configure encryption algorithm 'AES256';
new RMAN configuration parameters:
configure encryption algorithm 'AES256';

new RMAN configuration parameters are successfully stored

RMAN> show encryption algorithm;
RMAN configuration parameters are:
configure encryption algorithm 'AES256';
```

Again, anytime this configuration is cleared, the encryption algorithm can be returned to its default value as follows:

```
RMAN> configure encryption algorithm clear;

old RMAN configuration parameters:
configure encryption algorithm 'AES256';

RMAN configuration parameters are successfully reset to default value

RMAN> show encryption algorithm;
```

```
RMAN configuration parameters are:

configure encryption algorithm 'AES128'; # default
RMAN>
```

To use Oracle Encryption Wallet, configure RMAN to perform an encrypted backup of any tablespace or whole database automatically. For this, use the *configure encryption for* command. In the following example, RMAN is configured to create an encrypted backup of the database, and the users tablespace is excluded from encryption:

```
RMAN> show all;
RMAN configuration parameters are:
configure encryption for database off;

 # default

configure encryption algorithm 'AES128';

 # default

RMAN> configure encryption for database on;
new RMAN configuration parameters:
configure encryption for database on;

new RMAN configuration parameters are successfully stored

RMAN> configure encryption for tablespace users off;

tablespace users will not be encrypted in future backup sets
new RMAN configuration parameters are successfully stored

RMAN> show all;
RMAN configuration parameters are:
configure encryption for database on;
configure encryption algorithm 'AES128';

 # default

configure encryption for tablespace 'users' off;
```

To return back to default value, clear the *encryption configuration* parameter:

```
RMAN> configure encryption for database clear;
old RMAN configuration parameters:
configure encryption for database on;

RMAN configuration parameters are successfully reset to default value

RMAN> configure encryption for tablespace users clear;

tablespace users will default to database encryption configuration
old RMAN configuration parameters are successfully deleted
```

```
RMAN> show all;
RMAN configuration parameters are:
configure encryption for database off;

 # default
```

Validating Backups

To check the datafiles for any physical or logical corruption and verify whether a datafile is in the correct directory, use the *backup validate* command. This command does not create a backup of any datafile; it checks for validity of the datafiles and updates the *v$database_block_corruption* view in case it finds any corruption. After getting the list of corrupted data blocks, use the Block Media Recovery feature of RMAN to recover the corrupted blocks. This feature is explained in more detail in Chapter 4.

By default, RMAN checks for physical corruption. By using *check logical* syntax, the DBA can check for logical corruption as well. Next, an example is provided of checking and validating a datafile by first manually corrupting it.

To begin, create a tablespace and table by assigning it to that tablespace. Then insert data in the table as follows:

```
SQL>
create
tablespace tbs_test datafile 'c:\tbs_test.dbf' size 1M;

Tablespace created.

SQL>
create
table tbl_test (name varchar2(20)) tablespace tbs_test;

Table created.

SQL>
insert into
tbl_test values('oracle');

1 row created.

SQL>
commit;

Commit complete.
```

Then query the *v$database_block_corruption* view. As the datafile was not validated, it must be empty:

```
SQL>
select * from
v$database_block_corruption;

no rows selected
```

Bring the tablespace to the offline mode, and then corrupt the datafile using the manual corruption methods described in Chapter 4. Then bring the tablespace to the online mode and query the table. The following error occurs:

```
SQL>
alter
tablespace tbs_test offline;

Tablespace altered.

SQL>
alter
tablespace tbs_test online;

Tablespace altered.

SQL>
select * from
tbl_test;
select * from
tbl_test
            *

ERROR at line 1:
ORA-01578: ORACLE data block corrupted (file # 8, block # 13)
ORA-01110: data file 8: 'C:\tbs_test.dbf'
```

Now use the *backup validate* command to check that datafile for any corruption. Then query the *v$database_block_recovery* view:

```
RMAN> backup validate tablespace tbs_test;

SQL>
select * from
v$database_block_corruption;

     FILE#      BLOCK#     BLOCKS CORRUPTION_CHANGE# CORRUPTION
---------- ---------- ---------- ------------------ ---------
         8         13          1                  0 CHECKSUM
SQL>
```

This shows that datafile number 8 has a block corruption in block number 13. Only one block has been corrupted. This information will help to recover that block using Block Media Recovery.

To validate the tablespace, use the following command:

```
RMAN> backup validate tablespace tbs_test;
```

To validate a specific datafile, use the following command:

```
RMAN> backup validate datafile 8;
```

To check the whole database, use the following command:

```
RMAN> backup validate database;
```

To check all archived redo log files, use the following command:

```
RMAN> backup validate archivelog all;
```

To check the spfile, use the following command:

```
RMAN> backup validate spfile;
```

To check the current control file, use the following command:

```
RMAN> backup validate current controlfile;
```

Just as a datafile can be validated for a backup operation, a backup of a datafile can be validated for a restore. To check if a backup is valid and available for a restore operation, use the *restore .... validate* command.

To check backup of the control file, use the following command:

```
RMAN> restore control file validate;
```

To check backup of the spfile, use the following command:

```
RMAN> restore spfile validate;
```

To check backup of tablespace users, use the following command:

```
RMAN> restore tablespace users validate;
```

To check backup of a datafile, use the following command:

```
RMAN> restore datafile 4 validate;
```

To check backup of all archived redo log files, use the following command:

```
RMAN> restore archivelog all validate;
```

To check backup of the whole database, use the following command:

```
RMAN> restore database validate;
```

If RMAN is unable to find the backup file, it returns an error as follows:

```
RMAN> restore spfile validate;

Starting restore at 22-AUG-09
using channel ORA_DISK_1
.....................Output omitted
ORA-27041: unable to open file
OSD-04002: unable to open file
O/S-Error: (OS 3) The system cannot find the path specified
failover to previous backup

RMAN-00571: ===========================================================
RMAN-00569: =============== ERROR MESSAGE STACK FOLLOWS ===============
RMAN-00571: ===========================================================
RMAN-03002: failure of restore command at 08/22/2009 19:49:51
RMAN-06026: some targets not found - aborting restore
RMAN-06729: no backup of the SPFILE found to restore

RMAN>
```

In 10g, it is possible to check only backup sets for any corruptions by using the *validate backupset ...* command. To check a backup set, use:

```
RMAN> validate backupset 2;
```

In Oracle 11g, the *validate* command was expanded with new features. The syntax of the new *validate* command is the same as the syntax of the *backup validate* command. With the new *validate* command, almost everything that needs to be checked can be done. For example, to check validity of the backup of the spfile, use the following command:

```
RMAN> validate spfile
```

Moreover, parallelizing the validity process can be done by dividing it into specified section sizes using the *section size* command. It should be used when different channels have been allocated and the validity needs to be spread over those channels. In the following scenario, three different channels are opened and the validity is parallelized over these three channels with 300M per channel:

```
RMAN> run
{
```

Oracle Backup and Recovery

```
        allocate channel c1 divide type disk;
        allocate channel c2 divide type disk;
        allocate channel c3 divide type disk;
        validate database section size 300m;
}
```

Backing Up Backup Sets

In some circumstances, the backup of backup sets may need to be moved from one disk to another or from disk to tape. To do this using RMAN, use the *backup backupset* command. This command will not create a new backup set, it just creates copies of backup pieces. To understand it more clearly, look at this example. Here, first back up the datafile and use the *list backup* command to get information about that backup. This command is described in more detail later in this chapter. Then by using the *backup backupset* command, get a copy of the newly created backup piece without having a new backup set created as follows:

```
RMAN> backup datafile 4;

input datafile fno=00004
name=c:\oracle\product\10.2.0\oradata\test\users01.dbf
piece handle=../o1_mf_nnndf_tag20090823t124703_591wzqsd_.bkp

RMAN> list backup;

<....... output omitted .......>
Piece Name: ../o1_mf_nnndf_tag20090823t124703_591wzqsd_.bkp
  List of Datafiles in backup set 12

  File LV Type Ckp SCN    Ckp Time  Name
  ---- -- ---- ---------- --------- ----
   4      Full 569712     23-AUG-09
C:\oracle\product\10.2.0\oradata\test\users01.dbf
RMAN>

C:\oracle\product\10.2.0\flash_recovery_area\test\backupset\2009_08_23>dir
23.08.2009  12:47           385 024
o1_mf_nnndf_tag20090823t124703_591wzqsd_.bkp
            1 File(s)        385 024 bytes

RMAN> BACKUP backupset 12;

<....... output omitted .......>
channel ora_disk_1: backup piece
../o1_mf_nnndf_tag20090823t124703_591wzqsd_.bkp
piccc handle-../o1_mf_nnndf_tag20090823t124703_591x0nwb_.bkp

RMAN> list backup;

List of Backup Sets
===================
```

```
BS Key  Type LV Size
------- ---- -- ----------
12      Full    368.00K
  List of Datafiles in backup set 12
  File LV Type Ckp SCN    Ckp Time   Name
  ---- -- ---- ---------- --------- ----
  4       Full 569712     23-AUG-09
C:\oracle\product\10.2.0\oradata\test\users01.dbf
  Backup Set Copy #1 of backup set 12
  Device Type Elapsed Time Completion Time Compressed Tag
  ----------- ------------ --------------- ---------- ---
  DISK        00:00:01     23-AUG-09       NO         TAG20090823T124703
    List of Backup Pieces for backup set 12 Copy #1
    BP Key  Pc# Status     Piece Name
    ------- --- ----------- ----------
    39      1   AVAILABLE   o1_mf_nnndf_tag20090823t124703_591wzqsd_.bkp

  Backup Set Copy #2 of backup set 12
  Device Type Elapsed Time Completion Time Compressed Tag
  ----------- ------------ --------------- ---------- ---
  DISK        00:00:01     23-AUG-09       NO         TAG20090823T124703
    List of Backup Pieces for backup set 12 Copy #2
    BP Key  Pc# Status     Piece Name
    ------- --- ----------- ----------
    40      1   AVAILABLE   o1_mf_nnndf_tag20090823t124703_591x0nwb_.bkp
```

 # As we see, we have only one backupset - 12

```
C:\oracle\product\10.2.0\flash_recovery_area\TEST\BACKUPSET\2009_08_23>dir
23.08.2009  12:47  385 024  o1_mf_nnndf_tag20090823t124703_591wzqsd_.bkp
23.08.2009  12:47  385 024  o1_mf_nnndf_tag20090823t124703_591x0nwb_.bkp
               2 File(s)        770 048 bytes
```

#In case we delete backupset 12, both backups (backupset and its backup)
will be deleted as they are NOT separate backupsets

```
RMAN> backup backupset 12 delete input;

channel ora_disk_1: backup piece
o1_mf_nnndf_tag20090823t124703_591x0nwb_.bkp
piece handle=../o1_mf_nnndf_tag20090823t124703_591x1hbq_.bkp comment=none

deleted backup piece
backup piece handle= O1_mf_nnndf_tag20090823t124703_591x0nwb_.bkp recid=40
stamp=695652452

deleted backup piece
backup piece handle= o1_mf_nnndf_tag20090823t124703_591wzqsd_.bkp recid=39
stamp=695652423
```

#We have only one backup file which is taken with the above command.

```
RMAN> list backup;

List of Backup Sets
===================
BS Key  Type LV Size      Device Type Elapsed Time Completion Time
------- ---- -- ---------- ----------- ------------ ---------------
12      Full    368.00K    DISK        00:00:01     23-AUG-09
```

```
        BP Key: 41    Status: AVAILABLE  Compressed: NO  Tag:
TAG20090823T124703
        Piece Name:
C:\oracle\product\10.2.0\flash_recovery_area\test\backupset\2009_08_23\o1_mf
_nnndf_tag20090823t124703_591x1hbq_.bkp
  List of Datafiles in backup set 12
  File LV Type Ckp SCN    Ckp Time  Name
  ---- -- ---- ---------- --------- ----
  4      Full 569712      23-AUG-09
C:\oracle\product\10.2.0\oradata\test\users01.dbf

C:\oracle\product\10.2.0\flash_recovery_area\test\backupset\2009_08_23>dir
23.08.2009  12:47 385 024 O1_MF_NNNDF_TAG20090823T124703_591X1HBQ_.BKP
               1 File(s)         385 024 bytes
```

If all backup sets need to be copied to tape, this can be performed with one simple command:

```
RMAN> backup device type sbt backupset all;
```

This command connects to the tape and copies all backup pieces.

In the following example, how to use the *backupset all* option and back up backup sets according to the specific date range using the *completed before/after* option will be shown.

Do a backup of all archived redo log files as follows:

```
C:\>rman target /
RMAN> backup archivelog all;

Starting backup at 24-AUG-09
piece handle=C:\------\o1_mf_annnn_tag20090824t133908_594nfg3f_.bkp
c:\------->dir
24.08.2009  13:39        25 560 576
O1_mf_annnn_tag20090824t133908_594nfg3f_.bkp
               1 File(s)     25 560 576 bytes
```

Change the date of OS and add two days to the current date, then do a backup of datafile 4 as follows:

```
RMAN> backup datafile 4;

Starting backup at 26-AUG-09
piece handle=../O1_mf_nnndf_tag20090826t133934_599x66h4_.bkp
tag=TAG20090826T133934
RMAN>

C:\------->dir
26.08.2009  13:39  385 024 O1_mf_nnndf_tag20090826t133934_599x66h4_.bkp
               1 File(s)         385 024 bytes
```

Now change the date of OS again and add one day to the current date, then do a backup of all backup sets as follows. Note that as there are two backup sets, one for the archived redo logs and one for datafile 4, this command creates copies of each backup piece.

```
RMAN> backup backupset all;

C:\oracle\product\10.2.0\flash_recovery_area\test\backupset\2009_08_27>dir
27.08.2009  13:40         25 560 576
O1_MF_annnn_tag20090824t133908_59dkn0mk_.bkp
27.08.2009  13:40            385 024
o1_mf_nnndf_tag20090826t133934_59dkn3lk_.bkp
              2 File(s)      25 945 600 bytes
```

Two backup files have been copied to this directory. If the requirement is to back up backup sets which were created before or after a specific date, add the *completed before/after* option to the *backup* command. In this step, make two copies of the backup pieces as follows. One is the copy of the backup pieces which were created two days before. The other one is the copy of backup pieces which were created within the past two days.

```
RMAN> backup backupset completed before 'sysdate-2' format
'c:\backup_completed_before_2_days\backup_%u.bkp';

RMAN> backup backupset completed after 'sysdate-2' format
'c:\backup_completed_after_2_days\backup_%u.bkp';
RMAN>
```

Now, the listing of the files in these directories appears as follows:

```
C:\>dir backup_completed_before_2_days backup_completed_after_2_days

 directory of c:\backup_completed_before_2_days
27.08.2009  14:43         25 560 576 backup_02kngbft_1_4.bkp
              1 File(s)      25 560 576 bytes
 Directory of C:\backup_completed_after_2_days
27.08.2009  14:44            385 024 backup_03knlk8m_1_3.bkp
              1 File(s)         385 024 bytes
```

From this result, the backup piece of the archived redo log files created before the past two days is found in the first directory. In the second directory, the backup piece of datafile 4 which was created within two days (yesterday) is found.

Making Incremental Backups

If a full backup of a large database is done each time, each backup would take a long time and would require significant storage. Another option is to create RMAN incremental backups. A full backup can be done every Sunday with one incremental backup every night. By making incremental backups, RMAN makes a backup of only changed data blocks, thereby saving the time and space. When making an incremental backup, the level 0 incremental backup must be done which makes a backup of all data blocks. After that, the level 1 incremental backup is done which backs up only data blocks that were changed after the level 0 incremental backup.

> Note: Remember that when a restore needs to be done, first restore the Level 0 backup and then the incremental backups, so ensure that at least the latest Level 0 backup is always available for restoration.

There are two types of incremental backups: differential and cumulative. By using differential incremental backup, RMAN looks for the changed data blocks which were changed after the last level 1 incremental backup. If there is no level 1 backup made before that, it backs up the changed data blocks which were made after the level 0 incremental backup.

In cumulative incremental backup, RMAN backs up all changed data blocks after the level 0 backup even though there is a level 1 incremental backup that has been made. The advantage of cumulative incremental backup over differential backup is that it is faster to restore, because by using cumulative backup, only one incremental backup is restored over the level 0 backup. However, the main disadvantage of cumulative backup is that it requires more time to backup all the changed blocks made to the database after level 0 backup, and it also uses more space to hold all these changes. Select one of these incremental backup types according to the backup policy.

Here is how to do an incremental backup. First of all, do a backup of the database as usual and check its size as follows:

```
RMAN> backup database;

piece handle=./O1_mf_nnndf_tag20090905t131809_5b47p24d_.bkp
RMAN>
```

```
C:\-------->dir
05.09.2009  13:18        535 478 272
O1_mf_nnndf_tag20090905t131809_5b47p24d_.bkp
```

Then do a level 0 incremental backup and check the size:

```
RMAN> backup incremental level 0 database;

piece handle=../O1_mf_nnnd0_tag20090905t132414_5b481gl2_.bkp
RMAN>

C:\------->dir
05.09.2009  13:25        535 478 272
o1_mf_nnnd0_tag20090905t132414_5b481gl2_.bkp

05.09.2009  13:18        535 478 272
o1_mf_nnndf_tag20090905t131809_5b47p24d_.bkp
```

Both files have the same size because the level 0 backup is the same as the full backup which backs up only used data blocks. Now make changes to the database and create two differential incremental backups. Then make one cumulative backup:

```
SQL>
create
table tbl_test as
  2
select * from
all_objects;

Table created.

SQL> insert into
 tbl_test
  2
select * from
tbl_test;

49309 rows created.

SQL> /

98618 rows created.

SQL>
commit;

Commit complete.
SQL>

RMAN> backup incremental level 1 database;

piece handle=../o1_mf_nnnd1_tag20090905t133229_5b48jz6c_.bkp
rman>
```

```
C:\--------->dir
05.09.2009  13:32         23 371 776
O1_mf_nnnd1_tag20090905t133229_5b48jz6c_.bkp
```

Make additional changes to the database and take a differential level 1 incremental backup.

```
SQL>
insert into
 tbl_test
   2
select * from
 tbl_test;

197236 rows created.

SQL> /

394472 rows created.

SQL>
commit;

Commit complete.
SQL>

RMAN> backup incremental level 1 database;

piece handle=../o1_mf_nnnd1_tag20090905t133514_5b48p5oz_.bkp
RMAN>

C:\--------->dir
05.09.2009  13:32         23 371 776
O1_mf_nnnd1_tag20090905t133229_5b48jz6c_.bkp
05.09.2009  13:35         68 845 568
o1_mf_nnnd1_tag20090905t133514_5b48p5oz_.bkp
```

Now take a cumulative backup which backs up changed data blocks from the level 0 incremental backup as follows:

```
RMAN> backup incremental level 1 cumulative database;

piece
handle=C:\oracle\product\10.2.0\flash_recovery_area\test\backupset\2009_09_0
5\o1_mf_nnnd1_tag20090905t133735_5b48tjg5_.bkp

C:\----------->dir
o1_mf_nnnd1_tag20090905t133229_5b48jz6c_.bkp
o1_mf_nnnd1_tag20090905t133514_5b48p5oz_.bkp
o1_mf_nnnd1_tag20090905t133735_5b48tjg5_.bkp
```

Block Change Tracking Overview

Before talking about block change tracking, it should be mentioned that during recovery, RMAN verifies datafiles and checks incremental backups to update changes on the datafiles. If there are archived redo log files, RMAN prefers to apply incremental backups rather than archived redo log files. Starting from Oracle 11g, RMAN first looks for flashback logs if flashback is enabled in the database level, thus making the recovery process faster.

During incremental backup, RMAN checks every data block in all datafiles of the database and compares its SCN number with the SCN value that is at the incremental 0 backup. If the first value is greater than the second, it means that the data block has been changed after the last backup and needs to be backed up, so RMAN writes it to the backup file. This procedure is done for every data block in the database. Prior to 10gR2, RMAN was backing up the data block in case it was written once by any Oracle process even though it was empty. But in 10gR2, RMAN backs up only used extents.

So as RMAN checks all data blocks and writes down only changed ones during incremental backup, it takes more time for the checking procedure. Starting from Oracle 10gR1, the new feature called Block Change Tracking was presented, which uses a new process called Change Tracking Writer (CTWR). This tracks the changes made to the data blocks as redo is generated and stores their addresses to the special tracking file. When incremental backups are done, RMAN uses the tracking file and backs up only those data blocks that are written in this file, thus making incremental backups much faster, and it does not scan the unchanged data blocks. This feature is disabled by default. Only one tracking file is used for one database.

Enabling Block Change Tracking

To enable block change tracking for the database, use the following command:

```
alter database enable block change tracking using file
/u01/oracle/product/10.2.0/db_1/oradata/mydb/blk_track.trc';
```

If there is already a file named *blk_track.trc* and it needs to be overwritten, add a REUSE clause as follows:

```
alter database enable block change tracking using file
/u01/oracle/product/10.2.0/db_1/oradata/mydb/blk_track.trc' REUSE;
```

If the *db_create_file_dest* parameter is used, then the name of the tracking file should be omitted:

```
alter database enable block change tracking;
```

When enabling the change tracking feature, the following lines are added to the *alert.log* file:

```
alter database enable block change tracking using file
'/u01/oracle/product/10.2.0/db_1/oradata/mydb/blk_track.trc'

Mon Mar 8 16:07:20 2010
Block change tracking file is current.
Starting background process CTWR
CTWR started with pid=22, OS id=4796
Block change tracking service is active.
Mon Mar  8 16:07:21 2010
Completed: alter database enable block change tracking using file
'/u01/oracle/product/10.2.0/db_1/oradata/mydb/blk_track.trc'
```

And the new CTWR process will be created to track the changes:

```
[oracle@localhost ~]$ ps -ef | grep ctwr
oracle    4796    1  0 16:07 ?        00:00:00 ora_ctwr_mydb
```

Renaming and Disabling Block Change Tracking

To disable block change tracking, use the following:

```
alter database disable block change tracking;
```

To rename the tracking file, shut down the database, use an OS command to relocate/rename the file and then *startup mount* and use the *alter database rename file* command as follows:

```
SQL>
shutdown immediate;
SQL>
alter
database rename file
'/u01/oracle/product/10.2.0/db_1/oradata/mydb/blk_track.trc' TO
'/u01/oracle/product/10.2.0/db_1/oradata/mydb/blk_track_2.trc';
```

To rename the tracking file without having to shut down the database, use:

```
SQL>
alter
database disable block change tracking;
SQL>
```

```
alter
database enable block change tracking using file
'/u01/oracle/product/10.2.0/db_1/oradata/mydb/blk_track_2.trc'
```

Missing Tracking File

If a tracking file is missing or deleted, an error occurs when attempting to update the database:

```
SQL>
update
tbl_blk_change
set
owner='test';
update tbl_blk_change set owner='test'
      *

ERROR at line 1:
ORA-19755: could not open change tracking file
ORA-19750: change tracking file:
'/u01/oracle/product/10.2.0/db_1/oradata/mydb/blk_track.trc'
ORA-27037: unable to obtain file status
Linux Error: 2: No such file or directory
Additional information: 3
```

The block change tracking is disabled and the following lines are written to the *alert.log* file:

```
change tracking error 19755, disabling change tracking
Mon Mar 8 16:33:25 2010
Errors in file
/u01/oracle/product/10.2.0/db_1/admin/mydb/bdump/mydb_ctwr_4796.trc:
ORA-19755: could not open change tracking file
ORA-19750: change tracking file:
'/u01/oracle/product/10.2.0/db_1/oradata/mydb/blk_track.trc'
ORA-27037: unable to obtain file status
Linux Error: 2: No such file or directory
Additional information: 3
Block change tracking service stopping.
Deleted file /u01/oracle/product/10.2.0/db_1/oradata/mydb/blk_track.trc
```

Query the *v$block_change_tracking* view to be sure that it is disabled:

```
SQL>
select
status
from
v$block_change_tracking;

STATUS
```

```
----------
DISABLED
```

🔔 NOTE: In order to use the block change tracking feature, an incremental backup should be done after enabling that feature. Otherwise, it will not be used after being enabled with level 0 backup.

To get information about the status of the block change tracking, query the following view:

```
SQL>
select * from
v$block_change_tracking;

STATUS      FILENAME                             BYTES
----------  ------------------------------------ ----------
ENABLED     /tmp/test.trc                        11599872
SQL>
```

Moreover, the *used_change_tracking* column of the *v$backup_datafile* view indicates whether block change tracking was used to increase the incremental backup or not. This view shows information about control files and data files in backup sets. If the value is YES, then it means that block change tracking file was used to back up the current file. The *file#* column defines the file number of the datafile. If the value of this column is 0, then it is a control file. The following query shows that block change tracking was not used:

```
SQL>
select
a.file#,
decode
(a.file#,0,'control file',b.name) file_name, a.used_change_tracking from
v$backup_datafile a, v$datafile b
where
a.file#=b.file#(+);

FILE# FILE_NAME                                          USE
----- -------------------------------------------------- ---
0 Control File                                           NO
0 Control File                                           NO
1 /u01/oracle/product/10.2.0/db_1/oradata/newdb/system01.dbf    NO
2 /u01/oracle/product/10.2.0/db_1/oradata/newdb/undotbs01.dbf   NO
3 /u01/oracle/product/10.2.0/db_1/oradata/newdb/sysaux01.dbf    NO
4 /u01/oracle/product/10.2.0/db_1/oradata/newdb/users01.dbf     NO
6 rows selected.
SQL>
```

RMAN Reporting on Backups

To get detailed information on RMAN backups, two commands are used: *list* and *report*.

- *list*: Using this command enables obtaining very extensive and detailed information about backup of the database from the RMAN repository.

- *report:* Using this command helps determine whether it is possible to recover the database in accordance with backups taken.

Using the *list* Command

To use the *list* command, first back up database files. To review what has been seen in the earlier sections of this chapter, the following are commands to make backups:

```
RMAN> backup database;
RMAN> backup tablespace users;
RMAN> backup datafile 3;
RMAN> backup current controlfile;
RMAN> BACKUP spfile;
RMAN> backup archivelog all;
```

As different backups have been done of the database, by now using the *list* command, detailed information about all backups that have been made can be found. To get information about the whole database backup, use the following statement:

```
RMAN> list backup;

<....... output omitted .......>
Piece Name: C:\oracle\product\10.2.0\flash_recovery_area\test\backupset\
2009_08_27\o1_mf_nnndf_tag20090827t192821_59f6060z_.bkp
  List of Datafiles in backup set 1

  File LV Type Ckp SCN    Ckp Time  Name
  ---- -- ---- ---------- --------- ----
  1       Full 547482     27-AUG-09 c:\oracle\product\10.2.0\oradata\test\system01.dbf
  2       Full 547482     27-aug-09 c:\oracle\product\10.2.0\oradata\test\undotbs01.dbf
  3       Full 547482     27-aug-09 c:\oracle\product\10.2.0\oradata\test\sysaux01.dbf
  4       Full 547482     27-aug-09 c:\oracle\product\10.2.0\oradata\test\users01.dbf
<....... output omitted .......>

piece name: ../o1_mf_ncsnf_tag20090827t192821_59f61yqg_.bkp
  Control File Included: Ckp SCN: 547500      Ckp time: 27-AUG-09
  SPFILE Included: Modification time: 27-AUG-09

BS Key  Type LV Size       Device Type Elapsed Time Completion Time
------- ---- -- ---------- ----------- ------------ ---------------
3       Full   368.00K     DISK        00:00:01     27-AUG-09
        BP Key: 3   Status: AVAILABLE  Compressed: NO  Tag: TAG20090827T193040
<....... output omitted .......>
```

```
List of Archived Logs in backup set 7
  Thrd Seq    Low SCN    Low Time  Next SCN   Next Time
  ---- ------- ---------- --------- ---------- ---------
    2      543424   27-AUG-09 547766    27-AUG-09
```

This shows detailed information about each backup. To get information about backup of the control file, use the following statement:

```
RMAN> list backup of control file;

List of Backup Sets
===================
BS Key  Type LV Size       Device Type Elapsed Time Completion Time
------- ---- -- ---------- ----------- ------------ ---------------
2       Full    6.80M       DISK         00:00:02     27-AUG-09
        BP Key: 2   Status: AVAILABLE  Compressed: NO  Tag: TAG20090827T192821
        Piece Name: ../O1_MF_NCSNF_TAG20090827T192821_59F61YQG_.BKP
  Control File Included: Ckp SCN: 547500       Ckp time: 27-AUG-09
```

This result shows that there are two backups of the control file in the RMAN repository. One of them was created when the whole or full backup was done, and another one was created when the *backup current controlfile* command was run. To get information about backup of spfile, use the following statement:

```
RMAN> list backup of spfile;

List of Backup Sets
===================
BS Key  Type LV Size       Device Type Elapsed Time Completion Time
------- ---- -- ---------- ----------- ------------ ---------------
2       Full    6.80M       DISK         00:00:02     27-AUG-09
        BP Key: 2   Status: AVAILABLE  Compressed: NO  Tag: TAG20090827T192821
        Piece Name: ../O1_MF_ncsnf_tag20090827t192821_59f61yqg_.bkp
  spfile Included: Modification time: 27-AUG-09
RMAN>
```

The results above also show that the *list* command returned two backups of spfile. One of them was created when the whole database backup was done, and the other one was created with the *backup spfile* command.

To get information about backup of a specific datafile, use the following statement:

```
RMAN> list backup of datafile 3;

List of Backup Sets
===================
BS Key  Type LV Size       Device Type Elapsed Time Completion Time
------- ---- -- ---------- ----------- ------------ ---------------
1       Full    510.65M     DISK         00:00:49     27-AUG-09
        BP Key: 1   Status: AVAILABLE  Compressed: NO  Tag: TAG20090827T192821
        Piece Name: ../O1_mf_nnndf_tag20090827t192821_59f6060z_.bkP
  List of Datafiles in backup set 1
  File LV Type Ckp SCN    Ckp Time  Name
  ---- -- ---- ---------- --------- ----
    3     Full 547482     27-AUG-09 C:\oracle\product\10.2.0\oradata\test\sysaux01.dbf
RMAN>
```

RMAN Reporting on Backups

The first backup of the datafile was created from the *backup database* command. The second backup of the datafile was created from the *backup datafile 3* command. To get information about backup of a specific tablespace, use the following statement:

```
RMAN> list backup of tablespace users;

List of Backup Sets
===================
BS Key  Type LV Size       Device Type Elapsed Time Completion Time
------- ---- -- ---------- ----------- ------------ ---------------
1       Full    510.65M    DISK        00:00:49     27-AUG-09
        BP Key: 1   Status: AVAILABLE  Compressed: NO  Tag: TAG20090827T192821
        Piece Name: ../O1_mf_nnndf_tag20090827t192821_59f6060z_.bkp
  List of Datafiles in backup set 1
  File LV Type Ckp SCN    Ckp Time  Name
  ---- -- ---- ---------- --------- ----
  4       Full 547482     27-AUG-09 C:\oracle\product\10.2.0\oradata\test\users01.dbf
RMAN>
```

The output shows that there are two backups of user tablespace. The first backup was created by issuing the *backup database* command. The second backup was created from the *backup tablespace* users command. To get information about backup of all datafiles, use:

```
list backup of database;
```

By using this command, no information is obtained about control file, spfile and archived redo log files. This command returns information only about backup of datafiles as follows:

```
RMAN> list backup of database;

List of Backup Sets
===================
BS Key  Type LV Size       Device Type Elapsed Time Completion Time
------- ---- -- ---------- ----------- ------------ ---------------
1       Full    510.65M    DISK        00:00:49     27-AUG-09
        BP Key: 1   Status: AVAILABLE  Compressed: NO  Tag: TAG20090827T192821
        Piece Name: ../O1_mf_nnndf_tag20090827t192821_59f6060z_.bkp
  List of Datafiles in backup set 1
  File LV Type Ckp SCN    Ckp Time  Name
  ---- -- ---- ---------- --------- ----
  1       Full 547482     27-AUG-09 C:\oracle\product\10.2.0\oradata\test\system01.dbf
  2       Full 547482     27-aug-09 c:\oracle\product\10.2.0\oradata\test\undotbs01.dbf
  3       Full 547482     27-aug-09 c:\oracle\product\10.2.0\oradata\test\sysaux01.dbf
  4       Full 547482     27-aug-09 c:\oracle\product\10.2.0\oradata\test\users01.dbf
RMAN>
```

The result shows backup sets 1, 3 and 4. These backup sets were created as a result of the following commands:

```
backup database;
backup tablespace users;
backup datafile 3;
```

Oracle Backup and Recovery

Skipping a Tablespace from the Output of the *list* Command

To omit or skip any tablespace from appearing in the output of the *list* command, use the *list backup of database skip ...* command:

```
RMAN> list backup of database skip tablespace users;

List of Backup Sets
===================
BS Key  Type LV Size       Device Type Elapsed Time Completion Time
------- ---- -- ---------- ----------- ------------ ---------------
1       Full    510.65M    DISK        00:00:49     27-AUG-09
        BP Key: 1   Status: AVAILABLE  Compressed: NO  Tag: TAG20090827T192821
        Piece Name: ../O1_mf_nnndf_tag20090827t192821_59f6060z_.bkp
  List of Datafiles in backup set 1
  File LV Type Ckp SCN    Ckp Time  Name
  ---- -- ---- ---------- --------- ----
  1       Full 547482     27-AUG-09 C:\oracle\product\10.2.0\oradata\test\system01.dbf
  2       full 547482     27-aug-09 c:\oracle\product\10.2.0\oradata\test\undotbs01.dbf
  3       full 547482     27-aug-09 c:\oracle\product\10.2.0\oradata\test\sysaux01.dbf
  4       Full 547482     27-AUG-09
RMAN>
```

The results show that information about *users.dbf* was hidden in backup sets 1 and 3. To get backup information about a specific backup set, use the following:

```
RMAN> list backupset 5;


List of Backup Sets
===================
BS Key  Type LV Size       Device Type Elapsed Time Completion Time
------- ---- -- ---------- ----------- ------------ ---------------
5       Full    6.77M      DISK        00:00:01     27-AUG-09
        BP Key: 5   Status: AVAILABLE  Compressed: NO  Tag: TAG20090827T193119
        Piece Name: ../O1_mf_ncnnf_tag20090827t193119_59f65r6t_.bkp
  Control File Included: Ckp SCN: 547721     Ckp time: 27-AUG-09
RMAN>
```

Listing Information about Backup of Archived Redo Log Files

By using the *list* command, a list of archived redo log files' backup can be obtained by defining different criteria. To list backup of all archived redo log files, use the keyword *all* as follows:

```
RMAN> list backup of archivelog all;

List of Backup Sets
===================
BS Key  Size       Device Type Elapsed Time Completion Time
------- ---------- ----------- ------------ ---------------
7       21.37M     DISK        00:00:02     27-AUG-09
        BP Key: 7   Status: AVAILABLE  Compressed: NO  Tag: TAG20090827T193230
        Piece Name: ../O1_mf_annnn_tag20090827t193230_59f67znj_.bkp
```

```
List of Archived Logs in backup set 7
  Thrd Seq    Low SCN    Low Time  Next SCN    Next Time
  ---- -----  ---------- --------- ----------  ---------
  1    2      543424     27-AUG-09 547766      27-AUG-09

BS Key  Size        Device Type Elapsed Time Completion Time
------- ----------  ----------- ------------ ---------------
9       49.38M      DISK        00:00:04     28-AUG-09
        BP Key: 9   Status: AVAILABLE  Compressed: NO  Tag: TAG20090828T125407
        Piece Name:
C:\oracle\product\10.2.0\flash_recovery_area\test\backupset\2009_08_28\o1_mf_annnn_tag20090828t125407
_59h391c7_.bkp
  List of Archived Logs in backup set 9

  Thrd Seq    Low SCN    Low Time  Next SCN    Next Time
  ---- -----  ---------- --------- ----------  ---------
  1    2      543424     27-AUG-09 547766      27-AUG-09
  1    3      547766     27-AUG-09 578895      28-AUG-09
  1    4      578895     28-AUG-09 578897      28-AUG-09
  1    5      578897     28-AUG-09 578905      28-AUG-09
RMAN>
```

To get a list of archived redo log files according to SCN number, use one of the following keywords:

```
FROM SCN
SCN BETWEEN
UNTIL SCN
```

Using commands with these keywords, a list of archived redo log backups with different variations can be found as follows:

```
list backup of archivelog from scn 578895;
list backup of archivelog scn between 547766 and 578898;
list backup of archivelog until scn 578895;
```

By changing the keyword *scn* to *sequence* and *time*, a list of archived redo log backups according to redo sequence number or any point in time appear. Moreover, to check backup of the database according to its completion time, add the *completed* command with the *before*, *after* and *between* keywords.

To get the list of backup files of the users tablespace which were completed in the last one-day period, use:

```
RMAN> list backup of tablespace users completed after '(sysdate-1)';
```

There are two types of results that are obtained by using the *list* command. One is detailed information which is default and may be achieved also by adding the *verbose* keyword to the end of the command. Another is getting a summary of backups done which may be achieved by using the *summary* command. This is shown in the following example:

```
RMAN> list backup of datafile 4;

List of Backup Sets
===================
```

```
BS Key   Type LV Size      Device Type Elapsed Time Completion Time
-------  ---- -- ---------- ----------- ------------ ---------------
1        Full 368.00K       DISK        00:00:01     28-AUG-09
         BP Key: 1   Status: AVAILABLE  Compressed: NO  Tag: TAG20090828T172845
         Piece Name:
C:\oracle\product\10.2.0\flash_recovery_area\test\backupset\2009_08_28\o1_mf_nnndf_tag20090828t172845
_59hmcxsd_.bkp
   List of Datafiles in backup set 1
   File LV Type Ckp SCN    Ckp Time  Name
   ---- -- ---- ---------- --------- ----
   4       Full 548025     28-AUG-09 C:\oracle\product\10.2.0\oradata\test\users01.dbf

RMAN> list backup of datafile 4 summary;


List of Backups
===============
Key     TY LV S Device Type Completion Time #Pieces #Copies Compressed Tag
------- -- -- - ----------- --------------- ------- ------- ---------- ---
1       B  F  A DISK        28-AUG-09       1       1       NO         TAG20090828T172845
2       B  F  A DISK        29-AUG-09       1       1       NO         TAG20090829T172857
RMAN>
```

Listing Image Copies of Database Files

To list all image copies of database files, use the *list copy* command. Before getting started with the syntax of the *list copy* command, create some image copies using the following commands:

```
RMAN> backup as copy current control file format 'c:\image_copy_control
file.ctl';

RMAN> backup as copy tablespace users format 'c:\users01.dbf';
RMAN> backup as copy datafile 4 format 'c:\datafile4.dbf';
RMAN> backup as copy spfile format 'c:\image_copy_spfile.ora';
RMAN> backup as copy archivelog all format 'c:\arch_%U.arc';
```

Now get information about these image copies using *list copy* commands:

```
RMAN> list copy of control file;

List of Control File Copies

Key     S Completion Time Ckp SCN    Ckp Time        Name
------- - --------------- ---------- --------------- ----
1       A 31-AUG-09       551743     31-AUG-09       C:\image_copy_control file.ctl

RMAN> list backup of spfile;

List of Backup Sets
===================
BS Key   Type LV Size      Device Type Elapsed Time Completion Time
-------  ---- -- ---------- ----------- ------------ ---------------
6        Full 6.80M        DISK        00:00:02     31-AUG-09
         BP Key: 6   Status: AVAILABLE  Compressed: NO  Tag: TAG20090831T175010
         Piece Name:
C:\oracle\product\10.2.0\flash_recovery_area\test\backupset\2009_08_31\o1_mf_ncsnf_tag20090831t175010
_59qks89r_.bkp
   SPFILE Included: Modification time: 31-AUG-09

RMAN> list copy of tablespace users;

List of Datafile Copies
Key     File S Completion Time Ckp SCN    Ckp Time        Name
```

```
-------  ----  -  ---------------  ----------  ---------------  ----
3        4     A  31-AUG-09           551771   31-AUG-09        C:\datafile4.dbf
2        4     A  31-AUG-09           551756   31-AUG-09        C:\users01.dbf

RMAN> list copy of datafile 4;

List of Datafile Copies
Key      File S Completion Time Ckp SCN     Ckp Time         Name
-------  ----  -  ---------------  ----------  ---------------  ----
3        4     A  31-AUG-09           551771   31-AUG-09        C:\datafile4.dbf
2        4     A  31-AUG-09           551756   31-AUG-09        C:\users01.dbf
RMAN> list copy of database;

List of Datafile Copies
Key      File S Completion Time Ckp SCN     Ckp Time         Name
-------  ----  -  ---------------  ----------  ---------------  ----
3        4     A  31-AUG-09           551771   31-AUG-09        C:\datafile4.dbf
2        4     A  31-AUG-09           551756   31-AUG-09        C:\users01.dbf

RMAN> list copy of archivelog all;

List of Archived Log Copies
Key      Thrd Seq    S Low Time  Name
-------  ----  ------- -  --------- ----
2        1     2        A 28-AUG-09 C:\arch_arch_d-test_id-1994245513_s-2_t-1_a-696099081_0bko3ab1.arc
1        1     2        A 28-AUG-09
C:\oracle\product\10.2.0\flash_recovery_area\test\archivelog\2009_08_31\o1_mf_1_2_59qm8hd6_.arc
RMAN>
```

A list of backup from disk or tape can be obtained. To switch between them, add the *device type* keyword at the end of the *list* command as follows:

```
list backup of tablespace users device type disk;
list backup of database device type sbt;
```

A list of backups can be found according to their TAG names. Create a backup and assign it a TAG. Then get information about it using the *list* command:

```
RMAN> backup datafile 2 TAG 'datafile_2_tag';

RMAN> list backup summary TAG 'datafile_2_tag';

List of Backups
===============

Key      TY LV S Device Type Completion Time #Pieces #Copies Compressed Tag
-------  -- -- - ----------- --------------- ------- ------- ------- ------
10       B  F  A DISK        01-SEP-09       1       1       NO      datafile_2_tag

RMAN>
```

When the database opens using the *resetlogs* option, Oracle clears the redo log files and creates a new incarnation in the database. In normal circumstances, when the database opens using the *resetlogs* option, the database is not able to be recovered to the SCN that was before the *resetlogs* operation. But in RMAN, it is possible to add redo information from archived redo log files which belongs to the SCN number which was generated before the *resetlogs* operation. To get the list of database incarnations, use this command:

```
RMAN> list incarnation of database 'test';

List of Database Incarnations

DB Key  Inc Key DB Name  DB ID            STATUS  Reset SCN Reset Time
------- ------- -------- ---------------  --- ---------- ----------
1       1       TEST     1994571333       PARENT  1          30-AUG-05
2       2       TEST     1994571333       PARENT  534907     01-SEP-09
3       3       TEST     1994571333       CURRENT 548214     03-SEP-09
RMAN>
```

By using *list expired backup*, backup information of nonexistent backups can be found from the repository. To get a correct list, run the *crosscheck* command first to make RMAN check the status of files and verify their existence:

```
RMAN> BACKUP tablespace users format 'c:\tbs_users.bkp';

piece handle=c:\tbs_users.bkp tag=tag20090903t123551 comment=none

RMAN> list expired backup;
C:\>move tbs_users.bkp backup_tbs_users.bkp
C:\>rman target /
RMAN> list expired backup;

using target database control file instead of recovery catalog

RMAN> crosscheck backup of tablespace users;

<....... output omitted .......>
crosschecked backup piece: found to be 'expired'
backup piece handle=c:\tbs_users.bkp recid=3 stamp=696602152
Crosschecked 1 objects

RMAN> list expired backup of tablespace users;

List of Backup Sets
===================
BS Key  Type LV Size       Device Type Elapsed Time Completion Time
------- ---- -- ---------- ----------- ------------ ---------------
3       Full    368.00K    DISK        00:00:00     03-SEP-09
        BP Key: 3   Status: EXPIRED  Compressed: NO  Tag: TAG20090903T123551
        Piece Name: C:\TBS_USERS.BKP
  List of Datafiles in backup set 3
  File LV Type Ckp SCN    Ckp Time  Name
  ---- -- ---- ---------- --------- ----
  4       Full 547406     03-SEP-09 C:\oracle\product\10.2.0\oradata\test\users01.dbf
```

Now move the backup back, crosscheck and list backup:

```
C:\>move backup_tbs_users.bkp tbs_users.bkp

RMAN> list expired backup;

List of Backup Sets
===================
BS Key  Type LV Size       Device Type Elapsed Time Completion Time
------- ---- -- ---------- ----------- ------------ ---------------
3       Full    368.00K    DISK        00:00:00     03-SEP-09
        BP Key: 3   Status: EXPIRED  Compressed: NO  Tag: TAG20090903T123551
        Piece Name: C:\tbs_users.bkp
  List of Datafiles in backup set 3
  File LV Type Ckp SCN    Ckp Time  Name
  ---- -- ---- ---------- --------- ----
```

```
4      Full 547406    03-SEP-09 C:\oracle\product\10.2.0\oradata\test\users01.dbf
```

```
RMAN> crosscheck backup;

allocated channel: ORA_DISK_1
channel ORA_DISK_1: sid=142 devtype=DISK
crosschecked backup piece: found to be 'available'
backup piece handle=C:\TBS_USERS.BKP recid=3 stamp=696602152
Crosschecked 1 objects

RMAN> list expired backup;
RMAN>
```

In the above example, after doing a backup of *users* tablespace the name of the backup file is changed and the *list expired backup* command is used, but no result is obtained. It is because the *crosscheck* command has not been run to make verification on the deleted file. After running that command, the *list expired backup* command returns expired and nonexistent backup file information.

To get a list of backups which are recoverable, use:

```
list recoverable backup of database;
```

To test it, create a backup of *users* tablespace, then open it in any editor and make some changes. Then check whether this backup is recoverable or not as follows:

```
RMAN> backup tablespace users format 'c:\tbs_users.bkp';

piece handle=c:\tbs_users.bkp tag=tag20090903t133855 comment=none

RMAN> list recoverable backup of tablespace users;

List of Backup Sets
===================
BS Key  Type LV Size       Device Type Elapsed Time Completion Time
------- ---- -- ---------- ----------- ------------ ---------------
4       Full    368.00K    DISK        00:00:01     03-SEP-09
        BP Key: 4   Status: AVAILABLE  Compressed: NO  Tag: TAG20090903T133855
        Piece Name: C:\TBS_USERS.BKP
  List of Datafiles in backup set 4
  File LV Type Ckp SCN    Ckp Time  Name
  ---- -- ---- ---------- --------- ----
  4       Full 549647     03-SEP-09 C:\oracle\product\10.2.0\oradata\test\users01.dbf

#Here, backup file was opened in a text editor and changed (corrupted)

RMAN> crosscheck backup;

using channel ORA_DISK_1
crosschecked backup piece: found to be 'EXPIRED'
backup piece handle=C:\TBS_USERS.BKP recid=4 stamp=696605935
Crosschecked 1 objects

RMAN> list recoverable backup of tablespace users;
```

```
RMAN>
```

After the file was corrupted, it became *expired*. By running *list recoverable*, RMAN looks for backups with *available* status, so here it does not return any result. It means that there is no recoverable backup of *users* tablespace.

If the recovery catalog is used instead of the control file for storing repository information, RMAN scripts can be created and stored inside. Using the *list* command, information about these scripts appears. Create a small script, store it in the recovery catalog and get information about it using the following command:

```
RMAN> create script 'test_script'
2> {
3>   backup database plus archivelog;
4> }

created script test_script

RMAN> list all script names;

List of Stored Scripts in Recovery Catalog

    Scripts of Target Database test

        Script Name
        Description
        --------------------
        test_script
```

Reporting Information about RMAN Backups

Using the *report* command, information about RMAN backups can be acquired which corresponds to current retention policy. To know which files need to be backed up according to current retention policy, use the *report need backup* command.

```
report need backup;
```

First, be sure that there is no backup of the database as follows:

```
RMAN> list backup;

using target database control file instead of recovery catalog
```

Now get RMAN configuration for *retention policy*:

```
RMAN> show retention policy;
RMAN configuration parameters are:
configure retention policy to recovery window of 2 days;
```

A recovery windows of 2 days has been configured for retention policy. It means that after two days, the backups will be expired. Now using the *report need backup* command, check which files need to be backed up for future recovery processes. As there is no backup of the database at this point, get a list of all datafiles of the database:

```
RMAN> report need backup;

RMAN retention policy will be applied to the command
RMAN retention policy is set to recovery window of 2 days
Report of files that must be backed up to satisfy 2 days recovery window

File Days  Name
---- ----- -------------------------------------------------------
1    1463  c:\oracle\product\10.2.0\oradata\test\system01.dbf
2    1463  c:\oracle\product\10.2.0\oradata\test\undotbs01.dbf
3    1463  c:\oracle\product\10.2.0\oradata\test\sysaux01.dbf
4    1463  c:\oracle\product\10.2.0\oradata\test\users01.dbf
```

Backup the database using the *backup database* command as follows:

```
RMAN> backup database;
```

Run the same command again to see which files need to be backed up according to retention policy:

```
RMAN> report need backup;

RMAN retention policy will be applied to the command
RMAN retention policy is set to recovery window of 2 days
Report of files that must be backed up to satisfy 2 days recovery window

File Days  Name
---- ----- -------------------------------------------------------
```

This shows that no files need backup at this point because a backup of the database has already been done.

Now change the date of the operating system, add four days and run *report need backup* to know whether any backup will be needed after four days or not:

```
RMAN> report need backup;

RMAN retention policy will be applied to the command
RMAN retention policy is set to recovery window of 2 days
Report of files that must be backed up to satisfy 2 days recovery window

File Days  Name
---- ----- -------------------------------------------------------
1    3     c:\oracle\product\10.2.0\oradata\test\system01.dbf
2    3     c:\oracle\product\10.2.0\oradata\test\undotbs01.dbf
```

```
3    3     c:\oracle\product\10.2.0\oradata\test\sysaux01.dbf
4    3     c:\oracle\product\10.2.0\oradata\test\users01.dbf
```

As the retention policy has been configured to recovery windows of two days, after four days all backups will be expired. But if the backup retention policy were to be configured to a recovery window of four days, no backups will need to be made because there are backups of four days. To check it without changing RMAN configuration of retention policy, run:

```
RMAN> report need backup recovery window of 4 days;

Report of files that must be backed up to satisfy 4 days recovery window

File Days  Name
---- ----- -------------------------------------------------------
RMAN>
```

It is possible to check backup according to a retention policy of redundancy. In this example, the retention policy is changed to redundancy and backups are checked. Check backup of datafile 3 as follows:

```
RMAN> list backup of datafile 3;
```

This shows that there is no backup of datafile 3. So check the retention policy and change it to redundancy 2 as follows:

```
RMAN> show retention policy;

RMAN configuration parameters are:
configure retention policy to recovery window of 2 days;

RMAN> configure retention policy to redundancy 2;
old RMAN configuration parameters:
configure retention policy to recovery window of 2 days;
new RMAN configuration parameters:
configure retention policy to redundancy 2;

new RMAN configuration parameters are successfully stored
```

Backup datafile 3 and run the *report need backup* command for datafile 3 as follows:

```
RMAN> backup datafile 3;

RMAN> report need backup datafile 3;

RMAN retention policy will be applied to the command
RMAN retention policy is set to redundancy 2
Report of files with less than 2 redundant backups

File #bkps Name
```

```
---- -----  -------------------------------------------------------
3     1     C:\oracle\product\10.2.0\oradata\test\sysaux01.dbf
```

As the retention policy has been configured to redundancy 2, there needs to be two backups per file, so take another backup of datafile 3 and run the *report need backup* command again as follows:

```
RMAN> backup datafile 3;

RMAN> report need backup datafile 3;

RMAN retention policy will be applied to the command
RMAN retention policy is set to redundancy 2
Report of files with less than 2 redundant backups

File #bkps Name
---- -----  -------------------------------------------------------
```

Because there are two backups for datafile 3, there is no need for additional backup according to the retention policy, which was set to redundancy 2.

Whether another backup is needed is also reported if the retention policy is set to redundancy 3 by running the following command:

```
RMAN> report need backup redundancy 3 datafile 3;

Report of files with less than 3 redundant backups

File #bkps Name
---- -----  -------------------------------------------------------
  3     2   C:\oracle\product\10.2.0\oradata\test\sysaux01.dbf
```

If the backup strategy relies on a number of incremental backups for a specific datafile and how many incremental backups that the datafile needs to recover are to be checked, use the following:

```
report need backup incremental=specific_number
```

Look at the following example to understand it more clearly. Here, an incremental backup of a datafile is done and the above command is used to check how many incremental backups are needed to recover that file. Now check for backups for datafile 4:

```
RMAN> list backup of datafile 4;
```

Do a level 0 and two level 1 incremental backups of datafile 4 as follows:

```
RMAN> backup incremental level 0 datafile 4;
```

```
RMAN> backup incremental level 1 datafile 4;
RMAN> backup incremental level 1 datafile 4;
```

Now check if more than one incremental backup is needed to recover datafile 4:

```
RMAN> report need backup incremental=1 datafile 4;

Report of files that need more than 1 incrementals during recovery

File Incrementals Name
---- ------------ ----------------------------------------------
4    2            C:\oracle\product\10.2.0\oradata\test\users01.dbf
```

As can be seen, more than one incremental backup is needed to recover that file. Since there are two incremental backups, a third incremental backup is not needed to recover that file, so the following command will not return any result:

```
RMAN> report need backup incremental=2 datafile 4;

Report of files that need more than 2 incrementals during recovery

File Incrementals Name
---- ------------ ----------------------------------------------
RMAN>
```

To check which datafiles need a specific number of days of archived redo log files for recovery, run the following command:

```
report need backup days 3;
```

See the next example to look at this more closely. First, back up the database and check which file needs more than one day of archived redo log files for recovery:

```
RMAN> backup database;

RMAN> report need backup days 1;

Report of files whose recovery needs more than one day of archived logs

File Days  Name
---- ----- ------------------------------------------------------
```

Change the operating system date and add two days, then run the same report:

```
RMAN> report need backup days 1;

Report of files whose recovery needs more than 1 day of archived logs
```

```
File Days  Name
---- -----  --------------------------------------------------------
1    2      C:\oracle\product\10.2.0\oradata\test\system01.dbf
2    2      c:\oracle\product\10.2.0\oradata\test\undotbs01.dbf
3    2      c:\oracle\product\10.2.0\oradata\test\sysaux01.dbf
4    2      c:\oracle\product\10.2.0\oradata\test\users01.dbf
```

These files need more than one day of archived redo log files for recovery. Now, back up datafile 4 and run the report again as follows:

```
RMAN> backup datafile 4;

RMAN> report need backup days 1;

Report of files whose recovery needs more than 1 days of archived logs

File Days  Name
---- -----  --------------------------------------------------------
1    2      C:\oracle\product\10.2.0\oradata\test\system01.dbf
2    2      c:\oracle\product\10.2.0\oradata\test\undotbs01.dbf
3    2      c:\oracle\product\10.2.0\oradata\test\sysaux01.dbf
```

This shows that datafile 4 disappeared from the result because it is already backed up. Now add two more days to the OS date and run the report again as follows:

```
RMAN> report need backup days 1;

Report of files whose recovery needs more than 1 days of archived logs

File Days  Name
---- -----  --------------------------------------------------------
1    4      C:\oracle\product\10.2.0\oradata\test\system01.dbf
2    4      c:\oracle\product\10.2.0\oradata\test\undotbs01.dbf
3    4      c:\oracle\product\10.2.0\oradata\test\sysaux01.dbf
4    2      c:\oracle\product\10.2.0\oradata\test\users01.dbf
```

Now report the datafiles which need more than two and four days of archived redo log files and see the result as follows:

```
RMAN> report need backup days 2;

Report of files whose recovery needs more than 2 days of archived logs

File Days  Name
---- -----  --------------------------------------------------------
1    4      c:\oracle\product\10.2.0\oradata\test\system01.dbf
2    4      c:\oracle\product\10.2.0\oradata\test\undotbs01.dbf
3    4      c:\oracle\product\10.2.0\oradata\test\sysaux01.dbf
RMAN> report need backup days 4;

Report of files whose recovery needs more than 4 days of archived logs
```

```
File Days  Name
---- -----  -------------------------------------------------------
```

RMAN>

To find out which backups are not needed in the recovery process, i.e. are beyond the specified retention policy, use this command:

```
report obsolete
```

See the following example to understand this command more clearly. For this, list backup of the database, show the current retention policy and do two backups of datafile 4:

```
RMAN> list backup;

using target database control file instead of recovery catalog

RMAN> show retention policy;
RMAN configuration parameters are:
configure retention policy to redundancy 1;

 # default

RMAN> backup datafile 4;

piece handle=../o1_mf_nnndf_tag20090901t164959_59t2m7n0_.bkp

RMAN> backup datafile 4;

piece handle=../o1_mf_nnndf_tag20090901t165007_59t2mhj3_.bkp
```

As the retention policy has been configured to redundancy 1, one backup will be useless and should be deleted. To confirm that, use the *report obsolete* command and then by using the *delete obsolete* command, delete it as follows:

```
RMAN> report obsolete;

RMAN retention policy will be applied to the command
RMAN retention policy is set to redundancy 1
Report of obsolete backups and copies

Type                Key    Completion Time    Filename/Handle
------------------- ------ ------------------ --------------------
Backup Set          9      01-SEP-09
  Backup Piece      9      01-SEP-09
../O1_mf_nnndf_tag20090901t164959_59t2m7n0_.bkp

RMAN> delete obsolete;

deleted backup piece
backup piece handle=../O1_mf_nnndf_tag20090901t164959_59t2m7n0_.bkp
```

```
Deleted 1 objects
```

Any backup can be verified against any retention policy as follows:

```
RMAN> report obsolete redundancy 2;

no obsolete backups found

RMAN> report obsolete recovery window of 1 days;

no obsolete backups found
RMAN>
```

To get a list of all datafiles of the database, use the following command:

```
RMAN> report schema;

using target database control file instead of recovery catalog
Report of database schema

List of Permanent Datafiles
===========================
File Size(MB) Tablespace           RB segs Datafile Name
---- -------- -------------------- ------- ------------------------
1    480      system               ***     c:\oracle\product\10.2.0\oradata\test\system01.dbf
2    25       undotbs1             ***     c:\oracle\product\10.2.0\oradata\test\undotbs01.dbf
3    240      sysaux               ***     c:\oracle\product\10.2.0\oradata\test\sysaux01.dbf
4    5        users                ***     c:\oracle\product\10.2.0\oradata\test\users01.dbf

List of Temporary Files
=======================
File Size(MB) Tablespace           Maxsize(MB) Tempfile Name
---- -------- -------------------- ----------- --------------------
1    20       TEMP                 32767       C:\oracle\product\10.2.0\oradata\test\temp01.dbf
```

To get information about datafiles of a database according to a specific point in time, use the following:

```
report schema at time 'sysdate-1';
report schema at scn=554962;
report schema at sequence 3 thread 1;
```

In order to use this feature of the *report schema* command, connect to RMAN using Recovery Catalog, or an error like this will appear:

```
C:\>rman target /
RMAN> report schema at time 'sysdate-1';

using target database control file instead of recovery catalog
RMAN-00571: ===========================================================
RMAN-00569: =============== ERROR MESSAGE STACK FOLLOWS ===============
RMAN-00571: ===========================================================
RMAN-03002: failure of report command at 09/01/2009 17:04:07
RMAN-06137: must have recovery catalog for REPORT SCHEMA AT TIME
RMAN>
```

Connect to RMAN using Recovery Catalog, and issue the same command. This shows that yesterday there was no *tbs_rcat* datafile, but today it has been created as shown here:

```
C:\>rman target / catalog rcat/rcat
connected to target database: test (DBID=1994589404)
connected to recovery catalog database
RMAN> report schema;

Report of database schema
List of Permanent Datafiles
===========================
File Size(MB) Tablespace          RB segs Datafile Name
---- -------- ------------------- ------- ------------------------
1    490      system              yes     c:\oracle\product\10.2.0\oradata\test\system01.dbf
2    25       undotbs1            yes     c:\oracle\product\10.2.0\oradata\test\undotbs01.dbf
3    240      sysaux              no      c:\oracle\product\10.2.0\oradata\test\sysaux01.dbf
4    5        users               no      c:\oracle\product\10.2.0\oradata\test\users01.dbf
5    200      tbs_rcat            no      c:\tbs_rcat.dbf

List of Temporary Files
===========================
File Size(MB) Tablespace          Maxsize(MB) Tempfile Name
---- -------- ------------------- ----------- --------------------
1    20       temp                32767       c:\oracle\product\10.2.0\oradata\test\temp01.dbf

RMAN> report schema at time 'sysdate-1';

Report of database schema

List of Permanent Datafiles
===========================
File Size(MB) Tablespace          RB segs Datafile Name
---- -------- ------------------- ------- ------------------------
1    490      system              yes     c:\oracle\product\10.2.0\oradata\test\system01.dbf
2    25       undotbs1            yes     c:\oracle\product\10.2.0\oradata\test\undotbs01.dbf
3    240      sysaux              yes     c:\oracle\product\10.2.0\oradata\test\sysaux01.dbf
4    5        users               yes     c:\oracle\product\10.2.0\oradata\test\users01.dbf
```

The *report* command can be used in both disk and tape. To switch between them, add the *device type* keyword to the end of each *report* command and specify to which device being connected to as follows:

```
report schema device type disk;
```

Summary

This chapter has shown almost all the ways to back up the physical structure of the database using RMAN. Each physical file of the database can be backed up while it is open, compressed and encrypted using different algorithms to save more space and the backup can be protected using Oracle Wallet or any password.

Incremental backup types and techniques have been shown where RMAN backs up only the changed data blocks and not the whole database. By using incremental backups, space and time can be saved by not backing up those unchanged data blocks. Additionally, how to obtain information about backups that have been performed was shown. The two commands which are used for this purpose are the *list* and *report* commands. Both these commands were explained in detail with different examples in this chapter.

Restoring and Recovering the Database Using RMAN

Introduction

Life is not supposed to be perfect; there are good times, and there are bad times, too. When the tough times come, it is best to be prepared to deal with them. The Oracle database is a very robust piece of software code which is made to run for an indefinite period of time without any trouble. However, problems may arise that cause trouble despite best efforts.

No DBA would like to be in a situation where his database is down and he is getting calls, pages and text messages, asking him how long it will take to get the database up and running again! Then if the DBA is not sure how to recover from the error which has crashed his database, he may soon see even more serious problems than just the database being down. This chapter will review those spine-chilling issues which can bring the database down. The actions that can help in recovering from those horrific issues will also be introduced. Welcome to the world of database recovery!

Doing a Recovery Operation?

There are various situations where a recovery operation needs to be done. Not all of those would necessitate using restore and recover commands, which will be examined in just a while, and some can be just kicked off automatically and may not need any action to be taken at all. There are some cases where an explicit intervention of the DBA is required to start the recovery. The possible situations where a manual or automatic recovery is needed are listed here:

- An instance crash
- User created mistakes
- User process failure
- A media crash

- A complete disaster

These are the broad categories covering almost all recoveries. Regardless of what the recovery situation calls for, the resolution calls for the use of two concepts: restore and actual recovery. Now take a look at all those recovery situations.

Instance Crash Recovery

The instance crash probably is the easiest recovery for a DBA to do. In the instance crash, all that has been lost is the memory portion of the database which was running. That can be caused by a number of reasons, including where someone issued a *shut abort* command, did a *startup force* or where some kind of quick demo was done.

Even an awkward little reason like a power failure on the system can cause that. Any mandatory process that is dead can cause this, too. But that does not need the attention of a dedicated DBA. By simply restarting the database and using a SMON process, the recovery can be done. A good DBA should look for the trends which may be instigating those problems. A detailed explanation of the Instance Crash Recovery mechanism can be found in this chapter under the topic, "How is a Recovery Accomplished?"

User Created Mistake Recovery

This probably is the most common type of recovery which a DBA has to perform. Someone intent on listening to his favorite song and carelessly dropping a really important table is the kind of error that is being referred to here. These errors normally are not an error from the database prospective. For example, when a critical table is dropped or deleted and data from tables is updated without putting a WHERE clause at the end of the statement, that is surely an issue which needs quick and complete attention.

In the past, there was only one recovery method and that was to do a time-based incomplete recovery of the database. But with the current Oracle releases from 10g onwards, things have improved and become much simpler using flashback technology. In the past, there was only one method, to do a time-based incomplete recovery of the database.

User Process Failure Recovery

This is, again, a sort of recovery which probably is relatively easy to fix from the experienced DBA's perspective. This error often occurs when a client's machine or client user process has been killed abruptly. However, since this is just a process crash, Oracle's PMON process will be doing all the required tasks and will be recovering it all.

Like in an instance crash situation, the focus needs to be on whatever caused this and how to prevent it from happening time and time again. If a user fails, PMON performs recovery by rolling back the transaction and cleaning the database buffer cache, freeing user resources and releasing all locks that user holds.

Media Crash/Failure Recovery

This error is a serious one that requires the close attention of a DBA. In this situation, the underlying drive which contains the files is either corrupt or has somehow become inaccessible, leading to mandatory files becoming unavailable. Anything causing this has to be taken care of by the DBA, and they must perform a complete restore and recovery of the corrupted file(s). Here, it can still be assumed that not all of the files or the entire system has crashed. If that is the case, then read the next point.

Disaster Recovery

This means that something really serious has happened and everything has been lost, including the Oracle database, in the machine. That requires a complete restore and recover of the entire machine on a separate machine.

What is Recovery All About?

The situations where a recovery operation is needed have been covered, but what that term really means also needs to be known. So explore the what, when and how of recovery.

What Does Recovery Mean?

Here is the definition of recovery from *The Free Dictionary* at http://www.thefreedictionary.com/recovery:

1. The act, process, duration, or an instance of recovering

2. A return to a normal condition

3. Something gained or restored in recovering

4. The act of obtaining usable substances from unusable sources

Simply put, this means that something is corrupted and it needs to be fixed. It can be recovered by replacing what is corrupted with a good image of it. That is what will be demonstrated in the subsequent sections.

When is a Recovery Needed?

There are two major categories of recovery: instance (or crash) recovery and media recovery. There may be some further sub-categories as well, but generally, recoveries can be categorized into these two areas.

Instance recovery is the recovery when all that has been lost is the memory portion that Oracle was working on before the instance happened. There can be numerous reasons for this, including a mandatory process getting killed or being dead on its own, someone pulling out the power plug from the server (unlikely, but it can happen) or the database getting bounced due to some urgency. Any of the above, and more, can bring the instance down without letting it say a last goodbye to all of its control files and datafiles, thus leading to chaos in the next startup. The good news is that all that a DBA has to do is to issue a *startup* command.

A media crash is a serious problem. Not only is the database's functionality lost for a few moments or even long hours, but may also face hardware failure that needs replacement as soon as possible because using the same hardware may again give the same failure. The DBA must ensure that the recovery is successful, and that requires a complete understanding of how to perform that recovery beforehand.

Note that even though the name is media recovery, it is not necessarily just media that is the problem. It may be caused by hardware loss, database files being damaged or lost, a partial or total loss of the files of a tablespace or any other mandatory file loss.

How is a Recovery Accomplished?

Though both the instance and media recovery are different problems requiring recovery operations, they still primarily use the same steps to perform the recovery and use the same ingredient to perform it as well. That ingredient is redo data. The amount of redo and the source of it may be different for both, but that is still the component that is used in both recoveries. If that concept is explored a bit more, it is not even redo data, but instead is the redo vectors which are used in the recovery operation to reincarnate the lost transactions. Instance recovery uses the online redo logs, and media recovery uses online as well as archived redo logs.

In addition to using the same source for recovery, both recovery operations use the same steps to get out of their misery. These steps are roll forward and roll backward. Both steps are performed in this order, first roll forward following a roll backward. Roll forward is a way to get everything back, including committed and uncommitted data both. There is no concern that only committed data will be used and applied to the missing parts. All that was changed before the mishap happened will be reapplied blindly over the files.

It is important to note that in instance recovery, only the active portion of the redo log is used for the roll forward process. Active redo is that part of the redo log which failed to get checkpointed to the datafiles because of the instance crash. This essentially means that if the active redo content is too large, then the instance recovery will take a long time. This can be controlled through frequent checkpointing, or auto tuned checkpointing as well from 10gR2 onwards, which will reduce the active redo content by flushing it to the files.

However, this can lead to performance issues related to heavy I/O as well, which means that it is sort of a which came first situation, the chicken or the egg. There is no optimal write frequency or checkpoint frequency that can be used. That is why choosing the auto-tuned checkpointing option is a safer bet.

It is worthwhile to mention that the roll forward process is not limited to just the contents of the user changes and normal data files. This also brings back the changes which happened over the undo segments, or rollback segments prior to 9i, of the undo tablespace as well. This means that when the roll forward process is complete, not only do the data files receive all of their redo contents, but also the undo tablespace has all of its changes restored. That helps a lot in the next and final step, roll backward.

Roll backward is the next and final step in the recovery process. As was mentioned above, roll forward brings back everything that is in the active redo logs, committed and uncommitted both. As the default level of the isolation in Oracle is Read Committed, it means that only consistent data can stay in the database as permanent. Therefore, consistent data is only that data which has had a commit issued for it.

When the changes are being recorded in the redo log buffer and then subsequently to the redo log files, Oracle does not care whether the data is committed or uncommitted. This obviously means that when in the roll forward process and Oracle applies ALL over the datafiles, it also does uncommitted changes; or in other words, inconsistent data as well. This has to be rolled back before it can finally be said that the file(s) or even the whole database is consistent. This essential and very important roll forward process is followed up with the roll backward process where all the uncommitted changes are rolled back and for this, undo segments are used.

The last aspect worth mentioning regarding instance recovery is that this essentially means the recovery of a single instance. If the work is being done in a clustered environment and all the instances of the clustered database are lost, this calls for crash recovery. Here all the instances are lost and thus get recovered with the next *alter database open* command.

The terms crash recovery and instance recovery hold the same meaning when used in a single instance, a non-RAC database. In the case of the RAC database, if just one instance is lost and other surviving instances are available, this is called RAC instance recovery where cache loss of the failed server is undertaken by any surviving instance doing both roll forward and roll backward steps.

Media Recovery

This is among the most crucial recoveries that a DBA will need to be able to do. Media crash normally means that either some component of the database, like a datafile or a control file, is gone or the file with its underlying media is gone. Whatever the case may be, this recovery needs a proper restoration and recovery process to be done, and it can cause real headaches at times.

Later in this chapter, a look at the following scenarios with step-by-step explanations and demonstrations will be offered:

- Recovering when the control file is lost but a mirrored copy is available

- Restoring a control file with the redo logs being intact

- Recovering from the loss of the control file and data files but the redo logs are intact

- Recovering from the loss of control files when datafiles are from the backup where redo logs are lost as well

- Recovering from the loss of the control files with no backup available, but the redo logs are intact

- Restoration of spfile

- Restoration and recovery of a normal datafile

- Restoration and recovery of system tablespace

- Restoration and recovery of an undo datafile

- Recovering a datafile that is not backed up

- Restoring tablespaces

- Restoration of the archive logs

- Performing media block recovery

- Performing block recovery without having RMAN backups

- Restoring and recovering the *noarchivelog* database

- Performing disaster recovery

- Performing *scn*-based incomplete recovery

- Performing time-based incomplete recovery

- Performing change-based incomplete recovery

- Recovering to the restore point

- Restoring a database to a previous incarnation

- Performing Tablespace Point in Time Recovery (TSPITR)

> Note: Please remember that these scenarios must not be performed in the production database. Test them on any available copy of the production system in a test environment.

Restoring and Recovering Control Files

Because of media failure, control files as well as datafiles and redo log files can be lost. This section will go over different scenarios with control file loss and practical recovery procedures.

Recovering from the Loss of a Control File When a Mirrored Copy is Available

It is always best to have backup copies of the control files. Oracle recommends having at least three copies of the control file at all times. It is recommended to multiplex control files to different physical disks so that if one of them is lost due to media failure, it can be restored from the other physical disks.

Please note that more than three copies can be made, but here, "the more the merrier" is not the right thing to do. If multiplexed copies of the control file are going to be made and the database is doing a huge amount of control file updates, it leads to the control file parallel write wait event and also the control file enqueue will come into contention. So it is always better to use just the number of copies needed. If more than the maximum of eight copies of control files are made, the following error occurs:

```
ORA-00208: number of control file names exceeds limit of 8
```

If there is just one lost copy of the mirrored files, there is much less to do. See what happens in the following scenarios with the resident DBA, Bob:

1st Scenario

Due to media failure, Bob lost one of the control files of the database and got the following error:

```
ERROR at line 1:
ORA-00210: cannot open the specified control file
ORA-00202: control file: '/u02/oradata/db1/control01.ctl'
ORA-27041: unable to open file
Linux Error: 2: No such file or directory
Additional information: 3
```

As Bob has multiplexed controlfiles on the different hard drives, he performs the following actions:

- Shuts down the database (in abort mode)
- Copies available control file to the directory where the file was lost and renames it
- Starts the database

Here are the steps in detail to recover the database:

If the database is already up, bring it down immediately without invoking the checkpoint.

```
SQL> shut abort;
```

Copy one of the available control files to the location where the lost file is needed. Make sure that the location is intact, and use an operating system level command to do so.

```
$cp /u01/oradata/db1/control02.ctl /u02/oradata/db1/control01.ctl
```

As the file has already been copied, just issue the instance *startup* to open the database.

```
SQL> startup
```

It is also possible that even though there are multiplexed control files and *x* has been lost, not only one control file but the underlying location of the missing control file is also damaged. If that is the case, then the file cannot be restored to the same location. The existing control file copy can be used, but the location has to be different and this means that the initialization file of the database can be edited as well as updating the *control_files* parameter.

With all the steps mentioned above being the same, one more step needs to be performed: editing the parameter that has the new location with the corresponding missing file's name. After this has been done, issue a *startup* command and there will be a running database.

Restoring Control File with Redo Logs Intact

2nd Scenario

Due to a media failure, Bob has lost all control files and received the same error message as in Scenario 1 previously. Having control file backups, he decides to restore the backups of the control files and recover the database.

If all the copies of the control file have been lost but the datafiles and online redo logs are fine, then use the backup of the control file to recover from the loss. Create a small disaster scenario for Bob where he loses his control files. Please note that a backup was already completed and the database is running in archivelog mode.

To create Bob's disaster, very rudely move all the control files to a folder called control which is equivalent to losing all of them.

```
$ cd /u01/oradata/ORCL/
$ ls *ctl

control01.ctl   control02.ctl   control03.ctl

$ mkdir control
$ mv *.ctl control/
```

And just to make sure that an error occurs, access something which would only come from the control file. Now open a new SQL connection and try the following command, and note that sometimes the error may not be seen when still being connected to the previous SQL session.

```
SQL>
select * from
 v$database;
select * from
 v$database
              *

ERROR at line 1:
ORA-00210: cannot open the specified control file
ORA-00202: control file: '/u01/oradata/ORCL/control01.ctl'
ORA-27041: unable to open file
Linux Error: 2: No such file or directory
Additional information: 3
```

So there are no more control files there. Bob decides to shutdown the database, start up in nomount mode, restore control files from backup, recover the database and open it for use.

The first step would be to immediately shut down the database:

```
SQL>
 shut abort;

ORACLE instance shut down.
```

Fortunately, Bob has taken the backup using RMAN so he can use it to restore the control file. Moreover, he configured RMAN to do an automatic backup of the control file as follows:

```
RMAN> configure controlfile autobackup on;
```

But before that, he needs to at least have the instance started, as RMAN needs the instance to be up:

```
SQL>
startup nomount

ORACLE instance started.

Total System Global Area  171573248 bytes
Fixed Size                  1298668 bytes
Variable Size             134221588 bytes
Database Buffers           29360128 bytes
Redo Buffers                6692864 bytes
```

Now Bob fires up RMAN and restores the control files from the backup:

```
RMAN> restore controlfile from autobackup;
channel ORA_DISK_1: control file restore from autobackup complete
output file name=/u01/oradata/ORCL/control01.ctl
output file name=/u01/oradata/ORCL/control02.ctl
output file name=/u01/oradata/ORCL/control03.ctl
Finished restore at 17-NOV-09
```

This shows that all three control files have come up. This can also be verified as well.

```
$ ls *.ctl

control01.ctl  control02.ctl  control03.ctl
```

The next step would be to recover the database. So Bob brings the database in the *mount* stage and issues the *resetlogs* command to open it up afterwards.

```
RMAN> alter database mount;
RMAN> recover database;
```

Now the database can be opened easily.

```
SQL>
alter
 database open resetlogs;

Database altered.

SQL>
select
 status
from v$instance;

STATUS
-----------
OPEN
```

Recovery When Control Files and Data Files are Lost but the Redo Logs are Intact

3rd Scenario

Again, due to the media failure, Bob has lost all control files and datafiles which were in the same hard drive. However, the redo log files were saved as they were in a different hard drive.

This would be a semi-disaster situation. The reason for adding "semi" here is that almost everything has been lost with the loss of the datafiles and control files. Yet, there is a ray of hope left as the current redo logs still exist. In this case, as the current redo logs and archived logs both are available, it is possible to go ahead with the complete recovery.

Having full backup of the database, Bob does the following:

- Shuts down the database and starts it up in nomount mode

- Restores control files and starts the database in mount mode using newly restored control files

- Restores the datafiles, recovers the database and opens it for use

If this type of recovery scenario needs to be tested, follow these steps to move all control files and datafiles to another directory:

```
$ cd /u01/oradata/ORCL/
$ ls

control01.ctl   example01.dbf   redo03.log      temp01.dbf
control02.ctl   redo01.log      sysaux01.dbf    undotbs01.dbf
control03.ctl   redo02.log      system01.dbf    users01.dbf

$ mkdir backup
$ mv *.ctl *.dbf backup/
$ ls

backup   redo01.log   redo02.log   redo03.log
```

Bob begins the recovery process by shutting down the database in abort mode and starting it up with nomount mode as follows:

```
SQL>
shut abort;
SQL>
startup nomount;
```

Now, in the *nomount* stage, Bob tries to restore the control file from backup:

```
 RMAN> restore controlfile from autobackup;
```

As he has the control file restored, he mounts and restores the database:

```
RMAN> alter database mount;

database mounted

RMAN> restore database;
```

Bob now has all that he needs. Next, he tries to recover the database:

```
RMAN> recover database;
```

Please note that this is a complete recovery only. But he still needs to open the database using *resetlogs*.

```
RMAN> alter database open resetlogs;

database opened
```

And Bob is done!

Recovery When Control Files, Datafiles, and Redo Logs are Lost

This essentially would be a similar sort of recovery to those seen previously, but, and this matters the most, it will be an incomplete recovery as the current redo logs are not there to be recovered.

4th Scenario

Due to the media failure, Bob has lost all control files, datafiles and redo log files. He performs the steps which were mentioned in the previous scenario to bring the database back. However, when recovering the database, as RMAN looks for the current redo log file to add redo changes to the datafiles and cannot find it due to the media failure, the recovery is stopped and the database is opened with the *resetlogs* option.

To illustrate the point, create a table and put some data into it. Some of the entries are able to go to the redo logs and from there the archived logs come back to the DBA. The remaining is lost, confirming the incomplete recovery. With the database running, Bob creates a table and adds some data to it:

```
SQL>
create table
 test_recovery(a number);
SQL> insert into
 test_recovery values(1);

(output trimmed)
 .
 ..

SQL>
commit;
```

```
SQL>
select
 count(*)
from
 test_recovery;

  COUNT(*)
----------
        32
```

After this, he does a backup of the database and makes sure that the current archive logs are in that backup. Once finished with that, he adds a lot more data to the table. Finally, he has this many rows in the table:

```
SQL>
select
 count(*)
from
 test_recovery;

  COUNT(*)
----------
   1048576
```

And this was the last output for the redo logs:

```
SQL>
select
 group#, sequence#, status
from
 v$log;

GROUP#  SEQUENCE#     STATUS        FIRST_CHANGE#
------  ----------    ----------    -------------
1       4             CURRENT           593472
2       2             INACTIVE          593409
3       3             INACTIVE          593455
```

The Sequence #4 is the number of the current log group. At this moment, all hard drives failed and Bob lost all his data, i.e. all control files, datafiles and redo log files. To work along with Bob, introduce the crash as follows:

```
$ cd /u01/oradata/ORCL/
$ ls

backup          control03.ctl  redo02.log   system01.dbf   users01.dbf
control01.ctl   example01.dbf  redo03.log   temp01.dbf
control02.ctl   redo01.log     sysaux01.dbf undotbs01.dbf

$ mv *.* backup/
```

So Bob has nothing with him anymore. Naturally, the first step is to stop the database and start in the *nomount* stage.

```
SQL>
shut
 abort;
SQL>
startup
 nomount;
```

After this, the next step is to restore the control file from the backup.

```
RMAN> restore controlfile from autobackup;

channel ORA_DISK_1: control file restore from autobackup complete
output file name=/u01/oradata/ORCL/control01.ctl
output file name=/u01/oradata/ORCL/control02.ctl
output file name=/u01/oradata/ORCL/control03.ctl
Finished restore at 18-NOV-09
```

Now, Bob brings the database to the *mount* stage so that he can restore the rest of the database.

```
SQL>
alter
 database mount;

Database altered.
```

Now it is time to restore the datafiles and recover the database:

```
RMAN> restore database;
RMAN> recover database;

archived log file
name=/u01/app/oracle/flash_recovery_area/ORCL/archivelog/2009_11_18/o1_mf_1_
2_5j7gkddx_.arc thread=1 sequence=2
archived log file
name=/u01/app/oracle/flash_recovery_area/ORCL/archivelog/2009_11_18/o1_mf_1_
3_5j7glm85_.arc thread=1 sequence=3
unable to find archived log
archived log thread=1 sequence=4
RMAN-00571: ===========================================================
RMAN-00569: =============== ERROR MESSAGE STACK FOLLOWS ===============
RMAN-00571: ===========================================================
RMAN-03002: failure of recover command at 11/18/2009 14:48:07
RMAN-06054: media recovery requesting unknown archived log for thread 1 with
sequence 4 and starting SCN of 593472
```

Suddenly, Bob gets an error for the same Sequence #4 which was of the current log group. Oracle cannot find its archived file and the redo log is deleted. Therefore, whatever was inside it is lost and so this is an incomplete recovery. Bob opens the database with the *resetlogs* option and checks the number of rows in the table.

```
SQL>
alter
 database open resetlogs;

Database altered.

SQL>
select
 count(*)
from
 test_recovery;

  COUNT(*)
----------
        32
```

Indeed, he got only what he could save via the archivelogs in his backup. Since he has lost the redo logs with the *resetlogs*, he gets them back, but only as blank with nothing available in them yet:

```
SQL>
lect * from
 V$log;

GROUP#      SEQUENCE#      STATUS        FIRST_CHANGE#
----------  ----------     -------       ----------
1           1              CURRENT       593473
2           0              UNUSED        0
3           0              UNUSED
```

That is why Oracle recommends multiplexing the redo log files to different hard drives.

Recovery From the Loss of Control Files When No Backup Files are Available

5th Scenario

Bob has lost all control files and deleted RMAN backups of control files. Bob needs to create a new control file so as not to lose data in the redo log files. He uses the *sql* command which was generated before this failure occurred, creates the control file and recovers the database.

This is a serious situation. Bob has lost all of his control files and to top it off, he has no backup either. This means that he cannot simply restore the control file from the backup. Therefore, he needs to recreate the control file. Fortunately, Oracle gives Bob a way out by using its *create controlfile* command to recreate the control file. Take a look at this case.

To start with, Bob moves the control file. Please note that in this case, the redo logs need to be intact. Using the redo logs and archivelogs, Bob is able to open the database. To simulate the loss of the control files, move them to another location.

```
SQL>
alter
 database backup controlfile to trace;
$ mv *.ctl control_backup/
```

As Bob has lost the control files, he immediately kills the instance with the *abort* option.

```
SQL> shut
 abort;

Oracle instance shut down.
```

To create the control file again, Bob needs all the information of the database that this file stores and this must match exactly with his database structure. It is possible to get the current structure and the *create* command by using the following command:

```
alter database backup controlfile to trace.
```

This creates the text-based trace file in the user dump destination (in 10g) or in diagnostic destination (in 11g). If no changes have been made to the database structure, simply pick up this file and use it. This file contains two sections: with *resetlogs* and without *resetlogs*. The *resetlogs* option is required for incomplete recovery.

Also, as the control file is older than the rest of the database, use the *using backup controlfile* option to tell Oracle that an old file is being used as follows:

```
recover database using backup controlfile;
```

Fortunately, all this is already there in the trace file that is acquired from the *alter database* option. The trace natively contains lots of information which may not be needed; it is better to have only the content needed in the trace file. Run this script while being connected as the SYS user. It has all the commands to go ahead with the rest of the process. The following is the source of this file:

```
startup nomount
create controlfile reuse database "orcl" noresetlogs  archivelog
    maxlogfiles 16
    maxlogmembers 3
    maxdatafiles 100
    maxinstances 8
    maxloghistory 292
logfile
  group 1 '/u01/app/oracle/oradata/orcl/redo01.log'  size 50m,
  group 2 '/u01/app/oracle/oradata/orcl/redo02.log'  size 50m,
  group 3 '/u01/app/oracle/oradata/orcl/redo03.log'  size 50m
datafile
  '/u01/app/oracle/oradata/orcl/system01.dbf',
  '/u01/app/oracle/oradata/orcl/undotbs01.dbf',
  '/u01/app/oracle/oradata/orcl/sysaux01.dbf',
  '/u01/app/oracle/oradata/orcl/users01.dbf',
  '/u01/app/oracle/oradata/orcl/example01.dbf',
character set we8iso8859p1;
recover database;
```

So Bob puts this command into a script called *create_controlfile.sql* and runs it as follows:

```
SQL>
@/home/oracle/create_controlfile.sql

ORACLE instance started.

Total System Global Area  171573248 bytes
Fixed Size                  1298668 bytes
Variable Size             138415892 bytes
Database Buffers           25165824 bytes
Redo Buffers                6692864 bytes
Control file created.
Specify log: {<RET>=suggested | filename | AUTO | CANCEL}
/u01/app/oracle/oradata/orcl/redo01.log
Log applied.
Media recovery complete.
```

After creating control files and performing recovery, Bob opens the database with the *resetlogs* option if the *create controlfile … resetlogs* has been run:

```
SQL>
alter database
 open resetlogs;

Database altered.
```

In the creation of the control file, there may be cases when just going ahead with the default given file may not be sufficient here. One case may be a new tablespace has been added and then the control file is lost with no or old backup of it, which does not have the newly added tablespace. In this case, it is very important that the information on the newly added tablespace be saved to the previous control file and also to the *using backup controlfile* option with the recover database.

If there is not already a backup of the old control file stored somewhere already the option to create it from scratch with the *trace* option is being used, then take care that the path of all the datafiles and the names of all the tablespaces which were newly added are in the listing of this control file.

To illustrate this point, look at the same case here. Following are the files and tablespaces that are in the database:

```
SQL>
select
 name
from
 v$datafile;

NAME
------------------------------------------
/u01/app/oracle/oradata/orcl/system01.dbf
/u01/app/oracle/oradata/orcl/sysaux01.dbf
/u01/app/oracle/oradata/orcl/undotbs01.dbf
/u01/app/oracle/oradata/orcl/users01.dbf
/u01/app/oracle/oradata/orcl/example01.dbf

SQL>
select * from
 v$tablespace;

      TS# NAME                            INC BIG FLA ENC
---------- ------------------------------ --- --- --- ---
         0 SYSTEM                         YES NO  YES
         1 SYSAUX                         YES NO  YES
         2 UNDOTBS1                       YES NO  YES
         4 USERS                          YES NO  YES
         3 TEMP                           NO  NO  YES
         6 EXAMPLE                        YES NO  YES
6 rows selected.
```

Now add one more tablespace into the list:

```
SQL> create
 tablespace new
   2  datafile '/u01/app/oracle/oradata/orcl/new.dbf' SIZE 1M;

Tablespace created.
```

```
SQL>
select
 count(*)
from
 v$tablespace;

  COUNT(*)
----------
         7
```

Now one more file has been added to the database that is not in the backup control file. After the control file is lost, try to restore it from backup as follows:

```
RMAN> restore control file from
'/u01/app/oracle/flash_recovery_area/ORCL/backupset/2009_11_19/o1_mf_ncnnf_T
AG20091119T083712_5j9fm60b_.bkp';
RMAN> alter database mount;
RMAN> recover database;

. . . . . . . . . .
. . . . . . . . . .
. . . . . . . . . .
archived log file name=/u01/app/oracle/oradata/orcl/redo02.log thread=1
sequence=8
creating datafile file number=6 name=/u01/app/oracle/oradata/orcl/new.dbf
RMAN-00571: ============================================================
RMAN-00569: =============== error message stack follows ===============
RMAN-00571: ============================================================
RMAN-03002: failure of recover command at 11/19/2009 09:11:12
ORA-01119: error in creating database file
'/u01/app/oracle/oradata/orcl/new.dbf'
ORA-27038: created file already exists
Additional information: 1
```

When recovering the database and applying information from the archived redo log files, RMAN tries to create the new datafile *new.dbf* because information about creation of *new.dbf* was written in archived redo log files and was not in the control file. As the original file is there, rename and recover it as follows:

```
SQL> recover
 database using backup control file;

ORA-00283: recovery session canceled due to errors
ORA-01111: name for data file 6 is unknown - rename to correct file
ORA-01110: data file 6:
'/u01/app/oracle/product/11.1.0/db_1/dbs/UNNAMED00006'

SQL> alter
 database rename file '/u01/app/oracle/product/11.1.0/db_1/dbs/UNNAMED00006'
to '/u01/app/oracle/oradata/orcl/new.dbf';
```

Restoring and Recovering Control Files

```
Database altered.

SQL>
recover
 database using backup control file;

ORA-00279: change 564920 generated at 11/19/2009 08:43:22 needed for thread
1
ORA-00289: suggestion :
/u01/app/oracle/flash_recovery_area/ORCL/archivelog/2009_11_19/o1_mf_1_8_%u_
.arcORA-00280: change 564920 for thread 1 is in sequence #8

Specify log: {<RET>=suggested | filename | AUTO | CANCEL}
/u01/app/oracle/oradata/orcl/redo02.log

Log applied.
Media recovery complete.
SQL>

SQL> alter
 database open resetlogs;

Database altered.

SQL> select * from
 v$tablespace;

     TS# NAME                            INC BIG FLA ENC
---------- ------------------------------ --- --- --- ---
       0 SYSTEM                          YES NO  YES
       1 SYSAUX                          YES NO  YES
       2 UNDOTBS1                        YES NO  YES
       4 USERS                           YES NO  YES
       3 TEMP                            NO  NO  YES
       6 EXAMPLE                         YES NO  YES
       7 NEW                             YES NO  YES
7 rows selected.
```

In a worst-case scenario, all the control files have been corrupted or removed, no backup of control file is available, and unfortunately, the database is down. Also, no control file trace has ever been previously taken. Moreover, there is no chance left to take the control file trace using *alter database backup controlfile to trace*; because to run this command, the database must be in either mounted or opened state.

In this case, the control file has to be created manually using the *create controlfile* command. But for this, the qualified path for all the datafiles, redo log files and character set details needs to be remembered. It is a good practice to have a copy of the control file trace preserved somewhere for such a problem.

Restoring the Spfile

Spfile (System Parameter file and also known as Server Parameter file) is used at the time of the database startup. Since version 9i, Oracle has been promoting using it more as compared to the traditional parameter files. To continue encouraging DBAs to use those, Oracle's backup and recovery tool RMAN also includes the spfile in backups, making it a perfect solution to restore the file if it is lost.

It is likely that even if the spfile is lost, there will not be much that would be impacted. Most of the databases are not rebounced for a long time and parameter change is not something which is supposed to happen at repeated intervals. Also, the loss of spfile does not impact the normal working of the database. Still, a loss is a loss and if spfile is needed at any time and it is not there, it would likely at least cause some trouble if not more major problems. Therefore, it needs to be recovered as well. Now look at some different ways that the file can be restored.

A Dirty Workaround

So why was this title chosen? This section will be explaining dirty way(s) to get the file back in place. What is a spfile? It is nothing but a collection of all the parameters used and maintained by the database, and all of the database related information goes to the alert log file of it as well. Smell the dirty trick coming?!

So if the spfile is lost, the simplest way to get it back would be to open up the alert log file in a favorite editor, copy the parameter list and save the file as the parameter file. Once the parameter file is in place, all that needs to be done is create the spfile from it. This can be done by using the following command:

```
SQL>
create
 spfile from pfile='the_location_of_parameter_file';
```

In the same manner, if there are multiple databases or multiple clones running in the shop or a standby database, its parameter file can be copied, brought to the machine and from it, the spfile can be made. Remember to update the *db_name* and *control_files* and other parameters which are database specific!

Sure, it is a dirty way to do the task, but it is the simplest way when there are no backups of spfile to play around with. Also, if there is no backup, the very first rule of the backup/recovery playground has been broken.

In case the backup of the spfile has been done, either with the whole database or with the control file, RMAN can be used to restore the file as follows:

```
RMAN> restore spfile from autobackup;
```

Please note that for this command to be successful, the database must not be started from the spfile by default. This means the database must be shut down before this command can be used. If shutting down the database has not been done before issuing this command, RMAN – 06564 is hit, which essentially means that a restore of the spfile cannot be done if it has already been started up using spfile. So what needs to be done is to create a pfile and start the instance from that. Once that is done, use RMAN's *restore* command to restore the spfile.

The following code listing shows how to backup the spfile. The recovery catalog here for the database is not being used here:

```
$ rman target /
connected to target database: ORCL (DBID=1223106097)
RMAN> list backup of spfile;

using target database control file instead of recovery catalog
List of Backup Sets
===================
BS Key  Type LV Size       Device Type Elapsed Time Completion Time
------- ---- -- ---------- ----------- ------------ ---------------
2       Full    80.00K     DISK        00:00:01     21-OCT-09
        BP Key: 2    Status: AVAILABLE  Compressed: NO  Tag:
TAG20091021T013349
        Piece Name:
/u01/app/oracle/flash_recovery_area/ORCL/backupset/2009_10_21/o1_mf_nnsnf_TA
G20091021T013349_5fw5xyw6_.bkp
  spfile Included: Modification time: 21-OCT-09
```

As the database was already started with the spfile, the spfile is going to be restored to another location and */tmp* is the best place for this.

```
RMAN> restore spfile to '/tmp/spfileorcl.ora' ;
channel ORA_DISK_1: restoring spfile
output filename=/tmp/spfileorcl.ora
. . . . . . . . . .
. . . . . . . . . .
Finished restore at 21-OCT-09
```

If the autobackup feature of RMAN is to be used, there should be a backup of spfile done via autobackup. The following shows how to back up the system tablespace's datafile which would trigger the autobackup of the spfile as well.

```
RMAN> backup datafile 1;

Starting backup at 21-OCT-09
input datafile fno=00001 name=/u01/app/oracle/oradata/orcl/system01.dbf
channel ORA_DISK_1: starting piece 1 at 21-OCT-09
channel ORA_DISK_1: finished piece 1 at 21-OCT-09
piece
handle=/u01/app/oracle/flash_recovery_area/ORCL/backupset/2009_10_21/o1_mf_n
nndf_TAG20091021T055510_5fwo78jf_.bkp tag=TAG20091021T055510 comment=NONE
Finished backup at 21-OCT-09
Starting Control File and SPFILE Autobackup at 21-OCT-09
piece
handle=/u01/app/oracle/flash_recovery_area/ORCL/autobackup/2009_10_21/o1_mf_
s_700811738_5fwo83co_.bkp comment=NONE
Finished Control File and spfile Autobackup at 21-OCT-09
```

Once the autobackup of the spfile has been ensured, it can be used later for restoration. Since the recovery catalog is not being used, it is important to tell Oracle where to find the autobackup of the spfile. For this, the location of the backup and the *database_name* (even DBID will do) is required.

```
RMAN> restore spfile to '/tmp/spfiletemp.ora' from autobackup recovery area
='/u01/app/oracle/flash_recovery_area' db_name=orcl;
```

Once the backup is restored to the */tmp* folder, all that is needed is to copy the file from there to the database specific location, rename it and the restoration of the spfile is now done.

This process can be used even when there is no pfile. RMAN can jump-start the database instance with a dummy parameter file just for the sake of the restoration of the spfile afterwards. But after this, things may become complicated depending on whether the recovery catalog is being used or not. If it is being used, then it is a rather simple process. All to be done is to issue the following command:

```
RMAN> restore spfile from autobackup;
```

Oracle finds the backup of the spfile from the automatic backup and restores it. The location can be changed if so desired, but because the recovery catalog is being used, there will not be any sort of hassles supplying the database identifier (DBID). That is a must, and it can be a tricky thing if the catalog is not being used. If the recovery catalog is not being used, then it is a must to supply explicit DBID before continuing with the above command. That can be difficult if the DBID beforehand has not been noted beforehand.

Restoring and Recovering Datafiles

It is highly unlikely that a whole database is corrupted. Most of the time, the loss happens to a single datafile due to something like a hardware failure or disk crash. Losses like those can cause more than one file to get damaged, too. Be it a single file or multiple files, if there is proper backup, the restoration and recovery of the files is a simple task.

There are still some things to keep in mind depending on the type of file that has been lost. The method of recovering a normal user objects file is entirely different from that done for an undo tablespace datafile. The same applies to the whole tablespace as well if all of its datafiles have been lost.

There can also be situations when no physical file of the tablespace has been lost, but it still needs to be recovered, and that would be a different type of recovery. This type of recovery will be examined later but first of all, see what different kinds of recoveries can be done for different types of files.

In this section, the following types of recoveries will be reviewed:

- Restoration and recovery of a normal (non-system) datafile
- Restoration and recovery of a system datafile
- Restoration and recovery of an undo datafile

Restoration and Recovery of a Normal (Non-System) Datafile

A normal datafile is defined as any file which is not the part of the system, sysaux and undo tablespaces. Any other type of file which is lost can be recovered either at the open or mount stage of the database. If it is a normal datafile, the database can even be opened if it has been shut down, assuming it is in the archivelog mode. See how the resident DBA, Bob, handles this type of recovery in the following scenario. For this current setup, Bob is using RMAN without the recovery catalog.

6th Scenario

By mistake, Bob placed one of the datafiles to a different location in the OS and the system administrator accidently deleted it. It was a *users01.dbf* file which belongs to the users tablespace. Bob got a call from a user who was querying data from the table which resides on that datafile and was getting the following error:

```
ERROR at line 1:
ORA-01116: error in opening database file 4
ORA-01110: data file 4: '/u01/app/oracle/oradata/orcl/users01.dbf'
ORA-27041: unable to open file
```

As an experienced DBA, Bob immediately knew what to do:

- Take datafile to offline mode

- Restore datafile from backup

- Recover the datafile

- Take datafile to online mode

To test this scenario, move one of the datafiles to another folder as follows:

```
$ ls users01.dbf

users01.dbf

$ mv users01.dbf users01.dbf.old
$ ls users*
users01.dbf.old
```

This shows that there is a datafile *users01.dbf* which is now renamed to *users01.dbf.old*. Now to make sure that the cached data cannot be seen, flush the buffer cache:

```
SQL>
alter
 system flush buffer_cache;

System altered.
```

So now, as the buffer cache is flushed, try to access a table which is part of this datafile.

```
SQL>
select * from
test;
 select * from test
```

```
ERROR at line 1:
ORA-01116: error in opening database file 4
ORA-01110: data file 4: '/u01/app/oracle/oradata/orcl/users01.dbf'
ORA-27041: unable to open file
Linux Error: 2: No such file or directory
Additional information: 3
```

Bob now has a problem here as the datafile is renamed; hence, equivalent to lost, it or the underlying objects cannot be accessed as well. Now work with Bob to identify the error by looking at *v$recover_file* which can help to identify the issue with the datafile. Though it is obvious from the above error code, ORA-27041, that the file is not at its desired location, this can come in handy when notice of this error has suddenly been received in the mailbox. Sometimes, however, this view may not show any output. In that case, looking at the *alert.log* file is the best option to identify the error.

So as he has lost a normal file, Bob takes the file offline. It is a good practice to take a file offline before attempting any sort of recovery on it. This only applies to non-system or non-undo files.

```
SQL>
alter
 database datafile 4 offline;

Database altered.
```

Then, he checks whether he has backup of that file or not by querying the RMAN repository as follows:

```
RMAN> list backup of datafile 4;

List of Backup Sets
===================
BS Key Type LV Size       Device Type Elapsed Time Completion Time
------- ---- -- ---------- ----------- ------------ ---------------
1      Full   565.38M    DISK        00:00:30     23-OCT-09
       BP Key: 1    Status: AVAILABLE Compressed: NO Tag: TAG20091023T154137
       Piece Name:
/u01/app/oracle/flash_recovery_area/ORCL/backupset/2009_10_23/o1_mf_nnndf_TA
G20091023T154137_5g30bt6z_.bkp
 List of Datafiles in backup set 1
 File LV Type Ckp SCN    Ckp Time Name
 ---- -- ---- ---------- --------- ----
 4       Full 477201     23-OCT-09 /u01/app/oracle/oradata/orcl/users01.dbf
```

After checking the backup of that file, Bob restores it:

```
RMAN> restore datafile 4;
```

```
restoring datafile 00004 to /u01/app/oracle/oradata/orcl/users01.dbf
```

Bob can then veryify that the file is restored at the OS level:

```
$ ls user*

users01.dbf.old      users01.dbf
```

Before putting the file back online, Bob needs to recover it since it is not consistent with the database. If he tries to put it back online before recovering it, he will get the following error message:

```
SQL>
alter
 database datafile 4 online;
alter database datafile 4 online
*

ERROR at line 1:
ORA-01113: file 4 needs media recovery
ORA-01110: data file 4: '/u01/app/oracle/oradata/orcl/users01.dbf'
```

So he was told that the file needs to be recovered. Bob checks the status of the file and also the checkpoint position from where it is to where he needs to recover it.

```
SQL>
select
 d.file_name, v.checkpoint_change#,v.last_change#, v.status
  2  from
     dba_data_files d, v$datafile v
  3
     * where d.file_id=v.file#
SQL> /

FILE_NAME                            CHECKPOINT_CHANGE# LAST_CHANGE# STATUS
----------------------------------   ------------------ ------------ ------
/u01/app/oracle/oradata/orcl/system01.dbf  478422                   SYSTEM
/u01/app/oracle/oradata/orcl/undotbs01.dbf 478422                   ONLINE
/u01/app/oracle/oradata/orcl/sysaux01.dbf  478422                   ONLINE
/u01/app/oracle/oradata/orcl/users01.dbf   478422       478854      RECOVER
/u01/app/oracle/oradata/orcl/example01.db  478422                   ONLINE
```

The file status is *recover*. To check how many log sequence numbers would be applied to the file by bringing it to the current checkpoint number 478422, Bob runs the following query.

```
SQL>
select
 first_change#, next_change#, sequence#
from
 v$log_history;
```

```
FIRST_CHANGE# NEXT_CHANGE#  SEQUENCE#
------------- ------------  ----------
      446075       474826           1
      474826       478284           2
      478284       478286           3
      478286       478289           4
      478289       478291           5
      478291       478422           6
6 rows selected.
```

Now it is time to recover the datafile, so Bob performs the recovery operation:

```
RMAN> recover datafile 4;
```

Finally, the file has been recovered. Bob checks the status one last time before bringing it online.

```
SQL>
select
 d.file_name, v.checkpoint_change#,v.last_change#, v.status
from
 dba_data_files d, v$datafile v
  where
   d.file_id=v.file#;


FILE_NAME                          CHECKPOINT_CHANGE# LAST_CHANGE# STATUS
---------------------------------- ------------------ ------------ ------
............
............
/u01/app/oracle/oradata/orcl/sysaux01.dbf  478422               ONLINE
/u01/app/oracle/oradata/orcl/users01.dbf   478854     478854 OFFLINE
```

So the file status has now been changed from *recover* to *offline*. Now, Bob brings it online and issues a manual checkpoint to get all the files in synch.

```
SQL>
alter
 database datafile 4 online;

Database altered.

SQL>
select
 d.file_name, v.checkpoint_change#,v.last_change#, v.status
    from
     dba_data_files d, v$datafile v
  where
    d.file_id=v.file# and d.file_id=4;

FILE_NAME                          CHECKPOINT_CHANGE# LAST_CHANGE#    STATUS
---------------------------------- ------------------ ------------    ----
/u01/app/oracle/oradata/orcl/users01.dbf   481319                    ONLINE

SQL> alter
    system checkpoint;
```

```
System altered.

SQL>
 select
   d.file_name, v.checkpoint_change#,v.last_change#, v.status
     from
       dba_data_files d, v$datafile v
   where
     d.file_id=v.file#;

FILE_NAME                        CHECKPOINT_CHANGE# LAST_CHANGE# STATUS
-------------------------------- ------------------ ------------ ------
............
............
/u01/app/oracle/oradata/orcl/sysaux01.dbf 481328              ONLINE
/u01/app/oracle/oradata/orcl/users01.dbf  481328              ONLINE
SQL>
```

It should be mentioned that the database was recovered in *open* state as the non-system datafile is being recovered. When the system datafile is corrupted, the database will not operate and the recovery process will start from nomount mode.

Restoration and Recovery of a System Datafile

Unlike the normal datafile, the system datafile recovery tablespace is different. The biggest difference lies within the fact that the system tablespace contains the data dictionary which needs to be updated all the time. Any recovery of the datafile which contains the database's data dictionary information cannot be done at all when the database is operational. This would be sort of like which comes first, the chicken or the egg situation as some information be updated should but the location itself for that needs recovery.

Therefore, the restoration of the system datafile is done by bringing the database down and in the *mount* stage. The rest of the steps are the same as the normal datafile's recovery operation previously explored. Now see it in action.

7th Scenario

Due to media failure, Bob has lost the datafile of the system tablespace and received the following error message while querying data dictionary views:

```
ERROR at line 1:
ORA-00604: error occurred at recursive SQL level 1
ORA-01116: error in opening database file 1
```

```
ORA-01110: data file 1: '/u02/oradata/db1/system01.dbf'
ORA-27041: unable to open file
Linux Error: 2: No such file or directory
Additional information: 3
SQL>
```

Bob decides to recover the datafile. Thus, he needs to shut down the database, start it up in nomount mode, and then restore and recover the datafile. To test this scenario, delete the *system01.dbf* file. As this is on a Linux based system, the file can be removed even when the database is open. Please note that this is not possible if a Windows system is being worked on. Now try to query any data dictionary view. The same error message that was shown at the beginning of this scenario will appear.

Bob checks for any backups of the system tablespace in RMAN repository:

```
RMAN> list backup of tablespace system;

using target database control file instead of recovery catalog

List of Backup Sets
===================
BS Key  Type LV Size       Device Type Elapsed Time Completion Time
------- ---- -- ---------- ----------- ------------ ---------------
1       Full    565.38M    DISK        00:00:30     23-OCT-09
        BP Key: 1    Status: AVAILABLE Compressed: NO  Tag: TAG20091023T154137
        Piece Name:
/u01/app/oracle/flash_recovery_area/ORCL/backupset/2009_10_23/o1_mf_nnndf_TA
G20091023T154137_5g30bt6z_.bkp
  List of Datafiles in backup set 1
  File LV Type Ckp SCN    Ckp Time  Name
  ---- -- ---- ---------- --------- ----
  1       Full 477201     23-OCT-09 /u01/app/oracle/oradata/orcl/system01.dbf
```

As he has done a backup of the *system01.dbf* file, he is ready to recover it. However, since he is recovering the system datafile, he needs to shut down the database with abort mode and start it in mount mode as follows:

```
SQL>
shut
 abort;
SQL>
startup
 mount;
```

And now he attempts to restore the file from RMAN:

```
RMAN> restore datafile 1;
```

So the file has been restored. Bob checks the status of the physical file to be sure whether it is indeed restored or not. There should be no doubt with RMAN, but a cross check is always better!

```
$ ls system*

system01.dbf
```

Now he checks to see how much needs to be recovered, e.g. from which checkpoint position to another, for this file using the following query:

```
SQL>
select
 file#,checkpoint_change#, status, recover
from
 v$datafile_header;

    FILE# CHECKPOINT_CHANGE# STATUS   REC
---------- ------------------ ------- ---
        1             477201 ONLINE   YES
        2             503455 ONLINE   NO
        3             503455 ONLINE   NO
        4             503455 ONLINE   NO
        5             503455 ONLINE   NO
```

From checkpoint number 477201 to 503455, he needs to recover the file. He attempts to recover and check the status of the file again:

```
RMAN> recover datafile 1;
SQL>
select
 checkpoint_change#, status, recover FROM v$datafile_header;

CHECKPOINT_CHANGE# STATUS   REC
------------------ ------- ---
            509975 ONLINE   NO
            503455 ONLINE   NO
            503455 ONLINE   NO
            503455 ONLINE   NO
            503455 ONLINE   NO
```

As can be seen, the *recover*=YES status of the file has been changed to NO, and the file is in sync with the rest of the files as well. Now Bob is ready to open the database safely:

```
SQL>
alter
 database open;

Database altered.
```

> 🔔 It is a good practice, after any system related datafile is recovered, to do a fresh backup of the whole database immediately.

Restoration and Recovery of an Undo Datafile

An undo datafile is a special file as it contains the undo segments which are a must for the database to operate. This means that if any file is lost from this tablespace, the recovery of that file is not possible when the database is up and operational. In order to bring the datafile up, the database must be immediately brought down.

8th Scenario

Due to the media failure, Bob has lost undo tablespace. As he has a backup of this tablespace, he shuts down the database, restores it from backup, restarts the database and makes the restored datafile online. To test this scenario, move the datafile of the undo tablespace to the different directory.

Bob shuts down the database, brings it to the mount mode, makes the undo datafile offline, reopens the database, restores and recovers the undo datafile and brings it online as follows:

```
SQL>
startup

ORACLE instance started.

Total System Global Area   171966464 bytes
Fixed Size                   1247900 bytes
Variable Size               67110244 bytes
Database Buffers            96468992 bytes
Redo Buffers                 7139328 bytes
Database mounted.
ORA-01157: cannot identify/lock data file 2 - see DBWR trace file
ORA-01110: data file 2:
'D:\ORACLE\product\10.2.0\oradata\orcl\undotbs01.dbf'

SQL>
alter
 database datafile 2 offline;

Database altered.
```

```
SQL>
alter
 database open;

Database altered.

SQL>
RMAN> restore datafile 2;
RMAN> recover datafile 2;
SQL>
alter
 database datafile 2 online;

Database altered.
SQL>
```

Recovering a Datafile That is Not Backed Up

Amazing, is it not? A datafile can now be restored and recovered which had never been able to be backed up before. Think it is impossible? Not if Oracle Database is involved! So now it is time to prove it.

9th Scenario

Bob has scheduled backup of the database every night. One day, he decides to create a new tablespace and creates some database objects on it. At 15:00, one of the system administrators accidently deletes the file from the OS. The next time Bob wants to access that file, he gets an error. He understands that he has lost the datafile which has not already backed up. He does not panic, and he opens the RMAN session to get the datafile back. Although there is no backup of that datafile, he successfully restores and recovers it.

 Recovery of a datafile that has not been backed up requires **all** archived redo log files since the time the datafile was added to the database. For example, if the datafile was added one week ago and not backed up, restore all the archived redo log files over the past week as well.

When a datafile which has not been backed up is lost but there are archived redo log files that were created after the creation of that datafile, it means that the data in that datafile can be saved. How? It is easy. As there is information about that datafile in the control file, by issuing the *restore* command RMAN will check to see if there is backup of that file or not. If there is, then RMAN restores that datafile from backup. If not, then by using archived redo log files, RMAN simply creates a new datafile and applies all changes made to that file from archived redo log files. Now see it in action.

Back up the database using RMAN:

```
RMAN> backup database plus archivelog;
```

Create a new tablespace with one datafile:

```
SQL>
create
 tablespace test datafile '/tmp/test.dbf' SIZE 1M;

Tablespace created.
```

Create a table on that datafile and insert one row:

```
SQL>
create
 table tbl_test (id number) tablespace test;

Table created.

SQL>
insert into
 tbl_test values(1);

1 row created.

SQL>
commit;
Commit complete.
SQL>
```

Delete that file directly from the OS.

```
SQL> select
 file#, name
from
 v$datafile
where
 file#=5;

    FILE#  NAME
---------- --------------------
        5  /tmp/test.dbf

SQL>
host
 rm -rf /tmp/test.dbf
```

Now use *startup force* to shut down the database and then open it. Doing that, an error about the missing datafile will appear:

```
SQL>
startup force

<....output trimmed ....>
Database mounted.
ORA-01157: cannot identify/lock data file 5 - see DBWR trace file
ORA-01110: data file 5: '/tmp/test.dbf'
```

Then take this file to the offline mode and open the database:

```
SQL>
alter
 database datafile '/tmp/test.dbf' offline;

Database altered.

SQL>
alter
 database open;

Database altered.
SQL>
```

Next, open the new RMAN session and restore the datafile:

```
RMAN> restore datafile 5;

Starting restore at 09-FEB-10
using target database control file instead of recovery catalog
allocated channel: ORA_DISK_1
channel ORA_DISK_1: sid=139 devtype=DISK

creating datafile fno=5 name=/tmp/test.dbf
restore not done; all files readonly, offline, or already restored
Finished restore at 09-FEB-10
```

As can be seen, RMAN just creates the datafile based on the information on the control file. Now the datafile can be recovered.

```
RMAN> recover datafile 5;

Starting recover at 09-FEB-10
using channel ORA_DISK_1

starting media recovery
media recovery complete, elapsed time: 00:00:00

Finished recover at 09-FEB-10
RMAN>
```

A Dirty Workaround

Lastly, take the datafile to online mode and check its status.

```
SQL>
alter
  database datafile '/tmp/test.dbf' online;

Database altered.

SQL>
select
  file#, status, name
from
  v$datafile
where
  file#=5;

FILE#                 STATUS        NAME
------------          -------       ----------------------------------
5                     ONLINE        /tmp/test.dbf
SQL>
```

To check the table that was created on the deleted datafile, query it as follows:

```
SQL>
select * from
  tbl_test;

        ID
----------
         1
SQL>
```

Restoring Tablespaces

Tablespace recoveries are similar to datafile recoveries but differ in that normally when a datafile is lost, chances are that only a subset of the tablespace has been lost, and some of the data is still accessible. In that case, only the lost file can be recovered. When tablespace recovery is needed, this means that all or the majority of the files of the said tablespace have been lost and it is not feasible to recover them one by one.

The method of tablespace recovery, whether it is at the open stage of the database or not, is dependent on which tablespace has been lost. If it is tablespace belonging to the system's category, like *system*, *sysaux* and *undo*, the recovery would be done at the *mount* stage only. In the case of a normal tablespace like users, the recovery can be done at either the open stage or the closed stage, based on whether downtime is allowed or not.

The process remains exactly the same for the datafiles with the only difference that now, instead of issuing a restore and recover, it is done for the entire tablespace and the same is true for the recovery as well. Look at one example of recovering the users tablespace.

```
RMAN> restore tablespace users;
RMAN> recover tablespace users;
```

Restoration of the Archivelogs

Normally, there is no need to restore the archivelogs as they are used and requested by RMAN automatically. Oracle picks up the information of available archivelogs using the *log_archive_dest_1* and *log_archive_dest* parameters' system defined combination. If not there, it will look in the backup for the same information.

In any of the places they are not found, the recovery process triggers back and asks where the files are and their complete path needs to be supplied. In this process, the archivelogs may need to be sent to a destination other than the default one. Then the archivelogs can be restored to that other destination.

As Oracle picks up the default destination automatically, change that process using the *set archivelog destination to* command. This command must be used before the recovery is done and all the archivelogs must be restored to this destination as well. The way to restore the archivelogs can be either by choosing them manually or by using RMAN.

The following demo will show how the archivelogs can be restored to a specifically defined destination. Make a folder over the system and restore all the archivelogs there as follows:

```
mkdir d:\archive
rman target /
RMAN> run {
2> set archivelog destination to 'd:\archive';
3> restore archivelog all;
4> }
```

Archivelogs can be restored to different destinations in case one destination is not able to store them all. In that case, how many sequence numbers are supposed to get placed on each destination can be chosen and the corresponding files can be restored.

Using *set newname* to Change the Restored File Location

As default, RMAN restores a backup of a datafile to its default location. To change this behavior, use the *set newname* command to define a new location for the restored datafile.

Prior to Oracle 11gR2, this command was used to rename the datafiles and tempfiles. But starting from Oracle 11gR2, all datafiles in any tablespace can be renamed as whole database files. Moreover, these new options come with new substitution variables which help to change the set of filenames at once. See the usage of these options and substitution variables in real examples.

1. Using *set newname for datafile*

```
RMAN> run
    {
        set newname for datafile 4 to '/tmp/datafile4.dbf';
        restore datafile 4;
    }

executing command: set newname

channel ORA_DISK_1: restoring datafile 00004 to /tmp/datafile4.dbf
```

2. Using *set newname for tempfile*

To create a tempfile in a new directory while cloning the database, use the *set newname for tempfile ... to ....* command as follows:

```
RMAN> run
    {
            set newname for tempfile 1 to '/tmp/temp01.dbf';
            duplicate database;
    }
```

RMAN will create a new tempfile with a specified name after the database is recovered and opened.

3. Using *set newname for tablespace*

This option is used to change all datafiles in a specified tablespace. When using this option, a substitution variable must be used to avoid name collisions. Here is the list of substitution variables which are used during name conversion:

- *%b*: Specifies the file name without the directory that it locates

- *%N*: Specifies the tablespace name

- *%f*: Specifies the absolute file number of a datafile

- *%I*: Specifies DBID

- *%U*: Specifies system generated unique filename as a following format: *data-D-%d_id-%I_TS-%N_FNO-%f*

See the following example to understand these substitution variables. In the following example, the *%b*, *%N* and *%f* variables are used:

```
RMAN> run
2> {
3> set newname for tablespace users to '/tmp/db/%n_%f_%b';
4> restore tablespace users;
5> }

output file name=/tmp/db/USERS_4_users01.dbf RECID=8 STAMP=728496167
output file name=/tmp/db/USERS_5_user02.dbf RECID=9 STAMP=728496168
```

By using the *%U* variable, the system-generated unique filename can be found. Look at the following example:

```
RMAN> run
2> {
3> set newname for tablespace users to '/tmp/db/%u';
4> restore tablespace users;
5> }

output file name=/tmp/db/data_d-test_ts-users_fno-4 recid=10 stamp=728496242
output file name=/tmp/db/data_d-test_ts-users_fno-5 recid=11 stamp=728496243
```

4. Using *set newname for database*

This option is used to set a new name for all datafiles and tempfiles in a database. This option is also used with one of the above-mentioned substitution variables.

Performing Block Media Recovery

One of the main features of RMAN is its ability to recover the datafile in data block level. Using this feature, it is possible to recover only the corrupted blocks of the datafile instead of doing it offline and doing a time-consuming full datafile (many gigabytes in size) restoration.

As RMAN backs up each individual data block, it checks the block for any physical corruption and updates the *v$database_block_corruption* view. The corrupted block and datafile number can easily be viewed for further block media recovery operations. To use the block media recovery feature, the database should be in archivelog mode.

10th Scenario

During midday, Bob received a phone call where the user complained about the following error he got while querying a table:

```
ERROR at line 1:
ORA-01578: Oracle data block corrupted (file # 4, block # 76)
ORA-01110: data file 4: 'C:\ORACLE\product\10.2.0\oradata\db1\users01.dbf'
```

Getting this error, Bob understood that the datafile was corrupted due to the media corruption, i.e. a hard drive bad sector issue. He uses the *dbv* (dbverify) utility to get more information about all corrupted blocks, and then using the *blockrecover* command, he recovers the corrupted data blocks.

To practice the block media recovery operation, there needs to be corrupted blocks in the database. As it is a very rare situation to have blocks corrupted in a datafile, the data block can be manually corrupted in a datafile and then try to recover it in order to test the block recovery mechanism.

To corrupt the data block, open the datafile in any hexadecimal editor, find the row that should be corrupted and change it. To be in poor Bob's shoes and have some corrupted data blocks, take a look at the following example. Here, try to manually corrupt the data block and recover it using the block media recovery feature of RMAN.

Create a table in users tablespace and insert one row in it.

```
SQL>
create
 table test_corruption (str varchar2(10)) tablespace users;

Table created.

SQL>
insert into
 test_corruption values('Test');

1 row created.

SQL>
commit;

Commit complete.
```

SQL>

Now open *users01.dbf* and change the first letter by selecting it in hexadecimal mode and changing it.

```
) C:\oracle\product\10.2.0\oradata\db1\USERS01.DBF
               0  1  2  3  4  5  6  7  8  9  a  b  c  d  e  f
0099f50h: 00 00 00 00 00 00 00 00 00 00 00 00 00 00 00 00 ;  ................
0099f60h: 00 00 00 00 00 00 00 00 00 00 00 00 00 00 00 00 ;  ................
0099f70h: 00 00 00 00 00 00 00 00 00 00 00 00 00 00 00 00 ;  ................
0099f80h: 00 00 00 00 00 00 00 00 00 00 00 00 00 00 00 00 ;  ................
0099f90h: 00 00 00 00 00 00 00 00 00 00 00 00 00 00 00 00 ;  ................
0099fa0h: 00 00 00 00 00 00 00 00 00 00 00 00 00 00 00 00 ;  ................
0099fb0h: 00 00 00 00 00 00 00 00 00 00 00 00 00 00 00 00 ;  ................
0099fc0h: 00 00 00 00 00 00 00 00 00 00 00 00 00 00 00 00 ;  ................
0099fd0h: 00 00 00 00 00 00 00 00 00 00 00 00 00 00 00 00 ;  ................
0099fe0h: 00 00 00 00 00 00 00 00 00 00 00 00 00 00 00 00 ;  ................
0099ff0h: 00 00 00 00 2C 01 01 04 54 65 73 74 03 06 EB 6A ;  ....,...Test..ëj
009a000h: 06 A2 00 00 4D 00 00 01 EB 6A 08 00 00 00 01 04 ;  .¢..M...ëj......
009a010h: 26 E2 00 00 01 00 00 00 9E C8 00 00 E2 6A 08 00 ;  &â......žÈ..âj..
009a020h: 00 00 00 00 02 00 32 00 49 00 00 01 00 00 00 00 ;  ......2.I.......
009a030h: 00 00 00 00 00 00 00 00 00 00 00 00 00 00 00 00 ;  ................
009a040h: 00 00 00 00 00 00 00 00 00 00 00 00 00 00 00 00 ;  ................
009a050h: 00 00 00 00 00 00 00 00 00 00 00 00 00 00 00 00 ;  ................
009a060h: 00 00 00 00 00 00 00 00 FF FF 0E 00 98 1F 8A 1F ;  ........yy..".Š.
009a070h: 8A 1F 00 00 00 00 00 00 00 00 00 00 00 00 00 00 ;  Š...............
009a080h: 00 00 00 00 00 00 00 00 00 00 00 00 00 00 00 00 ;  ................
009a090h: 00 00 00 00 00 00 00 00 00 00 00 00 00 00 00 00 ;  ................
```

Figure 4.1: *users01.dbf Table*

Save the file and exit. Try to select the table. This error appears:

```
SQL>
select * from
 test_corruption
         *

error at line 1:
ORA-01578: ORACLE data block corrupted (file # 4, block # 76)
ORA-01110: data file 4: 'C:\ORACLE\product\10.2.0\oradata\db1\users01.dbf'
SQL>
```

Block number 76 of datafile 4 has been corrupted. Without using the block media recovery feature of RMAN, the file would have to be restored from backup by making all datafiles offline and performing whole datafile recovery. That would be very time consuming with a file gigabytes in size.

Note: To corrupt the specific data block from Linux, get the block number for that table from *dba_segments* view and corrupt it using the *dd os* command.

For this, create a table on the users tablespace, insert one row, commit data and then get the block number which contains the segment header. Add 1 to that value and use the *dd* command to corrupt the next data block of that table as follows:

```
SQL>
create
 table tbl_corrupted (id number);

Table created.

SQL>
insert into
 tbl_corrupted values(1);

1 row created.

SQL>
commit;

Commit complete.

SQL>
select * from
 tbl_corrupted;

        ID
----------
         1

SQL>
select
 header_block
from
 dba_segments
where
 segment_name='tbl_corrupted';

HEADER_BLOCK
------------
          67

[oracle@localhost mydb]$ dd
of=/u01/oracle/product/10.2.0/db_1/oradata/mydb/users01.dbf bs=8192
conv=notrunc seek=68 << EOF
> corruption
> EOF
0+1 records in
0+1 records out

SQL>
alter
 system flush buffer_cache;

System altered.

SQL>
```

```
select * from
 tbl_corrupted;
select * from tbl_corrupted
                     *

ERROR at line 1:
ORA-01578: ORACLE data block corrupted (file # 4, block # 68)
ORA-01110: data file 4:
'/u01/oracle/product/10.2.0/db_1/oradata/mydb/users01.dbf'
SQL>
```

In this situation, Bob decides to recover only corrupted blocks of the datafile using the block media recovery feature of RMAN.

First of all, Bob checks the *alert.log* file and a trace file which was generated for this corruption as follows:

```
Hex dump of (file 4, block 76) in trace file
c:\oracle\product\10.2.0\admin\db1\udump\db1_ora_2968.trc
Corrupt block relative dba: 0x0100004c (file 4, block 76)
Bad check value found during buffer read
Data in bad block:
 type: 6 format: 2 rdba: 0x0100004c
 last change scn: 0x0000.00086aeb seq: 0x3 flg: 0x06
 spare1: 0x0 spare2: 0x0 spare3: 0x0
 consistency value in tail: 0x6aeb0603
 check value in block header: 0xa13a
 computed block checksum: 0xb
Reread of rdba: 0x0100004c (file 4, block 76) found same corrupted data
```

By opening the trace file with the *.trc* extension that is written in the *alert.log* file, he gets more information:

```
Corrupt block relative dba: 0x0100004c (file 4, block 76)
Bad check value found during buffer read
Data in bad block:
 type: 6 format: 2 rdba: 0x0100004c
 last change scn: 0x0000.00086aeb seq: 0x3 flg: 0x06
 spare1: 0x0 spare2: 0x0 spare3: 0x0
 consistency value in tail: 0x6aeb0603
 check value in block header: 0xa13a
 computed block checksum: 0xb
Reread of rdba: 0x0100004c (file 4, block 76) found same corrupted data
```

To get more information, Bob uses the *dbv* (dbverify) utility to get a list of all the corrupted blocks:

```
C:\>dbv file=c:\oracle\product\10.2.0\oradata\db1\users01.dbf

DBVERIFY - Verification starting : FILE =
c:\oracle\product\10.2.0\oradata\db1\USERS01.DBF
Page 76 is marked corrupt
```

Performing Block Media Recovery

```
Corrupt block relative dba: 0x0100004c (file 4, block 76)
Bad check value found during dbv:
Data in bad block:
 type: 6 format: 2 rdba: 0x0100004c
 last change scn: 0x0000.00086aeb seq: 0x3 flg: 0x06
 spare1: 0x0 spare2: 0x0 spare3: 0x0
 consistency value in tail: 0x6aeb0603
 check value in block header: 0xa13a
 computed block checksum: 0xb

DBVERIFY - Verification complete
Total Pages Examined         : 640
Total Pages Processed (Data) : 29
Total Pages Failing   (Data) : 0
Total Pages Processed (Index): 2
Total Pages Failing   (Index): 0
Total Pages Processed (Other): 35
Total Pages Processed (Seg)  : 0
Total Pages Failing   (Seg)  : 0
Total Pages Empty            : 573
Total Pages Marked Corrupt   : 1
Total Pages Influx           : 0
Highest block SCN            : 551659 (0.551659)
C:\>
```

> 🔔 Note: If the count of corrupted data blocks is not too large, then use the *blockrecover* command and specify the corrupted blocks. If there are a lot of corrupted data blocks and they do not need to be specified one by one, then there is another option. Run the *blockrecover corruption list* command after running the *backup* or *backup validate* command. Upon running one of these commands, the *v$database_block_corruption* view will be populated with a list of the corrupted data blocks.

Now Bob has only one corrupted block. Bob then runs the *backup validate* command and populates the *v$database_block_corruption* view:

```
SQL>
select * from
 v$database_block_corruption;

no rows selected

RMAN> backup validate datafile 4;

SQL>
```

```
select * from
v$database_block_corruption;

    FILE#      BLOCK#      BLOCKS CORRUPTION_CHANGE# CORRUPTIO
---------- ---------- ---------- ------------------ ---------
        4         76          1                  0 CHECKSUM
```

Bob uses the first method to recover the corrupted block by running the *blockrecover* command as follows:

```
RMAN> blockrecover datafile 4 block 76;

Starting blockrecover at 17-OCT-09
using target database control file instead of recovery catalog

channel ORA_DISK_1: restoring block(s)
channel ORA_DISK_1: specifying block(s) to restore from backup set
restoring blocks of datafile 00004
channel ORA_DISK_1: reading from backup piece
C:\ORACLE\product\10.2.0\flash_recovery_area\db1\backupset\2009_10_17\o1_mf_
nnndf_tag20091017t163201_5fmbsl9r_.bkp
channel ORA_DISK_1: block restore complete, elapsed time: 00:00:02

starting media recovery
archive log thread 1 sequence 3 is already on disk as file
C:\ORACLE\product\10.2.0\flash_recovery_area\db1\archivelog\2009_10_17\o1_mf
_1_3_5fmbtrk2_.arc
.................
.................
media recovery complete, elapsed time: 00:00:01
Finished blockrecover at 17-OCT-09
RMAN>

SQL>
select * from
 test_corruption;

STR
----------
Test
```

This command restores the specific data block from the backup and recovers the datafile by applying archived redo log files.

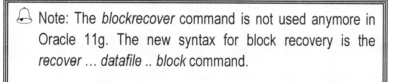

Note: The *blockrecover* command is not used anymore in Oracle 11g. The new syntax for block recovery is the *recover ... datafile .. block* command.

Another option to recover this block is running the *blockrecover corruption list* command. This command recovers all corrupted data blocks that are written in the *v$database_block_corruption* view. Starting from Oracle 11g, the *v$database_block_corruption* view is updated when any process or database utility encounters the data block corruption. Moreover, the specific block can be validated at the specific datafile using the *validate datafile ... block ...* command.

Here, Bob tries to recover the corrupted block using this command as follows:

```
RMAN> blockrecover corruption list;

restoring blocks of datafile 00004
......
......
starting media recovery
Finished blockrecover at 17-OCT-09

SQL>
select * from
 test_corruption;

STR
----------
Test
```

As can be seen, *blockrecover corruption list* recovered all the corrupted data blocks.

It is possible to recover more than one block of multiple datafiles. It is also possible to recover the data block using the tablespace name and Data Block Address (DBA). To test this, create two tablespaces and three tables, corrupt all tables and then recover them using different methods.

Create two tablespaces and three tables:

```
SQL>
create
 tablespace tbs_one datafile 'c:\tbs_one.dbf' SIZE 1M;

Tablespace created.

SQL>
create
 tablespace tbs_two datafile 'c:\tbs_two.dbf' size 1M;0

Tablespace created.

SQL>
create
 table tbl_one (str varchar2(10)) tablespace users;
```

```
Table created.

SQL>
drop
 table tbl_one;

Table dropped.

SQL>
create
 table tbl_one (str varchar2(10)) tablespace  tbs_one;

Table created.

SQL>
create
 table tbl_two (str varchar2(10)) tablespace tbs_two;

Table created.

SQL>
create
 table tbl_three (str varchar2(10)) tablespace users;

Table created.

SQL>
insert into
 tbl_one values('test');

1 row created.

SQL> insert into
 tbl_two values('test');

1 row created.

SQL>
insert into
 tbl_three values('test');

1 row created.

SQL> commit;

 Commit complete.

SQL>

RMAN> backup database plus archivelog;
```

Two tablespaces have been created with three tables and the whole database backed up. Now corrupt all three datafiles by opening them in hexadecimal editor and changing the first letter of the row (the letter t), save the file and exit.

To see the corruption, run the *backup validate database* command from RMAN and check the *v$database_block_corrupton* view.

```
RMAN> backup validate database;

SQL>
select * from
  v$database_block_corruption;

     FILE#     BLOCK#     BLOCKS CORRUPTION_CHANGE# CORRUPTION
---------- ---------- ---------- ------------------ ---------
         5         13          1                  0 CHECKSUM
         6         13          1                  0 CHECKSUM
         4         69          1                  0 CHECKSUM

SQL>
select * from
 tbl_one;

STR
----------
test

SQL> select * from
 tbl_two;

STR
----------
test

SQL> select * from
 tbl_three;

STR
----------
test
```

Here, although the datafiles have been corrupted, the tables are still able to be queried. In fact, the rows are queried from the database buffer cache, not from datafile. If the buffer cache is flushed, the tables would not be able to be queried because now they are queried directly from the datafiles.

```
SQL> alter
 system flush buffer_cache;

System altered.

SQL> select * from
 tbl_one;
select * from tbl_one
*

ERROR at line 1:
ORA-01578: ORACLE data block corrupted (file # 5, block # 13)
ORA-01110: data file 5: 'c:\tbs_one.dbf'
```

Oracle Backup and Recovery

```
SQL> select * from
 tbl_two;
select * from tbl_two
*

ERROR at line 1:
ORA-01578: ORACLE data block corrupted (file # 6, block # 13)
ORA-01110: data file 6: 'c:\tbs_two.dbf'

SQL> select * from
 tbl_three;
select * from tbl_three
*

ERROR at line 1:
ORA-01578: ORACLE data block corrupted (file # 4, block # 69)
ORA-01110: data file 4: 'C:\ORACLE\product\10.2.0\oradata\db1\users01.dbf'
SQL>
```

Recover the first two tablespaces by using the *datafile* parameter in one command line. The third tablespace will be recovered using the *tablespace* parameter. Now recover all the corrupted data blocks:

```
RMAN> blockrecover datafile 5 block 13 datafile 6 block 13;

Starting blockrecover at 18-OCT-09
restoring blocks of datafile 00005
restoring blocks of datafile 00006
...........
...........
starting media recovery
media recovery complete, elapsed time: 00:00:03
Finished blockrecover at 18-OCT-09
RMAN>
```

There are two different datafiles recovered using one command. Using information about Data Block Address (DBA) written in the *alert.log* file, recover the third tablespace. Here is the information from the *alert.log* file:

```
Hex dump of (file 4, block 69) in trace file
c:\oracle\product\10.2.0\admin\db1\udump\db1_ora_2460.trc
Corrupt block relative dba: 0x01000045 (file 4, block 69)
Bad check value found during buffer read
Data in bad block:
 type: 6 format: 2 rdba: 0x01000045
 last change scn: 0x0000.00086381 seq: 0x3 flg: 0x06
 spare1: 0x0 spare2: 0x0 spare3: 0x0
 consistency value in tail: 0x63810603
 check value in block header: 0xca6
 computed block checksum: 0x56
Reread of rdba: 0x01000045 (file 4, block 69) found same corrupted data
Sun Oct 18 14:59:27 2009
Corrupt Block Found
        tsn = 4, tsname = users
```

Performing Block Media Recovery

```
          rfn = 4, blk = 69, rdba = 16777285
          objn = 51349, objd = 51349, object = tbl_three, subobject =
          segment owner = sys, segment type = Table Segment
Sun Oct 18 15:18:11 2009
```

The data block number of the corrupted block is 16777285 and it resides in the users tablespace. Now using these values, recover the corrupted block as follows:

```
RMAN> blockrecover tablespace users dba 16777285;

Starting blockrecover at 18-OCT-09
using channel ORA_DISK_1
. . . . . . . . . . . . . .
. . . . . . . . . . . . . .
Finished blockrecover at 18-OCT-09
RMAN>
```

Next, query all tables to see whether the corrupted data blocks have been recovered or not using the following command:

```
SQL> select * from
   tbl_one
 2  union all
 3  select * from
   tbl_two
 4  union all
 5  select * from
   tbl_three;

STR
----------
test
test
test
SQL>
```

It is not possible to make backup with RMAN if there are corrupted data blocks in the database. If a backup is attempted, the following error will occur:

```
RMAN> backup database;
. . . . . . . . . . . . . . . . .
RMAN-00571: ===========================================================
RMAN-00569: =============== error message stack follows ===============
RMAN-00571: ===========================================================
RMAN-03009: failure of backup command on ORA_DISK_1 channel at 10/19/2009
17:17:41
ORA-19566: exceeded limit of 0 corrupt blocks for file c:\tbs_corrupt.dbf
```

In order to backup the corrupted datafile in spite of having corrupted data blocks in it, set the *maxcorrupt* parameter as follows:

```
RMAN> run
2> {
3> set maxcorrupt for datafile 5 to 2;
4> backup datafile 5;
5> }

executing command: set max corrupt

Starting backup at 19-OCT-09
channel ORA_DISK_1: backup set complete, elapsed time: 00:00:01
Finished backup at 19-OCT-09
```

However, if the corrupted datafile is possibly recovered with corrupted backup, there is failure:

```
RMAN> blockrecover datafile 5 block 15;

RMAN-00571: ===========================================================
RMAN-00569: =============== error message stack follows ===============
RMAN-00571: ===========================================================
RMAN-03002: failure of blockrecover command at 10/19/2009 17:28:47
RMAN-06026: some targets not found - aborting restore
RMAN-06023: no backup or copy of datafile 5 found to restore
```

 Note: A corrupted datafile is backed up and due to an attempted deletion of retention obsolete backups, RMAN considers the backup of the datafile which has corrupted the data blocks as valid backup and deletes other backups. In case of recovery, when this backup file is in use, all data blocks will be restored and recovered except the corrupted blocks.

It is possible to use specific *tag* names when using the *blockrecover* command. So assume that there are two backups of datafile. The first one with tag name *success* was taken before corruption, while the second one with tag name *corrupt* was taken after corruption by setting the *maxcorrupt* parameter.

In this situation, if a recovery of the data block using the *blockrecover* command is tried, RMAN first reads the last backup and restores the data block from that backup. As the corrupted datafile was backed up, RMAN will not be able to restore that datafile from the backup and searches for one previous backup. This can be seen from the following example:

```
RMAN> blockrecover datafile 5 block 15;

Starting blockrecover at 19-OCT-09
using channel ORA_DISK_1
# Here, RMAN reads the last backup (corrupted one)

channel ORA_DISK_1: block restore complete, elapsed time: 00:00:01
failover to previous backup
# As we see, RMAN finds that it can't restore the data block from this
backup, thus switches to the previous backup

channel ORA_DISK_1: restoring block(s)
starting media recovery
media recovery complete, elapsed time: 00:00:03
Finished blockrecover at 19-OCT-09
RMAN>
```

Try to use specific backup using the *tag* name as follows:

```
RMAN> blockrecover datafile 5 block 15 from tag corrupt;

Starting blockrecover at 19-OCT-09
using channel ORA_DISK_1
RMAN-00571: ===========================================================
RMAN-00569: =============== error message stack follows ===============
RMAN-00571: ===========================================================
RMAN-03002: failure of blockrecover command at 10/19/2009 18:22:39
RMAN-06026: some targets not found - aborting restore
RMAN-06023: no backup or copy of datafile 5 found to restore
```

By using the *corrupt* tag which is the corrupted backup of datafile, the data block is not able to be restored.

Using Flashback Logs to Improve Block Media Recovery Performance

Starting from Oracle 11g, RMAN uses flashback logs during block media recovery, thus improves the recovery performance. During block media recovery, RMAN checks flashback logs for required blocks before going to backups. The following example will demonstrate this. For this, enable flashback on a database, create a new tablespace and corrupt the data block. Then try to recover the corrupted datafile:

```
SQL>
alter
 database flashback on;
```

```
Database altered.

SQL>
create
 tablespace tbs_test datafile '/u01/home/ORACLE/oradata/test/tbs_test01.dbf'
SIZE 1M;

Tablespace created.
SQL>
host
[oracle@localhost ~]$ dd of=/u01/home/ORACLE/oradata/test/tbs_test01.dbf
bs=8192 conv=notrunc seek=2 <<EOF
> test corruption
> EOF
0+1 records in
0+1 records out
16 bytes (16 B) copied, 0.000522409 seconds, 30.6 kB/s

SQL>
alter
 system checkpoint;

System altered.

RMAN>
validate
 datafile 5;

<...output trimmed ...>
<...output trimmed ...>

List of Datafiles
=================
File Status Marked Corrupt Empty Blocks Blocks Examined High SCN
---- ------ -------------- ------------ --------------- ----------
5    FAILED 0              121          128             277432
  File Name: /u01/home/oracle/oradata/test/tbs_test01.dbf
  Block Type Blocks Failing Blocks Processed
  ---------- -------------- ----------------
  Data       0              0
  Index      0              0
  Other      1              7

validate found one or more corrupt blocks
See trace file /u01/home/ORACLE/diag/rdbms/test/test/trace/test_ora_3842.trc
for details

RMAN>

SQL>
select * from
 v$database_block_corruption;

     FILE#      BLOCK#     BLOCKS CORRUPTION_CHANGE# CORRUPTION
---------- ---------- ---------- ------------------ ---------
         5          2          1                  0 CORRUPT

RMAN> RECOVER DATAFILE 5 BLOCK 2;
```

Performing Block Media Recovery   **169**

```
Starting recover at 31-AUG-10
using target database control file instead of recovery catalog
allocated channel: ORA_DISK_1
channel ORA_DISK_1: SID=1 device type=DISK
searching flashback logs for block images
finished flashback log search, restored 1 blocks
starting media recovery
media recovery complete, elapsed time: 00:00:03

Finished recover at 31-AUG-10
RMAN>
```

RMAN has searched and restored the corrupted block from flashback logs.

```
searching flashback logs for block images
finished flashback log search, restored 1 blocks
```

The next section will examine performing block media recovery with no RMAN backups.

Performing Block Recovery Without RMAN Backups

It is possible to perform block media recovery using only OS-based hot backups and having no RMAN backups. For this, the hot backup file needs to be cataloged to the RMAN repository and use it as the image copy of the file and use the *blockrecover* command to recover only corrupted block from the image copy. To test it, create a table and insert one row.

```
SQL>
create
 table tbl_corrupt_test (id number);

Table created.

SQL>
insert into
 tbl_corrupt_test values(1);

1 row created.

SQL> commit;

Commit complete.
```

Get the filename where the *tbl_corrupt_test* table is and make its hot backup as follows:

```
SQL>
select
 segment_name, a.tablespace_name, b.name
from
```

```
 dba_segments a, v$datafile b
where
 a.header_file=b.file# and a.segment_name='tbl_corrupt_test';

SEGMENT_NAME     TABLESPACE_NAME NAME
--------------   --------------- -----------------------------------
tbl_corrupt_test users
/u01/oracle/product/10.2.0/db_1/oradata/newdb/users01.dbf

SQL>
alter
 tablespace users begin backup;

Tablespace altered.
SQL>
host
 cp /u01/oracle/product/10.2.0/db_1/oradata/newdb/users01.dbf
/u01/oracle/product/10.2.0/db_1/oradata/newdb/users01_backup.dbf

SQL>
alter
 tablespace users end backup;

Tablespace altered.
```

Now corrupt the table (datafile) using the techniques explained in the above section as follows:

```
SQL>
select
 header_block from dba_segments
where
 segment_name='tbl_corrupt_test';

HEADER_BLOCK
------------
          59

[oracle@localhost admin]$ dd
of=/u01/oracle/product/10.2.0/db_1/oradata/newdb/users01.dbf bs=8192
conv=notrunc seek=60 <<EOF
> corruption
> EOF
0+1 records in
0+1 records out
```

Test the corruption as follows:

```
SQL>
alter
 system flush buffer_cache;

System altered.

SQL>
select * from
```

```
 tbl_corrupt_test;
select * from tbl_corrupt_test
             *

ERROR at line 1:
ORA-01578: ORACLE data block corrupted (file # 4, block # 60)
ORA-01110: data file 4:
'/u01/oracle/product/10.2.0/db_1/oradata/newdb/users01.dbf'
SQL>
```

Connect to RMAN and try to recover the data block:

```
RMAN> blockrecover datafile 4 block 60;

RMAN-00571: ===========================================================
RMAN-00569: =============== error message stack follows ===============
RMAN-00571: ===========================================================
RMAN-03002: failure of blockrecover command at 03/09/2010 03:36:13
RMAN-06026: some targets not found - aborting restore
RMAN-06023: no backup or copy of datafile 4 found to restore
```

Next, store the online backup file to the repository of RMAN using the *catalog* command and make it act as an image copy:

```
RMAN> catalog datafilecopy
'/u01/oracle/product/10.2.0/db_1/oradata/newdb/users01_backup.dbf';

cataloged datafile copy
datafile copy
filename=/u01/oracle/product/10.2.0/db_1/oradata/newdb/users01_backup.dbf
recid=1 stamp=713158624
```

Try to recover the data block:

```
RMAN> blockrecover datafile 4 block 60;

<......output trimmed ......>
<......output trimmed ......>
starting media recovery
media recovery complete, elapsed time: 00:00:03
Finished blockrecover at 09-MAR-10
RMAN> exit
```

The block has been recovered. Now, query the table:

```
SQL> select * from tbl_corrupt_test;

        ID
----------
         1
SQL>
```

That is it! The corrupted data block has been recovered using the hot backup file taken by th *os* command.

Restore and Recover the Noarchivelog Database

As it was mentioned in the previous chapters, Oracle strongly recommends running the database in archivelog mode. If the database is not run in archivelog mode, the database cannot be recovered and changes cannot be applied to the restored datafiles due to missing archived redo log files.

From RMAN, a backup cannot be made of the database when it is open. If this is tried, the following error occurs:

```
RMAN-03009: failure of backup command on ORA_DISK_1 channel at 10/21/2009
11:00:45
ORA-19602: cannot backup or copy active file in noarchivelog mode
RMAN>
```

However, it is possible to backup the database from *mount* stage and even apply incremental backups and recover it to specific points in time. In the following scenario, the following steps are going to be performed to understand how the backup of the noarchivelog database could be restored and recovered.

- Backup the database running in noarchivelog mode

- Make some changes to the database and do an incremental backup

- Rename the folder which contains all physical files of the database

- Restore the backup and recover

Here are the steps in detail:

- Back up the database. Before backup, make sure RMAN has been configured to do an automatic backup of the control file. It will help to easily restore the control file.

- Connect to RMAN and run the following commands:

```
RMAN> shutdown immediate
RMAN> startup mount
RMAN> configure controlfile autobackup on;
RMAN> backup database;
RMAN> startup;

database is already started
database opened
```

Create a table and insert one row. Then take a level 1 incremental backup of the database:

```
SQL>
create
 table test (str varchar2(10));

Table created.

SQL>
insert into
 test values('test');

1 row created.

SQL>
commit;

Commit complete.

SQL>
select * from
 test;

STR
----------
TEST

SQL>
shutdown immediate
SQL>
startup mount

RMAN> backup incremental level 1 database;
RMAN> shutdown immediate;
```

Rename the *oradata* folder and create another empty *oradata* folder for destination of datafiles that will be restored. Open database in nomount mode and restore the control file from autobackup. Then switch to mount mode and restore all datafiles. Next, perform recovery using the *noredo* keyword to not look for redo log files that should be applied to datafiles.

```
RMAN> startup nomount;
RMAN> restore controlfile from autobackup;
RMAN> alter database mount;
RMAN> restore database;
RMAN> recover database;

RMAN-03002: failure of recover command at 10/21/2009 12:26:19
RMAN-06054: media recovery requesting unknown log: thread 1 seq 2 lowscn
549157

#As we see, RMAN looks for redo log files to be applied. Thus, we use NOREDO
keyword to bypass redo log files as we've lost them all
```

```
RMAN> recover database noredo;
RMAN> alter database open resetlogs;
```

Now, query the table *test* that was created between full and incremental backup:

```
SQL>
select * from
 test;

STR
-----
TEST
```

As this shows, RMAN restored backup of the datafiles and applied an incremental backup even though the database is running in noarchivelog mode.

More information about backup of the database while running in noarchivelog mode is contained in Chapter 3 under the "Backing Up a Database Running in Noarchivelog Mode" heading.

Performing Disaster Recovery

11th Scenario

One day, Bob comes to work and sees that all the hard drives of the production server have been damaged and he has lost all datafiles, controlfiles and redo log files. As Bob takes a backup of the database with RMAN, he knows that in this situation he needs to perform a disaster recovery to restore and recover the database. Knowing this, he starts to perform the following steps:

Bob first installs Oracle software to the new server and starts RMAN.

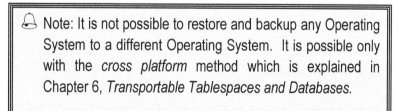

> ♤ Note: It is not possible to restore and backup any Operating System to a different Operating System. It is possible only with the *cross platform* method which is explained in Chapter 6, *Transportable Tablespaces and Databases.*

RMAN is started, and since he has no database running on the system, Bob gets the message that "the target database has not started":

```
C:\>rman target /
connected to target database (not started)
RMAN>
```

Bob starts the instance with a dummy parameter. As he has no parameter file in the system and he needs to get it from backup, he needs to start an instance to be able to get it from backup. Thus, he starts RMAN with default parameters using a dummy parameter file as follows:

```
RMAN> startup nomount;

startup failed: ORA-01078: failure in processing system parameters
ORA-01565: error in identifying file
'C:\oracle\product\10.2.0\db_1/dbs/spfiledb1.ora'
ORA-27041: unable to open file
OSD-04002: unable to open file
O/S-Error: (OS 2) The system cannot find the file specified.

starting Oracle instance without parameter file for retrieval of spfile
Oracle instance started
Total System Global Area      159383552 bytes
Fixed Size                      1247852 bytes
Variable Size                  54527380 bytes
Database Buffers              100663296 bytes
Redo Buffers                    2945024 bytes
RMAN>
```

In order to restore spfile from autobackup, Bob needs to set the database identifier (DBID) for the target database. DBID is the unique identifier which separates the databases. Oracle automatically creates this identifier when a database is created. In this situation, Bob does not know the DBID of the database, but he knows how to find it.

The first and most common way is to take it from the name of the autobackup of the control file. For this, before taking backup of the database, he set the autobackup of the control file ON and changed the format of the backup file to have autobackup of the control file, spfile and the DBID of the database. Do the following steps on the source database before making its backup:

```
RMAN> configure controlfile autobackup on;

new RMAN configuration parameters:
configure controlfile autobackup on;

new RMAN configuration parameters are successfully stored
```

```
RMAN> configure controlfile autobackup format for device type disk to
'c:\%f.bkp';

new RMAN configuration parameters:
configure controlfile autobackup format for device type disk to 'c:\%f.bkp';

new RMAN configuration parameters are successfully stored

RMAN> backup database plus archivelog all;

...............
...............
Starting Control File and SPFILE Autobackup at 22-OCT-09
piece handle=C:\C-1294811656-20091022-00.BKP comment=NONE
Finished Control File and SPFILE Autobackup at 22-OCT-09
RMAN>
```

As the *%of* element of the format string is made of *c-DBID-year month day –
sequence number.BKP*, the DBID of the database will be known if any disaster
recovery scenario is faced. Furthermore, the DBID might be taken from
RMAN logs of the previous backups if the *log* parameter was mentioned
during backup:

```
rman target / log='c:\rman.log'
```

Running the above command, log all output to the *rman.log* file as well as
DBID of the target database. After successfully connecting to RMAN, the
following three lines will be written to that file:

```
Recovery Manager: Release 10.2.0.1.0 - Production on Thu Oct 22 17:11:57 2009
```

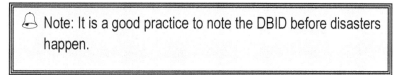

Note: It is a good practice to note the DBID before disasters happen.

```
Copyright (c) 1982, 2005, Oracle.  All rights reserved.
connected to target database: DB1 (DBID=1294811656)
```

Now by getting the DBID, Bob sets it and restores the spfile as follows:

```
RMAN> restore spfile from autobackup;

Starting restore at 22-OCT-09
using target database control file instead of recovery catalog
allocated channel: ORA_DISK_1
channel ORA_DISK_1: sid=36 devtype=DISK

RMAN-00571: ===========================================================
RMAN-00569: =============== error message stack follows ===============
RMAN-00571: ===========================================================
RMAN-03002: failure of restore command at 10/22/2009 20:02:28
```

```
RMAN-06495: must explicitly specify dbid with set dbid command
RMAN>
```

This means that the DBID needs to be set before restoring the spfile:

```
RMAN> set DBID=1294811656
executing command: set DBID

RMAN> restore spfile from autobackup;

channel ORA_DISK_1: no autobackup in 7 days found
RMAN-00571: ===========================================================
RMAN-00569: =============== error message stack follows ===============
RMAN-00571: ===========================================================
RMAN-03002: failure of restore command at 10/22/2009 20:06:22
RMAN-06172: no autobackup found or specified handle is not a valid copy or
piece
RMAN>
```

As the location of the backup files was changed to the *C:\backup* folder, RMAN cannot automatically find it. Using the following command, Bob sets the new location for the backup of the database and restores the spfile:

```
RMAN>  run {
        set controlfile autobackup format for device type disk to
'c:\backup\%f.bkp';
        restore spfile from autobackup;
        }

executing command: set controlfile autobackup format

Starting restore at 22-OCT-09
using channel ORA_DISK_1

channel ORA_DISK_1: looking for autobackup on day: 20091022
channel ORA_DISK_1: autobackup found: c:\backup\c-1294811656-20091022-00.BKP
channel ORA_DISK_1: SPFILE restore from autobackup complete
Finished restore at 22-OCT-09
RMAN>
```

Another way of restoring the spfile from backup is as follows:

```
RMAN> restore spfile from 'c:\backup\c-1294811656-20091022-00.bkp';

Starting restore at 22-OCT-09
using channel ORA_DISK_1
channel ORA_DISK_1: autobackup found: c:\backup\C-1294811656-20091022-00.BKP
channel ORA_DISK_1: SPFILE restore from autobackup complete
Finished restore at 22-OCT-09
RMAN>
```

Now he shuts down the instance and starts it back up using the restored spfile in nomount mode:

```
RMAN> shutdown immediate;

ORACLE instance shut down

RMAN> startup nomount

connected to target database (not started)
Oracle instance started
Total System Global Area      293601280 bytes
Fixed Size                      1248624 bytes
Variable Size                  96469648 bytes
Database Buffers              192937984 bytes
Redo Buffers                    2945024 bytes

RMAN> restore controlfile from 'c:\backup\c-1294811656-20091022-00.bkp';

Starting restore at 22-OCT-09
using channel ORA_DISK_1

channel ORA_DISK_1: restoring control file
channel ORA_DISK_1: restore complete, elapsed time: 00:00:05
output filename=C:\ORACLE\product\10.2.0\oradata\db1\control01.ctl
output filename=C:\ORACLE\product\10.2.0\oradata\db1\control02.ctl
output filename=C:\ORACLE\product\10.2.0\oradata\db1\control03.ctl
Finished restore at 22-OCT-09
RMAN>
```

Next, the database should be mounted as follows:

```
RMAN> alter database mount;

database mounted
released channel: ORA_DISK_1
RMAN>
```

As there is no information about the backup files in the restored control files, the backups should be registered in the RMAN repository using the *catalog start with* command as follows according to the capabilities of the specific version of Oracle. In Oracle 9i, only *catalog archivelog, catalog datafilecopy,* and *catalog controlfilecopy* commands can be used to catalog the backup. But starting with Oracle 10g, the capabilities of the *catalog* command have been expanded as follows:

- Using the *catalog start with* command, as in the following example, all files can be cataloged.

- Using the *catalog backuppiece* command, the backup piece can be cataloged if a backup piece was copied or moved to a new location.

- Using the *catalog recovery area* or *catalog db_recovery_file_dest*, all backup sets, image copies, and archive logs in the flash recovery area are cataloged.

The following example uses the *catalog start with* command:

```
RMAN> catalog start with 'c:\backup';

Starting implicit crosscheck backup at 22-OCT-09
allocated channel: ORA_DISK_1
channel ORA_DISK_1: sid=156 devtype=DISK
Crosschecked 3 objects
Finished implicit crosscheck backup at 22-OCT-09
Starting implicit crosscheck copy at 22-OCT-09
using channel ORA_DISK_1
Finished implicit crosscheck copy at 22-OCT-09

searching for all files in the recovery area
cataloging files...
no files cataloged

searching for all files that match the pattern c:\backup

List of Files Unknown to the Database
=====================================
File Name: C:\backup\C-1294811656-20091022-00.BKP
File Name: C:\backup\O1_mf_1_2_5g0wch6c_.arc
File Name: C:\backup\O1_mf_1_3_5g0wdsrf_.arc
File Name: C:\backup\O1_mf_annnn_tag20091022t195129_5g0wclnj_.bkp
File Name: C:\backup\O1_mf_annnn_tag20091022t195209_5g0wdv4d_.bkp
File Name: C:\backup\O1_mf_nnndf_tag20091022t195134_5g0wcpjm_.bkp

Do we really want to catalog the above files (enter YES or NO)? yes
cataloging files...
cataloging done

List of Cataloged Files
=======================
File Name: C:\backup\C-1294811656-20091022-00.bkp
File Name: C:\backup\O1_mf_1_2_5g0wch6c_.arc
File Name: C:\backup\O1_mf_1_3_5g0wdsrf_.arc
File Name: C:\backup\O1_mf_annnn_tag20091022t195129_5g0wclnj_.bkp
File Name: C:\backup\O1_mf_annnn_tag20091022t195209_5g0wdv4d_.bkp
File Name: C:\backup\O1_mf_nnndf_tag20091022t195134_5g0wcpjm_.bkp
RMAN>
```

Now Bob can restore the database as follows:

```
RMAN> restore database;

Starting restore at 22-OCT-09
using channel ORA_DISK_1
...............
...............
Finished restore at 22-OCT-09
RMAN>
```

In order to successfully restore all datafiles, the same mount point needs to be created as is in the source server. To restore datafiles to the different location, use the *set newname for datafile* command which is explained in detail in Chapter 5.

From the names of archived redo log files, Bob understands that he can restore the database until log sequence #4. By running the following command, he recovers the database and opens it with the *resetlogs* option.

```
RMAN> recover database until sequence 4;

Starting recover at 22-OCT-09
using channel ORA_DISK_1
starting media recovery

archive log thread 1 sequence 3 is already on disk as file
C:\backup\o1_mf_1_3_5g0wdsrf_.arc
archive log filename=C:\backup\o1_mf_1_3_5g0wdsrf_.arc thread=1 sequence=3
media recovery complete, elapsed time: 00:00:00
Finished recover at 22-OCT-09

RMAN> alter database open resetlogs;

database opened
RMAN>
```

At least Bob was able to perform disaster recovery and open the database. To automate this process, run the following script by making little changes to the DBID and autobackup file name:

```
set DBID =1294816684;
run {
  startup nomount;
  restore spfile from 'c:\backup\c-1294816684-20091022-00.bkp';
  shutdown immediate;
  startup nomount;
  restore controlfile from 'c:\backup\c-1294816684-20091022-00.bkp';
  alter database mount;
  catalog start with 'c:\backup' noprompt;
  restore database;
  recover database until sequence 4;
  alter database open resetlogs;
}
```

This script automatically performs disaster recovery, restores the spfile and controlfile from autobackup, then restores all datafiles, recovers the database and opens it for use!

Performing an Incomplete Recovery

There may be some circumstances where the database needs to be taken to a point-in-time condition. There may be a number of different reasons, including recovering a dropped table or taking a table to a point-in-time to recover changes made by a user incorrectly. When doing a complete recovery, add all the archived redo log files over restored datafiles, thus performing a complete recovery. However, while performing incomplete recovery, add only limited archived redo log files based on the situation. There are four types of incomplete recovery:

- SCN-based incomplete recovery
- Time-based incomplete recovery
- Change-based incomplete recovery
- Cancel-based incomplete recovery

In the following sections, all the above-mentioned incomplete recoveries will be performed on real examples.

SCN-based Incomplete Recovery

Bob was asked to create two tables from *all_tables* and *all_indexes* views to get the list of all tables and indexes in the database for a specific time. First of all, he creates a table *tbl_tables* and takes a backup of the database as follows:

```
SQL>
create
 table tbl_tables
as select * from
 all_tables;

Table created.

SQL>
select
 count(1)
from
 tbl_tables;

   COUNT(1)
----------
      1521

RMAN> backup database;
Starting backup at 26-OCT-09
...................
```

```
....................
Finished backup at 26-OCT-09
RMAN>
```

After awhile, he got a call from a user who accidentally deleted some rows from the table by running the following query:

```
SQL>
select
 current_scn, to_char(sysdate,'ddmmyyyy hh24:mi:ss') ddate
from
 v$database;

CURRENT_SCN DDATE                      SCN
----------- ------------------ ----------
    547063 26102009 09:46:40      547062

SQL>
delete
 tbl_tables
where
 rownum<=1000;

1000 rows deleted.

SQL>
commit;

Commit complete.

SQL>
select
 count(1)
from
 tbl_tables;

  COUNT(1)
----------
       521
```

The first query was run by the user to get the current time. But before this operation, there was a log switch in the database and Bob had made a backup of archived redo log files as follows:

```
RMAN> backup archivelog all;

Finished backup at 26-OCT-09
RMAN>
```

In this situation, Bob decides to make an incomplete recovery to get back the data which was accidently deleted by a user to its former version.

Although he knows the time when the user deleted the data from the *tbl_tables* table, he wants to use a *scn*-based incomplete recovery. To get a SCN number based on specific time, he uses the *timestamp_to_scn* function as follows:

```
SQL>
select
 ddate, timestamp_to_scn(to_date('26102009 09:46:40','ddmmyyyy hh24:mi:ss'))
scn
from
 v$database;

SCN
----------
547062
```

Now using this SCN number, Bob is ready to perform the incomplete recovery. Thus, he shuts down the database, then starts up in mount mode and performs the recovery as follows:

```
RMAN> shutdown immediate
RMAN> startup mount
RMAN> run
2> {
3> set until scn 547062;
4> restore database;
5> recover database;
6> }
RMAN> alter database open resetlogs;

database opened
RMAN>
```

After recovery is finished, he connects to the database and queries the table:

```
SQL>
select
 count(1)
from
 tbl_tables;

  COUNT(1)
----------
      1521
```

The data was recovered based on SCN value.

Time-based Incomplete Recovery

The previous scenario could also have been solved using the *until time* command. Look at the following example.

The table was created and populated with data as follows:

```
SQL>
create
 table tbl_indexes
as select * from
 all_indexes;

Table created.

SQL>
select
 count(1)
from
 tbl_indexes;

  COUNT(1)
----------
      1675
```

RMAN backup was taken after creation of the table:

```
RMAN> backup database;
```

As a user knows the approximate time when he issued the *drop table* command, query the current time just for demonstration:

```
SQL>
select
 to_char(sysdate,'dd/mm/yyyy hh24:mi:ss') ddate
from
 v$database;

DDATE
-----------------
26/10/2009 10:34:16
```

Then the table is dropped:

```
SQL>
drop
 table tbl_indexes;

Table dropped.

SQL>
select
 count(1)
from
 tbl_indexes;
select count(1) from tbl_indexes
                     *

ERROR at line 1:
```

```
ORA-00942: table or view does not exist
```

Now, it is time to recover the table. For this, shut down the database, start up in mount mode and perform the recovery as follows:

```
RMAN> shutdown immediate
RMAN> startup mount
RMAN> run
2> {
3> set until time="to_date('26102009 10:34:16','ddmmyyyy hh24:mi:ss')";
4> restore database;
5> recover database;
6> }
RMAN> alter database open resetlogs;

database opened
RMAN>
```

Lastly, connect to SQL*Plus and query the dropped table:

```
SQL>
select
 count(1)
from
 tbl_indexes;


  COUNT(1)
----------
      1675
SQL>
```

The table was recovered successfully.

Change-based Incomplete Recovery

It is possible to recover the database based on a log sequence number. Every time a log switch occurs, Oracle assigns a new log sequence number to the redo log file. If the DBA knows the exact sequence number of an archived redo log file which contains a damaged SQL command, they can easily make an incomplete recovery up to that sequence number and open the database without performing that SQL command. Look at the following scenario where Bob performs an incomplete recovery.

Bob creates a table based on the *all_tables* view as follows:

```
SQL>
create
```

```
 table test as
select * from
 all_tables;

Table created.
```

Then, due to some database operations, there were two log switches in the database. To make these log switches occur manually, use the following commands:

```
SQL>
alter
 system switch logfile;

System altered.

SQL>
alter
 system switch logfile;

System altered.

SQL>
select
 sequence#, name
from
 v$archived_log;

SEQUENCE#              NAME
----------            ----------
2  C:\ORACLE\product\10.2.0\flash_recovery_area\ db1\archivelog\o1_mf_1_2_5gcdbfoz_.arc
3  C:\ORACLE\product\10.2.0\flash_recovery_area\ db1\archivelog\2009_10_26\o1_mf_1_3_5gcdcr1g_.arc


SQL>
select
 sequence#, status
from
 v$log;

 SEQUENCE# STATUS
---------- ----------------
        2 ACTIVE
        3 ACTIVE
        4 CURRENT
```

There were two log switches which generated two archived redo log files.

To count the rows, the user runs the following query:

```
SQL>
select
 count(1)
from
 test;
```

```
  COUNT(1)
----------
      1521
```

Then she accidentally deletes the table and commits the session:

```
SQL>
delete from
 test;

1521 rows deleted.

SQL>
commit;

Commit complete.

SQL>
select
 count(1)
from
 test;

COUNT(1)
----------
         0
```

There was a one-log switch:

```
SQL>
alter
 system switch logfile;

System altered.
```

The user immediately contacted Bob and informed him of what happened. Knowing this, Bob decides to recover the database until the last archived redo log file. He gets the list of archived redo log files to have a log sequence number as follows:

```
SQL>
select
 sequence#, name
from
 v$archived_log;

SEQUENCE#             NAME
----------           ----------
2     C:\ORACLE\product\10.2.0\flash_recovery_area\ db1\archivelog\o1_mf_1_2_5gcdbfoz_.arc
3     C:\ORACLE\product\10.2.0\flash_recovery_area\
db1\archivelog\2009_10_26\o1_mf_1_3_5gcdcr1g_.arc
4     C:\ORACLE\product\10.2.0\flash_recovery_area\ db1\archivelog\2009_10_26\o1_mf_1_4_5gcdgqhn_.arc
```

By obtaining this query, Bob understands that the delete statement was performed after log sequence #3, so the database should be recovered until sequence #4. He shuts down the database, starts up in mount mode and performs recovery:

```
SQL>
shutdown immediate
SQL>
startup
 mount

RMAN> run
2> {
3> set until sequence 4;
4> restore database;
5> recover database;
6> }

RMAN> alter database open resetlogs;

database opened
RMAN>
```

To check the data of the table, Bob runs the following query:

```
SQL>
select
 count(1)
from
 test;

  COUNT(1)
----------
      1521
SQL>
```

This shows that by using change-based incomplete recovery, Bob was able to recover up to the specific archived redo log file and get the data back.

The next type of incomplete recovery is cancel-based incomplete recovery which is not done by RMAN. It can be used in the user-managed recovery process explained in Chapter 9.

Recovering to Restore Point

Restore point is the name associated with the SCN of the database. Before doing any bulk operation, in order to be able to recover to a specific SCN that is generated before this operation, create a restore point and there is no need to remember the SCN number or the time of the operation. As recovery can be done to any SCN and time, it is also possible to recover the database to any restore point.

Bob was asked to create a table which consists of a list of all the objects in the database. After creating the table, Bob decides to perform a test and deletes the table. But before that, he wants to be sure that he can recover the database up to the point before deletion of the table, so he creates a restore point. After performing his test, he decides to recover the table by performing incomplete recovery to restore point. Here is this scenario in detail.

Bob creates the table as follows:

```
SQL>
create
 table test
as select * from
 all_objects;

Table created.
```

Then he makes a backup of the database:

```
RMAN> backup database;
```

By listing the backup, he gets a SCN number of files when they were backed up:

```
RMAN> list backup;

  File LV Type Ckp SCN    Ckp Time   Name
  ---- -- ---- ---------- --------- ----
   1       Full 649848      28-OCT-09
C:\ORACLE\product\10.2.0\oradata\ db1\system01.dbf
```

So the SCN of the datafile is 649848.

Then Bob decides to delete the table that he created, and he creates a restore point to be able to recover to before the *delete* command. To get the list of restore points, use *v$restore_point* view:

```
SQL>
select
  current_scn from v$database;

CURRENT_SCN
-----------
    650143
```

```
SQL>
create
 restore point before_delete;

Restore point created.

SQL>
select
 scn, name
from
 v$restore_point;

SCN                      NAME
----------               --------------------
650149                          BEFORE_DELETE
```

Then he deletes the data of the table and commits the statement:

```
SQL>
delete from
 test;

49311 rows deleted.

SQL>
commit;

Commit complete.

SQL>
alter
 system switch logfile;

System altered.
SQL>
```

Now, he decides to recover the table and performs the following steps in RMAN:

```
RMAN> shutdown immediate
RMAN> startup mount
RMAN> run
2> {
3> set until restore point before_delete;
4> restore database;
5> recover database;
6> }

RMAN> alter database open resetlogs;

database opened
RMAN>
```

Now it is time to check the table:

Performing an Incomplete Recovery   **191**

```
SQL>
select
 count(1)
from
 test;

  COUNT(1)
----------
     49311
```

The table has successfully been recovered to the restore point which was created before the deletion of the table.

Recovering a Database to a Previous Incarnation

To perform an incomplete recovery to previous incarnation, first of all understand what database incarnation means. Actually, incarnation is a new version of the database. By opening the database with the *resetlogs* option, Oracle archives the current redo log file and clears them all by resetting the log sequence number to 1. This option is most often used after an incomplete recovery where information from archived redo log files is applied partly but not completely; therefore, the online redo log files need to be cleared.

If the database was opened with the *resetlogs* option, it is not possible to use backups that were taken before the newly created incarnation. Take a look at the following scenario to better understand the process.

This scenario will show how Bob must perform the second incomplete recovery to take the database back to the time before the first incomplete recovery, resetting the database to a time before that incarnation. Bob backs up the database and then creates a table by getting the SCN value of the database as follows:

```
RMAN> backup database;

SQL>
create
 table test
as select * from
 all_objects;

Table created.

SQL>
select
 current_scn
```

```
from
 v$database;

CURRENT_SCN
-----------
    547181
```

Then he deletes all the rows from the table and commits by taking the SCN value of the database:

```
SQL>
delete from
 test;

49309 rows deleted.

SQL>
commit;

Commit complete.

SQL>
select
 current_scn
from
 v$database;

CURRENT_SCN
-----------
    547891
```

Bob drops the table, takes the SCN value of the database and the switch log file:

```
SQL>
drop
 table test;

Table dropped.

SQL>
select
 current_scn
from
 v$database;

CURRENT_SCN
-----------
    547917

SQL>
alter
 system switch logfile;

System altered.
```

Performing an Incomplete Recovery

Next, he gets the list of all incarnations of the database:

```
SQL>
select
 incarnation#, resetlogs_change#
from
 v$database_incarnation;

INCARNATION# RESETLOGS_CHANGE#
------------ -----------------
           1                 1
           2            534907
```

He then performs an incomplete recovery to the state of the database before dropping the table, thus *until scn 547891* as follows:

```
SQL>
shutdown immediate
SQL>
startup
 mount
RMAN> run
2> {
3> set until scn=547891;
4> restore database;
5> recover database;
6> }
RMAN> alter database open resetlogs;
```

As he has opened the database using the *resetlogs* option, a new incarnation has been created. Below, he checks the new incarnation and the recovered table:

```
SQL>
select
 incarnation#, resetlogs_change#
from
 v$database_incarnation;

INCARNATION# RESETLOGS_CHANGE#
------------ -----------------
           1                 1
           2            534907
           3            547896

SQL>
select * from
 test;

no rows selected
SQL>
```

The new incarnation has been created and the table has been recovered successfully. After this operation, he recovers the database up to the *delete* command issued as follows:

```
RMAN> run
2> {
3> set until scn=547181;
4> restore database;
5> recover database;
6> }

executing command: set until clause
using target database control file instead of recovery catalog
RMAN-00571: ===========================================================
RMAN-00569: =============== error message stack follows ===============
RMAN-00571: ===========================================================
RMAN-03002: failure of set command at 10/29/2009 16:15:46
RMAN-20208: until change is before resetlogs change
```

Suddenly, Bob gets an error that he could not use the UNTIL SCN clause which will recover the data that was backed up before the database opened with the *resetlogs* option. He then creates a list of all the database incarnations from RMAN, and he resets the database to the previous incarnation and performs an incomplete recovery as follows:

```
RMAN> list incarnation of database;
List of Database Incarnations


DB Key  Inc Key DB Name  DB ID             STATUS  Reset SCN  Reset Time
------- ------- -------- ----------------  ---     ---------- ----------
1       1       DB1      1295402827        PARENT  1          30-AUG-05
2       2       DB1      1295402827        PARENT  534907     29-OCT-09
3       3       DB1      1295402827        CURRENT 547896     29-OCT-09

RMAN> shutdown immediate
RMAN> startup mount
RMAN> reset database to incarnation 2;

database reset to incarnation 2

RMAN> run
2> {
3> set until scn=547181;
4> restore database;
5> recover database;
6> }

RMAN> alter database open resetlogs;

database opened

RMAN> list incarnation of database;

using target database control file instead of recovery catalog

List of Database Incarnations
```

```
DB Key  Inc Key DB Name  DB ID              STATUS  Reset SCN  Reset Time
-------  ------- --------  ----------------  --- ---------- ----------
1       1       DB1      1295402827         PARENT  1          30-AUG-05
2       2       DB1      1295402827         PARENT  534907     29-OCT-09
4       4       DB1      1295402827         CURRENT 547183     29-OCT-09
3       3       DB1      1295402827         ORPHAN  547896     29-OCT-09

SQL>
select
 count(1)
from
 test;

   COUNT(1)
----------
     49309
SQL>
```

The table recovered to the previous incarnation successfully and a new incarnation has been created.

Tablespace Point-in-Time Recovery

To perform an incomplete recovery on a tablespace which consists of one or more datafiles, RMAN uses the Tablespace Point-in-Time Recovery (TSPITR) feature. This feature recovers erroneously updated data that was due to user's error or the batch process that stopped after updating some data on different datafiles of a tablespace while the database is running.

To use this type of recovery, there needs to be an auxiliary instance. It should be an instance created by RMAN automatically or a user-defined instance. To recover a tablespace to any point in time, RMAN performs the following steps:

- If there is not any user-managed auxiliary instance, RMAN creates an automatic auxiliary instance, assigns to it a random SID, starts it up and connects to it.

- As TSPITR is performed while the database is open, RMAN takes the tablespace that is recovering offline.

- It then restores the control file from backup of the target database to the auxiliary instance according to the *time/SCN value* specified in the UNTIL clause of the command.

- Next it restores datafiles of the system and undo tablespaces with the datafiles of the recovered tablespace from backup to the auxiliary destination, and then recovers it to the specified point in time and opens the auxiliary instance with *resetlogs* option.

- Then it exports metadata of the recovered tablespace from the auxiliary instance to a dump file and shuts down the auxiliary instance.

- If there were any changes to datafiles names, then RMAN issues *switch* commands to update the control file name with the recovered datafiles' information.

- It imports metadata of objects in the recovered tablespace to the target database.

- Then it removes the auxiliary instance and deletes all files associated with it.

Before starting to perform TSPITR, check the relationship between objects of the recovered tablespace and objects of the different tablespaces which will not be recovered. Also check on which objects will be lost after the recovery. To check on the relationship and the objects that will be lost after the recovery, two views are used: *ts_pitr_check* and *ts_pitr_objects_to_be_dropped* views. An example of how to use both views will be shown in the next scenario.

To recover the restored tablespace, RMAN needs an auxiliary instance. It is possible to leave it to RMAN to create it automatically, or a specific auxiliary instance can be created. In this section, both ways will be examined.

In the following scenario, Bob has recovered two dropped tables of one tablespace consisting of two datafiles. To perform this scenario, a tablespace with two datafiles and two tables in each datafile needs to be created. Now start the scenario.

Bob has created a tablespace and two tables in each datafile and backs up the database as follows:

```
SQL>
create
 tablespace tbs datafile 'c:\tbs1.dbf' size 1m autoextend on next 1m;

Tablespace created.

SQL>
create
 user bob identified by bob;
```

```
User created.

SQL>
grant
 dba to bob;

Grant succeeded.

SQL>
alter
user bob default tablespace tbs;

user altered.

SQL>
connect
 bob/bob

Connected.

SQL>
create
 table tbl_test1
as select * from
 dba_objects;

table created.

SQL>
alter
 tablespace tbs add datafile 'c:\tbs2.dbf' size 1m autoextend on next 1m;

Tablespace altered.

SQL>
select
 segment_name, a.tablespace_name, header_file, file_name
from
 dba_segments a, dba_data_files b
  2  where
a.header_file=b.file_id
  3  and
 segment_name
in
('tbl_test1','tbl_test2');

SEGMENT_NAME     TABLESPACE_NAME      HEADER_FILE    FILE_NAME
---------------  ------------------   -----------    ------------
tbl_test1        tbs                            5    c:\tbs1.dbf
tbl_test2        tbs                            6    c:\tbs2.dbf

SQL>

RMAN> backup database;
```

At 20:02, he gets a call from another DBA who says that two tables were suddenly dropped a minute ago from his schema. Bob decides to perform an incomplete recovery of the tablespace where these tables resided. As a first step, he tries to find out the SCN value of the database before the tables were dropped:

```
SQL>
select
 timestamp_to_scn(to_timestamp('05.11.2009 20.00.00','dd.mm.yyyy
hh24:mi:ss')) scn
from
 dual;

      SCN
----------
   604515
```

As noted here, before performing any TSPITR, two kinds of checks should be performed. The first check is the check of the relationship between objects of the recovered and non-recovered tablespaces. The second check is to identify the objects which will be lost after recovery. Therefore, Bob performs the first check as follows:

```
SQL>
select * from
 sys.ts_pitr_check
where
 (ts1_name='TBS' AND ts2_name<>'TBS') OR (ts2_name='TBS'
and
 ts1_name<>'TBS');

no rows selected
SQL>
```

If this query returns a row, the incomplete recovery might be unsuccessful. By investigating the *reason* column, the problem can be solved. To show one of the reasons why a row from this query can be found, see the following example. Here, a table is created on a different tablespace and a relationship created between the two tables using the ID column. As there is no ID column in the *tbl_test1* table, add it as follows:

```
SQL>
alter
 table tbl_test1 add (id number);

Table altered.
SQL>
create
 table tbl_pr (id number) tablespace users;

Table created.

SQL>
```

Performing an Incomplete Recovery

199

```
alter
 table tbl_pr add primary key (id);

Table altered.

SQL>
alter
 table tbl_test1 add foreign key (id) references tbl_pr(id);

Table altered.

SQL>
select
 obj1_name, ts1_name, obj2_name, ts2_name, reason
from
 sys.ts_pitr_check
where
 (ts1_name='TBS' AND ts2_name<>'TBS') OR (ts2_name='TBS'
and
 ts1_name<>'TBS');

OBJ1_NAME   TS1_NAME    OBJ2_NAME   TS2_NAME    REASON
----------- ----------- ----------- ---------   ----------
tbl_pr      users       tbl_test1   tbs         constraint between tables not
contained in recovery set
SQL>
```

If this message appears, then it means that it is not possible to successfully recover the tablespace at this point in time. In order to be successful, resolve the problem and get a "no result" message from the above query. Look at the error that comes up when an incomplete recovery is performed:

```
About to export Tablespace Point-in-time Recovery objects...
EXP-00008: ORACLE error 29308 encountered
ORA-29308: view ts_pitr_check failure
ORA-06512: at "sys.dbms_pitr", line 887
ORA-06512: at line 1
EXP-00000: Export terminated unsuccessfully
host command complete

About to import Tablespace Point-in-time Recovery objects...
import done in WE8ISO8859P1 character set and AL16UTF16 NCHAR character set
IMP-00009: abnormal end of export file

sql statement: alter tablespace  TBS online
RMAN-00571: ===========================================================
RMAN-00569: =============== ERROR MESSAGE STACK FOLLOWS ===============
RMAN-00571: ===========================================================
RMAN-03002: failure of recover command at 11/06/2009 11:12:34
RMAN-03015: error occurred in stored script Memory Script
RMAN-03009: failure of sql command on default channel at 11/06/2009 11:12:34
RMAN-11003: failure during parse/execution of SQL statement: alter
tablespace  T
BS online
ORA-01190: control file or data file 5 is from before the last RESETLOGS
ORA-01110: data file 5: 'C:\tbs1.dbf'
```

```
RMAN>
```

This concludes that the recovery process has failed.

The second check is to look at the objects that will be lost after the incomplete recovery. All objects that were created after deletion of those tables, that is, after the time to which tablespace recovery should be performed, will be lost. To see those, query the *ts_pitr_objects_to_be_dropped* view as follows:

```
SQL>
select
 name, to_char(creation_time,'dd.mm.yyyy hh24:mi:ss') creation_time,
tablespace_name from sys.ts_pitr_objects_to_be_dropped
where
 tablespace_name='TBS' AND creation_time>to_date('05.11.2009
20.00.00','dd.mm.yyyy hh24:mi:ss')

NAME                    CREATION_TIME           TABLESPACE_NAME
----------------        --------------------    ---------------
test_table              06.11.2009 01:41:04     TBS
SQL>
```

From the above result, Bob knows that the table which was created after the point in time to which he wants to recover the tablespace will be lost.

Now, it is time to perform the recovery. Here, Bob decides to perform the recovery using the automatic auxiliary instance created by RMAN. He creates a folder to keep the auxiliary database files in and runs the following command from RMAN prompt:

```
RMAN> recover tablespace tbs until scn 604515 auxiliary
destination='c:\aux_destination';
```

By running the above command, RMAN starts TSPITR. Examine the output of the recovery process step-by-step.

RMAN creates an automatic auxiliary instance and starts it using the default initialization parameter file.

```
Starting recover at 06-NOV-09
using target database controlfile instead of recovery catalog
allocated channel: ORA_DISK_1
channel ORA_DISK_1: sid=139 devtype=disk
List of tablespaces expected to have undo segments
tablespace system
tablespace undotbs1
Creating automatic instance, with SID='zxxu'
initialization parameters used for automatic instance:
```

```
db_name=DB1
compatible=10.2.0.1.0
db_block_size=8192
db_files=200
db_unique_name=tspitr_DB1_zxxu
large_pool_size=1M
shared_pool_size=110M
#No auxiliary parameter file used
db_create_file_dest=c:\aux_destination
control_files=c:\aux_destination/cntrl_tspitr_DB1_zxxu.f

starting up automatic instance DB1
Oracle instance started
Total System Global Area      201326592 bytes
Fixed Size                      1248092 bytes
Variable Size                 146801828 bytes
Database Buffers               50331648 bytes
Redo Buffers                    2945024 bytes
Automatic instance created
```

It restores the control file from backup of the target database and mounts an auxiliary database.

```
set until  scn 604515;
restore clone controlfile;
sql clone 'alter database mount clone database';
sql 'alter system archive log current';
```

It restores datafiles of the system, undo and the recovered tablespace and recovers them all to a past point in time. Then it opens the database with the *resetlogs* option.

```
set until  scn 604515;
set newname for clone datafile  1 to new;
set newname for clone datafile  2 to new;
set newname for clone tempfile  1 to new;
set newname for datafile  5 to "C:\tbs1.dbf";
set newname for datafile  6 to "C:\tbs2.dbf";
switch clone tempfile all;
restore clone datafile  1, 2, 5, 6;
switch clone datafile all;
sql clone "alter database datafile  1 online";
sql clone "alter database datafile  2 online";
sql clone "alter database datafile  5 online";
sql clone "alter database datafile  6 online";
recover clone database tablespace  "tbs", "system", "undotbs1" delete
archivelog;
alter clone database open resetlogs;
```

It exports metadata of objects of the recovered tablespace to a dump file. Then it shuts down the auxiliary instance and imports the data to the target database.

Oracle Backup and Recovery

```
# export the tablespaces in the recovery set
host 'exp userid
=\"/@(description=(address=(protocol=beq)(program=oracle)(argv0=oraclezxxu)(
args=^'(description=(local=yes)(address=(protocol=beq)))^')(envs=^'oracle_si
d=zxxu^'))(connect_data=(SID=zxxu))) as sysdba\" point_in_time_recover=y
tablespaces=TBS file=tspitr_a.dmp';
shutdown clone immediate
host 'imp userid =\"/@ as sysdba\" point_in_time_recover=y
file=tspitr_a.dmp';
```

It removes the auxiliary instance and deletes all database files.

```
Removing automatic instance
Automatic instance removed
auxiliary instance file C:\aux_destination\cntrl_tspitr_db1_zxxu.f deleted
auxiliary instance file
C:\aux_destination\tspitr_d\datafile\o1_mf_system_5h6lcxpg_.dbf deleted
auxiliary instance file
C:\AUX_destination\tspitr_d\datafile\o1_mf_undotbs1_5h6lcxrw_.dbf deleted
auxiliary instance file
C:\aux_destination\tspitr_d\datafile\o1_mf_temp_5h6lflrw_.tmp deleted
auxiliary instance file
C:\aux_destination\tspitr_d\onlinelog\o1_mf_1_5h6lffbq_.log deleted
auxiliary instance file
C:\aux_destination\tspitr_d\onlinelog\o1_mf_2_5h6lfgrw_.log deleted
auxiliary instance file
C:\aux_destination\tspitr_d\onlinelog\o1_mf_3_5h6lfj4w_.log deleted
Finished recover at 06-NOV-09
```

Now, Bob creates the tablespace online and checks to see whether the dropped tables were recovered or not as follows:

```
SQL>
alter
 tablespace tbs online;

Tablespace altered.

SQL>
select
 count(1)
from
 tbl_test1;

COUNT(1)
----------
     49746

SQL>
select
 count(1)
from
 tbl_test2;

  COUNT(1)
----------
```

```
        49747
SQL>
```

He has successfully recovered the dropped tables of the tablespace using TSPITR. It is suggested to back up the recovered tablespace after a successful recovery process.

It is also possible to use a customized auxiliary instance when the following customizations are desired:

- Using a self-customized different initialization parameter for an auxiliary instance

- Renaming datafiles of the recovered tablespace at the target database

- Changing the location of control files and datafiles of the auxiliary instance

- By using the SET *newname for datafile '....' to '...'* command, the location of datafiles of the recovered tablespace can be changed.

- By using the *db_file_name_convert* and *log_file_name_convert* parameters, the name of datafiles and redo log files of the auxiliary instance can be changed.

- By using the *control_files* parameter in the intialization parameter, the location of control files of an auxiliary instance can be changed.

If RMAN's automatic auxiliary instance needs to be used with the self-customized initialization parameter, create the file using the different parameters shown above and define it using the *set auxiliary instance parameter file* command before performing TSPITR.

If a specific auxiliary instance should be used, then create a password file, an initialization parameter file for an auxiliary instance, make changes to the *tnsnames.ora* and *listener.ora* files, start the auxiliary instance, connect to it from the RMAN client and perform the recovery.

Starting from Oracle 11g, tablespace point-in-time recovery can be performed on the dropped tablespace. If it is tried in Oracle 10g, the following error occurs:

```
RMAN-20202: tablespace not found in the recovery catalog
RMAN-06019: could not translate tablespace name "TBS_TEST"
```

Oracle Backup and Recovery

Another superiority of Oracle 11g is that TSPITR can be performed multiple times to any *scn*, *time* and *sequence*.

Using Data Recovery Advisor

One of the great new features of RMAN in Oracle 11g is the new tool named Data Recovery Advisor. This tool automates the diagnosis of the data failure and corruption, advises what recovery steps need to be taken and performs an automatic recovery of the database failure. This tool could be used from GUI as well as from CLI.

There are four new RMAN commands which help to use this tool, as follows:

1. List failure: Lists the failures that the database encountered. Using this command, detailed information about the error appears, specific failures are listed or some of them are excluded.

2. Advise failure: Automatically analyzes all backups and archived redo logs and provides a recovery script which recovers the required data failure. If there are already fixed errors, it closes them automatically.

3. Change failure: Changes the priority and the status of the failure

4. Repair failure: Repairs the failure using automatically created RMAN commands. The recovery process might be previewed before running to ensure which commands will be performed.

Each failure is identified by its status and the priority. The status could be OPEN or CLOSED. When a failure is repaired, the status is marked as CLOSED. If the problem is solved manually, then the failure can be closed using the *change failure* command.

There are three priority levels for each data failure: critical (when the database is unavailable), high (when the database is partly available) and low (when the failure can be ignored). If any high priority needs to be bypassed, change its status to low.

In the following scenario, use Data Recovery Advisor to recover the lost data as outlined in the following:

- There are three tablespaces (users, users02, users03).

- A table is created on each of two of the tablespaces (*tbl_test01* on users and *tbl_test02* on users02).

- The datafiles of users and users02 tablespaces are corrupted and the *users03* datafile is deleted.

- Using the *list failure* command shows that it lists three data failures (two data block corruption and one missing datafile).

- Advice for all these problems shows up and then the third datafile is manually restored and recovered.

- The *repair failure* command is used to make RMAN automatically repair the data block corruption.

Start performing the above outlined scenario. Create two new tablespaces (users02, user03) and create two tables, one table on each of the users and users02 tablespaces.

```
SQL>
create
 tablespace users02 datafile 'C:\app\administrator\oradata\tt\users02.dbf'
size 1M;

Tablespace created.

SQL>
create
 tablespace users03 datafile 'C:\app\administrator\oradata\tt\users03.dbf'
size 1M;

Tablespace created.

SQL>
create
 table tbl_test01 (name varchar2(10)) tablespace users;

Table created.

SQL>
create
 table tbl_test02 (name varchar2(10)) tablespace users02;

Table created.

SQL>
insert into
 tbl_test01 values('my_test01');

1 row created.

SQL>
insert into
 tbl_test02 values('my_test02');
```

Oracle Backup and Recovery

```
1 row created.

SQL>
commit;

Commit complete.
SQL>
```

Back up the database.

```
RMAN> backup database plus archivelog;
```

Corrupt the datafiles using the techniques that are described in the Block
Media Recovery subchapter. Next, flush the buffer cache and query the table.
An "ORA-01578: ORACLE data block corrupted" error occurs. Then query
the *v$database_block_corruption* view. This brings up an empty result. However,
after awhile Oracle automatically detects and updates the view. Next, shut
down the database, delete the datafile that belongs to the users03 tablespace,
mount the database and use the *alter database datafile 'path_of_the_users03.dbf'*
offline; command to take it offline and start the database:

```
SQL> alter system flush buffer_cache;

System altered.

SQL>
select * from
 tbl_test01;
select * from tbl_test01
              *

ERROR at line 1:
ORA-01578: ORACLE data block corrupted (file # 4, block # 72)
ORA-01110: data file 4: 'C:\app\administrator\oradata\tt\users01.dbf'

SQL>
select * from
 tbl_test02;
select * from tbl_test02
              *

ERROR at line 1:
ORA-01578: ORACLE data block corrupted (file # 5, block # 16)
ORA-01110: data file 5: 'C:\app\administrator\oradata\tt\users02.dbf'

SQL>
select * from
 v$database_block_corruption;

no rows selected
```

Wait awhile and run the command again:

```
SQL>
select * from
 v$database_block_corruption;
```

```
      FILE#      BLOCK#     BLOCKS CORRUPTION_CHANGE# CORRUPTIO
---------- ---------- ---------- ------------------ ---------
         4         72          1                  0 CHECKSUM
         5         16          1                  0 CHECKSUM

SQL>
shut abort
SQL>
startup
 mount;

SQL>
alter
 database datafile 'C:\app\administrator\oradata\tt\users03.dbf' offline;

Database altered.

SQL>
alter
 database open;

Database altered.
SQL>
```

Now use the *list failure* command to let RMAN gather the data failures present:

```
C:\>rman target /
RMAN> list failure;

using target database control file instead of recovery catalog

List of Database Failures
=========================
Failure ID Priority Status    Time Detected Summary
---------- -------- --------- ------------- -------
328        HIGH     OPEN      20-MAY-10     One or more non-system datafiles are  missing
308        HIGH     OPEN      20-MAY-10     Datafile 5: 'C:\APP\ADMINISTRATOR\ORADATA\TT\USERS02.DBF'
contains one or more corrupt blocks
122        HIGH     OPEN      20-MAY-10     Datafile 4: 'C:\APP\ADMINISTRATOR\ORADATA\TT\USERS01.DBF'
contains one or more corrupt blocks
```

Detailed information can be obtained on any listed failure:

```
RMAN> list failure 328 detail;

List of Database Failures
=========================
Failure ID Priority Status    Time Detected Summary
---------- -------- --------- ------------- -------
328        HIGH     OPEN      20-MAY-10     One or more non-system datafiles are missing
```

Oracle Backup and Recovery

```
    Impact: See impact for individual child failures
    List of child failures for parent failure ID 328

    Failure ID Priority Status    Time Detected Summary
    ---------- -------- --------- ------------- -------
    331        HIGH     OPEN      20-MAY-10     Datafile 6:
 'C:\app\administrator\oradata\tt\users03.dbf' is missing

      Impact: Some objects in tablespace users03 might be unavailable
```

Now use the *advise failure* command to get the necessary information and ready scripts to perform a recovery:

```
RMAN> advise failure all;

List of Database Failures
=========================
Failure ID Priority Status    Time Detected Summary
---------- -------- --------- ------------- -------
328        HIGH     OPEN      20-MAY-10     One or more non-system datafiles ar
 missing
308        HIGH     OPEN      20-MAY-10     Datafile 5: 'C:\app\administrator\o
adata\tt\users02.dbf' contains one or more corrupt blocks
122        high     open      20-MAY-10     Datafile 4: 'C:\app\administrator\o
adata\tt\users01.dbf' contains one or more corrupt blocks

analyzing automatic repair options; this may take some time
using channel ORA_DISK_1
analyzing automatic repair options complete

Mandatory Manual Actions
========================
no manual actions available

Optional Manual Actions
=======================
1. If file C:\APP\ADMINISTRATOR\ORADATA\TT\USERS03.DBF was unintentionally renamed or moved, restore
it

Automated Repair Options
========================
Option Repair Description
------ ------------------
1      Restore and recover datafile 6; Perform block media recovery of block 16 in file 5; Perform
block media recovery of block 72 in file 4
  Strategy: The repair includes complete media recovery with no data loss
  Repair script: c:\app\administrator\diag\rdbms\tt\tt\hm\reco_3231280737.hm
RMAN>
```

So there is detailed information on what is here and how a recovery can be performed. Now restoring and recovering datafile 6 and performing block media recovery on datafile 4 and 5 needs to happen. RMAN creates a script which could be run to perform the whole recovery. Here is the source of the script:

```
# restore and recover datafile
sql 'alter database datafile 6 offline';
restore datafile 6;
recover datafile 6;
sql 'alter database datafile 6 online';
# block media recovery
recover datafile 5 block 16
datafile 4 block 72;
```

Perform the first action manually by running the following commands in RMAN:

```
RMAN>    sql 'alter database datafile 6 offline';
RMAN>    restore datafile 6;
RMAN>    recover datafile 6;
RMAN>    sql 'alter database datafile 6 online';
```

Now use the *advise failure* command again. It will diagnose the failures and update the result:

```
RMAN> advise failure all;

List of Database Failures
=========================
Failure ID Priority Status    Time Detected Summary
---------- -------- --------- ------------- -------
308        HIGH     OPEN      20-MAY-10     Datafile 5: 'C:\app\administrator\or
adata\tt\users02.dbf' contains one or more corrupt blocks
122        high     open      20-may-10     datafile 4: 'c:\app\administrator\or
adata\tt\users01.dbf' contains one or more corrupt blocks

analyzing automatic repair options; this may take some time
using channel ORA_DISK_1
analyzing automatic repair options complete

Mandatory Manual Actions
========================
no manual actions available

Optional Manual Actions
=======================
no manual actions available

Automated Repair Options
========================
Option Repair Description
------ -------------------
1      Perform block media recovery of block 16 in file 5; Perform block media recovery of block 72
in file 4
  Strategy: The repair includes complete media recovery with no data loss
  Repair script: c:\app\administrator\diag\rdbms\tt\tt\hm\reco_1778061078.hm
```

Now preview the repair plan of RMAN and repair all data. For this, use the *repair failure preview* and *repair failure* commands as follows:

```
RMAN> repair failure preview;

Strategy: The repair includes complete media recovery with no data loss

Repair script: c:\app\administrator\diag\rdbms\tt\tt\hm\reco_1778061078.hm

contents of repair script:
   # block media recovery
   recover datafile 5 block 16
   datafile 4 block 72;

RMAN> repair failure;

Strategy: The repair includes complete media recovery with no data loss

Repair script: c:\app\administrator\diag\rdbms\tt\tt\hm\reco_1778061078.hm
```

```
contents of repair script:
   # block media recovery
   recover datafile 5 block 16
   datafile 4 block 72;

Do we really want to execute the above repair (enter YES or NO)? YES
executing repair script

Starting recover at 20-MAY-10
using channel ORA_DISK_1

channel ORA_DISK_1: restoring block(s)
channel ORA_DISK_1: specifying block(s) to restore from backup set
restoring blocks of datafile 00005
restoring blocks of datafile 00004
<...output trimmed ....>
<...output trimmed ....>
starting media recovery
media recovery complete, elapsed time: 00:00:07

Finished recover at 20-MAY-10
repair failure complete
RMAN>
```

Now query the tables:

```
SQL>
select * from
 tbl_test01;

NAME
----------
my_test01

SQL>
select * from
 tbl_test02;

NAME
----------
my_test02
SQL>
```

Conclusion

In this chapter, detailed information on recovery scenarios using RMAN has been presented along with examples of detailed step-by-step solutions. Failures and their common solutions, the difference between the terms restore and recovery, and the general recovery process were also examined.

Further, performing media recovery using RMAN and different scenarios which might be faced in daily work were covered. This chapter showed how to recover control files, archived redo log files, system and non-system datafiles, and tablespaces. Recovery processes including performing block media recovery, incomplete recovery and tablespace point-in-time recovery were reviewed. Demonstrations on how to create a media crash in order to have an example of corrupted databases for test scenarios were given, and the recovery steps were tested.

In the last section of the chapter, one of the new features of Oracle 11g, Data Recovery Advisor, was introduced and a media recovery was performed using the information that new tool provides. In the next chapter, the techniques of the database clone using RMAN will be illustrated in live scenarios, and the database will be duplicated on the remote host as well as on the local host using both different and same directory structures.

Cloning Database with RMAN

One of the RMAN advanced features is its ability to create a clone database when the database is running. In order to run and practice all tests and then apply them to the production database, every DBA should have at least one test copy of the production database. It is very dangerous to practice something directly on the production database without testing it on the test database. These practices may be any backup and recovery tests, applying a patch on the test database, generating reports on the database, a test upgrade of the database or application tests of developers and also preparing the environments for UAT, training and more.

Even though there are different and possible methods available for cloning a database, doing so by using RMAN's *duplicate database* command is easier and has significance. By using this command, a database can be duplicated both on the remote and local host. At the same time, it is possible to change the location of duplicated database files as well as skip any tablespace or create a clone of a database to its past point in time state. This chapter will cover the creation of a duplicate database with all its features in real examples.

Cloning Database with RMAN Overview

To understand all functionalities of the *duplicate database* command, create some practical scenarios as follows:

1. First of all, create a duplicate database on a remote host with both same and different directory structures.

2. Secondly, see how a duplicate database can be created on the local host.

3. At the end, create a clone of a database in local host by skipping tablespaces and recovering it to past point in time.

Creating a Duplicate Database on Remote Host with the Same Directory Structure

To create a clone of the database on the remote host, there should be two servers. Both servers should have Oracle software installed on them and make sure the operating system is the same on both the servers. On the first server, there should be one database which is duplicated to the second host. The first server is named as production server and the database on it is called the production database (SID of the production database is db1). However, the second server has a name as auxiliary server and the database which is created on it is called auxiliary database (SID of the auxiliary database is aux). The server name of the production database is *prod_server* and the server name of the auxiliary database is *dup_server*.

Initial Actions to Do Before Cloning Production Database

Before cloning the production database, some initial actions should be configured as follows.

Create a Password File for the Auxiliary Instance

It is possible to create a password file on the production server or on the auxiliary server. Because the passwords of target and auxiliary databases, password files should not be similar as it is a security threat. However, it should be mentioned that when creating a standby database from RMAN, the password file has to be same. However, since a standby database is not being created, the new password file should be created. Create a password file using the *orapwd* utility as follows:

```
$ orapwd file=$ORACLE_HOME/dbs/orapwaux password=test entries=3;
```

Configure the Auxiliary Instance Listener Net Configuration

To clone the production database to the auxiliary server, the connection should be configured between two servers, i.e. must be able to access the production database from the auxiliary server and vice versa. Thus, make changes to the *tnsnames.ora* and *listener.ora* files. If these files are not in the *$ORACLE_HOME/network/admin* directory, create them using the *netca* utility. First of all, change the *listener.ora* file on the auxiliary server and add the following lines:

```
listener.ora #auxiliary instance
    (SID_DESC =
      (SID_NAME = aux)
      (ORACLE_HOME = /u01/oracle/product/10.2.0/db_1)
    )
```

The reason a change was made to the *listener.ora* file is because the auxiliary server was made to listen for the connections that come from the production database. While duplicating the database, connect to the auxiliary instance from the production database. Since an auxiliary instance should understand and accept the connections which come from the production database, the *listener.ora* file has been configured. Without stopping and starting the listener, new changes are made to listener configuration by running the following command:

```
$ lsnrctl reload
```

Now, edit the *tnsnames.ora* file on the production database and add the entry about the auxiliary database to it:

```
aux =
  (description =
    (address_list =
       (address=(protocol=tcp)(host= dup_server)(port=1521))
    )
    (connect_data=
      (ORACLE_SID=aux)
    )
  )
```

After changing the file, make sure to connect to the auxiliary instance by using the *tnsping* utility:

```
$ tnsping aux

Attempting to contact (description = (address_list =
(address=(protocol=tcp)(host= dup_server)(port=1521))) (connect_data=
(ORACLE_SID=aux)))
OK (40 msec)
```

It means that there is access to the auxiliary server from the production server and the connection between two servers has been successfully configured.

Create a Parameter File for the Auxiliary Database

Use this parameter file to start the auxiliary instance in nomount mode. *pfile* can be created from the *spfile* of the production database and copied to the auxiliary server. A parameter file can also be created which consists only of the following few parameters:

1. *db_name*: As the duplicate database is created at the remote host, keep the database name the same as the production database name. However, this parameter will be different when the database is duplicated on the local host because it is impossible to have two databases with the same name in one host.

2. *control_files*: This parameter defines the name of the control files which will be restored to the auxiliary instance.

3. *db_block_size*: This parameter must be the same as in the target instance.

4. *compatible*: If the production database uses specific compatible parameters, add this parameter to the auxiliary parameter file with the same value.

5. *sga_target*: This parameter specifies the total size of all SGA components. To automatically size these components, make it the same as in the production database. It is not mandatory that this be the same size as in the production database. The cloning may be done to create a test/development environment on a smaller server with lesser RAM.

The following directories also need to be created on the auxiliary server and added to the parameter file:

- *adump*

- *bdump*

- *udump*

- *cdump*

- flash recovery area

```
$ cd $ORACLE_HOME
$ mkdir admin
$ cd admin/
$ mkdir aux
$ cd aux/
$ mkdir adump bdump cdump udump
$ cd ..
$ mkdir flash_recovery_area
```

After changes are made to the parameter file, it will look like the following:

```
db_name=aux
control_file=(/u02/oradata/aux/control01.ctl,/u02/oradata/aux/control02.ctl,
/u02/oradata/aux/control03.ctl')
db_block_size=8192
compatible='10.2.0.1.0'
SGA_TARGET=285212672
audit_file_dest='/u01/oracle/product/10.2.0/db_1/admin/aux/adump'
background_dump_dest='/u01/oracle/product/10.2.0/db_1/admin/aux/bdump'
core_dump_dest='/u01/oracle/product/10.2.0/db_1/admin/aux/cdump'
user_dump_dest='/u01/oracle/product/10.2.0/db_1/admin/aux/udump'
db_recovery_file_dest='/u01/oracle/product/10.2.0/db_1/flash_recovery_area'
db_recovery_file_dest_size=2147483648
```

Now to make Oracle automatically use this parameter file each time, create spfile as follows:

```
$ export ORACLE_SID=aux
$ export ORACLE_HOME=/u01/oracle/product/10.2.0/db_1/
$ sqlplus "/ as sysdba"

Connected to an idle instance.

SQL>
create spfile
from
pfile='/u01/oracle/product/10.2.0/db_1/dbs/pfile.ora';

File created.
SQL>
```

Start Up the Auxiliary Instance in Nomount Mode

```
SQL>
startup
nomount

ORACLE instance started.
Total System Global Area   285212672 bytes
Fixed Size                   1218992 bytes
Variable Size               92276304 bytes
Database Buffers           188743680 bytes
Redo Buffers                 2973696 bytes
SQL>
```

Back Up the Production Database and Copy All Backup Files to Auxiliary Server

As the auxiliary instance is ready, the production database and copy backup files need to be backed up to the auxiliary server. Since the backup will be recovered on the auxiliary server, the production database should be in archivelog mode.

Connect to the target instance and take the compressed backup of the database using *nocatalog*. The backup of the database can be taken by connecting to the RMAN catalog database as well.

```
$ export ORACLE_SID=db1
$ rman target /
RMAN> backup as compressed backupset database plus archivelog;
```

Create Datafile Locations in the Auxiliary Server

If the datafiles need to be created in the same directory as the production database, create the folder of datafiles on the auxiliary server:

```
# mkdir u02
# cd u02/
# mkdir oradata
# cd oradata/
# mkdir db1
# cd db1/
# chown -R oracle:oinstall /u02/
```

Copy the Backup of the Production Database to the Same Directory Residing on the Auxiliary Database Server

As the database is configured to use the flash recovery area, all RMAN backups will be stored under the flash recovery area folder. Therefore, the same folder should be created at the auxiliary server and all backup files should be copied to that folder. When the *duplicate database* command is issued, RMAN searches the auxiliary server for the backup files which should reside in the same folder where they were on the production server.

Identify the location of RMAN backups on the production server and create the same folders on the auxiliary server. Then copy all backup files from the production server to the auxiliary server.

Duplicate the Database

After all the above steps are done correctly, it is now time to create the clone database. For this, connect to both the production and auxiliary databases from RMAN and issue the command *duplicate target database to aux*.

```
$ rman target sys/my_pass auxiliary sys/test@aux

connected to target database: DB1 (DBID=1298725119)
connected to auxiliary database: AUX (not mounted)

RMAN> duplicate target database to aux nofilenamecheck;

Starting Duplicate Db at 06-DEC-09
==================
database opened
Finished Duplicate Db at 06-DEC-09
```

After performing all the steps, the production database is now successfully duplicated to the remote host (auxiliary server). RMAN performs the following steps automatically to duplicate the database:

1. Allocates automatic auxiliary channel

2. Creates a control file for the clone database

3. Performs an incomplete recovery of the clone database using incremental backups and archived redo log files up to the last backed up archived redo log file

4. Shuts down the database and opens it using the *resetlogs* option

5. Generates a new unique DBID for the clone database

Remember, all file locations were the same as in the production database. However, in case the clone database's directory structure needs to be changed, it can be done in different ways. The next section will examine these ways and demonstrate them with different examples.

Creating a Duplicate Database on a Remote Host

There are mainly three ways for creating duplicate databases on the remote host with different directory structure:

1. Making changes to the initialization parameter

2. Using the *set newname* command with the *duplicate* command

3. Using the *configure auxname* command before running the *duplicate* command

Now each of these methods will be demonstrated with real examples.

Duplicating Database to the Remote Host with Different Directory Structure

In this example, by making changes to the initialization parameter file of the auxiliary instance, RMAN is made to create all control files, redo log files and data files on the different directory.

In this process, all steps are the same as they were in the previous example except two parameters which are added to the initialization parameter file such as *db_file_name_convert* and *log_file_name_convert*:

1. *db_file_name_convert* parameter changes location of the production database's datafiles to a different location on the auxiliary database.

2. *log_file_name_convert* parameter changes location of the production database's redo log files to a different location on the auxiliary database.

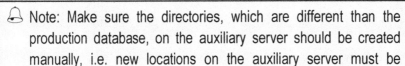

Note: Make sure the directories, which are different than the production database, on the auxiliary server should be created manually, i.e. new locations on the auxiliary server must be created manually.

At the end, the parameter file will be as follows:

```
*.compatible='10.2.0.1.0'
*.control_files='/u03/oracle/new_database/control01.ctl','/u03/oracle/new_da
tabase/control02.ctl','/u03/oracle/new_database/control03.ctl'
*.db_file_name_convert='/u01/oradata/test/','/u03/oracle/new_database/'
*.log_file_name_convert='/u01/oradata/test/','/u03/oracle/new_database/'
*.db_block_size=8192
*.db_name='test'
*.sga_target=285212672
```

Now if the *duplicate* command is run as in the previous example, all database files are created on the */u03/oracle/new_database* directory. It can be seen by querying the following views on the auxiliary database:

```
sys@TEST>
select
 name
from
 v$datafile;
```

```
NAME
-------------------------------------------------
/u03/oracle/new_database/system01.dbf
/u03/oracle/new_database/undotbs01.dbf
/u03/oracle/new_database/sysaux01.dbf
/u03/oracle/new_database/users01.dbf

sys@TEST>
select
 member
from
v$logfile;

MEMBER
-------------------------------------------------
/u03/oracle/new_database/redo03.log
/u03/oracle/new_database/redo02.log
/u03/oracle/new_database/redo01.log
sys@TEST>SELECT name FROM v$controlfile;

NAME
-----------------------------------------
/u03/oracle/new_database/control01.ctl
/u03/oracle/new_database/control02.ctl
/u03/oracle/new_database/control03.ctl
```

Creating Duplicate Database with Different Directory Structure

In the previous example, the creation of database files at a different location in the auxiliary server was accomplished by making changes to the parameter file. This is not the only way to achieve it. It can be performed directly from RMAN as follows:

1. Use *db_file_name_convert* and *logfile* parameters in the duplicate database command.

2. Use the *set newname* command to change location of files of the auxiliary database directly from RMAN.

The first way will be explained under this subtopic. The second way will be shown on the next subtopic on creating a duplicate database on a local host. To use the first solution, perform all the steps which were mentioned in the beginning of this chapter until the *duplicate* command. Change the *duplicate* command to:

```
RMAN> duplicate target database to clone_db
db_file_name_convert=('/u01/oradata/test/','/u03/oradata/new_database/')
LOGFILE '/u03/oradata/new_database/redo01.log' size 5m, '/u03/oradata
/new_database/redo02.log' size 5m,'/u03/oradata new_database/redo03.log'
size 5m;
```

Creating a Duplicate Database on a Remote Host   **221**

While running this command, all files are created on the */u03/oradata /new_database* directory.

Creating a Duplicate Database on a Local Host

Once the clone database has been created on the remote host, it is possible to duplicate a database to the local host, too. For this, the database name and location of database files should be different. Moreover, *tnsnames.ora* and *listener.ora* files should be configured correctly.

🔔 It is recommended NOT to clone the production database on the same server or host. As a practice, it can be done for any non-production databases.

In the following example, there is one production database called test and the goal is to clone it to the same host with the name *clone_db*. Now go through the steps of the process:

1. Make a copy of the password file for the second database:

```
$ cp $ORACLE_HOME/dbs/orapwtest $ORACLE_HOME/dbs/orapwclone_db
```

2. Configure both *listener.ora* and *tnsnames.ora* files to connect to the auxiliary database *(clone_db)* that is needed to change the *tnsnames.ora* and *listener.ora* file. Change these files as follows:

```
listener.ora:
   (SID_DESC =
     (SID_NAME = clone_db)
     (ORACLE_HOME = /u01/oracle/product/10.2.0/db_1)
   )
tnsnames.ora
clone_db =
  (description =
    (address = (protocol = tcp)(host = localhost.localdomain)(port = 1521))
    (connect_data =
      (server = dedicated)
      (service_name = clone_db)
    )
  )
```

Do not forget to apply changed parameters to the running listener by running the following command:

```
$ lsnrctl reload
```

3. Create a parameter file for the auxiliary (*clone_db*) database:

```
*.compatible='10.2.0.1.0'
*.control_files='/u03/oracle/clone_db/control01.ctl','/u03/oracle/clone_db/c
ontrol02.ctl','/u03/oracle/clone_db/control03.ctl'
*.db_block_size=8192
*.db_name='clone_db'
*.sga_target=285212672
```

4. Now, create spfile from this parameter file:

```
$ export ORACLE_SID=clone_db
$ cd $ORACLE_HOME/dbs
$ sqlplus "/ as sysdba"

SQL>
create
spfile from pfile='pfile_clone_db.ora';

File created.
SQL>
```

5. Start up the auxiliary instance in nomount mode:

```
$ export ORACLE_SID=clone_db
$ sqlplus "/ as sysdba"
SQL>
startup
nomount;
```

6. Back up the production database using RMAN:

```
$ export ORACLE_SID=test
$ rman target /
RMAN> backup database plus archivelog;
```

7. Duplicate database using the following script.

Now, as the database is cloned in the same host, a different location for datafiles of the new database needs to be defined. Here, use *set newname* to define the new location in run block. Ensure that this is done correctly for every datafile! Connect to both instances and run the following run block:

```
$ export ORACLE_SID=test
$ ./rman target sys/test auxiliary sys/test@clone_db

connected to target database: TEST (DBID=2003066891)
connected to auxiliary database: clone_db (not mounted)

RMAN> run {
        set newname for datafile 1 TO '/u03/oracle/clone_db/system01.dbf';
        set newname for datafile 2 TO '/u03/oracle/clone_db/undotbs01.dbf';
        set newname for datafile 3 TO '/u03/oracle/clone_db/sysaux01.dbf';
        set newname for datafile 4 TO '/u03/oracle/clone_db/users01.dbf';
        set newname for tempfile 1 TO '/u03/oracle/clone_db/temp01.dbf';
duplicate target database to clone_db
```

```
    logfile
'/u03/oracle/clone_db/redo01.log' SIZE 5M, '/u03/oracle/clone_db/redo02.log'
SIZE 5M, '/u03/oracle/clone_db/redo03.log' SIZE 5M;
}
. . . . . . . . . . . . . . . .
. . . . . . . . . . . . . . . .
database opened
Finished Duplicate Db at 06-DEC-09
RMAN>
```

If the exact number of the data file to specify in the *set newname for datafile <
datafile number> to* command is not known, then query in the database as
follows:

```
SQL>
select
file_id,file_name FROM dba_data_files;
```

For the *set newname for tempfile < tempfile number> to* command, then:

```
SQL>
select
file_id,file_name
from
dba_temp_files;
```

The data and tempfile numbers can also be found by connecting to the
production database with RMAN client as follows:

```
$ export ORACLE_SID=test
$ rman target /
RMAN> show schema;
```

Here the file number information can be seen. Now, connect to the auxiliary
instance and query datafile locations:

```
$ export ORACLE_SID=clone_db
$ sqlplus "/ as sysdba"
SQL>
select
name
from
v$database;

NAME
---------
clone_db

SQL>
 select
 name
from
 v$datafile;
```

```
NAME
-------------------------------------
/u03/oracle/clone_db/system01.dbf
/u03/oracle/clone_db/undotbs01.dbf
/u03/oracle/clone_db/sysaux01.dbf
/u03/oracle/clone_db/users01.dbf
SQL>
```

This shows that the clone database of the primary database test1 was created with a different database name (clone_db) and different directory structure.

Using *configure auxname* Configuration to Rename Datafiles

It is possible to specify the location of database files of the duplicated database directly from RMAN configuration. By doing so, RMAN will keep these configuration changes and there will be no need to specify them in the future.

To clear the auxname from the default *configure* settings, issue the following command at the RMAN command:

```
RMAN> configure auxname for datafile <data file number> clear;
```

Now, perform all the steps above until the run block and add the following steps:

1. Make changes to RMAN configuration default settings and configure the auxname parameter for each data file.

2. Connect to RMAN and perform the following configuration changes.

```
configure auxname for datafile 1 TO '/u03/oracle/clone_db/system01.dbf';
configure auxname for datafile 2 TO '/u03/oracle/clone_db/undotbs01.dbf';
configure auxname for datafile 3 TO '/u03/oracle/clone_db/sysaux01.dbf';
configure auxname for datafile 4 TO
'/u03/oracle/clone_db/users01.dbf';
```

Above, RMAN has been configured so that it will change the location of each file specified.

Run the following block to duplicate the database in the same host. Even though *auxname* is used for data files, the *configure auxname* cannot be used for tempfiles and redo log files. Thus, for tempfiles, use the SET NEWNAME clause and for redo log files, use the LOGFILE clause.

```
run {
set newname for tempfile 1 TO '/u03/oracle/clone_db/temp01.dbf';
duplicate target database to clone_db
```

```
logfile
'/u03/oracle/clone_db/redo log01.log' SIZE 5M,  '/u03/oracle/clone_db/redo
log02.log' SIZE 5M,  '/u03/oracle/clone_db/redo log03.log' SIZE 5M;
}
```

After fulfilling all steps, there is now a new database on the same host. If the RMAN configuration is checked for any changes, RMAN keeps the *auxname* configuration for each file in its configuration. No pre-configuration is needed to change file names because all changes reside at the RMAN configuration:

```
RMAN> show auxname;
RMAN configuration parameters are:
configure auxname for datafile '/u02/oradata/test/system01.dbf' TO
'/u03/oracle/clone_db/system01.dbf';
configure auxname for datafile '/u02/oradata/test/undotbs01.dbf' TO
'/u03/oracle/clone_db/undotbs01.dbf';
configure auxname for datafile '/u02/oradata/test/sysaux01.dbf' TO
'/u03/oracle/clone_db/sysaux01.dbf';
configure auxname for datafile '/u02/oradata/test/users01.dbf' TO
'/u03/oracle/clone_db/users01.dbf';
RMAN>
```

Skipping Tablespaces While Cloning RMAN Database

The next example will show how to skip Read Write, Read Only and Offline tablespaces. Then how to clone the database to a past point in time will be covered.

Perform all above steps up to Step 5 and bring the auxiliary database to the nomount mode. Then create three tablespaces in the production database:

- tbs_skip: This is a Read Write tablespace. This tablespace will be skipped during the clone process.

- tbs_readonly: This is a Read Only tablespace and will be skipped automatically by the *skip readonly* command during the clone process.

- tbs_offline: This is an offline tablespace and will be skipped automatically by RMAN during the clone process.

Then create a table and use it to show the result of the past point in time recovery. Look at this example in more details. Create three tablespaces:

```
sys@TEST>
create
tablespace tbs_skip datafile '/u02/oradata/test/tbs_skip.dbf' SIZE 1M;

Tablespace created.
```

```
sys@TEST>
create
tablespace tbs_readonly datafile '/u02/oradata/test/tbs_readonly.dbf' SIZE
1M;

Tablespace created.

sys@TEST>
create
tablespace tbs_offline datafile '/u02/oradata/ /test/tbs_offline.dbf' SIZE
1M;

Tablespace created.

sys@TEST>
```

Create two tables: *tbs_test* and *tbs_readonly*. The first table is used in the past point in time recovery scenario. The second table is used when the Read Only tablespace is recovered after the clone process. Create the *tbs_readonly* table and insert one row in it:

```
sys@TEST>
create
table tbl_test (id number);

Table created.

sys@TEST>
create
table tbl_readonly (col1 varchar2(15)) tablespace tbs_readonly;

Table created.

sys@TEST>
insert into
 tbl_readonly values('Readonly table');

1 row created.

sys@TEST>
commit;

Commit complete.
```

Change the status of the tablespace tbs_readonly to Read Only, tbs_offline to Offline:

```
sys@TEST>
alter
Tablespace tbs_readonly Read Only;

Tablespace altered.

sys@TEST>
alter
```

```
tablespace tbs_offline Offline Normal;

Tablespace altered.

sys@TEST>
```

Connect to RMAN and take a full backup:

```
RMAN> backup database plus archivelog delete input;

Starting backup at 01-OCT-09
.................
.................
Finished backup at 01-OCT-09
```

Make changes to the *tbl_test* table and take a backup of the database and archivelogs. Insert a row to the *tbl_test* table and commit it. Then take the current SCN value of the database that will be used during recovery of said database. A clone will be made of the database to this SCN value.

Next, insert one more row since it is assumed that this row is a mistake and will not be recovered during the clone process. Then switch the redo log file and take a backup of the archived redo log files:

```
sys@TEST>
insert into
tbl_test values(1);

1 row created.

sys@TEST>
commit;

Commit complete.

sys@TEST>
select * from
tbl_test;

        ID
----------
         1

sys@TEST>
select
current_scn
from
v$database;

current_scn
-----------
    471662
```

```
sys@TEST>
insert into
tbl_test  values(100000);

1 row created.

sys@TEST>
commit;

Commit complete.

sys@TEST>
select * from
 tbl_test;

        ID
----------
         1
    100000

sys@TEST>
alter
system switch logfile;

System altered.

sys@TEST>
exit
$ rman target /
RMAN> backup archivelog all delete input;

Starting backup at 01-OCT-09
..................
..................
Finished backup at 01-OCT-09
RMAN>
```

The database is ready to be cloned. To clone the database, connect to both databases and run the following script:

```
$ rman target sys/test auxiliary sys/test@clone_db

connected to target database: test (DBID=782965739)
connected to auxiliary database: clone_db (not mounted)

RMAN> run {
set newname for tempfile 1 to '/u03/oracle/new_clone/temp01.dbf';
set newname for datafile 1 to '/u03/oracle/new_clone/system01.dbf';
set newname for datafile 2 to '/u03/oracle/new_clone/undotbs01.dbf';
set newname for datafile 3 to '/u03/oracle/new_clone/sysaux01.dbf';
set newname for datafile 4 to '/u03/oracle/new_clone/users01.dbf';
set newname for datafile 5 to '/u03/oracle/new_clone/skip.dbf';
set newname for datafile 6 to '/u03/oracle/new_clone/readonly.dbf';
set newname for datafile 7 to '/u03/oracle/new_clone/offline.dbf';
duplicate target database to clone_db
skip tablespace tbs_skip
skip readonly
```

```
until scn 471662
logfile
    '/u03/oracle/new_clone/redo log01.log' SIZE 5M,
    '/u03/oracle/new_clone/redo log02.log' SIZE 5M,
    '/u03/oracle/new_clone/redo log03.log' SIZE 5M;
}
```

RMAN starts to clone and recovers the database until the specified SCN value by skipping the tbl_skip, Read Only and Offline tablespaces. With the SKIP TABLESPACE clause, the tablespaces can be excluded from the duplicate database, but not the system tablespace or undo tablespace which contains rollback or undo segments. Below is the part of the result of the script:

```
contents of Memory Script:
{
    set until scn  471662;
    recover
    clone database
    delete archivelog
    ;
}

executing Memory Script
executing command: set until clause
Starting recover at 01-OCT-09
allocated channel: ORA_AUX_DISK_1
channel ORA_AUX_DISK_1: sid=36 devtype=disk
datafile 5 not processed because file is offline
datafile 6 not processed because file is read-only
datafile 7 not processed because file is offline
starting media recovery
. . . . . . . . . . . . . . . .
. . . . . . . . . . . . . . . .
Finished recover at 01-OCT-09

contents of Memory Script:
{
    shutdown clone;
    startup clone nomount;
}

executing Memory Script
database dismounted
Oracle instance shut down
connected to auxiliary database (not started)
Oracle instance started
. . . . . . . . . . . . . . .
. . . . . . . . . . . . . . .

contents of Memory Script:
{
    Alter clone database open resetlogs;
}

executing Memory Script
database opened
```

Oracle Backup and Recovery

```
contents of Memory Script:
{
# drop offline and skipped tablespaces
sql clone "drop tablespace  tbs_skip including contents cascade
constraints";
# drop offline and skipped tablespaces
sql clone "drop tablespace  tbs_offline including contents cascade
constraints";
}

executing Memory Script

sql statement: drop tablespace  tbs_skip including contents cascade
constraints
sql statement: drop tablespace  tbs_offline including contents cascade
constraints
Finished Duplicate Db at 01-OCT-09

RMAN>
```

The database has been recovered to SCN 471662 and all tablespaces have been skipped.

```
datafile 5 not processed because file is offline
datafile 6 not processed because file is read-only
datafile 7 not processed because file is offline
```

Datafile 5 was manually skipped because the skip tablespace *tbs_skip* command was used. Datafile 6 was skipped because it was a Read Only tablespace and all Read Only tablespaces were skipped by the *skip readonly* command. Datafile 7 was skipped automatically by RMAN because it is an offline tablespace. Then the database was opened with the *resetlogs* option and the tbs_skip and tbs_offline tablespaces dropped by RMAN.

Now, query the *tbl_test* table:

```
sys@clone_db>
select * from
 tbl_test;

        ID
----------
         1
```

The last time when this table was queried, there were two lines; however, as the database was recovered until a specific *SCN value*, at that *scn* there was only one row.

Now, query the *tbl_readonly* table:

Creating a Duplicate Database on a Remote Host

```
sys@clone_db>
select * from
tbl_readonly;
select * from
 tbl_readonly
                  *

ERROR at line 1:
ORA-00376: file 6 cannot be read at this time
ORA-01111: name for data file 6 is unknown - rename to correct file
ORA-01110: data file 6:
'/u01/oracle/product/10.2.0/db_1/dbs/MISSING00006'
```

This shows that since the tbs_readonly tablespace was skipped with the *skip readonly* command, the table which resides on Datafile 6 cannot be queried. It was dropped after the database had been cloned and opened. Check the status of the datafile in the *v$datafile* view:

```
sys@clone_db>
set
 linesize 1000
sys@clone_db>
select
status, enabled, name
from
v$datafile;

STATUS   ENABLED     NAME
-------  ----------  ------------------------------------
SYSTEM   READ WRITE  /u03/oracle/new_clone/system01.dbf
ONLINE   READ WRITE  /u03/oracle/new_clone/undotbs01.dbf
ONLINE   READ WRITE  /u03/oracle/new_clone/sysaux01.dbf
ONLINE   READ WRITE  /u03/oracle/new_clone/users01.dbf
OFFLINE  READ ONLY   /u01/oracle/product/10.2.0/db_1/dbs/MISSING00006
```

To recover this tablespace, copy it from the production database to the location where the auxiliary database's files are located and recover them by performing the following steps:

1. Copy it from the production database's file location to the auxiliary database's location:

```
sys@clone_db>host
$ cp /u01/oracle/test/tbs_readonly.dbf /u03/oracle/new_clone/
```

Note: Now is the time to use a cp copy of the datafile without taking a fresh backup because the tablespace is Read Only.

---

2. Then rename it and change the status to online in the clone_db database:

```
sys@clone_db>
alter tablespace
 tbs_readonly rename datafile
'/u01/oracle/product/10.2.0/db_1/dbs/MISSING00006' TO
'/u03/oracle/new_clone/tbs_readonly.dbf';

Tablespace altered.

sys@clone_db>
alter tablespace
 tbs_readonly online;

Tablespace altered.
```

3. Now view the status and datafile name of that file from the *v$datafile* view:

```
sys@clone_db>
select
status, enabled, name
 from
 v$datafile;

STATUS   ENABLED     NAME
-------  ----------  ---------------------------------
SYSTEM   READ WRITE  /u03/oracle/new_clone/system01.dbf
ONLINE   READ WRITE  /u03/oracle/new_clone/undotbs01.dbf
ONLINE   READ WRITE  /u03/oracle/new_clone/sysaux01.dbf
ONLINE   READ WRITE  /u03/oracle/new_clone/users01.dbf
ONLINE   READ ONLY   /u03/oracle/new_clone/tbs_readonly.dbf
```

4. Now the *tbl_readonly* table can be queried:

```
sys@clone_db>
select * from
 tbl_readonly;

COL1
---------------
Readonly table
sys@clone_db>
```

Resynchronize a Duplicate Database

Sometimes there is the need to refresh the clone database which was created from the production database. For this, run the *duplicate* command which was used to create the clone database. As RMAN uses backups to clone the database, the last backup of the database should be taken:
```
Configure AUXNAME configuration of RMAN
```

In order to not provide the location for datafiles each time, make changes on the RMAN configuration. These changes are kept in RMAN so it can be used in every resynchronization of the duplicate database. Connect to the target and auxiliary instance from RMAN and make changes to the RMAN configuration as follows:

```
$ rman target sys/test axuiliary sys/test@aux
RMAN> configure auxname for datafile 1 to
'/u03/oracle/new_clone/system01.dbf';
RMAN> configure auxname for datafile 2 to
'/u03/oracle/new_clone/undotbs01.dbf';
RMAN> configure auxname for datafile 3 to
'/u03/oracle/new_clone/sysaux01.dbf';
RMAN> configure auxname for datafile 4 to
'/u03/oracle/new_clone/users01.dbf';
RMAN> show
auxname;
RMAN configuration parameters are:
configure auxname for datafile '/u01/oradata/test/system01.dbf' to
'/u03/oracle/new_clone/system01.dbf';
configure auxname for datafile '/u01/oradata/test/undotbs01.dbf' to
'/u03/oracle/new_clone/undotbs01.dbf';
configure auxname for datafile '/u01/oradata/test/sysaux01.dbf' to
'/u03/oracle/new_clone/sysaux01.dbf';
configure auxname for datafile '/u01/oradata/test/users01.dbf' to
'/u03/oracle/new_clone/users01.dbf';
RMAN>
```

By any means, after the clone and before the resynchronizing of a duplicate database, if a new datafile is added or an existing datafile is moved to/renamed to another location, then the auxname configuration must be changed for those datafiles.

Now take a whole backup of the database and clone it:

```
RMAN> backup database plue archivelog delete input;

Starting backup at 04-OCT-09
. . . . . . . . . .
. . . . . . . . . . .
Finished backup at 04-OCT-09
```

Connect to both databases (target and auxiliary) and clone the production database:

```
$ rman target sys/test@test axuiliary sys/test@aux
connected to target database: test (DBID=1293202509)
connected to auxiliary database: aux (not mounted)

RMAN> run
{
set newname for tempfile 1 to '/u03/oracle/new_clone/temp01.dbf';

duplicate target database to aux
logfile '/u03/oracle/new_clone/redo01.log' SIZE 5M,
```

```
'/u03/oracle/new_clone/redo02.log' SIZE 5M,
'/u03/oracle/new_clone/redo03.log' SIZE 5M;
}
```

Now, the clone database is ready. Create a new table on the target host and synchronize it with the clone database:

```
sys@test>
create
table new_table (id number);

Table created.

sys@test>
insert into
 new_table values(1);

1 row created.

sys@test>
commit;

Commit complete.

sys@test>
select * from
 new_table;

        ID
----------
         1

sys@test>
alter
system switch logfile;

System altered.
```

Back up the archived redo log files, shut down the clone database and bring it to the nomount stage and run the same *duplicate* command once more:

```
RMAN> backup archivelog all delete input;
RMAN> exit;
$ export ORACLE_SID=aux
$ sqlplus "/as sysdba"
SQL>
shutdown immediate
SQL>
startup
nomount
$rman target sys/test@test auxiliary sys/test@aux

connected to target database: test(DBID=1293202509)
connected to auxiliary database: aux (not mounted)

RMAN> run
```

```
{
set newname for tempfile 1 to '/u03/oracle/new_clone/temp01.dbf';
duplicate target database to aux
logfile '/u03/oracle/new_clone/redo01.log' size 5m,
'/u03/oracle/new_clone/redo02.log' size 5m,
'/u03/oracle/new_clone/redo03.log' size 5m;
}
```

Connect to the clone database and query the *new_table*:

```
sys@aux>
select * from
 new_table;

        ID
----------
         1
```

The database has been resynchronized and all changes were applied to the clone database.

Duplicate on Windows Host

To make a clone of the database which was created on Windows OS, follow the steps above with an additional step where a Windows service of the database is created using the *oradim* utility. In this example, a clone of the database is created on the Windows host. Follow the subsequent steps which have been seen in the previous examples when the clone database was created on the local host.

Make a copy of the password file for the second database:

1. Configure both *listener.ora* and *tnsnames.ora* files

2. Create a parameter file for the auxiliary (clone_db) database

3. Create a new directory for the clone_db and make changes to the auxiliary database parameter file by adding the *db_file_name_convert* and *log_file_name_convert* parameters as follows:

```
db_file_name_convert=('C:\oracle\product\10.2.0\oradata\test','C:\new_databa
se')
log_file_name_convert=('C:\oracle\product\10.2.0\oradata\test','C:\new_datab
ase')
```

4. Create a Windows service for the database using the *oradim* tool and start up the database in nomount mode as follows:

```
C:\>oradim -new -sid clone_db -startmode auto -pfile
'c:\oracle\product\10.2.0\db_1\dbs\pfile.ora'
```

Oracle Backup and Recovery

```
Instance created.

C:\> set ORACLE_SID=clone_db
C:\> sqlplus "/ as sysdba"

Connected to an idle instance.

SQL>
create
 spfile
 from
pfile='c:\oracle\product\10.2.0\db_1\dbs\pfile.ora';

SQL>
startup
 nomount

ORACLE instance started.

Total System Global Area  293601280 bytes
Fixed Size                   1248624 bytes
Variable Size               92275344 bytes
Database Buffers           197132288 bytes
Redo Buffers                 2945024 bytes
SQL>
```

5. Back up the production database using RMAN.

6. Duplicate the database using the following command:

```
RMAN> duplicate target database to clone_db;

Starting Duplicate Db at 11-OCT-09
......................
......................
database opened
Finished Duplicate Db at 11-OCT-09
RMAN>
```

Duplicate Database Without Any Backup (11g New Feature)

In 11g, there is no need to have any backups for duplication of the database. This is a cloning of an active database instance that is running while the clone is being created. All that is needed is to configure the database for duplication as it was made in the previous scenarios. Next is to create a clone database in the same host by performing the following steps:

1. Make a copy of the password file for the second database

2. Configure both *listener.ora* and *tnsnames.ora* files

3. Create a new directory for the clone_db

4. Create a parameter file for the auxiliary (aux) database as follows:

```
*.compatible='11.1.0.0.0'
*.control_files='C:\clone_11g\control01.ctl','C:\clone_11g\control02.ctl','C
:\clone_11g\control03.ctl'
*.db_block_size=8192
*.db_name='aux'
db_file_name_convert='C:\app\oradata\db1','c:\clone_11g'
log_file_name_convert='C:\app\oradata\db1','c:\clone_11g'
log_archive_dest_1='location=c:\clone_11g\arc'
```

5. If Windows OS is being used, create a service using the *oradim* utility and bring it to the nomount mode.

6. Connect to both target and auxiliary instances and run the following command:

```
RMAN>duplicate target database to aux from active database;
```

By running this command, RMAN starts cloning the active production database without any backup. To check backups made by production database, run:

```
RMAN> list backup;
```

```
using target database control file instead of recovery catalog
RMAN>
```

No backup has been taken.

Duplicate Database Without Connecting to the Target Database

Oracle 11gR2 comes with a great new feature where the database can be cloned without connecting to the target database and recovery catalog. So the database can be cloned using only backups of the database directly from the auxiliary server. For this, a new syntax, backup location, is added to the *duplicate* command. In the following example, the steps of database duplication are shown without target database connection and recovery catalog:

1. Take a backup of the target database:

```
RMAN> backup database plus archivelog delete input;
```

2. Create a table, get the current date and time, and drop the table. During the database clone, perform an incomplete recovery until the time of the table drop and get the table back:

```
SQL>
create
 table tbl_test (id number);

Table created.

SQL>
insert into
 t values(1);

1 row created.

SQL>
commit;

Commit complete.

SQL>
select
 to_char(sysdate,'dd-mm-yyyy hh24:mi:ss') ddate
from
 dual;

DDATE
-------------------
31-08-2010 13:31:18

SQL>
drop
 table t;

Table dropped.
SQL>
```

3. Connect to RMAN and take a backup of the current redo log file. By taking backup of archived redo log files, the current redo will be archived and backed up.

```
RMAN> backup archivelog all;
```

4. Switch to the auxiliary server and create necessary folders for the backup files of the target database and datafiles that will be restored. Then copy all backup files from the target server to the auxiliary server.

5. In the auxiliary server, create a directory that will hold backup files:

```
[oracle@localhost /]$ cd /tmp/
[oracle@localhost tmp]$ mkdir backup
```

6. Create a folder for datafiles of the cloned database:

```
[oracle@localhost tmp]$ cd /u01/home/oracle/
[oracle@localhost oracle]$ mkdir oradata
[oracle@localhost oracle]$ cd oradata/
[oracle@localhost oradata]$ mkdir test
```

7. Switch to the target database and copy all backup files to the auxiliary server.

8. After all files are copied, switch to the auxiliary server and create a parameter file to start the auxiliary instance. This parameter file contains only one parameter: *db_name*. Then start the instance using this parameter with nomount mode:

```
db_name=test
```

9. Start the instance:

```
[oracle@localhost oracle]$ export ORACLE_SID=test
[oracle@localhost oracle]$ sqlplus "/ as sysdba"

Connected to an idle instance.

SQL> startup nomount pfile='/tmp/pfile.ora';

ORACLE instance started.

Total System Global Area  146472960 bytes
Fixed Size                  1335080 bytes
Variable Size              92274904 bytes
Database Buffers           50331648 bytes
Redo Buffers                2531328 bytes
SQL>
```

10. After the instance is started, connect to the auxiliary instance with RMAN and start cloning the database. In this example, assume that the name of the database and all file locations are same:

```
RMAN> duplicate database to "test" nofilenamecheck
until time "to_date('31-08-2010 13:31:18','dd-mm-yyyy hh24:mi:ss')"
backup location '/tmp/backup';
```

Running this command, RMAN starts automatically performing the following actions:

- Creates server parameter file and starts the database with it in nomount mode

- Restores the control file from backup and opens the database in mount mode

- Restores all datafiles and performs incomplete recovery

- Recreates new control file in case renaming the name of the cloned database is desired

- Opens database with *resetlogs* option

Cloning Database Using Enterprise Manager

It is possible to clone the database directly from Oracle Enterprise Manager (OEM). By using the OEM cloning feature, this makes it possible to clone the database with some simple mouse clicks without running any RMAN script. Take a backup of the database to the same host using OEM.

Open OEM and switch to the Maintenance tab and in the Data Movement section, select the Clone Database link:

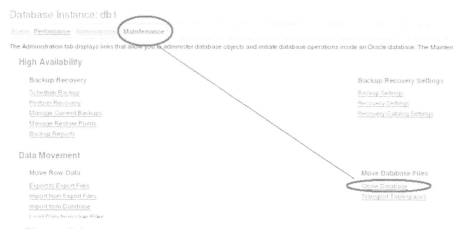

Figure 5.1: *Selection in the Maintenance Tab*

As a source type, select "A running database instance" and click Continue:

Figure 5.2: *Choice in Clone Database for Source Type*

In this step, provide the location for the working directory. The backup of the database will be stored in this directory. If the working directory needs to be deleted after the clone operation, select the first option. Below that, enter the username and password of the user who owns the Oracle software and click Next.

Clone Database: Source Working Directory

Source Database **db1**
Source Host **localhost.localdomain**

Cancel   Step 1 of 5   Next

Source Working Directory

A working directory on the source host is required in order to clone a running database. A backup is performed on the database and the backup files are stored in the working directory.

TIP The working directory can optionally be retained for future cloning operations to avoid doing another backup.

* Working Directory Location   /home/oracle/working_directory/

Subdirectory db1_1 will be created at this location

☐ Compress the backup datafiles in the working directory

Compression reduces backup file size and transfer time when cloning between hosts, but it may also slow down datafile backup and recomstion.

⦿ Delete db1_1 working directory after the cloning operation. Minimum temporary disk space required is 490 MB
This option requires only enough disk space to contain a backup of the largest datafile.

◯ Retain db1_1 working directory for a future cloning operation. Minimum disk space required is 950 MB
This option requires enough disk space to contain a full database backup.

Source Host Credentials

Enter the credentials of the user who owns the source database Oracle server installation.

* Username   oracle

* Password   ••••••••••

☑ Save as Preferred Credential

Figure 5.3: *Clone Database: Source Working Directory Screen*

In the next screen, enter the name of the new clone database and click Next:

Clone Database: Select Destination

Source Database **db1**
Source Host **localhost.localdomain**

Cancel   Back   Step 2 of 5   Next

Destination Database

* Global Database Name   db2

* Instance Name   db2

Database Storage   File System

Destination Host Credentials

Enter the credentials of the user who owns the Oracle installation in the Oracle Home selected below.

* Username   oracle

* Password   ••••••••••

Figure 5.4: *Clone Database: Select Destination Screen*

Now provide the destination for the database files of the clone database. If a different directory needs to be given, then click the Customize button. Next, select the network configuration file location and provide passwords for specific users.

Clone Database: Destination Options

Source Database **db1**
Source Host **localhost.localdomain**
Destination Host **localhost.localdomain**

(Cancel) (Back) Step 3 of 5 (Next)

Database File Locations

Specify the database file locations. The cloned database will reside on the same host as the source database. Optionally, you can customize the locations by clicking the Customize button.

Customize

Total Disk Space Required **950 MB**

The locations configuration has been automatically applied.

☑ Convert to Oracle Optimal Flexible Architecture (OFA)
The subdirectories will be created using Oracle Optimal Flexible Architecture. Click Customize to customize the subdirectory structure.

○ Use Oracle Managed Files (OMF)
The subdirectory files will be created using Oracle managed files. Click Customize to customize the database files and their base directory.

Network Configuration File Location

Specify the network configuration file location. The configuration files include listener.ora, tnsnames.ora, and sqlnet.ora. Clone Database will read these files and, if necessary, add configuration information about the destination database to listener.ora and tnsnames.ora.

• Configuration File Location /home/oracle/oracle/product/10.2.0/db_1/network/admin

Database Control Configuration

☐ Configure Enterprise Manager Database Control for this database

SYS Password	......	Confirm SYS Password	......
DBSNMP Password	......	Confirm DBSNMP Password	......
SYSMAN Password	......	Confirm SYSMAN Password	......
HTTP Port	5500		

Figure 5.5: *Clone Database: Destination Options Screen*

By clicking the Customize button, a different directory for every file of the database is able to be provided as follows:

Destination Options: Customize Destination Options

Source Database **db1**
Source Host **localhost.localdomain**
Destination Host **localhost.localdomain**

(Cancel) (OK)

Override database file locations or edit file names and locations below.

Datafiles

Set location for all files [   ] (Go)

Source Name	Tablespace	Status	Size (KB)	Destination Name
/home/oracle/oracle/product/10.2.0/db_1/oradata/db1/system01.dbf	SYSTEM	SYSTEM	491520	/home/oracle/new_clone/system01.dbf
/home/oracle/oracle/product/10.2.0/db_1/oradata/db1/undotbs01.dbf	UNDOTBS1	ONLINE	25600	/home/oracle/new_clone/undotbs01.dbf
/home/oracle/oracle/product/10.2.0/db_1/oradata/db1/sysaux01.dbf	SYSAUX	ONLINE	235520	/home/oracle/new_clone/sysaux01.dbf
/home/oracle/oracle/product/10.2.0/db_1/oradata/db1/users01.dbf	USERS	ONLINE	5120	/home/oracle/new_clone/users01.dbf

Tempfiles

Set location for all files [   ] (Go)

Source Name	Tablespace	Status	Size (KB)	Destination Name
/home/oracle/oracle/product/10.2.0/db_1/oradata/db1/temp01.dbf	TEMP	ONLINE	20480	/home/oracle/new_clone/temp01.dbf

Log Files

Set location for all files [   ] (Go)

Group	Source Member	Size (KB)	Destination Member
1	/home/oracle/oracle/product/10.2.0/db_1/oradata/db1/redo01.log	51200	/home/oracle/new_clone/redo01.log

Figure 5.6: *Customize Destination Options Screen*

Cloning Database Using Enterprise Manager

Here, Oracle schedules a job to clone the database. This job can be run immediately or be made to run anytime that is desired. Just click Next to make it run immediately.

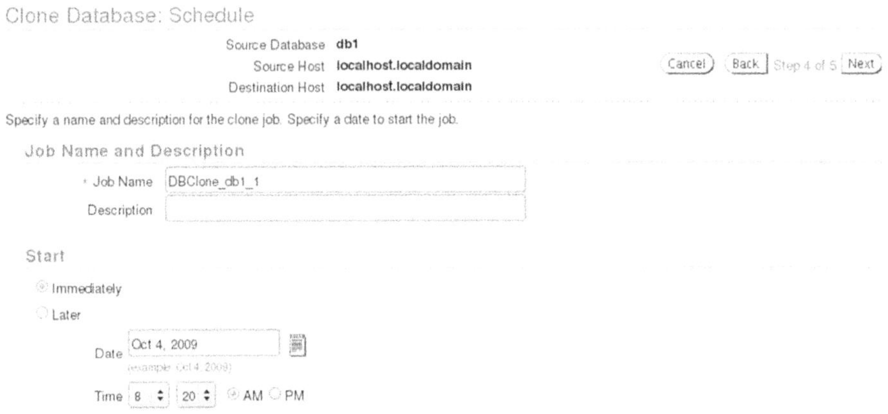

Figure 5.7: *Clone Database: Schedule*

This is the last page of configuring the clone of the database. Just click the Submit Job button and the clone process begins:

Figure 5.8: *Reviewing the Clone Database Process*

Here, a message that cloning has been started will appear:

Figure 5.9: *Clone Database Confirmation Message*

The status of the clone operation can be viewed by clicking on the View Status button:

Figure 5.10: *Viewing the Status of the Clone Operation*

Click on the name of the job to get more information about the job:

Figure 5.11: *Job Information Screen*

Click on the status of the job:

Cloning Database Using Enterprise Manager

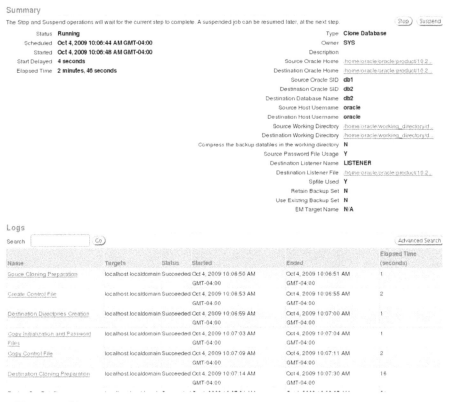

Figure 5.12: *Summary Status of the Job*

The clone operation has started and this shows that the steps that were performed were successful. Now press F5 to refresh the pages and see that the steps are performing automatically. At last, the final summary appears and the cloning process ends.

Souce Cloning Preparation	localhost.localdomain Succeeded Oct 4, 2009 10:06:50 AM GMT-04:00	Oct 4, 2009 10:06:51 AM GMT-04:00	1
Create Control File	localhost.localdomain Succeeded Oct 4, 2009 10:06:53 AM GMT-04:00	Oct 4, 2009 10:06:55 AM GMT-04:00	2
Destination Directories Creation	localhost.localdomain Succeeded Oct 4, 2009 10:06:59 AM GMT-04:00	Oct 4, 2009 10:07:00 AM GMT-04:00	1
Copy Initialization and Password Files	localhost.localdomain Succeeded Oct 4, 2009 10:07:03 AM GMT-04:00	Oct 4, 2009 10:07:04 AM GMT-04:00	1
Copy Control File	localhost.localdomain Succeeded Oct 4, 2009 10:07:09 AM GMT-04:00	Oct 4, 2009 10:07:11 AM GMT-04:00	2
Destination Cloning Preparation	localhost.localdomain Succeeded Oct 4, 2009 10:07:14 AM GMT-04:00	Oct 4, 2009 10:07:30 AM GMT-04:00	16
Backup One Datafile	localhost.localdomain Succeeded Oct 4, 2009 10:07:34 AM GMT-04:00	Oct 4, 2009 10:08:05 AM GMT-04:00	31
Restore One Datafile on Same Host	localhost.localdomain Succeeded Oct 4, 2009 10:08:09 AM GMT-04:00	Oct 4, 2009 10:08:41 AM GMT-04:00	32
Backup One Datafile	localhost.localdomain Succeeded Oct 4, 2009 10:08:45 AM GMT-04:00	Oct 4, 2009 10:08:48 AM GMT-04:00	3
Restore One Datafile on Same Host	localhost.localdomain Succeeded Oct 4, 2009 10:08:50 AM GMT-04:00	Oct 4, 2009 10:08:53 AM GMT-04:00	3
Backup One Datafile	localhost.localdomain Succeeded Oct 4, 2009 10:08:55 AM GMT-04:00	Oct 4, 2009 10:09:07 AM GMT-04:00	12
Restore One Datafile on Same Host	localhost.localdomain Succeeded Oct 4, 2009 10:09:11 AM GMT-04:00	Oct 4, 2009 10:09:22 AM GMT-04:00	11
Backup One Datafile	localhost.localdomain Succeeded Oct 4, 2009 10:09:26 AM GMT-04:00	Oct 4, 2009 10:09:28 AM GMT-04:00	2
Restore One Datafile on Same Host	localhost.localdomain Succeeded Oct 4, 2009 10:09:31 AM GMT-04:00	Oct 4, 2009 10:09:33 AM GMT-04:00	2
Skip Creating Standby Control File	localhost.localdomain Succeeded Oct 4, 2009 10:09:35 AM GMT-04:00	Oct 4, 2009 10:09:36 AM GMT-04:00	1
Archive Current Log for New Backup on Same Host	localhost.localdomain Succeeded Oct 4, 2009 10:09:41 AM GMT-04:00	Oct 4, 2009 10:09:44 AM GMT-04:00	3
Restore Current Logs for Existing Backup on Same Host	localhost.localdomain Succeeded Oct 4, 2009 10:09:46 AM GMT-04:00	Oct 4, 2009 10:09:49 AM GMT-04:00	3
Recover Database	localhost.localdomain Succeeded Oct 4, 2009 10:09:51 AM GMT-04:00	Oct 4, 2009 10:10:42 AM GMT-04:00	51
Add Temporary Files	localhost.localdomain Succeeded Oct 4, 2009 10:10:46 AM GMT-04:00	Oct 4, 2009 10:20:01 AM GMT-04:00	555
Skip Adding EM Target	localhost.localdomain Succeeded Oct 4, 2009 10:20:04 AM GMT-04:00	Oct 4, 2009 10:20:05 AM GMT-04:00	1
Cleanup Source Temporary Directory	localhost.localdomain Succeeded Oct 4, 2009 10:20:09 AM GMT-04:00	Oct 4, 2009 10:20:11 AM GMT-04:00	2

Figure 5.13: *Final Summary of the Clone Process*

Now connect to the db2 database and check the status of the instance to be sure that it was cloned successfully.

```
$ export ORACLE_SID=db2
$ sqlplus "/ as sysdba"
sys@DB2>
select
status
from
 v$instance;

status
------------
OPEN
```

The production database was successfully cloned.

Pre & Post Cloning Changes

- To avoid the confusion between the production and test/development databases, do not set the clone database name as a production database name.

- It is not mandatory to have the initialization parameter's value of the cloned instance similar to the production instance. Of course, the source, i.e. the production database, must be in archivelog mode for the duration of the cloning.

- It is not compulsory to have the cloned instance in archivelog mode because unnecessary archivelog files are generated which consume hard disk space.

- If the cloned instance crashes and needs to be recovered, it can easily be cloned again from the production database.

- After the clone, change the system users' passwords, i.e. SYS and SYSTEM, and any critical and application users' passwords.

- Disable the jobs which are not required to be run in the cloned instance.

- Change any application users' tables from the cloned database that are still referring the production database, i.e. server IP, port details, printer details and such.

Creating Standby Database Using RMAN

RMAN simplifies and automates the creation of the standby database. For this, it is enough to make some prerequisite changes and run the *duplicate target database for standby* command. The following example will show the main plan and step-by-step instruction on preparing a standby database on a different machine using RMAN. As some steps are the same with the previous database clone scenarios, those steps will be passed. Here are the main steps:

- Make a format of the backup to make backups to the specific destination

- Take a backup of the database with all archived redo log files

- Take a backup of the control file for the standby database

- Create necessary directories on the standby server

Oracle Backup and Recovery

- Create the initialization parameter, make necessary changes and copy it to the standby server

- Copy password file to the standby server

- Make changes to the network files on both servers

- Copy all backups to the standby server

- Start the standby database in nomount mode

- Connect to both the primary and standby database and run *duplicate target database for standby* command to create a standby database

- Recover the standby database

Now perform all the above steps one by one:

1. Create a directory (*/u02/rman_backup/*) in both servers and make the following changes in the RMAN configuration:

```
RMAN> show all;
configure controlfile autobackup on;
configure controlfile autobackup format for device type disk to
'/u02/rman_backup/ct_%F';
configure channel device type disk format
'/u02/rman_backup/testdb_backup_%U';
```

2. Take a backup of the target database:

```
RMAN> backup database plus archivelog delete input;
```

3. Take a backup of the current control file to use it in the standby database.

```
RMAN> backup current controlfile for standby format
 ='/u02/rman_backup/standby_control_%U';
```

It is not possible to create a standby database automatically after creating a standby backup of control file. If this is tried, the following error will appear after running the *duplicate database ... for standby* command:

```
RMAN-06026: some targets not found - aborting restore
RMAN-06024: no backup or copy of the control file found to restore
```
The reason for getting this error is explained in Metalink note 466321.1:

"When *dorecover* is specified in the duplicate for the *standby* command, then an *untilscn* is chosen. The *untilscn* is calculated by looking at the latest *scn* in the *v$archived_log* table. So the issue is, there was no switch of the archivelog after taking the *controlfile backup for standby*."

To keep from getting the following error during the standby database creation, do some redo log switches.

```
SQL>
alter
system switch logfile;

System altered.

SQL>
/

System altered.
SQL>
```

Get the last archived redo log sequence number and take a backup of newly created archived redo log files:

```
SQL>
select
MAX(sequence#)
 from
v$archived_log;

MAX(SEQUENCE#)
--------------
            36

RMAN> backup archivelog all delete input;
```

4. Refer to the "Creating a Duplicate Database on Remote Host" scenario in this chapter to create necessary directories on the standby server to change network files, copy password files and parameter files and copy all backups to the standby server.

5. Start the standby database in nomount mode using the changed parameter file as follows:

```
SQL>
 create
spfile from pfile ='/u02/rman_backup/pfile.ora';

File created.

SQL>
startup nomount

ORACLE instance started.
SQL>
```

6. Connect to both primary and standby databases and create the standby database as follows:

```
[oracle@localhost rman_backup]$ rman target sys/kamran auxiliary
sys/kamran@test

connected to target database: TEST (DBID=2018653477)
connected to auxiliary database: TEST (not mounted)

RMAN> run
{
        set until sequence =36;
        duplicate target database for standby dorecover nofilenamecheck;
}

<....output trimmed .....>
<....output trimmed .....>
archive log
filename=/u01/oracle/product/10.2.0/db_1/flash_recovery_area/TEST/archivelog
/2010_06_02/o1_mf_1_35_60dgx2pr_.arc thread=1 sequence=35
channel clone_default: deleting archive log(s)
archive log
filename=/u01/oracle/product/10.2.0/db_1/flash_recovery_area/TEST/archivelog
/2010_06_02/o1_mf_1_35_60dgx2pr_.arc recid=8 stamp=720601698
media recovery complete, elapsed time: 00:00:04
Finished recover at 02-JUN-10
Finished Duplicate Db at 02-JUN-10
RMAN>
```

As can be seen, RMAN applied archived redo log files until sequence 36. The sequence 35 was applied and recover has stopped.

7. Switch to the standby database and perform the recovery to apply all archived redo log files. Oracle applies archived redo log file number 36 and searches for the next archived redo log file which is not available for now:

```
SQL>
recover
standby database;

ORA-00279: change 459718 generated at 06/02/2010 06:08:39 needed for thread
1
ORA-00289: suggestion :
/u01/oracle/product/10.2.0/db_1/flash_recovery_area/TEST/archivelog/2010_06_
02/o
1_mf_1_36_%u_.arc
ORA-00280: change 459718 for thread 1 is in sequence #36

Specify log: {<RET>=suggested | filename | AUTO | CANCEL}
AUTO
ORA-00279: change 459735 generated at 06/02/2010 06:09:06 needed for thread
1
ORA-00289: suggestion :
/u01/oracle/product/10.2.0/db_1/flash_recovery_area/TEST/archivelog/2010_06_
02/o
1_mf_1_37_%u_.arc
ORA-00280: change 459735 for thread 1 is in sequence #37
ORA-00278: log file
```

```
'/u01/oracle/product/10.2.0/db_1/flash_recovery_area/TEST/archivelog/2010_06
_02/
o1_mf_1_36_60dgwkl0_.arc' no longer needed for this recovery


ORA-00308: cannot open archived log
'/u01/oracle/product/10.2.0/db_1/flash_recovery_area/TEST/archivelog/2010_06
_02/
o1_mf_1_37_%u_.arc'
ORA-27037: unable to obtain file status
Linux Error: 2: No such file or directory
Additional information: 3
```

8. Change the *log_archive_dest_2* parameter on the primary database to make archived redo log files sent to the standby server automatically:

```
SQL>
alter
system set log_archive_dest_2='service test optional reopen 30';

System altered.
SQL>
```

9. To test the standby database, create a table on the primary database and switch the redo log file. The archived redo log file is automatically copied to the standby side. Then open the standby database with read only mode and check the table:

```
SQL>
create
table tbl_test (id number );

Table created.

SQL>
insert into
tbl_test values (1);

1 row created.

SQL>
commit;

Commit complete.

SQL>
alter
system switch logfile;

System altered.

SQL>
select
max (sequence#)
from
v$archived_log;
```

```
MAX ( sequence #)
--------------
            37
SQL>
```

Switch to the standby server and run the *recover standby database* command. The shipped new archived redo log file will be automatically added.

```
SQL>
recover
standby database;

ORA-00279: change 459735 generated at 06/02/2010 06:09:06 needed for thread
1
ORA-00289: suggestion :
/u01/oracle/product/10.2.0/db_1/flash_recovery_area/TEST/archivelog/2010_06_
02/o
1_mf_1_37_%u_.arc
ORA-00280: change 459735 for thread 1 is in sequence #37

Specify log: {<RET>=suggested | filename | AUTO | CANCEL}
AUTO
ORA-00279: change 460659 generated at 06/02/2010 06:45:12 needed for thread
1
ORA-00289: suggestion :
/u01/oracle/product/10.2.0/db_1/flash_recovery_area/TEST/archivelog/2010_06_
02/o
1_mf_1_38_%u_.arc
ORA-00280: change 460659 for thread 1 is in sequence #38
ORA-00278: log file
'/u01/oracle/product/10.2.0/db_1/flash_recovery_area/TEST/archivelog/2010_06
_02/
o1_mf_1_37_60dhm0gx_.arc' no longer needed for this recovery

ORA-00308: cannot open archived log
'/u01/oracle/product/10.2.0/db_1/flash_recovery_area/TEST/archivelog/2010_06
_02/
o1_mf_1_38_%u_.arc'
ORA-27037: unable to obtain file status
Linux Error: 2: No such file or directory
Additional information: 3
```

Now open the database with read only mode and query the table:

```
SQL>
select
status
from
v$instance;

STATUS
------------
MOUNTED

SQL>
alter
```

```
database open read only;

Database altered.

SQL>
desc
tbl_test;

  Name                                    Null?    Type
  --------------------------------------  -------  --------------------------
  ID                                               NUMBER
SQL>
```

While creating the standby database, if the *dorecover* option is specified, RMAN automatically recovers the standby database by restoring necessary archived redo log files from backup. In both situations, RMAN mounts the standby database and does not put it on manual or managed recovery mode.

A standby database can be created on the same host with the primary database; however, Oracle does not recommend it. For this, define a different location of standby datafiles and use the *db_unique_name* initialization parameter in both databases.

Recovering Standby Database Using Incremental Backups

The standby database might be recovered using incremental backups taken from the primary database. For this, perform the following steps:

1. Take the current SCN value on the standby side:

```
SQL>
select
current_scn
from
v$database;

CURRENT_SCN
-----------
     485263
```

From the primary side, use the *backup incremental from scn* command and provide the SCN value taken from the standby database to take a backup of the changes made after the specified SCN value:

```
RMAN> backup incremental from scn 485263 database format
'/u02/inc_backup_%U';
```

Switch to the standby database and register the incremental backup using the *catalog* command:

```
RMAN> catalog start with '/u02/';
```

Now recover the standby database using the *noredo* option to apply only incremental backups:

```
RMAN> recover database noredo;
```

RMAN will apply only incremental backups to the standby database.

Then switch the redo log file on the primary database and apply it on the standby side:

```
# On the primary side
SQL>
alter
system switch logfile;

System altered.

#On the standby side
SQL>
recover
standby database;
```

Now the standby database has been recovered.

Resolving Archived Redo Log Gaps Using Incremental Backups

Imagine that due to the network failure, some archived redo log files were not shipped to the standby database and were deleted from the primary database according to the defined RMAN retention policy. Since the next generated archived redo log file cannot be jumped into before successfully applying all of them one by one in subsequent order, either create a standby database from scratch, or ...

Sure, there is another option. By applying the necessary incremental backup taken from the primary database, take the database forward and bypass applying missing archived redo log files. The following scenario shows the steps of recovering the standby database without having archived redo log files.

At first, there needs to be a standby database with missing redo log files. For this:

1. Change the *log_archive_dest_2* parameter on the primary site

2. Manually switch log files to create some archived redo log files

3. Delete generated archived redo log files from the primary site

First of all, check the *v$archived_log* file and get the last generated archived redo log sequence value on both databases, then change the *log_archive_dest_2* initialization parameter on the primary site to block archived redo log shipping to the standby site as follows:

```
# Run the following code on the primary database:
SQL>
 select
max(sequence#)
from
v$archived_log;

MAX(SEQUENCE#)
--------------
            54

# Run the following code on the standby database:
SQL>
select
 max(sequence#)
from
v$archived_log;

MAX(SEQUENCE#)
--------------
            54

SQL>
show
parameter log_archive_dest_2

NAME                          TYPE         VALUE
----------------------------- ------------ ----------------------------
log_archive_dest_2            string       service=test optional reopen=15

SQL>
alter
system set log_archive_dest_2='service=noservice';

System altered.

SQL>
```

```
show
parameter log_archive_dest_2;

NAME                          TYPE         VALUE
--------------------------    -----------  --------------------------
log_archive_dest_2            string       service=noservice
```

Now make some manual redo log switches and check the *v$archived_log* view on both sites again:

```
# Run the following codes on the primary database:
SQL>
alter
system switch logfile;

System altered.

SQL>
 /

System altered.


SQL>
/

System altered.

SQL>
select
 max(sequence#)
from
 v$archived_log;

MAX(SEQUENCE#)
--------------
            57
SQL>

# Run the following code on the standby database:
SQL>
select
 max(sequence#) FROM v$archived_log;

MAX(SEQUENCE#)
--------------
            54
```

This shows that the last three archived redo log files were not shipped to the standby site. Go to the primary site and delete the last generated three archived redo log files with sequence 55, 56 and 57:

```
[oracle@localhost 2010_06_06]$ rm -rf o1_mf_1_5[5-7]_60rp*
```

Now cancel the managed recovery operation on the standby site, take the last sequence value and shut down the standby database:

```
SQL>
alter
database recover managed standby database cancel;

SQL>
select

current_scn
from
v$database;

CURRENT_SCN
-----------
     507189

SQL>
shutdown immediate
```

Switch to the primary site and take an incremental backup of the database starting from the SCN value that has been taken from the standby database:

```
RMAN> backup incremental from scn 507189 database
FORMAT='/u02/rman_backup/incremental/incr_backup_%U';
```

Create the standby controlfile, change the *log_archive_dest_2* initialization parameter and switch the current redo log file:

```
SQL>
alter
database
create
standby controlfile as '/u02/rman_backup/standby_control.ctl';

SQL>
alter
system set log_archive_dest_2='service=test optional reopen=15';

System altered.

SQL>
alter
system switch logfile;
```

Copy the standby controlfile and incremental backup file to the standby side, start up the standby database in nomount mode and change the parameter file to make the instance use the standby control file:

```
SQL>
alter
```

```
system set control_files='/u02/rman_backup/standby_control.ctl'
SCOPE=spfile;

System altered.

SQL>
shutdown immediate
SQL>
startup
nomount
```

Mount the standby database and catalog the incremental backup to its repository:

```
SQL>
alter
database mount standby database;
RMAN> catalog ackuppiece'/u02/rman_backup/incr_backup_1mlfj8pq_1_1';
```

Now, recover the database using incremental backup:

```
RMAN> recover database;

channel ORA_DISK_1: starting incremental datafile backupset restore
channel ORA_DISK_1: reading from backup piece
/u02/rman_backup/incr_backup_1mlfj8pq_1_1
channel ORA_DISK_1: restored backup piece 1
piece handle=/u02/rman_backup/incr_backup_1mlfj8pq_1_1
tag=TAG20100606T224202
channel ORA_DISK_1: restore complete, elapsed time: 00:00:02

starting media recovery

archive log thread 1 sequence 58 is already on disk as file
/u01/oracle/product/10.2.0/db_1/flash_recovery_area/TEST/archivelog/2010_06_
07/o1_mf_1_58_60s4sjbc_.arc
archive log
filename=/u01/oracle/product/10.2.0/db_1/flash_recovery_area/TEST/archivelog
/2010_06_07/o1_mf_1_58_60s4sjbc_.arc thread=1 sequence=58
unable to find archive log
archive log thread=1 sequence=59
RMAN-00571: ===========================================================
RMAN-00569: =============== ERROR MESSAGE STACK FOLLOWS ===============
RMAN-00571: ===========================================================
RMAN-03002: failure of recover command at 06/07/2010 02:38:36
RMAN-06054: media recovery requesting unknown log: thread 1 seq 59 lowscn
508306
RMAN> exit
```

RMAN tries to apply archived redo log with sequence 59 which was not generated yet on the primary database. Perform a manual redo log switch on the primary database. The new archived redo log file is, with sequence 59, created and shipped to the standby server. Take the current *scn* on the primary database to compare it with the standby database:

```
SQL>
alter
system switch logfile;

System altered.

SQL>
select
current_scn
from
v$database;

CURRENT_SCN
-----------
     511308
SQL>
```

Now switch to the standby database and run the *recover standby database* command. RMAN looks for the next archived redo log file and apply it automatically:

```
SQL>
recover
standby database;
```

Then query the current SCN value on the standby database:

```
SQL>
select
current_scn
from
v$database;

CURRENT_SCN
-----------
     511301
SQL>
```

Conclusion

In this chapter, the method of cloning a database using the *duplicate database* command of RMAN has been shown. The database has been cloned to the remote and local host with the same and different directory structures. Then the new feature of Oracle 11g – a network enabled database clone without having any backups – was examined where the database was cloned using live datafiles.

Next, the way of the database clone was shown using Enterprise Manager. The end of the chapter demonstrated the standby database creation steps using the *duplicate database for standby* command. The next chapter will focus on transporting tablespaces and the whole database to a different platform using RMAN.

Transportable Tablespaces and Databases

There are different solutions to satisfy the need to transport the data between databases in Oracle. Data Pump can be used to export logical backup of the database and import it to another database or database links can be used to copy the objects between databases. But these basic methods are more time consuming than a more advanced way, particularly if dealing with terabytes of data.

Transportable Tablespace (TTS) Feature

The advanced way to do this is by using the Transportable Tablespace (TTS) feature of RMAN. Using this feature, the datafiles which contain actual data can be copied, thus making the migration faster. This feature was firstly introduced in Oracle 8i which allowed copying the data between databases that used the same block size faster than a traditional export/import.

In version 9i, Oracle introduced a multiple block size feature, and so removed that restriction from TTS. In Oracle 10g Release 1, the Cross Platform transportable tablespace feature was introduced that allows the moving of datafiles between platforms that use different endian formats. In Oracle 10g Release 2, a transportable database feature was introduced which allows transporting the whole database to the different platform with the same endian format.

This chapter will explain and demonstrate in practical terms the following TTS methods:

- Transporting tablespaces between two databases with the same platform using both RMAN backups and live datafiles

- Transporting a single tablespace between two databases running on the different platforms (Cross-Platform transportable tablespace)

- Transporting the whole database to the different platform (Cross-Platform transportable database)

The first scenario is divided into two parts: in the first part, the tablespace is transported using RMAN backup, while in the second part, no backup is used and tablespaces are copied from the running database instance. In the second scenario, a cross-platform transportation of the tablespace from Solaris OS to Linux is performed. In the third scenario, the whole database that runs on Windows OS is transported to the Linux OS.

Transportable Tablespace can be used to:

- Transport the tablespace from the test environment to the production database

- Transport data from a production database to a data warehouse system

- Publish data to customers

- Perform Tablespace Point in Time Recovery (TSPITR)

- Upgrade the database to the new release

The following are the limitations of the Transporting Tablespace feature:

- It is not possible to transport the system tablespace and the objects that are owned by the user SYS.

- Both databases must be running with a *compatible* parameter set to 10.0 or higher.

- In Oracle 10g, the tablespace must be set to read/write so it can be transported to another platform. However this restriction is not available in Oracle 11g. The tablespace does not have to be put in read/write mode before transporting it to another platform in Oracle 11g.

- The character set and national character set must be the same for both source and target databases.

- The tablespace cannot be transported that is already present in the target database until and unless either the source tablespace or target tablespace is renamed before the tablespace transport.

Transportable Tablespace (TTS) Feature

Transporting Tablespace Using RMAN Backups

Starting from Oracle 10gR2, RMAN simplified tablespace transportation by providing the *transport tablespace* command which automatically does almost everything that was performed in prior releases by the DBA to transport the tablespace. The main advantage of this command after it is automated is that the tablespace does not need to be put in the read-only mode. To use this command, only the necessary RMAN backups are needed. Look at the following scenario and perform tablespace transportation using RMAN backups right now!

Note: This method is similar to that used for TSPITR (Tablespace Point In Time Recovery) using an auxiliary instance for the required tablespace.

Scenario 1

Bob received a request to transport the whole tablespace with all its datafiles and objects from one database (TTSone) to another (test) with no downtime. Therefore, he decides to use the *transport tablespace* command of RMAN as follows:

1. Connect to the first database (TTSone), and then create a new tablespace and one object in it. This tablespace is transported to the second database. Do not create the table with the SYS user, because SYS-owned objects are not transported by transportable tablespaces.

```
SQL>
 create
 tablespace tbs_test datafile
'/u01/oracle/product/10.2.0/db_1/oradata/TTSone/tbs_test01.dbf' SIZE 1M;

Tablespace created.

SQL>
conn
 test/test

Connected.

SQL>
create
 table tbl_test (id number) tablespace tbs_test;

Table created.

SQL>
insert into
 tbl_test values(1);
```

```
1 row created.

SQL>
commit;

Commit complete.
```

2. As RMAN needs to put the dump file that contains metadata of the transported tablespace and datafile in the auxiliary instance, create a folder for both files. Moreover, create an Oracle directory that will be used in the RMAN command to define the output folder of the *data pump export* file. Do all the above actions in the first database as follows:

```
SQL>
create directory
 ora_dump
as
 '/home/oracle/ora_dump';

Directory created.

SQL>
[oracle@localhost ~]$ cd /home/oracle/
[oracle@localhost ~]$ mkdir ora_dump aux
```

3. Now connect to RMAN and back up the database:

```
RMAN> backup database plus archivelog;
```

4. Get the current SCN number, insert one row into the table. This is done because the tablespace will be transported until the above SCN number and should not see the second added row.

```
SQL>
select
 current_scn
from
 v$database;

CURRENT_SCN
-----------
     459822

SQL>
conn
 test/test

Connected.

SQL>
insert into
 tbl_test values(2);

1 row created.
```

```
SQL>
commit;

Commit complete.

SQL> select * from
 tbl_test;

        ID
----------
         1
         2
```

5. Now connect to RMAN and run the following commands to create a transportable set of the newly created tablespace:

```
run
      {
               transport tablespace 'tbs_test'
               auxiliary destination '/home/oracle/aux'
               tablespace destination '/home/oracle/aux'
               datapump directory ora_dump
               dump file 'tbs_dump.dmp'
               export log 'tbs_log.log'
               import script 'tbs_script.sql'
               until scn 459822;
      }
```

Using the above commands, RMAN performs the following:

- Creates transportable tablespace set for the tablespace tbs_test

- Uses the */home/oracle/aux* folder to store the files that are used for the auxiliary instance

- Uses the */home/oracle/aux* folder to store the datafiles of the transported tablespace which will be used on the second host during import process

- Creates a dump file for the metadata of the objects that are stored in the transported tablespace as well as the export logfile and the *sql* script that is used to automate the import process

- Recovers the tablespace up to the specified SCN number

After running the above run block, RMAN automatically performs the following actions:

1. Creates an automatic instance with random name and default initialization parameters using the *auxiliary instance* parameter of the run block to store necessary datafiles (and control file) as follows:

```
Creating automatic instance, with SID='xqhB'

initialization parameters used for automatic instance:
db_name=TTSONE
compatible=10.2.0.1.0
db_block_size=8192
db_files=200
db_unique_name=tspitr_TTSONE_xqhB
large_pool_size=1M
<....output trimmed .....>
```

2. Starts the instance in nomount mode:

```
starting up automatic instance TTSONE
Oracle instance started
Total System Global Area      201326592 bytes
Fixed Size                      1218508 bytes
Variable Size                 146802740 bytes
Database Buffers               50331648 bytes
Redo Buffers                    2973696 bytes
Automatic instance created
```

3. Restores control file from the backup file and starts the database in mount mode as follows:

```
channel ORA_AUX_DISK_1: starting datafile backupset restore
channel ORA_AUX_DISK_1: restoring control file
<....output trimmed .....>
```

4. Restores system, undo and sysaux tablespaces and datafiles that belong to the transported tablespace set:

```
<....output trimmed .....>
restoring datafile 00001 to
/home/oracle/aux/TSPITR_TTSONE_XQHB/datafile/o1_mf_system_%u_.dbf
restoring datafile 00002 to
/home/oracle/aux/TSPITR_TTSONE_XQHB/datafile/o1_mf_undotbs1_%u_.dbf
restoring datafile 00003 to
/home/oracle/aux/TSPITR_TTSONE_XQHB/datafile/o1_mf_sysaux_%u_.dbf
restoring datafile 00005 to /home/oracle/aux/tbs_test01.dbf
<....output trimmed .....>
```

5. Recovers datafiles by applying the necessary archived redo log files:

```
Starting recover at 02-APR-10
using channel ORA_AUX_DISK_1

starting media recovery
archive log thread 1 sequence 8 is already on disk as file
/u01/oracle/product/10.2.0/db_1/flash_recovery_area/TTSONE/archivelog/2010_0
4_02/o1_mf_1_8_5vd85l8w_.arc
<....output trimmed .....>
<....output trimmed .....>
media recovery complete, elapsed time: 00:00:01
Finished recover at 02-APR-10
```

6. Opens the auxiliary instance with the *resetlogs* option:

```
<....output trimmed .....>
```

```
alter clone database open resetlogs;
<....output trimmed .....>
```

7. Places the transported tablespace in read-only mode:

```
<....output trimmed .....>
sql statement: alter tablespace tbs_test read only
<....output trimmed .....>
```

8. Uses Data Pump to get the metadata of the objects in the transported tablespace:

```
Starting "sys"."sys_export_transportable_01":
userid="/********@(description=(address=(protocol=beq)(program=/u01/oracle/p
roduct/10.2.0/db_1//bin/oracle)(argv0=oraclexqhb)(args=\(description=\(local
=yes\)\(address=\(protocol=beq\)\)\)\))(envs=oracle_sid=xqhb))(connect_data=(s
id=xqhb))) as sysdba" transport_tablespaces= tbs_test dumpfile=tbs_dump.dmp
directory=ora_dump logfile=tbs_log.log
processing object type transportable_export/plugts_blk
processing object type transportable_export/table
<....output trimmed .....>
dump file set for sys.sys_export_transportable_01 is:
  /home/oracle/ora_dump/tbs_dump.dmp
```

9. Creates a *sql* script that automates the import procedure of the tablespace set on the target database using the *dbms_streams_tablespace_adm* package:

```
<....output trimmed .....>
-------------------------------------------------------------
-- Start of sample PL/SQL script for importing the tablespaces
-------------------------------------------------------------

-- creating directory objects
create directory streams$dirobj$1 as  '/home/oracle/aux/';
/* PL/SQL Script to import the exported tablespaces */
DECLARE
  -- the datafiles
  tbs_files    dbms_streams_tablespace_adm.file_set;
  cvt_files    dbms_streams_tablespace_adm.file_set;
<....output trimmed .....>
<....output trimmed .....>
-------------------------------------------------------------
-- End of sample PL/SQL script
-------------------------------------------------------------
```

10. Removes all files of the auxiliary instance:

```
<....output trimmed .....>
Removing automatic instance
shutting down automatic instance
Oracle instance shut down
Automatic instance removed
auxiliary instance file /home/oracle/aux/cntrl_tspitr_TTSONE_xqhB.f deleted
auxiliary instance file
/home/oracle/aux/TSPITR_TTSONE_XQHB/datafile/o1_mf_system_5vd8mjgm_.dbf
deleted
<....output trimmed .....>
```

```
An auxiliary instance is being automatically created to perform TSPITR
The ORACLE_SID of the auxiliary instance is: xqhB
If for any reason this instance is not removed automatically
Do the following for Windows platform
  - Connect to target instance used for TSPITR
  SQL>
execute
 dbms_backup_restore.manageAuxInstance(' xqhB ',1)
Do the following for non-Windows platform
  - Set ORACLE_SID to: xqhB
  - sqlplus '/ as sysdba'
  SQL>
shutdown abort
Auxiliary instance with ORACLE_SID: xqhB has been shutdown
```

Now switch to the second database and create the folders
/home/oracle/ora_dump and */home/oracle/aux*, copy all files from the source
server to the target server at the same location as they were in the source
server, create an Oracle directory and run the *sql* script that was generated in
the previous step:

```
SQL>
create directory
 ora_dump
as
 '/home/oracle/ora_dump';

Directory created.

SQL>
@/home/oracle/aux/tbs_script.sql

Directory created.

PL/SQL procedure successfully completed.

Directory dropped.

SQL>
select
 name
from
 v$tablespace;

NAME
-----------------------------
system
undotbs1
sysaux
users
temp
tbs_test
6 rows selected.
```

```
SQL>
conn
 test/test

Connected.

SQL>
select * from
 tbl_test;

        ID
----------
         1
SQL>
```

This shows how RMAN simplified and automated tablespace transformation using this simple command: *transport tablespace*. In this example, the tablespace has been successfully transported between two databases and recovered up to a specific *SCN value*. Remember that the second row has been added to the table after getting the *scn* value and as that *scn* value has been recovered, the second row was not applied.

Transporting Tablespace Manually Without RMAN Backups

If RMAN backup is not present, which may be used to create a Transportable Tablespace Set, live datafiles can be used instead. However, the one disadvantage of this procedure is that the transported tablespaces should be taken to the read-only mode and all steps that were performed by RMAN in the previous example should be performed by the DBA manually. Here is an outline of this procedure:

- Verify the self-contained status of the tablespaces using the *dbms_tts.transport_set_check* procedure

- Place the tablespace in the read-only mode

- Take metadata of all objects that are stored in transported tablespace using Data Pump

- Transfer all datafiles that consist in the transported tablespace and export dump to the target server

- Import metadata of the tablespace to the target database

- Bring the transported tablespaces to the read/write mode

Now transport the tablespace to the new host using live datafiles:

1. Create a new tablespace and new user as in the previous example:

```
SQL>
create tablespace
 tbs_test_manual datafile
'/u01/oracle/product/10.2.0/db_1/oradata/TTSone/tbs_test_manual01.dbf'  SIZE
1M;

Tablespace created.

SQL>
grant dba to
 test
identified by
 test;

Grant succeeded.
```

2. Though this step is not necessary when transporting the tablespace, to demonstrate the self-contained object, create a table with SYS user, create another table and a foreign key for the first table that references the second one, run the *transport_set_check* procedure and check the *transport_set_violations* view as follows:

```
SQL>
show user

user is "SYS"

SQL>
create table
 tbl_test (id number) tablespace tbs_test_manual;

Table created.

SQL>
create table
 tbl_test2 (id number primary key);

Table created.

SQL>
alter table
 tbl_test add constraint fk_tbl_test foreign key (id) references
tbl_test2(id);

Table altered.

SQL>
exec
dbms_tts.transport_set_check(ts_list=>'tbs_test_manual',incl_constraints=>tr
ue);
```

```
PL/SQL procedure successfully completed.

SQL>
select * from
 transport_set_violations;


violations
---------------------------------------------------------------------
Constraint fk_tbl_test between table sys.tbl_test2 in tablespace system and
table sys.tbl_test in tablespace tbs_test_manual
sys owned object tbl_test in tablespace tbs_test_manual not allowed in
pluggable set
```

It is not possible to transport the table which is owned by the SYS user or which has reference to the objects that do not belong to the transported tablespace set.

3. If the previous step regarding the self-contained object has been done, then drop both tables that are owned by the SYS user, connect with the new user and create a table at the newly created tablespace, then use the *dbms_tts.transport_set_check* function to see whether the tablespace could be transported with no issues.

> **Note:** Checking and verifying that all references are self-contained is highly recommended. Thus, referential integrity constraints on data can be maintained by ensuring that the transported set preserves the constraints (indexes).

```
SQL>
drop table
 tbl_test;

Table dropped.

SQL>
drop table
 tbl_test2;

Table dropped.

SQL>
conn
 test/test

Connected.

SQL>
create table
 tbl_test (id number) tablespace tbs_test_manual;
```

```
Table created.

SQL>
exec
sys.dbms_tts.transport_set_check(ts_list=>'tbs_test_manual',incl_constraints
=>true);
PL/SQL procedure successfully completed.

SQL>
select *from
 sys.transport_set_violations;

no rows selected
```

4. Take the tablespace to read-only mode:

```
SQL>
alter tablespace
 tbs_test_manual read only;

Tablespace altered.
SQL>
```

5. Use Data Pump to export the metadata of the tablespace and copy the datafile to the different location. This datafile will be transferred to the second database.

```
SQL>
create directory
 ora_dump
as
 '/home/oracle/ora_dump';

Directory created.
SQL>
exit

[oracle@localhost    ~]$    expdp    test/test    dumpfile=tbs_test_manual
directory=ora_dump transport_tablespaces=tbs_test_manual;

<.....output trimmed .....>
<.....output trimmed .....>
starting "test"."sys_export_transportable_01":  test/********
dumpfile=tbs_test_manual directory=ora_dump
transport_tablespaces=tbs_test_manualprocessing object type
transportable_export/plugts_blk
processing object type transportable_export/table
processing object type transportable_export/post_instance/plugts_blk
master table "test"."sys_export_transportable_01" successfully
loaded/unloaded
************************************************************************
Dump file set for test.sys_export transportable 01 is:
  /home/oracle/ora_dump/tbs_test_manual.dmp
job "test"."sys_export_transportable_01" successfully completed at 08:52:00

[oracle@localhost ~]$ cp
/u01/oracle/product/10.2.0/db_1/oradata/TTSone/tbs_test_manual01.dbf
/home/oracle/ora_dump/
```

Transporting Tablespace Manually Without RMAN Backups   **273**

6. Make the tablespace read/write:

```
SQL>
alter tablespace
 tbs_test_manual read write;

Tablespace altered.
SQL>
```

7. Copy the dump file and datafiles of the transported tablespace to the second server and switch over to it:

```
[oracle@localhost ~]$ scp /home/oracle/ora_dump/*
second_server:/home/oracle/ora_dump/
```

8. Create the same user, OS and an Oracle directory on the second host and use Data Pump to import the tablespace set:

```
[oracle@localhost ora_dump]$ impdp test/test
transport_datafiles='/home/oracle/ora_dump/tbs_test_manual01.dbf'

directory=ora_dump dumpfile=tbs_test_manual.dmp
<.....output trimmed .....>
<.....output trimmed .....>
master table "test"."sys_import_transportable_02" successfully
loaded/unloaded
starting "test"."sys_import_transportable_02":  test/********
transport_datafiles=/home/oracle/ora_dump/tbs_test_manual01.dbf
directory=ora_dump dumpfile=tbs_test_manual.dmp
processing object type transportable_export/plugts_blk
processing object type transportable_export/table
processing object type transportable_export/post_instance/plugts_blk
job "test"."sys_import_transportable_02" successfully completed at 09:32:15
[oracle@localhost ora_dump]$
```

Now, check the tablespace and the table on the second server:

```
SQL>
select
 name
from
 v$tablespace;

NAME
-----------------------------
system
undotbs1
sysaux
users
temp
tbs_test_manual
6 rows selected.

SQL>
conn
 test/test
```

```
Connected.

SQL>
desc
 tbl_test;

 Name                                    Null?    Type
 --------------------------------- -------- ---------------------------
 ID                                                NUMBER
SQL>
```

Transporting the Tablespace across Different Platforms

Scenario 2

Bob gets a call from his IT Manager, "Hi Bob. We need to plug the tablespace from the production database that runs on Solaris OS into the data warehouse system that runs on Linux OS (Solaris->Linux). We also need to get the tablespace from the warehouse system and plug it into the test server that runs on Windows OS for testing purposes (Linux->Windows). Please try to finish this request by the end of the day."

Having received these requests, Bob decides to use the cross-platform tablespace transportation method to transport the whole tablespace from one platform to another and vice versa. When the tablespace is transporting to a different platform, it should be converted to match the destination platform type. RMAN provides two commands for the conversion of the tablespaces:

■ Convert tablespace: Used to convert the whole tablespace (with all its datafiles) on the source host

■ Convert datafile: Used to convert specific datafiles on the destination host

In this section, both methods will be tried as follows:

■ Transporting the tablespace from Solaris to Linux using the first method (convert tablespace)

■ Transporting the tablespace from Linux to Windows using the second method (convert datafile)

This is further illustrated in Figure 6.1:

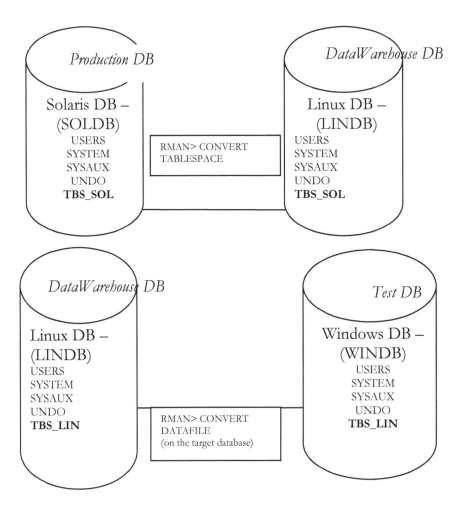

Figure 6.1: *Transporting Tablespaces from Solaris to Linux and from Linux to Windows*

In the following sections, three different databases will be used:

- SOLDB: Production database that runs on Solaris OS

- LINDB: DataWarehouse database that runs on Linux OS

- WINDB: Test database that runs on Windows OS

Using the *convert tablespace* Command

The following scenario involves transporting the tablespace from the Solaris OS to the Linux OS. All steps will be the same as in the previous scenario where a manual transport of the tablespace was done with live datafiles.

1. Login to the database that is running on Solaris OS, and create a tablespace that will be transferred to the target server. Then create a user and an object on that tablespace:

```
[oracle@localhost ~]$ export ORACLE_SID=SOLDB
[oracle@localhost ~]$ sqlplus "/ as sysdba"
SQL>
create tablespace
 tbs_sol datafile '/export/home/oracle//oradata/soldb/tbs_sol01.dbf' size
1M;

Tablespace created.

SQL>
grant dba to
 test
identified by
 test;

Grant succeeded.

SQL>
conn
 test/test

Connected.

SQL>
create table
 tbl_sol (id number) tablespace tbs_sol;

Table created.
SQL>
```

2. Verify the self-contained status of the tablespace, place it in read-only mode, create the necessary directory object and use Data Pump to export the metadata of the objects of that tablespace:

```
SQL>
execute
 sys.dbms_tts.transport_set_check('tbs_sol',true);

PL/SQL procedure successfully completed.

SQL>
elect * from
 sys.transport_set_violations;
```

```
no rows selected

SQL>
alter tablespace
 tbs_sol read only;

Tablespace altered.

SQL>
create directory
 ora_dump AS '/export/home/oracle';

Directory created.

SQL>
exit
bash-3.00$ expdp test/test dumpfile=tbs_sol.dmp directory=ora_dump
transport_tablespaces=tbs_sol
Starting "test"."sys_export_transportable_01":  test/********
dumpfile=tbs_sol.dmp directory=ora_dump transport_tablespaces=tbs_sol
processing object type transportable_export/plugts_blk
processing object type transportable_export/table
processing object type transportable_export/post_instance/plugts_blk
master table "test"."sys_export_transportable_01" successfully
loaded/unloaded
********************************************************************
Dump file set for test.sys_export_transportable_01 is:
  /export/home/oracle/tbs_sol.dmp
job "test"."sys_export_transportable_01" successfully completed at 15:38:37
bash-3.00$
```

3. In this step, use the *convert tablespace* command with the necessary platform
    name where the conversion should be performed. Use Linux IA (32-bit)
    platform name in this conversion process:

```
RMAN> convert tablespace tbs_sol
2> to platform 'linux ia (32-bit)'
3> db_file_name_convert '/export/home/oracle/oradata/soldb'
'/export/home/oracle';

Starting backup at 11-APR-10
using target database control file instead of recovery catalog
allocated channel: ORA_DISK_1
channel ORA_DISK_1: sid=141 devtype=DISK
channel ORA_DISK_1: starting datafile conversion
input datafile fno=00005 name=/export/home/ oradata/soldb/tbs_sol01.dbf
converted datafile=/export/home/oracle/tbs_sol01.dbf
channel ORA_DISK_1: datafile conversion complete, elapsed time: 00:00:01
Finished backup at 11-APR-10
RMAN>
```

4. Place the tablespace to read/write mode, copy the dump file and convert
    datafiles to the target server. Then create a user and directory object on
    the target database and use Data Pump to import the tablespace to the
    target database:

```
SQL>
```

```
alter tablespace
 tbs_sol read write;

Tablespace altered.
SQL>
-- Perform the following steps on the target database after copying the
converted datafiles and export dump file to it
[oracle@localhost ~]$ export ORACLE_SID=LINDB
[oracle@localhost ~]$ sqlplus "/ as sysdba"

SQL>
grant dba to
 test
identified by
 test;

Grant succeeded.

SQL>
create or replace directory
 ora_dump AS '/home/oracle/ora_dump';

Directory created.

[oracle@localhost ~]$ impdp test/test dumpfile=tbs_sol.dmp
directory=ora_dump transport_datafiles='/home/oracle/ora_dump/tbs_sol01.dbf'
<......output omitted ......>
<......output omitted ......>
Processing object type transportable_export/plugts_blk
processing object type transportable_export/table
processing object type transportable_export/post_instance/plugts_blk
job "test"."sys_import_transportable_01" successfully completed at 11:47:23

SQL>
select
 name
from
 v$tablespace;

NAME
-----------------------------
system
undotbs1
sysaux
users
temp
tbs_sol
6 rows selected.

SQL>
conn
 test/test

Connected.

SQL>
desc
 tbl_sol;
```

```
Name                                    Null?    Type
-------------------------------- -------- ------------------------
 ID                                               NUMBER
SQL>
```

The tablespace was successfully converted and plugged into the second database that is running on the different platform.

If the size of the tablespace is huge and there is more than one datafile in the tablespace, then add *parallelism* and *format* options to run the process in any parallel degree that is desired and generate user defined file names. In the following command, convert the tablespace *tbs_sol_two*, which has three datafiles, into five parallel sessions and user-defined filenames:

```
SQL>
select
 tablespace_name, name
from
 v$datafile_header
where
 tablespace_name='tbs_sol_two';

TABLESPACE_NAME                  NAME
-------------------------------- --------------------------------
tbs_sol_two                      /export/home/oracle/ oradata/soldb/tbs_sol_1.dbf

tbs_sol_two                      /export/home/oracle/ oradata/soldb/tbs_sol_2.dbf

TBS_SOL_TWO                      /export/home/oracle/ oradata/soldb/tbs_sol_3.dbf
SQL>

RMAN> convert tablespace tbs_sol_two
2> to platform 'linux ia (32-bit)'
3> parallelism 5
4> format '/tmp/converted/file_%N_%f';

Starting backup at 12-APR-10
using channel ORA_DISK_1
using channel ORA_DISK_2
using channel ORA_DISK_3
using channel ORA_DISK_4
using channel ORA_DISK_5
channel ORA_DISK_1: starting datafile conversion
input datafile fno=00006 name=/export/home/oracle/ oradata/soldb/tbs_sol_1.dbfchannel ORA_DISK_2:
starting datafile conversion
input datafile fno=00007 name=/export/home/oracle/ oradata/soldb/tbs_sol_2.dbfchannel ORA_DISK_3:
starting datafile conversion
input datafile fno=00008 name=/export/home/oracle/ oradata/soldb/tbs_sol_3.dbfconverted
datafile=/tmp/converted/file_TBS_SOL_TWO_6
channel ORA_DISK_1: datafile conversion complete, elapsed time: 00:00:00
converted datafile=/tmp/converted/file_TBS_SOL_TWO_7
channel ORA_DISK_2: datafile conversion complete, elapsed time: 00:00:00
converted datafile=/tmp/converted/file_TBS_SOL_TWO_8
channel ORA_DISK_3: datafile conversion complete, elapsed time: 00:00:01
Finished backup at 12-APR-10
RMAN>

bash-3.00$ ls -ltr
total 6192

-rw-r-----  1 oracle  dba   1056768 apr 12 09:49 file_tbs_sol_two_6
-rw-r-----  1 oracle  dba   1056768 apr 12 09:49 file_tbs_sol_two_7
-rw-r-----  1 oracle  dba   1056768 apr 12 09:49 file_tbs_sol_two_8
```

Using the *convert datafile* Command on the Destination Host

In case a single datafile or set of datafiles needs to be converted to any platform that RMAN supports, use the *convert datafile … to platform* command on the destination host. Since all the steps are the same as in the previous scenario, only the *rman* command that will be used on the destination host (Windows OS) to convert the datafile that was copied from the source host (Linux OS) will be shown. Here are two options:

One is to use the *to platform* command and mention the platform name to which the conversion is going to be performed:

```
RMAN> convert datafile 'c:\test\tbs_lin01.dbf'
2> to platform 'microsoft windows ia (32-bit)'
3> format 'c:\tmp\file_%U';
```

The other is to use the *from platform* command and mention the platform name from which the conversion is being performed:

```
RMAN> convert datafile 'c:\test\tbs_lin01.dbf'
2> from platform 'linux ia (32-bit)'
3> format 'c:\tmp\file_%U';
```

If an attempt is made to convert the datafile on the source host (Linux OS) using the TO PLATFORM clause to the Windows OS, the following error occurs:

```
RMAN> convert datafile
'/u01/oracle/product/10.2.0/db_1/oradata/lindb/tbs_lin01.dbf'
2> to platform 'microsoft windows ia (32-bit)'
3> format '/tmp/converted_to_win_%U';

Starting backup at 07-APR-10
using channel ORA_DISK_1
RMAN-00571: ===========================================================
RMAN-00569: =============== ERROR MESSAGE STACK FOLLOWS ===============
RMAN-00571: ===========================================================
RMAN-03002: failure of backup command at 04/07/2010 16:45:41
RMAN-06595: platform name 'Microsoft Windows IA (32-bit)' does not match
database platform name 'Linux IA (32-bit)'
```

Cross-Platform Database Migration

Starting from 10gR2, Oracle introduced the next magical feature of RMAN: its ability to convert the database from one platform to a different one which shares the same endian format. This feature is called cross-platform database migration. It is very easy and can be performed with some basic steps to convert the whole database from one platform to another. The following scenario explains step-by-step the mechanism of database migration from Windows OS (Source) to Linux OS (Target) using the *convert database* command of RMAN.

Scenario 3

Bob got a call from his IT manager "Hi Bob. Our application developers created a big project that uses an Oracle database which runs on Windows OS. The whole project should be migrated to the Linux OS. It is very urgent, so try to finish it before the end of the day."

After receiving this call, Bob decides to use RMAN's cross platform migration feature to migrate the whole Oracle database that runs on Windows OS to the Linux OS. Here are the following steps to perform the migration process.

1. To convert the database from one platform to another, the endian format of both databases should be the same. So as a first step, check the *v$transportable_platform* view for both platforms.

```
SQL>
column
 platform_name
format
 a35
SQL>
set
 pagesize 1000
SQL>
select * from
 v$transportable_platform
order by
 2;

PLATFORM_ID PLATFORM_NAME                       ENDIAN_FORMAT
----------- ----------------------------------- --------------
          6 AIX-Based Systems (64-bit)          Big
         16 Apple Mac OS                        Big
         15 HP Open VMS                         Little
          5 HP Tru64 UNIX                       Little
          3 HP-UX (64-bit)                      Big
          4 HP-UX IA (64-bit)                   Big
         18 IBM Power Based Linux               Big
```

```
 9 IBM zSeries Based Linux            Big
13 Linux 64-bit for AMD               Little
10 Linux IA (32-bit)                  Little
11 Linux IA (64-bit)                  Little
12 Microsoft Windows 64-bit for AMD   Little
 7 Microsoft Windows IA (32-bit)      Little
 8 Microsoft Windows IA (64-bit)      Little
17 Solaris Operating System (x86)     Little
 1 Solaris[tm] OE (32-bit)            Big
 2 Solaris[tm] OE (64-bit)            Big

17 rows selected.
```

It is seen from the output that both the Windows and Linux operating systems are in the little endian format. So in this case, RMAN can be easily used to convert the whole database.

2. Bring database to the mount mode and open it with the *read only* option.

```
SQL>
shutdown immediate
SQL>
startup mount
SQL>
alter database
 open read only;

Database altered.
SQL>
```

3. Use *dbms_tdb.check_db* function to check whether the database can be transported to a target platform and the *dbms_tdb.check_external* function to check for existence of external objects, directories and BFILEs. Pass the name of the destination platform as a parameter to the first function. The return type of the function is *boolean*, so declare a variable with *boolean* type and call the function as follows:

```
SQL>
set
serveroutput on
SQL>
declare
  2  v_return boolean;
  3  begin
  4  v_return:=dbms_tdb.check_db('linux ia (32-bit)');
  5  end;
  6  /

PL/SQL procedure succcosfully completed.
```

If nothing was returned, then it means that the database is ready to be transported to the destination platform.

Cross-Platform Database Migration

Now call the second function *dbms_tdb.check_external*:

```
SQL>
declare
  2  v_return boolean;
  3  begin
  4  v_return:=dbms_tdb.check_external;
  5  end;
  6  /

the following directories exist in the database:
sys.data_pump_dir, sys.admin_dir, sys.work_dir, sys.ora_dump

PL/SQL procedure successfully completed.
```

These objects will not be created on the transported database.

4. Run the *convert database* command to convert the whole database to the Linux platform.

```
RMAN> convert database new database 'linuxdb'
2> transport script 'c:\test\transport.sql'
3> db_file_name_convert 'C:\oracle\product\10.2.0\oradata\windb' 'c:\test'
4> to platform 'Linux IA (32-bit)';

Starting convert at 07-APR-10
using target database control file instead of recovery catalog
allocated channel: ORA_DISK_1
channel ORA_DISK_1: sid=154 devtype=DISK
<.....output trimmed .....>
<.....output trimmed .....>
channel ORA_DISK_1: datafile conversion complete, elapsed time: 00:00:01
Run SQL script C:\test\transport.sql on the target platform to create
database
Edit init.ora file
C:\ORACLE\product\10.2.0\db_1\database\init_00lahuto_1_0.ora.
This PFILE will be used to create the database on the target platform
To recompile all PL/SQL modules, run utlirp.sql and utlrp.sql on the target
plat
form
To change the internal database identifier, use dbnewid Utility
Finished backup at 07-APR-10
RMAN>
```

While performing the *convert database* command, RMAN does not convert and transfer redo log files, control files, password files and temporary tablespaces to the destination platform.

RMAN converted all datafiles to the destination platform type. Now copy the parameter file *transport.sql* script, which is located at the *$ORACLE_HOME/dbs directory*, that is used to create the database and all datafiles to the destination host.

5. Perform the following prerequisite actions on the destination host before running the *transport.sql*.

Create dump directories:

```
[oracle@localhost ~]$ cd $ORACLE_HOME/admin
[oracle@localhost ~]$ mkdir linuxdb
[oracle@localhost ~]$ cd linuxdb/
[oracle@localhost linuxdb]$ mkdir adump bdump cdump udump
[oracle@localhost ~]$ cd $ORACLE_HOME/oradata
[oracle@localhost ~]$ mkdir linuxdb
```

Move all datafiles to the necessary folder. Edit parameter file and convert paths from Windows syntax to the Linux syntax:

```
  control_files            =
"/u01/oracle/product/10.2.0/db_1/oradata/linuxdb/control01.ctl"
  db_recovery_file_dest    =
"/u01/oracle/product/10.2.0/db_1/flash_recovery_area"
  db_recovery_file_dest_size= 2147483648
  audit_file_dest          =
"/u01/oracle/product/10.2.0/db_1/admin/linuxdb/adump"
  background_dump_dest      =
"/u01/oracle/product/10.2.0/db_1/admin/linuxdb/bdump"
  user_dump_dest           =
"/u01/oracle/product/10.2.0/db_1/admin/linuxdb/udump"
  core_dump_dest           =
"/u01/oracle/product/10.2.0/db_1/admin/linuxdb/cdump"
  db_name                  = "LINUXDB"
```

Edit *transport.sql* script and correct paths of datafiles, control files and trace directories.

6. Now check all changes made above once more, export the *ORACLE_SID* environment variable and run the *transport.sql* command from SQL*Plus:

```
SQL>@
transport.sql
```

By running this *sql* file, Oracle performs the following steps:

- Creates *spfile* from the provided *pfile* that was generated by RMAN

- Creates control files and opens the database with *resetlogs* option

- Creates temporary tablespace

- Brings the database down, starts it using the upgrade mode and runs *utlirp.sql*. This script recompiles all PL/SQL objects in the format required by the target database platform.

- Runs the *utlrp.sql* file which recompiles all PL/SQL objects with *invalid* status.

After all the above steps are finished, the database can be used successfully.

Copying Datafiles from ASM Storage

There is often a need to move the files from the file system to the ASM storage and vice versa. This may come in handy when one of the file systems is corrupted by some means and then the file may need to be moved to the other file system. How to do this is demonstrated in the following scenario where the file from the file system is copied to ASM using the *convert datafile* command.

1. Get the list of all datafiles:

```
SQL>
select
 name
from
 V$datafile;

NAME
---------------------------------------------
/u01/app/oracle/oradata/orcl/system01.dbf
/u01/app/oracle/oradata/orcl/undotbs01.dbf
/u01/app/oracle/oradata/orcl/sysaux01.dbf
/u01/app/oracle/oradata/orcl/users01.dbf
/u01/app/oracle/oradata/orcl/example01.dbf
/u01/app/oracle/oradata/orcl/testtbs.dbf
```

2. Use the *convert datafile* command to convert the datafile from the file system to ASM:

```
RMAN> convert datafile '/u01/app/oracle/oradata/orcl/testtbs.dbf' format
'+data';

<....output trimmed ....>
input filename=/u01/app/oracle/oradata/orcl/testtbs.dbf
converted datafile=+DATA/orcl/datafile/test_tbs.256.716418819
<....output trimmed ....>
RMAN>
```

3. Take the original datafile offline and rename it with the newly converted one.

```
SQL>
alter
 database datafile '/u01/app/oracle/oradata/orcl/testtbs.dbf' offline;

Database altered.
```

```
SQL>
alter
 database rename file '/u01/app/oracle/oradata/orcl/testtbs.dbf' to
'+data/orcl/datafile/test_tbs.257.716426835';

Database altered.

SQL>
select
 name
from
 V$datafile;

NAME
-------------------------------------------
/u01/app/oracle/oradata/orcl/system01.dbf
/u01/app/oracle/oradata/orcl/undotbs01.dbf
/u01/app/oracle/oradata/orcl/sysaux01.dbf
/u01/app/oracle/oradata/orcl/users01.dbf
/u01/app/oracle/oradata/orcl/example01.dbf
+DATA/orcl/datafile/test_tbs.257.716426835
SQL>
```

It is also possible to convert the datafile from ASM to the file system. For that scenario, use the *convert datafile* command to convert the ASM datafile to file system type.

```
RMAN> convert datafile '+data/orcl/datafile/test_tbs.257.716426835' format
'/u01/app/oracle/testtbs%u';

<....output trimmed ....>
input filename=+data/orcl/datafile/test_tbs.257.716426835
converted datafile=/u01/app/oracle/testtbsdata_d-orcl_i-1243929761_ts-
test_tbs_fno-6_041b7jn4
<....output trimmed ....>
```

Now take the ASM datafile to offline mode and plug the converted datafile to the database by renaming it as follows:

```
SQL>
select
 name
from
 V$datafile;

NAME
-------------------------------------------
/u01/app/oracle/oradata/orcl/system01.dbf
/u01/app/oracle/oradata/orcl/undotbs01.dbf
/u01/app/oracle/oradata/orcl/sysaux01.dbf
/u01/app/oracle/oradata/orcl/users01.dbf
/u01/app/oracle/oradata/orcl/example01.dbf
+DATA/orcl/datafile/test_tbs.257.716426835

SQL>
```

Copying Datafiles from ASM Storage

```
alter
 database datafile '+data/orcl/datafile/test_tbs.257.716426835' offline;
Database altered.

SQL>
alter
 database rename file '+data/orcl/datafile/test_tbs.257.716426835' to
'/u01/app/oracle/testtbsdata_d-orcl_i-1243929761_ts-test_tbs_fno-6_04lb7jn4'
;

Database altered.

SQL>
select
 name
from
 V$datafile;

NAME
---------------------------------------------------
/u01/app/oracle/oradata/orcl/system01.dbf
/u01/app/oracle/oradata/orcl/undotbs01.dbf
/u01/app/oracle/oradata/orcl/sysaux01.dbf
/u01/app/oracle/oradata/orcl/users01.dbf
/u01/app/oracle/oradata/orcl/example01.dbf
/u01/app/oracle/testtbsdata_D-ORCL_I-1243929761_ts-test_tbs_fno-6_04lb7jn4
```

Conclusion

RMAN greatly facilitates the transportation of data as physical backups of datafiles can simply be plugged into a database on a different server/different platform. Using logical backups via Export-Import or Data Pump has the expense in time and money of actually having to reformat data blocks and insert rows and rebuild indexes. With tablespace transportation, indexes do not have to be rebuilt! That is a big time saver.

Transportable tablespaces and the use of the *convert* command are quicker ways to migrate data to a new platform than rebuilding the whole database. Also, as noted earlier, OLTP data can be moved to a data warehouse, e.g. as a staging tablespace.

Be aware of the limitations of transportable tablespaces, i.e. tablespaces holding XML types, tables with VARRAYs, nested tables, replicated master tables and snapshots cannot be transported.

Managing the Recovery Catalog

Introduction

As has been seen in previous chapters, RMAN uses the control file of the target database to store its metadata information by default. The target database's control file is updated with every operation of RMAN. But there are some capabilities of RMAN which do not come alive by just using the control file. By using the recovery catalog, it is possible to store the repository data of RMAN for different databases, thereby centralizing metadata for all databases. It is also possible to store metadata of multiple incarnations of each database in order to restore from any incarnation. In addition, it is possible to create RMAN scripts in the recovery catalog and use them in different databases.

Furthermore, the recovery catalog stores metadata of backups longer than the control file does. If the metadata of RMAN backups is kept in control files and they are lost due to media failure, it means that all metadata about backups have been lost. This metadata can only be regained by restoring a control file backup which would not have metadata about database and archivelog backups made after the control file backup itself. In this case, the recovery becomes difficult.

From the following table, the difference between storing metadata of RMAN backups in the recovery catalog and the control file are shown:

Feature	Recovery Catalog	Control File
Centralizing backup repository	It is possible to register more than one database to the same recovery catalog.	Store only backup metadata of the target database in the control file.
Restore to any incarnation of the database	It is easier to restore to any incarnation of the database that is registered in the recovery catalog.	Only reset to the database incarnation of which the control file is aware.
Using backup scripts	It is possible to store and use backup scripts using the recovery catalog for every database that is registered in it.	It is not possible to store any script in the control file.
Limitation of storing backup metadata	It is possible to store unlimited backup data of any database that is registered in the recovery catalog.	The initialization parameter *control_file_record_ keep_time* stores backup metadata for seven days as a default. The maximum limit is one year (365 days).
Disaster recovery	In case of disaster recovery, it is very easy to restore the control file from backup and perform a recovery as the recovery catalog contains RMAN backup information in itself.	In case of control file loss, the information about RMAN backup is also lost until the control file is restored.
Control file (binary) backups		Binary backups of control files are critical as RMAN metadata about database is in the control file.

Table 7.1: *Recovery Catalog Vs Control File*

This chapter will show how the recovery catalog can be created and managed.

Creating the Recovery Catalog

Although it is advisable to create the recovery catalog in the same version as the target database, this is not strictly necessary, as in the case of a single recovery catalog serving a mix of 9i, 10g and 11g databases! In this case, the recovery catalog must be created in a database that is running the same version as the highest version of the target databases. However, a catalog in a 9i or 10g database cannot be used to backup an 11g target. The RMAN Compatibility Matrix is included in the RMAN documentation and available on Oracle's support site.

Since the recovery catalog is capable of holding backup-related metadata longer than the target database's control file, this essentially depicts that the storage should be persistent compared to the control file. In Oracle, the persistent storage lies only in the form of datafiles managed via tablespaces. The same goes for the recovery catalog as well, which is going to be managed within a dedicated tablespace that will be used for it only. Recovery catalog creation demands the creation of its owner which would be used to manage it.

Although Oracle does not prevent creating the recovery catalog schema in the target database, such an implementation would be unacceptable. It is recommended that this schema be created on a different database that resides at the remote host. If this schema is created on the same database, then if the database is lost, all backup metadata is lost as well. If this schema is created in a different database in the same host, then again due to the media failure, all hard drives can be lost, thus the backup metadata is lost. Therefore, it is recommended that this schema be put in a different database that resides on a different server.

In order to create the recovery catalog, a user needs to be created, i.e. a separate schema to hold the metadata of backups, and then a catalog which is created holds RMAN backup metadata of registered databases. Following are the main steps in creating the recovery catalog:

1. Create a tablespace that holds backup metadata

2. Create a user that owns the catalog

3. Grant *recovery_catalog_owner* privilege to that user

4. Using RMAN executable, connect to the catalog database

5. Use *create catalog* command to create a recovery catalog

Now, connect to the second database where the catalog should be created and create a separate tablespace for the recovery catalog as follows:

```
sys@RC>create tablespace rcat_ts datafile
'/u01/oracle/product/10.2.0/db_1/oradata/RC/rcat_ts.dbf' SIZE 400M;

Tablespace created.
```

Then create a user which should own the recovery catalog and make the previous tablespace be the default tablespace of this user:

```
sys@RC>create user rcat_owner identified by rcat
  temporary tablespace temp
  default tablespace rcat_ts
  quota unlimited on rcat_ts;

User created.
```

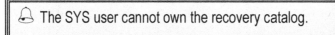

The recovery catalog owner must have the role *recovery_catalog_owner* granted to him. So grant this role to the user in addition to the normal roles of *connect* and *resource* as follows:

```
sys@rc>grant recovery_catalog_owner to rcat_owner;

Grant succeeded.

sys@rc>grant connect, resource to rcat_owner;

Grant succeeded.
```

Once this part is over, the next step is to actually create a recovery catalog connecting with the user that owns it and run the *create catalog* command. There are two options to connect to the recovery catalog. Either connect directly from the OS:

```
$ export ORACLE_SID=rc
$ rman catalog rcat_owner/rcat

connected to recovery catalog database
RMAN>
```

Or run *rman* executable and connect to the catalog database using the *connect catalog* command:

```
$ rman
RMAN> connect catalog rcat_owner/rcat

connected to recovery catalog database
RMAN>
```

Now, using the *create catalog* command, create a catalog on that database:

```
RMAN> create catalog;

recovery catalog created
RMAN>
```

The recovery catalog has been successfully created. To check the objects that were created after running the *create catalog* command, connect to the recovery catalog database and query the *dba_segments* table:

```
sys@RC>select count(*) from dba_segments where owner='rcat_owner';

  count(*)
----------
       132
sys@RC>
```

By running the *create catalog* command, RMAN created objects to hold metadata information of the databases that registered in that catalog.

Registering a Database in the Recovery Catalog

To make RMAN store the metadata information, register the database in the recovery catalog. Before the database is registered, the metadata is written to the control file of the target database. So in order to register the database, connect to both the target and catalog database. For this, connect to the catalog database via Oracle Net by configuring both *tnsnames.ora* and *listener.ora* files. After making changes to both these files, connect to the target and catalog databases and register the target database as follows:

```
$ export ORACLE_SID=db1
$ rman target / catalog rcat_owner/rcat@RC

connected to target database: DB1 (DBID=1302506781)
connected to recovery catalog database

RMAN> register database;
```

```
database registered in recovery catalog
starting full resync of recovery catalog
full resync complete
```

Note: The target database *db1* is the database that will be backed up with RMAN. The recovery catalog database *RC* contains the recovery catalog shema.

The database is registered to the recovery catalog. To verify it, run the *report schema* command and the registered database's structure appears:

```
RMAN> report schema;

Report of database schema
List of Permanent Datafiles
===========================
File Size(MB) Tablespace           RB segs Datafile Name
---- -------- -------------------- ------- ------------------------
1    480      SYSTEM               YES
/u01/oracle/product/10.2.0/db_1/oradata/db1/system01.dbf
2    25       UNDOTBS1             YES
/u01/oracle/product/10.2.0/db_1/oradata/db1/undotbs01.dbf
3    230      SYSAUX               NO
/u01/oracle/product/10.2.0/db_1/oradata/db1/sysaux01.dbf
4    5        USERS                NO
/u01/oracle/product/10.2.0/db_1/oradata/db1/users01.dbf

List of Temporary Files
=======================
File Size(MB) Tablespace           Maxsize(MB) Tempfile Name
---- -------- -------------------- ----------- --------------------
1    20       TEMP                 32767
/u01/oracle/product/10.2.0/db_1/oradata/db1/temp01.dbf
RMAN>
```

NOTE: Schema in the context of the above RMAN command is the physical structure of the target database.

Since all files of the target database can be seen by querying the recovery catalog, the recovery catalog has been created and the database is registered in it successfully.

The database is registered in the catalog based on their DBID number. This is always going to be unique for a database as long as the database is not registered that was created from the cold copy of the database that was already registered in the recovery catalog. In this case, make sure that if another database with the same DBID is to be added (it may be a cold backup of an already added database) in the same catalog where its source is also registered, then its DBID number must be changed using the *dbnewid* utility. In the instance of dataguard environments, both primary and secondary, if they are a part of the same catalog, they must have the parameter *db_unique_name* set within their parameter files.

Now assume that the database *db1* has been registered which has a DBID equal to 1302506781 to the recovery catalog:

```
$ rman target / catalog rcat_owner/rcat@rc

connected to target database: DB1 (DBID=1302506781)
connected to recovery catalog database

RMAN> register database;

database registered in recovery catalog
starting full resync of recovery catalog
full resync complete

RMAN> list incarnation;

List of Database Incarnations


DB Key  Inc Key DB Name  DB ID            STATUS  Reset SCN  Reset Time
-------  ------- -------- ---------------- ------- ------  ----------
1        8       DB1      1302506781       PARENT  1         30-JUN-05
1        2       DB1      1302506781       CURRENT 446075    18-JAN-10
RMAN> exit
```

Since that database is cloned to a different server using cold backup, some changes are made on it and the decision is made to register it to the same recovery catalog. As a cold copy of datafiles, redo logs and control files was done, the DBID was not changed. This means that the database cannot be registered with the same DBID to the same recovery catalog. If an attempt is made to register it, the following error occurs:

```
$ rman target / catalog rcat_owner/rcat@rc

connected to target database: DB1 (DBID=1302506781)
connected to recovery catalog database

RMAN> register database;

RMAN 00571: ---------------------------------------------------------
RMAN-00569: =============== ERROR MESSAGE STACK FOLLOWS ===============
RMAN-00571: ===========================================================
RMAN-03009: failure of register command on default channel at 01/24/2010
19:12:12
RMAN-20002: target database already registered in recovery catalog
```

In this case, change the DBID of the second database using the *dbnewid* utility. For this example, change the DBID and *db_name* of the database.

```
$ nid target=sys/pass dbname=db1clone

Connected to database DB1 (DBID=1302506781)
Connected to server version 10.2.0
Control Files in database:
    /u01/oracle/product/10.2.0/db_1/oradata/db1/control01.ctl
    /u01/oracle/product/10.2.0/db_1/oradata/db1/control02.ctl
    /u01/oracle/product/10.2.0/db_1/oradata/db1/control03.ctl

Change database ID and database name DB1 to DB1CLONE? (Y/[N]) => y
Proceeding with operation
Changing database ID from 1302506781 to 2551771250
Changing database name from DB1 to DB1CLONE
    Control File /u01/oracle/product/10.2.0/db_1/oradata/db1/control01.ctl -
modified
    Control File /u01/oracle/product/10.2.0/db_1/oradata/db1/control02.ctl -
modified
    Control File /u01/oracle/product/10.2.0/db_1/oradata/db1/control03.ctl -
modified
    Datafile /u01/oracle/product/10.2.0/db_1/oradata/db1/system01.dbf - dbid
changed, wrote new name
    Datafile /u01/oracle/product/10.2.0/db_1/oradata/db1/undotbs01.dbf -
dbid changed, wrote new name
    Datafile /u01/oracle/product/10.2.0/db_1/oradata/db1/sysaux01.dbf - dbid
changed, wrote new name
    Datafile /u01/oracle/product/10.2.0/db_1/oradata/db1/users01.dbf - dbid
changed, wrote new name
    Datafile /u01/oracle/product/10.2.0/db_1/oradata/db1/temp01.dbf - dbid
changed, wrote new name
    Control File /u01/oracle/product/10.2.0/db_1/oradata/db1/control01.ctl -
dbid changed, wrote new name
    Control File /u01/oracle/product/10.2.0/db_1/oradata/db1/control02.ctl -
dbid changed, wrote new name
    Control File /u01/oracle/product/10.2.0/db_1/oradata/db1/control03.ctl -
dbid changed, wrote new name
    Instance shut down

Database name changed to DB1CLONE.
Modify parameter file and generate a new password file before restarting.
Database ID for database DB1CLONE changed to 2551771250.
All previous backups and archived redo logs for this database are unusable.
Database is not aware of previous backups and archived logs in Recovery
Area.
Database has been shutdown, open database with RESETLOGS option.
Succesfully changed database name and ID.
DBNEWID - Completed successfully.
```

Now the DBID of the second cloned database from 1302506781 to 2551771250 has been successfully created. As the database name has been changed (skip changing *db_name* of the database), perform the following steps in order to successfully complete the operation:

```
$ cd $ORACLE_HOME/dbs/
$ cp spfiledb1.ora spfiledb1clone.ora
$ sqlplus "/ as sysdba"

Connected to an idle instance.

SQL>
 startup mount

ORACLE instance started.
Total System Global Area  285212672 bytes
Fixed Size                  1218992 bytes
Variable Size              92276304 bytes
Database Buffers          188743680 bytes
Redo Buffers                2973696 bytes
ORA-01103: database name 'DB1CLONE' in control file is not 'DB1'

SQL>
 alter system
set db_name=db1clone scope=spfile;

System altered.

SQL>
 shutdown immediate

ORA-01507: database not mounted

ORACLE instance shut down.

SQL>
 startup mount;

ORACLE instance started.

Total System Global Area  285212672 bytes
Fixed Size                  1218992 bytes
Variable Size              92276304 bytes
Database Buffers          188743680 bytes
Redo Buffers                2973696 bytes
Database mounted.

SQL>
 alter database
 open resetlogs;

Database altered.

SQL> exit
Disconnected from Oracle Database 10g Enterprise Edition Release 10.2.0.1.0
- Production
With the Partitioning, OLAP and Data Mining options

$ rman target / catalog rcat_owner/rcat@rc

connected to target database: DB1CLONE (DBID=2551771250)
connected to recovery catalog database

RMAN> register database;
```

Creating the Recovery Catalog   **297**

```
database registered in recovery catalog
starting full resync of recovery catalog
full resync complete
RMAN>
```

Next, check the recovery catalog:

```
$ export ORACLE_SID=rc
$ sqlplus "/ as sysdba"
sys@RC> conn rcat_owner/rcat

Connected.

rcat_owner@RC> select distinct dbid, name FROM rc_database;

DBID NAME
---------- --------
1302506781 DB1
2551771250 DB1CLONE
```

There are now two databases registered in the recovery catalog.

Unregistering the Database From the Catalog

If the database should not be managed through the catalog for any reason, it can be unregistered from the catalog. The database can still be backed up using the target database control file. This can be done through the *unregister* command which takes the input of three types: DBID, the name of the database and the parameter value of *db_unique_name* for the standby database.

The DBID can be found while connecting to the recovery catalog with the database as follows:

```
$ export ORACLE_SID=db2
$ rman target / catalog rcat_owner/rcat@RC

connected to target database: DB2 (DBID=1872103512)
connected to recovery catalog database
RMAN>
```

The database name can be used as well for unregistering, but it is very likely that there are multiple databases with the same name registered in the same catalog. Remember, a catalog can manage more than one database of more than one version. So it is always a best practice to set the DBID before unregistering the database which will make sure that the operation is done on

Oracle Backup and Recovery

the correct database only. To do so, using the run block is suggested. Now unregister the database DB2 from the catalog.

First, connect to the catalog. Though not necessary, if the DBID of the database is being looked for, then connect to the target database first, get the DBID and then connect to the catalog. As the DBID is already present, connect directly to the catalog and unregister the database:

```
$ rman catalog rcat_owner/rcat@rc
RMAN> set DBID=1872103512

executing command: set dbid
database name is "DB2" and DBID is 1872103512

RMAN> unregister database db2;

database name is "DB2" and DBID is 1872103512

Do we really want to unregister the database (enter YES or NO)? yes
database unregistered from the recovery catalog
RMAN>
```

Once unregistered, all the records related to the backup and about the stored scripts will be removed permanently. It is a good practice to find and keep handy the listing of all backups and stored scripts unregistering the database. If the same database should be registered with either the same or a new catalog, the lost records will not come back. Only the information that is there at that time in the target control file will be registered in the catalog. Also, the information that is older than the value of the *control_file_record_keep_time* parameter in the initialization parameter file would not be registered in the database of the catalog.

Dropping the Recovery Catalog

Since there is no database registered in the catalog, i.e. it has just been removed in the previous section, this essentially means that the catalog is not needed anymore. Therefore, if it is not needed, simply say goodbye to it by using the *drop* command. Like dropping any other database object, this operation cannot be undone.

To do so, be connected to the recovery catalog, but there is no need to connect to the target database. Obviously, if the catalog is dropped, the entire database's metadata also would be gone from it permanently. The databases can still be worked with regarding their backups from their control files, though. RMAN will prompt the DBA for confirmation twice for the operation and if confirmed, the deed is done!

As there is also nothing in the catalog database, it can be dropped as well.

```
$ rman catalog rcat_owner/rcat

connected to recovery catalog database

RMAN> drop catalog;

recovery catalog owner is rcat_owner
enter drop catalog command again to confirm catalog removal

RMAN> drop catalog;

recovery catalog dropped
RMAN>
```

Managing the Recovery Catalog

The recovery catalog is such a vital thing in the backup stack and it needs serious management related to its space consumption, its own backup and things like this. The following sections examine these areas.

Capacity Planning of Recovery Catalog

As the metadata of the backup is stored in the recovery catalog, it becomes essential to make sure that the recovery catalog is managed properly. In management, the first thing that should be taken care of is that there must not be any records not needed to be stored in it. For this, the retention policy should be properly set based on the requirement and commands to check and delete the obsoleted backups should be periodically fired. This would limit the space consumption of the catalog file, storing only what is needed.

It is also important that the size of the tablespace used by the recovery catalog owner should be big enough to hold not just the current database's information, but also the subsequent backups of various files and backup scripts whose information is stored in it. Note that it is directly proportional to the number of the databases that need to be managed in a single recovery catalog. This is a quote from the 11.2 Backup and Recovery User's Guide:

"Assume that the target database has 100 files, and the database is backed up once a day, producing 50 backup sets containing one backup piece each. If is assumed that each row in the backup piece table uses the maximum amount of space, then one daily backup will consume less than 170 KB in the recovery catalog. So if a backup is done once a day for a year, then the total storage in this period is about 62 MB. Assume approximately the same amount for archived logs. Thus, the worst case is about 120 MB for a year for metadata storage. For a more typical case in which only a portion of the backup piece row space is used, 15 MB for each year is realistic.

If the plan is to register multiple databases in the recovery catalog, then remember to add up the space required for each one based on the previous calculation to arrive at a total size for the default tablespace of the recovery catalog schema."

Using the above calculation, estimate the size of the recovery catalog needed by the database by looking at the number and size of the various files whose backup would be a part of the recovery catalog. If recovery catalog tablespace is being added in an existing database (which is a really bad idea), than make sure that the space is available for it. If a new database is being created for the storage of the recovery catalog, than in addition to the recovery catalog owner's tablespace, space for the other tablespaces like system, sysaux, undo and temp must also be taken into consideration.

Synching a Catalog

RMAN stores the information of the backup in the target database's control file, and then it is pushed into the catalog once it is in place. This happens on its own without any manual intervention needed from the DBA. But at times, a DBA needs to do it manually as well. This section covers the details of the synching including the types of synching and the ways to do it.

RMAN maintains two kinds of information in the catalog. One is related to the backup metadata of the various types of the files. This includes the information related to the archive logs generated, number of log switches that have happened so far, the current incarnation number of the database and the backup information. The other type of information maintained is the knowledge of the physical structure of the database, meaning the number of files, their names and paths.

Both types of information come from the target control file of only the database for which the catalog is being maintained. The information on the backup will get refreshed, but the other information will not get updated within the catalog in case the target database's current control file is lost and is either recreated or is restored from the backup.

Whenever the *backup* command is issued from RMAN, it does an automatic resynchronization of the information stored as new in the control file in the catalog. This needs no intervention from a DBA other than making sure that the command is completely successful. Three types of resynchronization are possible in RMAN:

1. Full resynchronization

2. Partial resynchronization

3. Reverse resynchronization

In the full resync, RMAN updates all the records of the catalog, including the records of the physical database as well. To do this, the snapshot control file is used by RMAN which essentially is nothing but a copy of the target database control file. Using the snapshot control file, RMAN compares the information of the target database's control file with it and the missing information is refreshed in the catalog. This is done when any kind of structural changes are done on the database; for example, adding a tablespace or adding a new datafile to a tablespace. For any action like this, the full resynchronization is initiated by RMAN.

In the partial resynchronization, only the information of the newly created backups and the archivelogs is updated in the catalog. This is done anytime the backup of the archivelogs and other files is initiated through reading the control file of the target database. This does not refresh new tablespaces or data files that were added in the database since the last full resync.

The reverse resynchronization is specifically for a data guard environment. In the case of a data guard environment, only one out of the primary or secondary is part of the catalog. All the databases in the data guard configuration do not need to be in the catalog. With whichever database the connection is established, information about that is refreshed in the catalog, i.e. in the target switch of which ever database is used, and only that information is updated and not for all the databases. The following command can be used to update the other database:

```
RMAN>resync catalog from db_unique_name <name goes here>
```

To understand this, take an example of two databases, *prod* and *stdby*. Assume that connection is always made to the *prod* database and the backups are performed. Now, after some time, connect to the *stdby* database and issue:

```
RMAN>resync catalog from db_unique_name stdby
```

This pulls the information from the catalog and updates the control file of the *stdby* database. By doing this, the metadata kept in RMAN becomes consistent across all the databases in a dataguard configuration.

Normally, the metadata in the control file and in the catalog is updated automatically. But there is still a chance that it may not happen on its own. Following are some of the reasons:

1. When the catalog becomes available

This is the simplest and probably most obvious reason. This means that the backup is being taken while not being connected to the recovery catalog. This would only be a partial resynchronization happening in the target control file. The next time the catalog database is connected to, the information maintained in the control file will not be in it. So this would surely need a manual resynchronization of the catalog. Now see it in an example.

Take a backup of the target database (*db1*) by not connecting to catalog database:

```
$ export ORACLE_SID=db1
$ rman target / nocatalog

connected to target database: DB1 (DBID=1302506781)
using target database control file instead of recovery catalog

RMAN> backup spfile;
```

Query the *rc_backup_spfile* view which should be updated if a backup was taken of spfile by connecting to the recovery catalog:

```
$ export ORACLE_SID=RC
$ sqlplus "rcat_owner/rcat"
rcat_owner@RC>select count(*) from rc_backup_spfile;
```

```
   COUNT(*)
----------
         0
rcat_owner@RC>
```

As this shows, there is no information about the backup taken without connecting to the recovery catalog. Now, connect to both the target and catalog databases and synchronize the control file of the target database with the recovery catalog as follows:

```
$ export ORACLE_SID=db1
$ rman target / catalog rcat_owner/rcat@rc

connected to target database: DB1 (DBID=1302506781)
connected to recovery catalog database

RMAN> resync catalog;

starting full resync of recovery catalog
full resync complete
RMAN>
```

After the resynchronization has been finished, check whether the data is added to the recovery catalog repository:

```
$ export ORACLE_SID=RC
$ sqlplus "rcat_owner/rcat"

rcat_owner@RC>select count(*) from rc_backup_spfile;
  COUNT(*)
----------
         1
rcat_owner@RC>
```

After the resynchronization, the information about the backup that was recorded in the control files is added to the recovery catalog repository.

Note: A good practice is to include the *resync catalog* command explicitly in the Daily Backup script so that it handles the case of the catalog schema being unavailable on any day.

---

2. Database in archivelog and infrequent backups

Information about the archivelogs generated and the log sequence numbers is maintained in the catalog. This information is not updated automatically in the catalog at the time of these events, but is available when a backup command is issued. So if there is a highly volatile database with lots of log switches happening resulting in lots of archivelogs being generated but backups are not being taken daily, then there is a need to manually resynchronize the recovery catalog. How frequently this needs to be done depends on the frequency of the redo log switching and the archivelog generation.

3. In a dataguard environment

In a dataguard environment, not all the databases have to be connected in the catalog. Only one database is used as a maintained target and normally this is the primary database. For the other databases using the reverse resynchronizaion, the information is updated from the catalog manually.

4. Before the control file gets overwritten

The information in the catalog is nothing but the permanent repository of the same information kept in the target database's control file. In the control file, this information is kept up till the time limit of the *control_file_record_keep_time* parameter, which is defaulted to seven days. This parameter's value needs to be that much so that the control file does not need to overwrite the information contained in it to make space for the new metadata. As the same information is going to be kept in the catalog also, this means that before this time period passes, make sure the records are updated in the catalog. Therefore, either do the resynchronization of the catalog manually before this parameter is overridden or issue a *backup* command more frequently which would do the synching on its own in the catalog.

If the control file overwrites the information contained in it, there is no chance to get the same information updated in the catalog afterwards. That is why setting the *keep time* parameter to a value of 0 is never suggested. Note that if the control file has already grown to its maximum possible size and cannot grow any further, then a message is recorded in the alert log resulting in the database overwriting the records on its own even though there is a time period left in the *keep time* parameter. If this is experienced, then decrease the value of the *keep time* parameter and do more manual resynchronization.

Upgrading the Catalog

It is good practice to have the catalog the same version as the RMAN client that is being used. This ensures the complete compatibility between the two of them. However, if the recovery catalog is older than the RMAN client that is used, then it is a must that the recovery catalog be upgraded to match with the client's version.

To determine the version of the catalog, connect to the recovery catalog using the catalog owner's credentials and issue:

```
SQL> select * from rcver;
```

This would result in either a single row or multiple row output of the version of the catalog. In the case of the multi-line output, the highest version given is the version of the catalog which should be compatible with the RMAN client. The reason for finding multiple rows here would be because of the upgrades that happened to this catalog in the past from one release to another.

Once it has been determined that the recovery catalog is the older version compared to the RMAN client, it needs to be upgraded. Follow the below set of commands to do so. If the catalog owner is from a release older than 10gR1, it would lack a privilege of *create type* in the *recover_catalog_owner*. So this needs to be granted manually to the owner.

```
SQL>
grant
 create type to catalog_owner;
```

In the following scenario, after applying patch 10.2.0.4.0, log in to the catalog database and the following message appears:

```
[oracle@localhost ~]$ rman catalog rc/rc@rc

connected to recovery catalog database
PL/SQL package RC.DBMS_RCVCAT version 10.02.00.00 in RCVCAT database is not
current
PL/SQL package RC.DBMS_RCVMAN version 10.02.00.00 in RCVCAT database is not
current
```

RMAN says that the recovery catalog needs to be upgraded also. Therefore, upgrade it using the *upgrade catalog* command. This asks for the confirmation twice. Issue the confirmation and the catalog gets upgraded to the current release:

```
RMAN> upgrade catalog;

recovery catalog owner is RC
enter upgrade catalog command again to confirm catalog upgrade

RMAN> upgrade catalog;
```

```
recovery catalog upgraded to version 10.02.00.04
dbms_rcvman package upgraded to version 10.02.00.00
dbms_rcvcat package upgraded to version 10.02.00.00
RMAN>
```

Now connect to the catalog database from SQL*Plus with the user which is the owner of the catalog and query the *rcver* view:

```
[oracle@localhost ~]$ sqlplus rc/rc
SQL>
select * from
 rcver;

VERSION
------------
10.02.00.00
10.02.00.04
SQL>
```

Saving RMAN Scripts in the Recovery Catalog

There must be something that is unique to the recovery catalog other than the persistent storage of metadata related to backup. This section goes over the feature of creating the stored scripts which is not possible if just the target database control file is being used. If it is certain that some commands will be run repeatedly, they can be stored in the form of a script and permanently stored in the catalog. Furthermore, the running of the script can be scheduled as well. By having RMAN scripts stored in the recovery catalog, everyone who connects to the recovery catalog will have the option to run it by not having any access to the file system.

As the name says itself, the scripts can be stored in the catalog of commonly performed operations. RMAN provides the flexibility to create the scripts within the recovery catalog which makes the handling and usage of them much easier. There are two possible types of RMAN scripts, local scripts and global scripts.

Local scripts are the scripts which, as the name says, are local to a specific database instance. This means they are created while being connected to a specific database and their usage is also limited to the scope of that database itself. These are useful for catering different kind of environments solely which cannot otherwise be managed through a generic script. Global scripts, on the other hand, are not tied up to a specific instance but are available for any instance which is a part of that catalog where this script is stored. That is why they are called global scripts.

Creation of RMAN Scripts

RMAN scripts are only created from the RMAN prompt with the *create script* command. There is one difference in the making of the global or local scripts and that is the word *global* while using the *create script* words. Create a local script first.

```
$ rman target / catalog rcat_owner/rcat@rc

connected to target database: DB1 (DBID=1302506781)
connected to recovery catalog database

RMAN> create script spfile_backup
{
    backup spfile;
}

created script spfile_backup
RMAN>
```

This has created a local script, as the word *global* has not been used while making it. For making the local script, ensure that the same named script in the local database catalog is not already present. For the global script, the name must not be used by any of the scripts in the catalog.

Getting Content of the Stored Script

To see the contents of the scripts, use the *print script* command. Now print the script to see what it contains:

```
RMAN> print script spfile_backup;
printing stored script: spfile_backup
{
        backup spfile;
}
RMAN>
```

Since a local script has now been created, create a global one as well. For this, all that is needed is use the word *global* in the syntax. So create a global script, print it and try to see if the output is any different from the local one.

```
RMAN> create global script g_spfile_backup
{
    backup spfile;
```

```
}
created global script g_spfile_backup
RMAN>
RMAN> print script g_spfile_backup;

printing stored global script: g_spfile_backup
 {backup spfile;
}
RMAN>
```

If this has been examined carefully, there is a keyword *global* that is shown in the creation of the script.

Running the Script

Now that the script is ready, see how to execute it. To execute the script, call it from the *run* block with its name. Run the local script with the same procedure:

```
RMAN> run
2> {
3> execute script spfile_backup;
4> }

executing script: spfile_backup

Starting backup at 19-JAN-10
......<output trimmed>
Finished backup at 19-JAN-10
RMAN>
```

For running the global script, it is mandatory to supply the keyword *global* with the script name. The rest of the procedure remains the same.

```
RMAN> run
2> {
3>   execute global script backup_database;
4> }

executing global script: backup_database
......<output trimmed>
RMAN>
```

To call the RMAN stored script directly from the RMAN client, use the *script* parameter as follows:

```
$ rman target / catalog rcat_owner/rcat@rc script 'spfile_backup'
```

Creating Dynamic Scripts

It is also possible to pass a value to the stored RMAN script. It is an 11g new feature to create a dynamic script in RMAN. In this example, a dynamic script is created and two values are passed to it: the name and extension of the backup file.

```
RMAN> create script backup_db {
2> allocate channel ch1 device type disk;
3> backup format='c:\&1..&2' database;
4> }

created script backup_db
RMAN>
```

Next, run this script inside a *run* block and pass the values as shown here:

```
RMAN> run
2> {
3> execute script backup_db
4> using 'db_backup'
5> 'bkp';
6> }

executing script: backup_db

allocated channel: ch1
channel ch1: SID=131 device type=DISK

Starting backup at 01-FEB-10
......<output trimmed>
Finished backup at 01-FEB-10
```

It is possible to call the script directly from the OS command line and pass the values as follows:

```
C:\>rman target / catalog rc_owner/rc@rc script backup_db using 'backup_db'
'bkp'
```

Running the above command, RMAN connects to the target and catalog databases and runs the script *backup_db* by passing it two parameters: *backup_db* as a file name and *bkp* as an extension.

Like all the other options, the *list script names* command can be used to print the scripts that are in the catalog; local and global as well as a complete listing. Below is output from the catalog where two scripts have just been created.

```
RMAN> list script names;
```

```
List of Stored Scripts in Recovery Catalog

    Scripts of Target Database DB1
        Script Name
        Description
        ----------------------------
        spfile_backup

    Global Scripts
        Script Name
        Description
        ----------------------------
        backup_database
RMAN>
```

Create Script From a File

It is also possible to create a script directly from a file. Assume that there is a file called *backup_database.txt* and it needs to be put in the recovery catalog as a global script in order to use it in each database that registered in this recovery catalog. To do so, use the *create script … from file …* command as follows:

```
$ cat backup_database.txt
run
{
backup database plus archivelog;
}
$ rman target / catalog rcat_owner/rcat@rc

connected to target database: DB1 (DBID=1302506781)
connected to recovery catalog database

RMAN> create global script backup_db from file '/tmp/backup_database.txt';

script commands will be loaded from file /tmp/backup_database.txt
created global script backup_db

RMAN> print script backup_db;
printing stored global script: backup_db
run
{
backup database plus archivelog;
}
RMAN> run
2> {
3> execute global script backup_db;
4> }

executing global script: backup_db
Starting backup at 19-JAN-10
......<output trimmed>
RMAN>
```

Replacing and Deleting the Existing Scripts

There may be times when the content of the script should be changed. It is not required that the existing script be deleted in order to do so. Simply replace the current script contents with the new ones by using the *replace script* command. Replace the global script with some new content. But before that, print and see its current contents:

```
RMAN> print global script backup_db;
printing stored global script: backup_db
run
{
backup database plus archivelog;
}

RMAN> replace global script backup_db {
2> backup database plus archivelog;
3> crosscheck backup;
4> delete noprompt obsolete;
5> }

replaced global script backup_db

RMAN> print global script backup_db;
printing stored global script: backup_db
 {backup database plus archivelog;
crosscheck backup;
delete noprompt obsolete;
}
RMAN>
```

It is also possible to replace the script using the OS file as follows:

```
RMAN> replace global script spfile_backup from file
'/tmp/backup_database.txt';
```

Delete the Stored Script

Finally, if the DBA is not willing to use the script anymore, it can be deleted with the *delete script* command. Once deleted, there is no way to get the script back, so this command should be executed only when it is certain that the script is not needed anymore.

```
RMAN> delete global script backup_db;

deleted global script: backup_db
```
And the script is no more!

Cataloging the Copies of the Files

The other benefit of RMAN is to catalog when the backup is done without the use of the recovery catalog or from the user-managed procedure, but still be able to use them just like they are RMAN backups only.

It should be acknowledged that RMAN is not something that is the first choice when it comes to the backup of the Oracle database. There are plenty of people who still think that using RMAN is actually much tougher. Even still, the preferred method is the user-managed backup which means image copies of the database are made through the operating system commands.

Now facing this truth, imagine a DBA is hired by such a company where RMAN does not get much of the love. By having the knowledge that RMAN is actually much easier and a better way to do Oracle backups, it is proposed to use it as the preferred method for doing the backups and this gets approved. But wait a minute, what about the backups which were done without it? And just to make things a little worse, suppose some of the backups were indeed done through the RMAN but without the recovery catalog. It is known that using the target control file alone as the repository of the metadata is like walking on a sword, a small mistake is all it would take to make a DBA regret for a long time this decision!

So what can be the way out to make a unified solution for such issues? The answer lies in the capability of RMAN to catalog the backups which were done either through the simply copy or without the catalog. Using this feature of RMAN, the image copies can even be used as though they are RMAN's own backups. All this is done through a simple command, *catalog*.

Using the *catalog* command, the backup information can again be stored in the catalog which either was never stored or was stored in the control file and from there, it is either now gone or will be gone soon! Now see an example of the *catalog* command where an operating system image copy is recorded to the catalog.

Scenario 1

Before Bob was hired in a new job, there was a table created in a separate tablespace which was backed up using the old hot backup technique instead of using RMAN. One day, the system administrator suddenly deleted it using the *os* command. Having only the hot backup of that file, Bob decided to catalog that file to RMAN and use it to restore/recover the datafile.

To be in a Bob's situation, perform the following steps:

1. Create a new tablespace, connect with a user and create a table in that tablespace:

```
SQL>
create
 tablespace tbs datafile '/tmp/tbs.dbf' size 1M;

Tablespace created.

SQL>
conn
 usr/usr

Connected.

SQL>
create
 table test (id number) tablespace tbs;

Table created.

SQL>
insert into
 test values(1);

1 row created.

SQL>
commit;

Commit complete.

SQL>
select * from
 test;

        ID
----------
         1
```

2. Take a backup of that file, delete it and query the table again:

```
SQL>
alter
 tablespace tbs begin backup;

Tablespace altered.

SQL>
```

```
host
[oracle@localhost tmp]$ cp tbs.dbf tbs2.dbf
[oracle@localhost tmp]$ exit

exit

SQL>
alter
 tablespace tbs end backup;

Tablespace altered.

SQL>
host
[oracle@localhost tmp]$ rm -rf tbs.dbf
[oracle@localhost tmp]$ exit

exit

SQL>
alter
 system switch logfile;

System altered.

SQL>
select * from
 test;
select * from
 test
*

ERROR at line 1:
ORA-00376: file 5 cannot be read at this time
ORA-01110: data file 5: '/tmp/tbs.dbf'
SQL> exit
```

3. By having only the host backup of that file, login to the RMAN using the recovery catalog and catalog it:

```
[oracle@localhost tmp]$ rman target / catalog rc_owner/rc@rc

connected to target database: testdb (DBID=2493091955)
connected to recovery catalog database

RMAN> catalog datafilecopy '/tmp/tbs2.dbf';

starting full resync of recovery catalog
full resync complete
cataloged datafile copy
datafile copy filename=/tmp/tbs2.dbf recid=27 stamp=709826172

RMAN> list copy;

List of Datafile Copies
Key      File S Completion Time Ckp SCN    Ckp Time        Name
-------  ---- - --------------- ---------- --------------- ----
764      5    A 01-FEB-10       486473     01-FEB-10 /tmp/tbs2.dbf
```

4. Now, place the tablespace in the offline mode and restore/recover the file as follows:

```
RMAN> sql 'alter tablespace tbs offline immediate';

sql statement: alter tablespace tbs offline immediate

RMAN> restore datafile 5;

Starting restore at 01-FEB-10
......<output trimmed>
output filename=/tmp/tbs.dbf recid=28 stamp=709826182
Finished restore at 01-FEB-10

RMAN> recover datafile 5;

Starting recover at 01-FEB-10
using channel ORA_DISK_1

starting media recovery
media recovery complete, elapsed time: 00:00:02

Finished recover at 01-FEB-10

RMAN> SQL 'alter tablespace tbs online';

sql statement: alter tablespace tbs online
RMAN>
```

5. Connect to the database and query the table:

```
[oracle@localhost tmp]$ sqlplus "/ as sysdba"er/rc@rc
SQL>
conn
 usr/usr

Connected.

SQL>
select * from
 test;
        ID
----------
         1
```

Wow! The image copy of the datafile has been successfully cataloged to the recovery catalog and the datafile is restored/recovered using RMAN!

Just like the datafile, control files and archivelogs can also be cataloged into the recovery catalog. In addition to these files, the backup pieces which may have been created without the recovery catalog can also become a part of the recovery catalog using the same command.

If the Flash Recovery Area (FRA) for the backup storage is used, catalog all the files stored over it using:

```
RMAN>catalog recovery area;
```

There is another variant of the above command where the parameter *db_recovery_area_dest* can be directly used as well. Both the commands have the exact same meaning.

If there are backup files located at a non-FRA location but under a common folder, for example */u01/app/oracle/backup* under the *backup* folder, there are various files like datafiles, control files and archivelogs that can be cataloged using the *catalog start with* command. This command asks for the confirmation before adding the information to the recovery catalog. If the prompt for each file is not desired, use the *noprompt* switch:

```
RMAN>catalog start with '/u01/app/oracle/backup' noprompt;
```

It is worth mentioning that the name of the folder in the above command is taken as a prefix. This means that any files under the *backup* folder and folders which have *backup* as their prefix are cataloged by RMAN. Care must be taken if this is not what needs to happen. The check can be done by ending the path with a backslash after the desired folder beyond which should not be traversed; for example, the above command would then look like:

```
RMAN>catalog start with '/u01/app/oracle/backup/' noprompt;
```
This would mean only the files under the folder with the name *backup* would be cataloged and nothing else.

Note: The *catalog start with, catalog backuppiece, and catalog recovery area/db_recovery_file_dest* commands are new from Oracle 10g.

In the same way the file information can be filed into the catalog, the information from the catalog can be uncataloged as well. But interestingly, for this, there is no direct command like *uncatalog* that is available; it is done through the *change* command. This can come in handy when some metadata regarding a particular backup piece which is not needed anymore or is not available at all over the physical media should be removed. So to illustrate the command, uncatalog the same datafile copy which had been cataloged just a while ago:

```
RMAN> change datafilecopy 'e:\users01.dbf' uncatalog;
```

```
uncataloged datafile copy
datafile copy filename=E:\USERS01.DBF recid=7 stamp=706666372
Uncataloged 1 objects
```

Backing Up and Recovering the Recovery Catalog

As the recovery catalog contains such vital information concerning the backups, it is important that it must be protected as well. The backup of the recovery catalog database or even of the tablespace of it becomes a serious matter of concern.

The very first thing to be sure of is that the database where the catalog is stored and the target database are not the same! This sounds like a very obvious thing, but still many shops do not bother with it and realize what they have done only when they lose the target database containing their backup metadata as well. Therefore, the first step would be to have a separate and if possible, separately located database for the storage of the catalog. This would ensure the availability of at least the recovery catalog, thereby making the backup information available even when the target database has been lost.

The first option to back up the recovery catalog is RMAN itself. As the recovery catalog should be in a separate database, it is preferable to back up the database on a regular basis. To be able to perform a disaster recovery on the recovery catalog, the controlfile autobackup configuration should be ON. Also make sure that there are at least three copies of the catalog database backup available at different physical locations; for example, one on the hard disk and two on the tape drive. This means that the retention policy should also be changed to keep at least three copies of the backup as available backup which means redundancy should be set to more than one.

As the recovery catalog is nothing but the information stored in the catalog owner's schema objects, the logical backup done with the help of the Data Pump should be the second option. As this is going to be the logical backup, care should be taken that the frequency of doing this backup matches with the physical backup done via RMAN because it is important to make sure that all the recent information is kept in the dump file of the backup. In the case of loss of either the schema or of the entire catalog database, all that is needed is to create another new database and through import, create the catalog schema once again.

If both RMAN and Data Pump have not been configured to take a backup of the recovery catalog and it has been lost, then there are two options. After creating a new recovery catalog, either use the *resync catalog* command to synchronize the backup repository information between control file and catalog database, or use the *catalog* command to update the recovery catalog with information of available backups.

RMAN brings tons of options with it. Though it is not mandatory to use the catalog, some of its options only become alive with the help of the catalog. In this chapter, the ways to create, manage, protect and use the recovery catalog have been shown. As has been said, the real power of RMAN comes alive when used from the command line. In the same manner, the real benefits of it come alive when used with a recovery catalog!

Creating Virtual Private Catalogs

In Oracle 11g, there is a new feature called Virtual Catalog which lets the administration of any database that is registered in the recovery catalog be granted to any user. Imagine that there are more than 100 databases that are registered in one recovery catalog. As the administration of the whole recovery catalog becomes harder, the decision is made to grant the administration of the specific databases to the specific DBAs. None of them will be able to view the recovery catalog of the databases where access was not granted. Now see the following scenario:

Scenario 2

Bob administers more than 50 databases and uses one recovery catalog to store the RMAN backup repository. Due to the new project, Bob registers some more databases to the recovery catalog. After a while, the managers ask Bob to give permission for DBAs that supports the project to view the RMAN repository of their own databases. So Bob decides to use the new feature of Oracle 11g, the Virtual Private Catalog, and grants the DBAs access to view the repository of only their databases.

To show it practically, look at the following example. Here there are three databases and the recovery catalog database:

■ testdb: First target database ˙

- db1: Second target database

- db2: Third target database

- rc: The database that keeps the recovery catalog

And two users:

- rc: The main recovery catalog owner

- usr: The second user that owns the virtual private catalog

First, register testdb to the main recovery catalog. Then create a new user in the recovery catalog database (rc) and register the second database (db1) to the base recovery catalog. Next, grant the user (usr) to view the repository of the second database (db1) by running the *grant catalog for database* command. Then connect to the catalog database with the new user name and create a virtual private catalog using the *create virtual catalog* command. Next, the decision is made to let the user (usr) register another database to its virtual catalog by running *grant register database* from RMAN.

Now, follow the next steps to successfully implement the above scenario. Create both users and grant them necessary privileges and roles:

```
C:\>set ORACLE_SID=rc
C:\>sqlplus "/ as sysdba"
SQL>
create
 user rc identified bY rc;

User created.

SQL>
grant
 connect, resource, recovery_catalog_owner
to
 rc;

Grant succeeded.

SQL>
create
 user usr
identified
 by usr;

User created.

SQL>
grant
 connect, resource, recovery_catalog_owner
to
```

```
  usr;

Grant succeeded.
SQL>
```

Connect both to the first target (testdb) and the catalog (rc) database. Create the catalog and register the database in the recovery catalog as follows:

```
C:\>set ORACLE_SID=testdb
C:\>rman target / catalog rc/rc@rc
RMAN> create catalog;

recovery catalog created

RMAN> register database;

database registered in recovery catalog
starting full resync of recovery catalog
full resync complete

RMAN> list incarnation;

List of Database Incarnations

DB Key  Inc Key DB Name  DB ID             STATUS   Reset SCN  Reset
                                                               Time
------- ------- -------- ---------------- --- ---------- ----------
1       14      TESTDB   2493084339        PARENT  1          15-OCT-07
1       2       TESTDB   2493084339        CURRENT 886308     31-JAN-10
RMAN>
```

Now connect to the second target database (db1) and the recovery catalog (rc) and register the second database as well:

```
C:\>set ORACLE_SID=db1
C:\>rman target / catalog rc/rc@rc
RMAN> register database;

database registered in recovery catalog
starting full resync of recovery catalog
full resync complete
RMAN>
```

Now connect to RMAN using the rc user and grant the *catalog for database* command to let the user usr view the backup repository of the database db1 through the virtual catalog:

```
RMAN> connect catalog rc/rc@rc

connected to recovery catalog database

RMAN> grant catalog for database db1 TO usr;

Grant succeeded.
```

Creating Virtual Private Catalogs

```
RMAN>
```

Connect to the recovery catalog using the usr username and create the virtual catalog:

```
RMAN> connect catalog db1/db1@rc
connected to recovery catalog database

RMAN> create virtual catalog;

found eligible base catalog owned by RC
created virtual catalog against base catalog owned by RC
RMAN>
```

Here, issue the *list incarnation* command to be sure that only the db1 database is viewed:

```
RMAN> list incarnation;

List of Database Incarnations
DB Key  Inc Key DB Name  DB ID             STATUS   Reset SCN  Reset
                                                               Time
-------  ------- --------  ----------------  ---  ----------  ----------
62       75      DB1      1304505053        PARENT 1           15-OCT-07
62       63      DB1      1304505053        CURRENT 886308     11-FEB-10
RMAN>
```

Run the same command again by connecting with the owner of the recovery catalog (rc):

```
C:\>rman catalog rc/rc@rc
RMAN> list incarnation;

List of Database Incarnations
DB Key  Inc Key DB Name  DB ID             STATUS   Reset SCN  Reset
                                                               Time
-------  ------- --------  ----------------  ---  ----------  ----------
62       75      DB1      1304505053        PARENT 1           15-OCT-07
62       63      DB1      1304505053        CURRENT 886308     11-FEB-10
1        14      TESTDB   2493084339        PARENT 1           15-OCT-07
1        2       TESTDB   2493084339        CURRENT 886308     31-JAN-10
RMAN>
```

Although there are two databases registered in the recovery catalog, a user can easily be granted access to view the specific database's backup repository.

Next, let the user register the third database (db2) to its virtual catalog by running the *grant register database* command from RMAN:

```
C:\>set ORACLE_SID=rc
C:\>rman
RMAN> connect catalog rc/rc
```

```
connected to recovery catalog database

RMAN> grant register database to usr;

Grant succeeded.
RMAN>
```

It is time to register the third database (db2) to the virtual catalog:

```
C:\>set oracle_sid=db2
C:\>rman target / catalog usr/usr@rc

connected to target database: DB2 (DBID=1874133855)
connected to recovery catalog database

RMAN> register database;

database registered in recovery catalog
starting full resync of recovery catalog
full resync complete

RMAN> list incarnation;

List of Database Incarnations
DB Key  Inc Key DB Name  DB ID            STATUS  Reset SCN  Reset
                                                             Time
-------  ------- -------- ---------------- --- ---------- ----------
62       75      DB1      1304505053       PARENT  1          15-OCT-07
62       63      DB1      1304505053       CURRENT 886308     11-FEB-10
82       95      DB2      1874133855       PARENT  1          15-OCT-07
82       83      DB2      1874133855       CURRENT 886308     11-FEB-10
RMAN>
```

Having registered two databases to the virtual private catalog, the scenario was finished successfully.

To get the user list of virtual catalog owners, query the *vpc_users* view. To get the list of registered databases, use the *vps_databases* view. Since catalog privilege can be granted to the user, it can also be revoked if needed using the *revoke* command. So revoke this privilege for the user (usr):

```
C:\>rman
RMAN> connect catalog rc/rc@rc

connected to recovery catalog database

RMAN> revoke catalog for database db1 from usr;

Revoke succeeded.
```

To revoke both privileges, use the *revoke all privileges* command as follows:

```
RMAN> revoke all privileges from usr;

Revoke succeeded.
RMAN>
```

To drop the catalog, use the *drop catalog* command:

```
C:\>rman
RMAN> connect catalog usr/usr@rc

connected to recovery catalog database
recovery catalog is not installed

RMAN> drop catalog;

recovery catalog owner is USR
enter drop catalog command again to confirm catalog removal

RMAN> drop catalog;

virtual catalog dropped
RMAN>
```

Merging and Moving the Recovery Catalog

One of the new features of Oracle 11g is the *import catalog* command which is used to merge or move recovery catalogs. If there are different recovery catalogs for different databases with different Oracle versions and the RMAN repository of all databases should be centralized under one recovery catalog, they can all be moved into one general catalog. By using the *import catalog* command, RMAN unregisters the database from the source target and imports all databases that were registered on the catalog to the new recovery catalog.

In the following example, there are two databases which run on two different Oracle versions. The first database is named dbone and the database that stores its repository is named dbonecat. Both databases run on Oracle 10gR2. The second database is the target database called dbtwo and its backup repository database named dbtwocat run on Oracle 11gR1. The repository of the first database should be moved to the second recovery catalog. Before starting the process, the first catalog should be upgraded. For this, connect to the recovery catalog of the first database (dbonecat) from 11g RMAN binary and issue the *upgrade catalog* command (twice).

```
RMAN> connect catalog usr_one_cat/test@dbonecat;

connected to recovery catalog database
PL/SQL package usr_one_cat.dbms_rcvcat version 10.02.00.00 in RCVCAT
database is too old
```

```
RMAN> upgrade catalog;

recovery catalog owner is USR_ONE_CAT
enter upgrade catalog command again to confirm catalog upgrade

RMAN> upgrade catalog;

recovery catalog upgraded to version 11.01.00.06
DBMS_RCVMAN package upgraded to version 11.01.00.06
DBMS_RCVCAT package upgraded to version 11.01.00.06
RMAN>
```

Now, connect to the recovery catalog of the second database (dbtwocat) and use the *import catalog* command by connecting to the backup repository of the first database (dbonecat) as follows:

```
C:\>RMAN catalog usr_two_cat/test@dbtwocat;

connected to recovery catalog database

RMAN> import catalog usr_one_cat/test@dbonecat;

Starting import catalog at 23-MAR-10
connected to source recovery catalog database
import validation complete
database unregistered from the source recovery catalog
Finished import catalog at 23-MAR-10
RMAN>
```

The import process has now finished. Check the registered database list by running the *list incarnation* command:

```
RMAN> list incarnation;

List of Database Incarnations
DB Key  Inc Key DB Name  DB ID             STATUS   Reset SCN  Reset
                                                               Time
------- ------- -------- ---------------- --- ---------- ----------
1       16      DBTWO    3816644412        PARENT  1         15-OCT-07
1       2       DBTWO    3816644412        CURRENT 886308    23-MAR-10
32      39      DBONE    3840858402        PARENT  1         30-AUG-05
32      33      DBONE    3840858402        CURRENT 534907    23-MAR-10
RMAN>
```

The first database has now been registered successfully.

> 🔔 Note: During *import catalog*, the RMAN will create two underlying temporary objects: Table – used to store the DBID of the databases which need to be imported. Database link –used to query the information from the original catalog.

In case the database should not be unregistered from the source catalog and only a specific database is registered, use the *db_name* and *no unregister* commands with the *import catalog* command. As has been mentioned above, a default RMAN unregisters and imports all databases from the source catalog. In the following example, only the specific database named dbthree is registered by not unregistering the database from the source catalog.

```
RMAN> connect catalog usr_two_cat/test@dbtwocat

connected to recovery catalog database

RMAN> import catalog usr_one_cat/test@dbonecat db_name=dbthree no
unregister;

Starting import catalog at 23-MAR-10
connected to source recovery catalog database
import validation complete
Finished import catalog at 23-MAR-10
```

Check the list of all registered databases from the target catalog:

```
RMAN> list incarnation;
```

```
List of Database Incarnations
DB Key  Inc Key DB Name  DB ID             STATUS   Reset SCN  Reset
                                                               Time
------- ------- -------- ----------------- --- ---------- ----------
101     114     DBTHREE  3116112601        PARENT  1          30-AUG-05
101     102     DBTHREE  3116112601        CURRENT 534907     23-MAR-10
1       16      DBTWO    3816644412        PARENT  1          15-OCT-07
1       2       DBTWO    3816644412        CURRENT 886308     23-MAR-10
32      39      DBONE    3840858402        PARENT  1          30-AUG-05
32      33      DBONE    3840858402        CURRENT 534907     23-MAR-10
RMAN>
```

Query the source catalog and check whether the database was unregistered or not:

```
RMAN> list incarnation;

List of Database Incarnations
```

```
DB Key   Inc Key DB Name  DB ID            STATUS  Reset SCN  Reset
                                                              Time
-------  ------- -------- ---------------- --- ---------- ----------
41       54      DBTHREE  3116112601       PARENT  1          30-AUG-05
41       42      DBTHREE  3116112601       CURRENT 534907     23-MAR-10
RMAN>
```

The database was not unregistered from the source catalog.

Querying the Recovery Catalog

To get information about the backup taken by RMAN, use the *report*, *list* or *show* commands. All these commands were explained in Chapter 3, *Backing Up the Database Using RMAN*. However, it is also possible to get backup information from views that store everything about backup of all databases that registered in the recovery catalog. These views can be accessed by connecting to the database as the owner of the catalog and by querying the view which starts with the *rc_* prefix, i.e. *rc_spfile_backup*, *rc_datafile* and such.

To get the list of all the views, run the following query:

```
SQL> conn rc_owner/rc

Connected.

SQL>
select
 view_name
from
 user_views
where
 view_name
like 'rc_%';
```

There are more than 50 views, but the most commonly used are the following:

View name	Explanation
rc_archived_log	Historical information about archived and non-archived redo logs (Corresponds to the v$archived_log view)
rc_backup_controlfile	Contains information about control files in backup sets
rc_backup_corruption	Contains list of corrupted blocs in datafile backups. Corresponds to the v$backup_corruption view.

rc_database_block_corruption	Lists information about data blocks that were corrupted after last backup
rc_backup_datafile	Contains information about datafiles in backup sets
rc_backup_piece	Lists information about backup pieces
rc_backup_set	Contains information about backup sets of all incarnations of the database
rc_backup_spfile	Lists information about server parameter file in backup sets
rc_controlfile_copy	Lists information about controlfile copy in backup sets
rc_database	Contains information about all databases that registered in the recovery catalog
rc_database_incarnation	Lists information about all databases registered in the recovery catalog
rc_datafile	Lists information about all datafiles registered in the recovery catalog
rc_resync	Lists information about recovery catalog resynchronizations
rc_rman_configuration	Contains information about RMAN configuration settings
rc_rman_status	Contains information about all operations on all databases made by connecting to the recovery catalog
rc_stored_script and *rc_stored_script_line*	Both contain information about the scripts that stored in the recovery catalog.

Table 7.2: *Main Recovery Catalog Views*

Conclusion

This chapter provided detailed information on creating and managing the recovery catalog. After creating a recovery catalog for the RMAN repository, the target database was registered in that catalog. Then the resynchronization process that happens between target database control file and recovery catalog was covered.

As the recovery catalog can store scripts and share it between databases that are registered in the catalog, how to create global, local and dynamic scripts and use them in backup procedures was shown. Moreover, an example was provided on cataloging older backups that were taken using the old hot backup technique to the recovery catalog and using them in restore/recover procedures.

As the recovery catalog contains everything about RMAN backups of the databases that are registered in it, it should be backed up on a daily basis. So the procedures on backing up the recovery catalog have been examined thoroughly. Lastly, the main views have been provided which are useful to be queried and which display any information needed from the recovery catalog.

Troubleshooting, Monitoring and Tuning RMAN

Oracle is a big and very complex piece of software code. With so many features, it is easy to get errors while working with them. It is as important to understand how to troubleshoot an error as it is to use the software itself. Just like the Oracle database or any other software, RMAN has a number of errors and error messages associated with it which may come and haunt the DBA when least expected and sometimes when something is actually done wrong.

This chapter is not devoted to troubleshooting all of those errors as there may be numerous reasons and each reason is based on many types of environmental conditions as well. What this chapter will tell is how to understand the error message better in order to decide what to do about it and why.

RMAN Troubleshooting Overview

There can be several places which can be helpful while trying to debug RMAN. Not all of them need to dig up, but all of these listed below contain information that can often be vital to troubleshoot the error in a precise manner.

- RMAN terminal
- RMAN *debug* file
- Alert log
- Oracle Server trace file
- *Sbtio.log*

RMAN is recommended as a command line tool. Whenever an error message of RMAN is seen, its error stack first appears in the terminal window itself where the RMAN client is/was running. RMAN error messages have the format RMAN-nnnn; for example, RMAN-06043. By default, when connected to the RMAN client, the error messages as well as messages/output of the command issued are printed on the same terminal itself. This can be changed if the messages of the command are logged in a log file that can be created when the *log* option is used while connecting to RMAN.

There is no debugging that is enabled by default for RMAN operations. At the most, what are printed are the standard error messages. No information is provided about anything that is peeking into the operations that are running in the back end. But this information can be enabled by the *trace* option which may go into a debug file. This information is not normally meant to be read by the DBA; it is best suited for an Oracle Support professional to understand and troubleshoot the issue in a better way. It shall be seen in a subsequent topic how to enable this tracing facility for RMAN as well as see a small trace file.

As usual, the alert log is the first place where a DBA should look when any sort of errors are reported. This contains the information about all the parameters used in the instance startup and the log of all the operations along with the errors and many more things. In general, specific RMAN issues are meant to be issued at its prompt only, but there may be a possibility that the error in RMAN is coming based on some issue in the database. For example, connecting to RMAN when the database is down may be desired. For this, surely there is an error reported on the RMAN prompt related to this and the message is also recorded in the alert log. Using that information, it is easier to diagnose the error.

There may be a chance that the database has undergone some serious error like *ORA-04031* or some internal error like *ORA-00600*. For example, a channel dies abnormally; as it is also a session connected to the database, it generates a trace file like any other process trace and is available in the *user_dump_dest* destination at the server side.

Sbtio.log contains the error information about the vendor-supplied media management software. This file does not contain any information about Oracle or RMAN errors. The destination of this file is also like the server trace, i.e. in the *user_dump_dest* destination at the server side.

It is worth mentioning that even though the file *sbtio.log* is supposed to contain the information about the MML software of the vendor, this file does not contain anything if the vendor has not enabled the logging of the error messages into this file in its scripts. If this is not done, then there will not be any information that is recorded in this file and the entire log is logged into the client side log file only. The file can become very large over time and should be purged after some defined interval decided by the DBA.

Interpreting RMAN Error Stack

RMAN does not present just one error message when there is some issue. It presents an error stack that can be a tough nut to crack if it is not known where to start reading from. For example, look at this error message issued.

```
RMAN-03002: failure of backup command at 12/28/2009 00:10:20
RMAN-03014: implicit resync of recovery catalog failed
RMAN-06403: could not obtain a fully authorized session
ORA-01034: ORACLE not available
ORA-27101: shared memory realm does not exist
```

Looking straight at this error code is not very meaningful as it has five lines of errors. To start with the RMAN errors, it is always better to start from the bottom up. This error stack is actually a mix of both RMAN and ORA errors. So using the bottom-up route, the first error reported is *ORA-27101* which depicts that the shared memory realm is not there.

Normally, this message comes for one of two reasons. One, a database which does not exist is being tried. Second, the correct database only should be worked with, but it has not started yet. Looking further, doubt turns into confirmation as the next message is *ORA-01034* saying that Oracle is not available which means that the database is not yet started. So far, so good!

The next lines start with the error of RMAN as the prefix now is changed from ORA to RMAN here and the first error is *RMAN-06403*. The error code range is between 6000 to 6999, which is basically the series of errors dealing with generic compilation failures. The mentioned error, 06403, has this error description from the 11.2 Error Message Guide, "The most likely cause of the error is that one of the databases to which RMAN had previously connected is not started up or has been shut down. Other error messages should identify exactly which database is the problem."

The action for this is "Startup the database causing the problem". The error messages make perfect sense and correlate exactly with what had just been figured out from the ORA messages that the database is down. Now move above one step where it shows that the next RMAN error code is 03014 which lies in the range of 3000 to 3999 and is related to the main layer of the RMAN. Proceeding above, the next code is 03002 which defines the command failure and it is indeed correct as a backup command is issued which failed right away because the database was down! The same information is also given by the error code *RMAN-03009*, but this also includes the channel ID as well.

If a wrong command has been typed, the *RMAN-00508* error code occurs which is for the failed parsing of the command. It is always easy to create this error like below:

```
RMAN> bkup tablespace users;

RMAN-00571: ===========================================================
RMAN-00569: =============== ERROR MESSAGE STACK FOLLOWS ===============
RMAN-00571: ===========================================================
RMAN-00558: error encountered while parsing input commands
RMAN-01009: syntax error: found "identifier": expecting one of: "allocate,
alter, backup, beginline, blockrecover, catalog, change, connect, copy,
convert, create, crosscheck, configure, duplicate, debug, delete, drop,
exit, endinline, flashback, host, {, library, list, mount, open, print,
quit, recover, register, release, replace, report, renormalize, reset,
restore, resync, rman, run, rpctest, set, setlimit, sql, switch, spool,
startup, shutdown, send, show, test, transport, upgrade, unregister,
validate"
RMAN-01008: the bad identifier was: bkup
RMAN-01007: at line 1 column 1 file: standard input
```

There is a spelling mistake in the word *backup* and this resulted in a *RMAN-00508* error code. The error range of 550-999 is for the command line interpreter and the next error code after that is *RMAN-01009* whose range, 1000-1999, is the category for analyzing keywords. Also, a bad identifier called *bkup* was used which failed the command. The principle of bottom-up did not fail once again.

If there is a question about the syntax of the command, checking the Backup and Recovery Reference Guide is a good place to start with the following link (11.2): http://download.oracle.com/docs/cd/E11882_01/backup.112/e10643/toc.htm.

If there is no time to check the above guide, RMAN comes with the switch *checksyntax* that specifically checks the syntax of issued input, both standalone and in the script. So try it:

```
[oracle@localhost ~] rman checksyntax
RMAN> backup tablespace users;

The command has no syntax errors

RMAN> backup tablespace users:

RMAN-00571: ===========================================================
RMAN-00569: =============== ERROR MESSAGE STACK FOLLOWS ===============
RMAN-00571: ===========================================================
RMAN-00558: error encountered while parsing input commands
RMAN-01009: syntax error: found "colon": expecting one of: "archivelog,
backup, backupset, channel, comma, copy, controlfilecopy, current, database,
datafile, datafilecopy, delete, diskratio, db_recovery_file_dest,
filesperset, format, from, force, include, keep, (, maxsetsize, noexclude,
nokeep, not, pool, plus, reuse, recovery, ;, skip, spfile, setsize,
tablespace, tag, to"
RMAN-01007: at line 1 column 24 file: standard input
```

It clearly stated for the first time that there was no error with the command but the next time, as a colon was entered rather than a semi-colon, the error was reported.

The complete list of the error code range of RMAN is available from the 11.2 Backup and Recovery Reference Guide.

Error Range	Cause
0550-0999	Command-line interpreter
1000-1999	Keyword analyzer
2000-2999	Syntax analyzer
3000-3999	Main layer
4000-4999	Services layer
5000-5499	Compilation of *restore* or *recover* command
5500-5999	Compilation of *duplicate* command
6000-6999	General compilation
7000-7999	General execution
8000-8999	PL/SQL programs
9000-9999	Low-level keyword analyzer
10000-10999	Server-side execution
11000-11999	Interphase errors between PL/SQL and RMAN

Error Range	Cause
12000-12999	Recovery catalog packages

Table 8.1: *RMAN Error Message Ranges*

All the error messages of RMAN are well explained with their possible cause and actions in the 11.2 Error Message Guide. Please refer to it at the following link: http://download.oracle.com/docs/cd/E11882_01/ server.112/e17766/toc.htm.

RMAN in Debug Mode

The information given at any error should be enough to troubleshoot the underlying failed operation and command. However, there are times when digging much deeper than what is available on the outer side is required. For example, how the I/O calls for a backup and how restore and recover operations are working should be checked. For this, the standard error messaging or logging will not be helpful.

Similarly, if a channel is dying abruptly when allocated, reasoning for that will not be clear from the standard logging. Oracle database has capabilities to enable tracing and debugging sessions for almost all parts of it. In the same way, RMAN can also be run in the debug mode where the flow of the underlying and somewhat hidden operations can be revealed.

The *debug* option is a resource-consuming option, both in the terms of physical and computational resources. Even a simple command like *report, list* would be very slow when run with the *debug* option. The resultant trace files also come up with a huge size and the contents also do not make much sense if there is not familiarity with reading raw trace files like trace files of 10046 and 10053 trace events! For these reasons, an explanation of the contents of the trace file are beyond the scope of this book, but an introduction on how to enable the *debug* option and its various options will be given.

The *debug* option can be used in three different places while working with RMAN:

1. In a RMAN command line input

2. At the RMAN prompt

3. In a *run* block

The *debug* option is capable of debugging five different areas. The default is to provide the information about all five categories and is given as the category ALL. Other than this, the categories are I/O, SQL, PL/SQL, RCVMAN, and RPC. The default option if nothing else is mentioned would be to debug all five. Doing so will greatly impact the working of the RMAN. Here are some of the examples using the *debug* option:

▪ From the command prompt

The simplest way to enter into debug mode is while connecting to the RMAN. As the *debug* option creates a huge amount of feedback, it is always better to store it in a log file which can be given with the *log* option so that the entire feedback can be read after the command finishes.

```
$rman target / debug=ALL log=/u01/app/oracle/rmandebug.txt
```

The above command records all the info of the commands issued in the *rmandebug.txt* file and the debugging information is for all the five categories.

▪ At the RMAN prompt

Specify the *debug* option at the RMAN prompt itself with any other RMAN standalone command like below:

```
RMAN>debug on;
RMAN>backup database;
RMAN>debug off;
```

▪ From a *run* block

If multiple commands are being run in one go, start the debugging of all of them by supplying the option of *debug* inside the *run* block as shown below:

```
RMAN> RUN {
            debug on;
            allocate channel c1 type disk;
            backup database;
            debug off;
        }
```

In general, there will almost never be that requirement to enable the *debug* option; it will only occur if Oracle Support asks that it be done. Therefore, it is advisable to start RMAN in this mode. Also look at the MOS document, Note:132941.1 – RMAN: Quick Debugging Guide.

Dealing with MML and 3rd Party Errors

Most of the time, RMAN backups are done over a tape drive which is configured to work with RMAN through a Media Management Layer (MML). The MML loads the driver software which is required to make the tape drive work with RMAN. As each vendor makes and configures its media in its own way, most of the time errors related to tape media are best suited for the particular vendor of that tape drive.

So it would actually be the responsibility of the vendor to troubleshoot the error. But from RMAN itself, an error stack with error codes and messages is provided that may help in diagnosing the issue. If it is a media manager error, the error code *ORA-19511* is returned. This contains the informative message as well about the error and its reasoning. RMAN uses SBT (System Binary to Tape) to talk to the tape drives. For this, there is a whole range of errors which can be found to identify the actual reasoning of the error.

To illustrate the point, see a sample output.

```
RMAN-00571: ===========================================
RMAN-00569: ======= ERROR MESSAGE STACK FOLLOWS =======
RMAN-00571: ===========================================
RMAN-03009: failure of backup command on c1 channel at
09/09/2009 13:18:19
ORA-19506: failed to create sequential file,
name="07d36ecp_1_1", parms=""
ORA-27007: failed to open file
SVR4 Error: 2: No such file or directory
Additional information: 7005
Additional information: 1
ORA-19511: Error from media manager layer,error text:
```

The error *ORA-19511* is shown here and the additional information section also shows the number 7005. This is an example of a media management issue.

From RMAN or from Oracle's side, only a generic idea can be drawn about what is wrong about the 3rd party vendor software. The real information can be found in the vendor specific documentation and error logs only.

Using the *sbttest* Utility

Oracle ships a utility to check and diagnose the media management API called *sbttest*. This utility does not do an actual backup but tries to communicate with the media management software to see if it is working properly or not. There is no need to download anything to start using this utility since it is shipped on the Unix platforms out-of-the-box and can be found under *$ORACLE_HOME/bin*. If the installation does not have it and there is a valid Oracle Support contract, ask OSS to send the same and they will gladly do so.

If this is going to be used over Solaris, there is no need to do any relinking of binaries, but on other platforms, using it requires a relink and would depend on the operating system and the product that is being used to take the backup.

Now specify the correct API file that has to be used with the *sbttest* utility. If nothing is mentioned, then the default API file for Unix platforms is *libobk.so* which is used for testing. For Windows, the API file name is *orasbt.dll*. The location of the files can vary and if some MML software is already configured and is now being upgraded, redundant copies of the file may be found as well. Make sure that only the most current version of the API file is used.

Once the utility has been relinked successfully, all that is needed is to go to the terminal and issue:

```
$sbttest -help
```

This produces a long listing of the options available that can be used.

sbttest can work for any file which is required to work with the media management API or directly with some mentioned datafile of which the backup should be taken. It is normally a good practice to include a trace file to record the output of the feedback.

Once the required configuration has been finished, a successful run of *sbttest* should look like this:

```
$sbttest test.out -trace sbttest.trace

The sbt function pointers are loaded from libobk.so library.
-- sbtinit succeeded
-- sbtinit (2nd time) succeeded
sbtinit: Media manager supports SBT API version 2.0
sbtinit: vendor description string=NMO v4.2.0.0
sbtinit: allocated sbt context area of 1176 bytes
sbtinit: Media manager is version 4.2.0.0
sbtinit: proxy copy is supported
sbtinit: maximum concurrent proxy copy files is 0
-- sbtinit2 succeeded
```

```
-- regular_backup_restore starts

In case the utility doesn't work for any reason the output would be similar
like shown below,
The sbt function pointers are loaded from libobk.so library.
-- sbtinit succeeded
-- sbtinit (2nd time) succeeded
sbtinit: Media manager supports SBT API version 2.0
sbtinit: Media manager is version 5.0.0.0
sbtinit: vendor description string=VERITAS NetBackup for Oracle - Release
5.0GA (2003103006)
sbtinit: allocated sbt context area of 8 bytes
sbtinit: proxy copy is supported
-- sbtinit2 succeeded
-- regular_backup_restore starts .............................
MMAPI error from sbtbackup: 7501, Failed to process backup file <test>

-- sbtbackup failed
[billtemp]oracle:/bill/appl/oracle/product/10.2.0/bin>
```

There is not just one set of error messages that may occur if the test fails. The errors depend on what has gone wrong. Also, it is worth mentioning that even though *sbttest* runs successfully, it may still be possible that the tape media may not be used properly. For example, if there is not a proper configuration done between the server and the media management layer, the actual backup may fail but *sbttest* results in a successful test.

Monitoring RMAN

To monitor and administer RMAN, use either OEM or the command line views, both from the recovery catalog as well as from the SQL prompt. There are a couple of views from the SQL prompt which can help in knowing about RMAN and details related to it.

- *v$rman_configuration*

- *v$rman_status*

- *v$rman_output*

- *v$rman_backup_job_details*

The details of the columns of all the views are in the Oracle documentation. It is suggested that the description be checked from there. These views are introduced next.

- *v$rman_configuration*

RMAN in Debug Mode

This view shows the RMAN persistent configuration. Any setting that has been done through the *configure* command is shown from this view. As default RMAN parameters are changed, the view is automatically updated. The following example shows that only one row is there because the default location of backup has been changed:

```
SQL>
select * from
 v$rman_configuration;

CONF#          NAME           VALUE
---------      -------------  -----------------------
1              CHANNEL        DEVICE TYPE DISK FORMAT   'c:\rman_backup\test_backup_%U'
```

Now change another configuration and query the view again:

```
RMAN> configure controlfile autobackup on;
SQL>
select * from
 v$rman_configuration;

CONF# NAME            VALUE
--    -------------   ----------------------------
1     CHANNEL         DEVICE TYPE DISK FORMAT   'c:\rman_backup\test_backup_%U'
2     CONTROLFILE AUTOBACKUP          ON
SQL>
```

- *v$ rman_status*

This view explains the status of the operations which are either running or have been completed with its respective details. From here, which session is doing what can be found. To demonstrate the usage of this view, connect to RMAN and query the view:

```
C:\Documents and Settings\Administrator>rman target /
RMAN>
SQL>
select
 sid, row_type, operation, status, to_char(start_time,'dd-mm-yyyy
hh24:mi:ss') start_time, to_char(end_time,'dd-mm-yyyy hh24:mi:ss') end_time
from
 v$rman_status;

SID ROW_TYPE   OPERATION STATUS     START_TIME          END_TIME
-- ---------- --------- ---------- ---------------- ----------------
159 SESSION    RMAN   RUNNING  08-07-2010 16:52:38 08-07-2010 16:56:12
SQL>
```

By getting the *sid* value, more information about this session can be obtained from the *v$session* view:

```
SQL>
select
 sid, username, osuser, terminal, program, action from v$session where
 sid=159;
```

```
SID USERNAME OSUSER                          TERMINAL             PROGRAM     ACTION
--------- ------------------                 -------------------- ----------  --------------
159 SYS       KAMRAN-979959CB\Administrator  KAMRAN-979959CB      rman.exe    0000001 FINISHED70
```

Next, take a backup of the database using the following command:

```
RMAN> backup database plus archivelog;

Starting backup at 08-JUL-10
channel ORA_DISK_1: starting archive log backupset
Finished backup at 08-JUL-10

Starting backup at 08-JUL-10
channel ORA_DISK_1: starting full datafile backupset
Finished backup at 08-JUL-10

Starting backup at 08-JUL-10
channel ORA_DISK_1: starting archive log backupset
Finished backup at 08-JUL-10

RMAN>
```

By running this command, the following result appears:

```
SQL>
select
 sid, row_type, operation, status, to_char(start_time,'dd-mm-yyyy
hh24:mi:ss') start_time, to_char(end_time,'dd-mm-yyyy hh24:mi:ss') end_time
from
 v$rman_status;

SID ROW_TYPE   OPERATION  STATUS     START_TIME          END_TIME
--------- ---------- ---------- ---------- ------ -------------------
0 COMMAND    BACKUP     COMPLETED  08-07-2010 17:02:43 08-07-2010 17:02:50
0 COMMAND    BACKUP     COMPLETED  08-07-2010 17:02:50 08-07-2010 17:03:39
0 COMMAND    BACKUP     COMPLETED  08-07-2010 17:03:39 08-07-2010 17:03:41
159 SESSION    RMAN       RUNNING    08-07-2010 16:52:38 08-07-2010 17:11:38
```

Since there is a current connection to RMAN, the status of the session 159 is *running*. If RMAN is not active, then the third row will be changed as follows:

```
SID ROW_TYPE   OPERATION  STATUS     START_TIME          END_TIME
--------- ---------- ---------- -------------------- -----------             0 SESSION    RMAN
COMPLETED   08-07-2010 16:52:38    08-07-2010 17:13:15
```

Now delete one of the backupsets and check the *v$rman_status* view:

```
RMAN> delete backupset 1;

SID ROW_TYPE   OPERATION  STATUS     START_TIME          END_TIME
--------- ---------- ---------- =========
0  COMMAND    DELETE     COMPLETED  08-07-2010 17:14:43  08-07-2010 17:14:47
```

If the RMAN session was failed due to the unexpected error, the status column is *failed*. Take a backup of the database and interrupt it by pressing Ctrl+C to check the query again:

```
RMAN> backup database;

Starting backup at 08-JUL-10
using channel ORA_DISK_1
channel ORA_DISK_1: starting full datafile backupset
^C

C:\>
SQL>
select
 sid, row_type, operation, status, to_char(start_time,'dd-mm-yyyy
hh24:mi:ss') start_time, to_char(end_time,'dd-mm-yyyy hh24:mi:ss') end_time
from
 v$rman_status;

SID ROW_TYPE   OPERATION  STATUS    START_TIME          END_TIME
--------- ---------- ---------- ---------- ------------------- ----    0 COMMAND    BACKUP
FAILED      08-07-2010 17:26:59
SQL>
```

- *v$rman_output*

The *running* command's output can be seen either from the RMAN terminal or from the log file that was mentioned while connecting to the RMAN. In addition to these two sources, the in-memory output of the issued commands can also be seen through this view. This has the logging of the feedback produced by the issued command in a live RMAN session. Here is an example output from the *v$rman_output* view:

```
SQL>
select
 sid, output
from
 v$rman_output;

       SID OUTPUT
---------- -------------------------------------------
       147 connected to target database: TEST (DBID
           =2022494986)

       147
       147
       147 Starting backup at 14-JUL-10
       147 using target database control file inste
           ad of recovery catalog

       147 allocated channel: ORA_DISK_1
       147 channel ORA_DISK_1: sid=144 devtype=DISK
       147 channel ORA_DISK_1: starting full datafi
```

- *v$rman_backup_job_details*

Like the above view, this also shows the information about the jobs running within RMAN, but this gives the information of each job individually. This means if there are two backup jobs and four restore jobs running, this view shows all individually.

Before querying the view, take some backups. Connect to RMAN and take the following backups:

```
C:\>rman target /

RMAN> backup database;

RMAN> exit

C:\>rman target /
RMAN> backup archivelog all;

RMAN> exit

C:\>rman target /
RMAN> BACKUP SPFILE;

RMAN> exit

C:\>rman target /
RMAN> backup incremental level 1 database;

input datafile fno=00004
name=C:\ORACLE\product\10.2.0\oradata\test\users01.dbf
channel ora_disk_1: starting piece 1 at 16-JUL-10
^C
```

Above, the backup is interrupted by pressing Ctrl+C:

```
C:\>rman target /
RMAN> backup datafile 4;

RMAN> exit

SQL>
select
 session_key, input_type, status, input_bytes, output_bytes,
to_char(start_time, 'dd.mm.yyyy hh24:mi:ss') start_time, to_char(end_time,
'dd.mm.yyyy hh24:mi:ss') end_time, output_device_type, elapsed_seconds
from
 v$rman_backup_job_details;

SESSION_KEY INPUT_TYPE    STATUS                  INPUT_BYTES OUTPUT_BYTES  START_TIME
END_TIME            OUTPUT_DEVICE_TYP ELAPSED_SECONDS
----------- ------------- ----------------------- ----------- ------------ -------------------- -----
-------------- ---------------- ----------------
1 DB FULL       COMPLETED                 772505600    532733952  16.07.2010 16:22:41 16.07.2010
16:23:33 DISK                  52
```

```
6 SPFILE         COMPLETED    0        81920    16.07.2010 16:25:23 16.07.2010 16:25:26          3

8 DB INCR        FAILED       777748480  533078016    16.07.2010 16:25:45 16.07.2010 16:26:13 DISK
28

12 DATAFILE FULL COMPLETED             5242880       376832 16.07.2010 16:27:11 16.07.2010
16:27:19 DISK                     8

3 ARCHIVELOG     COMPLETED   46302208   46385664    16.07.2010 16:24:01 16.07.2010 16:24:23 DISK
22
SQL>
```

To make sure that there is nothing hung, it is good practice to keep a check on RMAN either through the command line or from the Oracle Enterprise Manager. When a job of backup or recovery is scheduled through RMAN from 10g onwards using either the database console or Grid console, it can be monitored graphically. From the command line of RMAN, there is no direct way of monitoring the progress of the command issued. So use the database view *v$session_longops* which can check and report back the progress of RMAN. If the output does not seem to be moving ahead, it may mean some issue(s) which can be looked for afterwards.

Since RMAN also connects to the target database like any other normal session, it also can be tracked through the same views from where the normal sessions can be tracked. When an RMAN backup is running, *v$session_longops*, *v$session_wait*, *v$session* and *v$rman_backup_job_details* can be used to monitor it.

Using the views depends on specific requirements. Since these views use the session details of the channel(s) which RMAN communicates to the database, they can be used for a variety of requirements starting from checking the active session of RMAN to monitoring progress of the operation.

> Tip: Set *nls_date_format* only in the RMAN session so that RMAN displays *Hours:Minutes:Seconds* as well. Do not change the *nls_date_format* at the instance level as that can affect the behavior of the applications.

Therefore, for a session that has issued,

```
ora10204>NLS_DATE_FORMAT=DD_MON_HH24_MI_SS;export NLS_DATE_FORMAT
ora10204>rman target /

connected to target database: ORT24FS (DBID=4163910544)

RMAN> backup database;

Starting backup at 25_JUL_12_45_29
```

```
using target database control file instead of recovery catalog
allocated channel: ORA_DISK_1
channel ORA_DISK_1: sid=145 devtype=DISK
channel ORA_DISK_1: starting full datafile backupset
channel ORA_DISK_1: specifying datafile(s) in backupset
input datafile fno=00004 name=/oracle_fs/Databases/ORT24FS/users01.dbf
input datafile fno=00001 name=/oracle_fs/Databases/ORT24FS/system01.dbf
input datafile fno=00006 name=/oracle_fs/Databases/ORT24FS/undotbs.dbf
input datafile fno=00003 name=/oracle_fs/Databases/ORT24FS/sysaux01.dbf
input datafile fno=00005 name=/oracle_fs/Databases/ORT24FS/example01.dbf
channel ORA_DISK_1: starting piece 1 at 25_JUL_12_45_31
```

it can be monitored with queries such as:

```
SQL> l
  1  select
to_char(sysdate,'DD-MON HH24:MI:SS') Collection_DateStamp, sid, opname,
target, sofar, totalwork,
  2   units, to_char(start_time,'HH24:MI:SS') StartTime,
  3   time_remaining, message, username
  4   from
 v$session_longops
  5   where
 sofar != totalwork
  6* order by
 start_time
SQL> /

COLLECTION_DATE        SID OPNAME
--------------- ---------- -----------------------------------------------------
TARGET                                                       SOFAR   TOTALWORK UNITS
STARTTIM
---------------------------------------------------------- ---------- ---------- --------------
----------------- --------
TIME_REMAINING
--------------
MESSAGE
------------------------------------------------------------------------------------------------
-----------------------------
USERNAME
-----------------------------
25-JUL 12:46:04        159 RMAN: aggregate input
20                                                               0      855840 Blocks
12:45:28

RMAN: aggregate input: backup 20: 0 out of 855840 Blocks done
SYS

25-JUL 12:46:04        145 RMAN: full datafile backup
70                                                           50616      855840 Blocks
12:45:31
         477
RMAN: full datafile backup: Set Count 70: 50616 out of 855840 Blocks done
SYS

25-JUL 12:46:04        145 RMAN: full datafile backup
70                                                           35915           0 Blocks
12:45:31

RMAN: full datafile backup: Set Count 70: 35915 out of 0 Blocks done
SYS

SQL>
SQL>
select
 sid, serial#, status, event, seq#, state, p1,p2,p3, seconds_in_wait
```

RMAN in Debug Mode   **345**

```
   2  from
v$session where sid=145;

     SID   SERIAL# STATUS   EVENT                                     SEQ# STATE
P1        P2    P3
---------- ---------- -------- ------------------------------------ ---------- ------------------- ---
------- ---------- ----------
SECONDS_IN_WAIT
---------------
     145         24 ACTIVE   RMAN backup & recovery I/O                 626 WAITING
1       256 4294967295
             0


SQL>
```

After a short while, Session 149 for the RMAN output can be seen as well:

```
SQL> l
  1  select
to_char(sysdate,'DD-MON HH24:MI:SS') Collection_DateStamp, sid, opname,
target, sofar, totalwork,
  2   units, to_char(start_time,'HH24:MI:SS') StartTime,
  3   time_remaining, message, username
  4   from
v$session_longops
  5   where
sofar != totalwork
  6* order by
start_time
SQL> /

COLLECTION_DATE      SID OPNAME
--------------- ---------- -----------------------------------------------------------------
TARGET                                                           SOFAR  TOTALWORK UNITS
STARTTIM
----------------------------------------------------------- ---------- ---------- --------------
----------------- --------
TIME_REMAINING
--------------
MESSAGE
-----------------------------------------------------------------------------------------
-----------------------------
USERNAME
-----------------------------
25-JUL 12:49:07      159 RMAN: aggregate input
20                                                             194170     855840 Blocks
12:45:28
        429
RMAN: aggregate input: backup 20: 194170 out of 855840 Blocks done
SYS

25-JUL 12:49:07      145 RMAN: full datafile backup
70                                                             398270     855840 Blocks
12:45:31
        245
RMAN: full datafile backup: Set Count 70: 398270 out of 855840 Blocks done
SYS

25-JUL 12:49:07      145 RMAN: full datafile backup
70                                                             315354          0 Blocks
12:45:31

RMAN: full datafile backup: Set Count 70: 315354 out of 0 Blocks done
SYS

25-JUL 12:49:07      149 RMAN: aggregate output
20                                                             157307          0 Blocks
12:47:34

RMAN: aggregate output: backup 20: 157307 out of 0 Blocks done
```

```
SYS
SQL>
select sid, serial#, status, event, seq#, state, p1,p2,p3, seconds_in_wait
  2  from
 v$session
where sid in (145,149,159)
order by 1;

       SID    SERIAL# STATUS   EVENT                                   SEQ# STATE
P1         P2         P3
---------- ---------- -------- ------------------------------------ ---------- ------------------- ---
------- ---------- ----------
SECONDS_IN_WAIT
---------------
       145         24 ACTIVE   RMAN backup & recovery I/O                 1360 WAITING
1          256 4294967295
             3

       149         35 INACTIVE SQL*Net message from client                167 WAITING
1650815232          1          0
             6

       159         20 INACTIVE SQL*Net message from client                700 WAITING
1650815232          1          0
           352


SQL>
```

Similarly, the processes can be identified. Note how all three database sessions have been created by the single RMAN client process OS process 4363. In fact, four or more can be seen when using multiple channels.

```
SQL>
  1  select
 s.sid, p.spid, s.program , s.process
from
 v$session s, v$process p
  2* where
 s.sid in (145,149,159) and s.paddr=p.addr
order by 1
SQL> /

       SID SPID         PROGRAM                                          PROCESS
---------- ------------ ------------------------------------------------ ------------
       145 4374         rman@linux64 (TNS V1-V3)                         4363
       149 4373         rman@linux64 (TNS V1-V3)                         4363
       159 4369         rman@linux64 (TNS V1-V3)                         4363
SQL> !ps -fp4363
UID        PID  PPID  C STIME TTY          TIME CMD
ora10204  4363  4198  0 12:45 pts/1    00:00:03 rman target /

SQL> !ps -fp4374
UID        PID  PPID  C STIME TTY          TIME CMD
ora10204  4374  4363 48 12:45 ?        00:04:45 oracleORT24FS
(DESCRIPTION=(LOCAL=YES)(ADDRESS=(PROTOCOL=beq)))

SQL> !ps -fp4373
UID        PID  PPID  C 3TIME TTY          TIME CMD
ora10204  4373  4363  0 12:45 ?        00:00:00 oracleORT24FS
(DESCRIPTION=(LOCAL=YES)(ADDRESS=(PROTOCOL=beq)))

SQL> !ps -fp4369
UID        PID  PPID  C STIME TTY          TIME CMD
ora10204  4369  4363  0 12:45 ?        00:00:02 oracleORT24FS
(DESCRIPTION=(LOCAL=YES)(ADDRESS=(PROTOCOL=beq)))
```

RMAN in Debug Mode

```
SQL>
```

The job can also be monitored using the *v$rman_backup_job_details* view as was mentioned above.

When the backup finishes,

```
channel ORA_DISK_1: finished piece 1 at 25_JUL_12_53_17
piece
handle=/oracle_fs/FRAs/ORT24FS/ORT24FS/backupset/2010_07_25/o1_mf_nnndf_TAG2
0100725T124531_64qjcf3b_.bkp tag=TAG20100725T124531 comment=NONE
channel ORA_DISK_1: backup set complete, elapsed time: 00:07:46
Finished backup at 25_JUL_12_53_17

Starting Control File Autobackup at 25_JUL_12_53_17
piece
handle=/oracle_fs/FRAs/ORT24FS/ORT24FS/autobackup/2010_07_25/o1_mf_n_7252879
97_64qjsybz_.bkp comment=NONE
Finished Control File Autobackup at 25_JUL_12_53_21

RMAN>
```

it comes up with this:

```
SQL>
select
to_char(start_time,'DD-MON HH24:MI') StartTime,
  2  to_char(end_time,'DD-MON HH24:MI') EndTime,
  3  (end_time-start_time)*1440 RunMin,
  4  input_bytes/1048576 Read_MB, output_bytes/1048576 Write_MB, input_type,
status
  5  from
v$rman_backup_job_details
  6  where
start_time > sysdate-1
order by
start_time
  7  /

STARTTIME    ENDTIME      RUNMIN  READ_MB WRITE_MB INPUT_TYPE    STATUS
------------ ------------ ------- -------- -------- ------------- ----------------------
25-JUL 12:45 25-JUL 12:53    7.92    5,924    5,629 DB FULL       COMPLETED

SQL>
```

However, note that if another RMAN command is issued in the same interactive session, it updates the same record in *v$rman_backup_job_details*:

```
RMAN> backup archivelog all;

Starting backup at 25_JUL_12_57_28
current log archived
using channel ORA_DISK_1
channel ORA_DISK_1: starting archive log backupset
channel ORA_DISK_1: specifying archive log(s) in backup set
```

```
input archive log thread=1 sequence=1 recid=97 stamp=721058820
input archive log thread=1 sequence=2 recid=99 stamp=721058831
input archive log thread=1 sequence=3 recid=101 stamp=721061092
.........
input archive log thread=1 sequence=42 recid=179 stamp=721070601
channel ORA_DISK_1: starting piece 1 at 25_JUL_12_57_37

channel ORA_DISK_1: backup set complete, elapsed time: 00:00:02
Finished backup at 25_JUL_13_04_16
Starting Control File Autobackup at 25_JUL_13_04_16
piece
handle=/oracle_fs/FRAs/ORT24FS/ORT24FS/autobackup/2010_07_25/o1_mf_n_7252886
56_64qkgk4m_.bkp comment=NONE
Finished Control File Autobackup at 25_JUL_13_04_19

RMAN>

SQL>
select
 to_char(start_time,'DD-MON HH24:MI') StartTime,
  2  to_char(end_time,'DD-MON HH24:MI') EndTime,
  3  (end_time-start_time)*1440 RunMin,
  4  input_bytes/1048576 Read_MB, output_bytes/1048576 Write_MB, input_type,
status
  5  from
 v$rman_backup_job_details
  6  where
 start_time > sysdate-1
order by
 start_time
  7  /

STARTTIME    ENDTIME       RUNMIN  READ_MB  WRITE_MB INPUT_TYPE   STATUS
------------ ------------  ------- -------- -------- ------------ -----------------------
25-JUL 12:45 25-JUL 13:04  18.85   9,679    9,384 DB FULL        COMPLETED

SQL>
```

Notice above how the same record, with the same *start_time* in *v$rman_backup_job_details*, was updated and the total backup size appears to show both the database and the archivelog backupsets together as *db full* since that is how the record was created.

So exit RMAN, start a new RMAN session and issue a *backup as compressed backupset*:

```
RMAN> exit
ora10204>rman target /
RMAN> backup as compressed backupset database;

Starting backup at 25_JUL_13_07_29
using target database control file instead of recovery catalog
allocated channel: ORA_DISK_1
channel ORA_DISK_1: sid=159 devtype=DISK
channel ORA_DISK_1: starting compressed full datafile backupset
channel ORA_DISK_1: specifying datafile(s) in backupset
```

RMAN in Debug Mode

```
input datafile fno=00004 name=/oracle_fs/Databases/ORT24FS/users01.dbf
input datafile fno=00001 name=/oracle_fs/Databases/ORT24FS/system01.dbf
input datafile fno=00006 name=/oracle_fs/Databases/ORT24FS/undotbs.dbf
input datafile fno=00003 name=/oracle_fs/Databases/ORT24FS/sysaux01.dbf
input datafile fno=00005 name=/oracle_fs/Databases/ORT24FS/example01.dbf
channel ORA_DISK_1: starting piece 1 at 25_JUL_13_07_31
channel ORA_DISK_1: finished piece 1 at 25_JUL_13_13_56
piece
handle=/oracle_fs/FRAs/ORT24FS/ORT24FS/backupset/2010_07_25/o1_mf_nnndf_TAG2
0100725T130731_64qknmqj_.bkp tag=TAG20100725T130731 comment=NONE
channel ORA_DISK_1: backup set complete, elapsed time: 00:06:25
Finished backup at 25_JUL_13_13_56

Starting Control File Autobackup at 25_JUL_13_13_57
piece
handle=/oracle_fs/FRAs/ORT24FS/ORT24FS/autobackup/2010_07_25/o1_mf_n_7252892
37_64q10p1k_.bkp comment=NONE
Finished Control File Autobackup at 25_JUL_13_14_01

RMAN>
```

This shows that the *output_bytes* for the second compressed backup is less:

```
SQL>
select
 to_char(start_time,'dd-mon hh24:mi') starttime,
  2   to_char(end_time,'dd-mon hh24:mi') endtime,
  3   (end_time-start_time)*1440 runmin,
  4   input_bytes/1048576 read_mb, output_bytes/1048576 write_mb, input_type,
status
  5   from v$rman_backup_job_details
  6   where start_time > sysdate-9 order by start_time
  7   /

STARTTIME     ENDTIME        RUNMIN    READ_MB WRITE_MB INPUT_TYPE    STATUS
------------ ------------   --------- -------- -------- ------------ ----------------------
25-JUL 12:45 25-JUL 13:04     18.85    9,679    9,384 DB FULL       COMPLETED
25-JUL 13:07 25-JUL 13:14      6.55    5,924      814 DB FULL       COMPLETED

SQL>
```

Exit again and then reconnect and run a *backup archivelog*:

```
RMAN> exit
ora10204>rman target /
RMAN> backup archivelog all not backed up 1 times;

Starting backup at 25_JUL_14_36_00
current log archived
using target database control file instead of recovery catalog
allocated channel: ORA_DISK_1
channel ORA_DISK_1: sid=145 devtype=DISK
skipping archive log file /oracle_fs/ArchiveLogs/ORT24FS/1_3_720302233.dbf;
already backed up 2 time(s)
skipping archive log file /oracle_fs/ArchiveLogs/ORT24FS/1_4_720302233.dbf;
already backed up 2 time(s)
...
channel ORA_DISK_1: starting archive log backupset
```

```
channel ORA_DISK_1: specifying archive log(s) in backup set
input archive log thread=1 sequence=2 recid=293 stamp=725294161
channel ORA_DISK_1: starting piece 1 at 25_JUL_14_36_05
channel ORA_DISK_1: finished piece 1 at 25_JUL_14_36_06
piece
handle=/oracle_fs/FRAs/ORT24FS/ORT24FS/backupset/2010_07_25/o1_mf_annnn_TAG2
0100725T143604_64qptoo5_.bkp tag=TAG20100725T143604 comment=NONE
channel ORA_DISK_1: backup set complete, elapsed time: 00:00:02
Finished backup at 25_JUL_14_36_06

Starting Control File Autobackup at 25_JUL_14_36_06
piece
handle=/oracle_fs/FRAs/ORT24FS/ORT24FS/autobackup/2010_07_25/o1_mf_n_7252941
66_64qptq5t_.bkp comment=NONE
Finished Control File Autobackup at 25_JUL_14_36_07

RMAN> exit
```

Since this is a new RMAN backup job session initiated as a *backup archivelog*, it appears more accurately in *v$rman_backup_job_details*:

```
SQL>
select
 to_char(start_time,'DD-MON HH24:MI') StartTime,
  2  to_char(end_time,'DD-MON HH24:MI') EndTime,
  3  (end_time-start_time)*1440 RunMin,
  4  input_bytes/1048576 Read_MB, output_bytes/1048576 Write_MB, input_type,
status
  5  from
 v$rman_backup_job_details
  6  where
 start_time > sysdate-9 order by start_time
  7  /

STARTTIME       ENDTIME       RUNMIN  READ_MB  WRITE_MB INPUT_TYPE    STATUS
-----------     -----------   ------  -------  -------- ------------  ----------------------
25-JUL 12:45 25-JUL 13:04    18.85    9,679    9,384 DB FULL       COMPLETED
25-JUL 13:07 25-JUL 13:14     6.55    5,924      814 DB FULL       COMPLETED
25-JUL 14:36 25-JUL 14:36      .13       12       12 ARCHIVELOG    COMPLETED

SQL>
```

Kill Hanged RMAN Session

Sometimes killing the RMAN session is needed when it is hanging and does not respond. For this, there are two options. The first option is using the *alter system kill session* command, so the *sid* and *serial#* values need to taken from the *v$process* and *v$sessions* views. See the following example:

1. Connect to RMAN and run the *backup database* command:

```
RMAN> backup database;
```

2. Use the following query to get the *sid* and *serial#* values of the connected RMAN session:

```
SQL>
select b.sid, b.serial#, a.spid, b.client_info
from
 v$process a, v$session b
where
 a.addr=b.paddr and client_info
like
 'rman%';

      SID    SERIAL# SPID          CLIENT_INFO
---------- ---------- ------------ --------------------------------
      141         22 976          rman channel=ORA_DISK_1
```

3. Use the *alter system kill session* command to kill the running backup session:

```
SQL>
alter
 system kill session '141,22' immediate;

system altered.
SQL>
```

After killing the session, the following message appears in the RMAN output:

```
input datafile fno=00004
name=C:\ORACLE\PRODUCT\10.2.0\ORADATA\TEST\USERS01.DBF
channel ORA_DISK_1: starting piece 1 at 20-JUL-10
RMAN-03009: failure of backup command on ORA_DISK_1 channel at 07/20/2010
18:47:39
ORA-00028: the session has been killed
ORA-00028: the session has been killed
continuing other job steps, job failed will not be re-run
RMAN-00571: ===========================================================
RMAN-00569: =============== ERROR MESSAGE STACK FOLLOWS ===============
RMAN-00571: ===========================================================
RMAN-03009: failure of backup command on ORA_DISK_1 channel at 07/20/2010
18:47:39
ORA-00028: the session has been killed
ORA-00028: the session has been killed
RMAN>
```

The RMAN session can also be killed directly from the OS. See the following example. Here, take a backup of the database and get the process ID of the RMAN process from the OS, then kill it using the *kill -9* command:

```
RMAN> backup database plus archivelog;

[oracle@locahost ~]$ ps -ef | grep rman
oracle    4669  4513  3 01:28 pts/1    00:00:00 rman target /
oracle    4712  4689  0 01:28 pts/2    00:00:00 grep rman
[oracle@locahost ~]$ kill -9 4669
[oracle@locahost ~]$
```

After killing the session, here is the following output from RMAN:

```
input datafile fno=00004
name=/u01/oracle/product/10.2.0/db_1/oradata/db3/users01.dbf
channel ORA_DISK_1: starting piece 1 at 19-JUL-10
Killed
```

RMAN Tuning Introduction

There is always a need to optimize things and this is a goal which is shared by all the administrators. When it comes to RMAN, the same goal is anticipated by the administrators on how they can improve the performance of the backups and recoveries done via RMAN. It is possible to make RMAN take a backup of multiple terabytes of the database in a blink of an eye! Though it is not a bad thing to have expectations, it is important to make realistic goals.

Imagine that someone is walking on a very busy road filled with lots of people and they are late reaching their office. What should be done to optimize this situation? Buy better, more expensive shoes? Would they blame their shoes for being slow and, therefore, making them late? No, it is not the shoes but the traffic on the road which is causing them to be slower. Maybe the road is not smooth and walking very fast over it is not possible.

This is the case with RMAN. It is the shoe that is being worn. Trying to make it better will not always help; not that it will never help because soccer shoes will not let anyone walk properly on a road! However, there are many other moving pieces which would actually impact the performance. This section will cover some guidelines which can be used to optimize the performance of RMAN.

It is All About I/O

As stated before, it is not the shoe that causes lower quality, but either the traffic on the road or the road itself being so messy! The poor shoe becomes the culprit despite the fact that it is actually the victim. So is the case with RMAN. It deals with many moving pieces and one of the most important terms in those moving pieces is the I/O; either while reading from the source of the backup or writing the same to the target device, it is I/O all around!

When RMAN is doing the operation of the backup, it will essentially be reading the information from the source of the media. The read information is then sent for final processing and copied into the memory area from where it is written out to the output device. The read phase of RMAN is the phase which can be really tricky and is governed by several factors.

RMAN can read the data from multiple sources as well. What this means is that it is possible for RMAN to read two datafiles at the same time and then write them to an output device in the form of a backup piece. This is governed primarily by the *filesperset* parameter which tells RMAN how many files can be part of a backup set. Another parameter which is a channel's property, *maxopenfiles*, tells how many files can be opened by RMAN for simultaneous read. So when the multiplexing limits are calculated, it is a minimum of this number and *filesperset*. The defaults of *filesperset* and *maxopenfiles* are 64 and 8.

Based on the level of multiplexing, RMAN allocates the number of buffers and also decides the size of the allocated memory buffer. The number of buffers remains fixed to 16 and a size of 1 MB with the multiplexing level 4 or less. With the level greater than 4, the number becomes varied and also the size of the buffers is reduced from 1 MB to 512 KB or 128 KB. For ASM, this is a fixed equivalent to the number of the disks within the disk group.

For backups done over the tape drives, each RMAN channel working over that device allocates four buffers and each buffer is sized to 1 MB of memory. So if settings for the multiplexing are carefully chosen which further govern the overall memory consumed by RMAN, it can give control over the memory consumed by it. Without unnecessarily consuming the memory, RMAN's impact over the system is minimal and with a planned multiplexing rate, backup operations also are faster. Since the memory buffers are allocated from PGA, having a control over their size also keeps the PGA tuned and does not let it overgrow.

Be In Synch With Asynchronous I/O

RMAN is doing its work over the storage device and this device has two kinds of I/O modes supported, synchronous and asynchronous. RMAN's performance is heavily impacted with what mode is used in the environment.

Synchronous I/O

This can also be called Slow I/O! The reason is, using this mode makes the DBA wait to get a YES from all those processes that have been assigned work before anything else could be done. To understand it more clearly, take an example of an Oracle process like DBWR that asks the O/S to write a few dirty buffers to the disk. If synchronous I/O is used, then follow these steps:

1. DBWR sends the dirty buffers to write on disk.

2. Operating system gets the notification that there are some buffers meant to be written on disk.

3. From Oracle's cache, the buffers are copied to the operating system's cache.

4. DBWR is now idle waiting for the write to be completed from the operating system.

5. Operating system finishes writing buffers to the disk and once complete, it notifies DBWR.

6. DBWR is now active and carries on its normal routines.

As this whole process reveals, DBWR is sitting completely idle as long as it does not get the response back from the operating system. This kind of mechanism is an absolute killer of performance in a highly concurrent and active system. There is no way to expect a good performance from the database using this kind of mechanism.

If this is the same routine followed by the backups, either going on disk or on tape, the slowness of the operation can easily be imagined. In order to overcome this, there are two possible ways out. One, try to change the behavior of the synchronous I/O and make it a little better. This needs some of the parameters to be used which can change the default way of working. Other than this, simply use the asynchronous I/O. Before the asynchronous I/O is understood, see what parameters can be used which can optimize the synchronous I/O.

dbwr_io_slaves

If RMAN is being used to take the backup on the disk drive and the operating system is not using and/or supporting asynchronous I/O, this parameter may be set and some benefit of the slave processes attained that are used by DBWR to segregate the backup. Normally, it is recommended that multiple DBWRs be deployed rather than slaves but that is applicable only when the system supports the asynchronous I/O. This parameter is set for the backup-related operations; four processes for RMAN.

For ARCH and LGWR, this sets the same number of processes. Using this parameter is effective in segregating the workload on multiple processes, thus making it a little faster. If using this parameter is desirable, consider setting *large_pool_size* to a non-zero value as well since the memory required for the slaves' processing is allocated from it if it is set. If large pool is not set, the same would be done either from the shared pool if it has sufficient memory or from the PGA, both of which are not the right places to get the memory for the slaves.

backup_tape_io_slaves

If a backup is going to be taken on the tape drives, regardless whether async or sync are being used, it would be good to set this parameter. Using this parameter, Oracle allocates multiple slave processes to talk to the tape drives which are otherwise accessed on the basis of one process per tape drive. So using this parameter, there are multiple allocations of the slave processes which optimize the performance. The same rule for memory allocation which is there for the disk slaves is applicable to the tape slaves as well. It is better to allocate the large pool for such operations; otherwise, the memory is allocated from the shared pool or from the PGA, both which are not the optimal locations for the memory allocation.

Though it is better to put this parameter when the synchornous I/O is not there, it is not going to hurt to use it as well.

Asynchronous I/O

Although the above given parameters can take care of the performance when the synchronous I/O is used, it is better to have asynchronous I/O in place if the best performance is desired. Most of the operating systems now offer it out-of-the-box for the same reason. Comparing it with the above-mentioned synchronous I/O, the following steps are followed by Oracle when it has asynchronous I/O available:

1. DBWR sends the dirty buffers to write on disk.

2. The operating system gets notification that there are some buffers meant to be written on disk. From Oracle's cache, the buffers are copied to the operating system's cache.

3. DBWR is not idle waiting for the write to be completed from the operating system and instead, will keep on doing its actions normally.

4. Operating system finishes writing buffers to the disk and once complete, it notifies DBWR.

5. DBWR acknowledges it.

As can be seen by using this behavior, it becomes much easier and optimized to work. Though the above-mentioned points were specific to disk as a media, the same happens for the tape drive as well. There is an additional layer of the media management layer which is doing the final course of action: writing the content over the tape that may further impact the performance.

Some prominent factors are the network traffic and the rate at which the data is transferred to the tape drive when the final writing is happening. Since tape drives offer streaming of the data to and from the drive, they also impact the performance of the backup. Additionally, just like in any I/O operation, the block size offered by the tape drive, managed by the software governing it, is also a very prominent factor in the performance of the backup stored over it.

The More the Merrier

RMAN allocates channels to do all the operations of backups and restores. There is by default a disk channel and maintenance channel configured by RMAN so that disk backup can be started immediately. For a large database, using just one channel is not sufficient, so the easiest way to make the RMAN backup faster would be to use more than one channel whether the backup is done over disk or tape. When configuring the channels, allocation of the parameter *rate* for them is also crucial since this decides how much a channel is allowed to read. Setting this parameter to a reasonable value does not let RMAN accomplish a huge amount of I/O while doing backup or restore from a channel.

Conclusion

At times, even a doctor needs to be cured when he falls sick. The same applies to RMAN. It is a doctor to cure the databases when they behave oddly by having a missing component. However, at times RMAN needs to be cured itself. This chapter covered the techniques to troubleshoot and diagnose RMAN-related errors and issues.

The possible reasons for RMAN having to deal with issues have also been reviewed. Its related errors, their possible causes and also what actions to take regarding them have been examined. Happy troubleshooting!

User-managed Backup and Recovery Scenarios

Though RMAN is and should be the preferred tool for doing and maintaining Oracle database backups, the same can be done incorporating user-managed techniques as well. Since the title of this chapter is user-managed, this essentially means that the backup is maintained and done by the DBA through some commands which are not Oracle-managed. The only way other than RMAN is to manually copy the file(s) which need to be backed up. The entire operations of backing up the files, maintaining the backups, getting the lists of the backups done and even deleting the backups which are not needed anymore are done manually only, hence the name user-managed backups.

Modes of the Backup

In the same manner in which RMAN takes the backup, user-managed backups can also be in hot (online) and cold (offline) modes. As has just been mentioned, the backup is done with the O/S commands so various commands like *copy* (Windows), *cp/dd* (UNIX) and other commands like these can be used to do the backup.

When the backup has to be taken in noarchivelog mode, unlike RMAN, the database needs to be completely closed because other than that, there is no way to ensure that all the datafiles are consistent with the control and redo log files. So in noarchivelog mode, the only option to take the backup would be a cold (offline) backup. And since the database is completely down, take the complete copy of the entire folder containing all of the database files.

It is very important to make sure that in the backup, when done over the database, all the datafiles must be consistent. In noarchivelog mode, this is ensured when the database is shut down with the *immediate*, *transactional* or *normal* options since this makes all the datafiles' checkpoints the same which are used to assure the database's consistency.

Backing Up Database Running in Noarchivelog Mode

If the database is not in archivelog mode, it is important to make sure that before the copy of the database files is started, the entire database has to be consistent and for this purpose, the database must be shut down. It is also important to make sure that none of the files are missed. To ensure that all the data, control and log files' locations and names are correctly known, use the views *v$datafile*, *v$controlfile*, and *v$logfile*. Once where the files are known that need to be backed up, push the backup like the following:

```
SQL>
archive
 log list;

Database log mode              No Archive Mode
Automatic archival             Disabled
Archive destination            use_db_recovery_file_dest
Oldest online log sequence     28
Current log sequence           30

SQL>
select
 name
from
 v$datafile
union all
select
 name
from
 v$controlfile
union all
select
 member
from
 v$logfile;


NAME
------------------------------------------------------------
/u01/oracle/product/10.2.0/db_1/oradata/lindb/system01.dbf
/u01/oracle/product/10.2.0/db_1/oradata/lindb/undotbs01.dbf
/u01/oracle/product/10.2.0/db_1/oradata/lindb/sysaux01.dbf
/u01/oracle/product/10.2.0/db_1/oradata/lindb/users01.dbf
/u01/oracle/product/10.2.0/db_1/oradata/lindb/control01.ctl
/u01/oracle/product/10.2.0/db_1/oradata/lindb/control02.ctl
/u01/oracle/product/10.2.0/db_1/oradata/lindb/control03.ctl
/u01/oracle/product/10.2.0/db_1/oradata/lindb/redo03.log
/u01/oracle/product/10.2.0/db_1/oradata/lindb/redo02.log
/u01/oracle/product/10.2.0/db_1/oradata/lindb/redo01.log

SQL>
shutdown
 immediate
```

```
SQL>
host
[oracle@localhost ~]$ cp /u01/oracle/product/10.2.0/db_1/oradata/lindb/*
/tmp/backup/
```

NOTE: The above *cp* command is on the basis that all datafiles, control files and redo log files are in the same directory. If they are distributed into separate directories and mount points, each location must be backed up.

It is a frequent debate about whether online redo logs should be backed up, even when doing a cold backup. Most experts and Oracle documentation recommend that online redo logs should not be backed up.

If these files are backed up, there may a risk to restoring these files and overwriting any good online redo log files still present on disk when all that is needed is to restore datafiles for a complete database recovery. Therefore, review the list of files before doing a restore.

Alternatively, if the online redo log files are not backed up, a dummy *recover database* will need to be issued and an *open resetlogs* done to have Oracle recreate the online redo logs when the database is restored and the online redo logs need to be recreated. Once the copy is complete, start the database again. To automate the above cold backup procedure, a batch (Windows) or a shell (Unix/Linux) script can be written.

Never perform the cold backup when the database is in *shutdown abort* as the backup will not be in consistent. In this case, if the database was taken down with shutdown abort mode, then *startup restrict*, *shutdown immediate*, and perform the cold backup for a consistent backup.

Back Up the Database Running in Archivelog Mode

In noarchivelog mode, the only option available for the backup is when the database is down. Since most of the databases at the moment are 24/7, this option is pretty much useless. So make sure that the backup is done when the database is online. However, doing so presents another problem which is that the database is constantly changing and in this case, the backup that has been done is useless. Seems like a chicken-egg kind of issue, does it not? But a backup still needs to be done.

So what can be the solution for this? Well, the very first thing is that what is the issue if the backup is taken when the database is changing? What would happen? The answer lies in the fact that there are ever-changing checkpoint numbers over the database. And if a backup is taken in this case and, later on, that backup file is used in any sort of recovery, it is impossible for Oracle to determine that from where it has to start recovering that file. In other words, from where it has to apply the archivelog files over that backup file, it would become consistent with the rest of the database. Seems to be a tough problem.

Indeed it is, but fortunately there is a solution for it as well. If Oracle could somehow be told that the file is in backup mode and it would be able to remember that, it would solve this issue. But how is that done and even if the file is in backup mode and Oracle also tracks this, what about the ever increasing checkpoints?

There is yet another issue that needs to be taken care of. If it has not been forgotten, this is about user-managed backups which means that the backup is essentially done by some O/S command like *cp* which is pretty much a dumb command when viewed in the context of Oracle and its files. In other words, the *cp* command neither knows nor cares about how Oracle files are maintained and how the inside mechanism works.

This means that when the *cp* command is told to take a backup of the online Oracle database file, what the *cp* command does is to start copying that file to the chosen location without caring or knowing that there is some constant change happening over the file. It cannot know it anyway since the I/O unit of the operating system and Oracle database is different.

Where Oracle does I/O in a chunk of kb of data starting from 2 to 32 kb, O/S does I/O most of the time in a hardcoded size for the program, e.g. 512 bytes, or in filesystem blocksizes of 2 k or 4 k or such in the sector size of the physical media, 512 bytes, e.g. when doing a dd backup of a raw device. Therefore, even if Oracle sends a block of 8 kb for the backup, it would take 16 I/O calls for O/S to completely copy it.

During the time the file is online, it may be requested by Oracle processes again for work which surely may corrupt the underlying block, i.e. the block sent for backup may contain all 4s but the final copy may contain half 4 and half 0. This is thanks to the context switching which would have happened before the OS I/O calls could return from finishing backup as a part of the block and asking for the rest which is already changed now. This concept is called fractured block, meaning a block which is fractured because the block's image that is in the backup is not the same as what was originally sent for the backup and contains discrepancies, thus making it completely useless for recovery purposes. Fortunately for all of these questions, there lies one answer: the backup mode.

Diving Deep into the Backup Mode

As has been shown, there can be many issues in the hot known as online backup. Oracle introduced the *alter tablespace ... begin backup* command to support hot backups. Since the online backup was a drastic need, that is why there was a requirement that something should take care of all the issues that were mentioned earlier and it happens with this command. This command works on both tablespaces and datafiles both and using it puts the respective database or datafile into the backup mode which tells Oracle that the backup is now on.

Since it has been stated that checkpointing is the way to manage the database's consistency, this command maintains that perfectly as well. When this command is run, a partial checkpoint is issued for the buffers of the tablespace in this mode. With the checkpoint, all the dirty buffers of the file are written into it and also the entry is recorded into the control file. Once the checkpoint write completes, the header for the respective file is marked frozen!

After this checkpoint, the datafile will not get updated but the rest of the database moves on. From this checkpoint number, in the case of the recovery, Oracle comes to know from where it has to start applying the archivelogs to make the datafile become consistent with the rest of the database. That is the reason that it is important to bring the datafile out of the backup by the *alter tablespace ... end backup* command. If the datafile is in this mode and the database gets shutdown illegally like in an instance crash because Oracle will not let the database shut down otherwise, stating that the file is in the backup mode, Oracle assumes that the file is restored from the previous backup. Therefore, it would need recovery and throw out the error, *ORA-3113*.

Also shown was that there might be a problem with the *cp* command being unaware about the Oracle data file structure and this leads to a fractured block issue. This also is optimized by Oracle. The fractured block essentially means that the datablock sent for the backup and the actual block which was supposed to be backed up are not matching. And this happens because of the ignorance of *cp*, *dd* and any other commands like these to understand how Oracle files work.

Since, by default, only the changed buffers for a block are logged into the redo log buffer, it will not be possible for Oracle to recover the blocks which are newer than the image that was sent for the backup since the recovery process is designed to bring the corrupted blocks forward rather than take care of the ahead blocks. Also, by default only the change vectors of a dirty buffer are logged into the log buffer, so it would not be possible even with using the redo and archive logs that would be able to be matched that gap between the two images.

To overcome this issue, Oracle logs the entire block for the first time whose file is in the backup mode. This ensures that the image is stored in the archivelog files which are actually need to be restored in case there is a need for recovery. From this block onwards, all the other change vectors are logged as usual in the redo buffer. This explains the reason why there is an extra redo generated if the datafile is in backup mode. Using the complete image logged for the first time and then the subsequent change vectors for the same buffer even though there is a fractured block in the copy of the file by using the archivelogs and current logs, troubleshooting that issue is done as well.

Before this section of online backups is concluded, it is worth mentioning that, at times, there may be a fuzzy issue that will come up. If this happens, do not get carried away with it. In some older threads found over the Web and also in the Oracle documentations, there is mention of the fuzzy bit being set over the datafile and visible from *v$datafile_header* with the fuzzy column as YES. The older theory is that the fuzzy bit is set when the file is in backup mode and is unset once the file is brought out of the backup.

This was true of the version prior to 9i where the fuzzy bit was set when there was at least one write done over the file. From the version 9i, this bit is set when the file is open and there is a write that has happened over the datafile at least one time higher than the current checkpoint information recorded over its header. That is why in the current releases of Oracle, even though there is no active user-managed backup there, all the datafile headers are shown with fuzzy as YES only.

If the file last time is closed in a legal manner, for example with *shutdown immediate*, *transactional* or any other way which would force a complete checkpoint, this bit would be unset. If this bit is still set and an opening of the database is attempted, this means that the last status of the files was *open* and they were not closed properly which would cause an instance recovery of the database. That is why in the latest releases of Oracle, it is not advisable to use the *v$datafile_header* view to see whether the backup is going on or not using fuzzy bit as a reference. This would always be shown as YES, thereby leading to a possible misunderstanding. The right way to check whether there is a user-managed backup going on or not would be to use the *v$backup* view where the file which is in the backup mode is shown with the checkpoint information from where it has been put in that mode.

Remember that in the backup mode, when Oracle freezes the header, it does not really know when the OS command, such as *cp* or *dd* or any other command, actually starts reading the datafile! Similarly, it does not know when the OS command has finished reading the datafile. It is up to the DBA or his script to inform Oracle via the *begin backup* and *end backup* commands to set markers for Oracle with the actual OS copy of the datafile being initiated and completed sometime between the *begin backup* and the *end backup*.

All the datafiles of the database can be found by using the following query:

```
SQL>
select
   t.name "tablespace", f.name "datafile"
  from
     v$tablespace t, v$datafile f
  where
    t.ts# = f.ts#
  order by
 t.name

Tablespace                      Datafile
----------------------------    ------------------------------------
EXAMPLE                         D:\ORACLE\ORADATA\ORCL\EXAMPLE01.DBF
SYSAUX                          D:\ORACLE\ORADATA\ORCL\SYSAUX01.DBF
SYSTEM                          D:\ORACLE\ORADATA\ORCL\SYSTEM01.DBF
UNDOTBS1                        D:\ORACLE\ORADATA\ORCL\UNDOTBS01.DBF
USERS                           D:\ORACLE\ORADATA\ORCL\USERS01.DBF
```

The status of the datafiles can be checked as to whether or not they are in the backup from the *v$backup* view. A very simple query over it would give a result like this:

```
SQL>
select * from
v$backup;

     FILE# STATUS              CHANGE# TIME
---------- ------------------- ---------- ---------
         1 NOT ACTIVE                0
         2 NOT ACTIVE                0
         3 NOT ACTIVE                0
         4 NOT ACTIVE                0
         5 NOT ACTIVE                0
```

As there is no backup running at the moment, the status column shows *not active*. The query can also be tweaked a little to include the datafile name as well with a view like the following:

```
SQL>
select
 t.name as "tb_name", d.file# as "df#", d.name as "df_name", b.status
  from
   v$datafile d, v$tablespace t, v$backup b
  where
  d.ts#=t.ts#
  and
    b.file#=d.file#
  and
    b.status='active';

no rows selected
SQL>
```

Again, the result is nothing since there is no backup going on at the moment. To put one of the files into the backup mode, issue the *alter tablespace ....begin backup* command.

```
SQL>
alter tablespace
 users
begin backup;

Tablespace altered.
```

And then see the status from the above query one more time:

```
SQL>
select t.name as "tb_name", d.file# as "df#", d.name as "df_name", b.status
  from
   v$datafile d, v$tablespace t, v$backup b
```

```
where
d.ts#=t.ts#
and
  b.file#=d.file#
and
  b.status='active'

TB_NAME      DF#      DF_NAME                                 STATUS
-----------  -------- --------------------------------------- ---------
USERS                 4 D:\ORACLE\ORADATA\ORCL\USERS01.DBF  ACTIVE
SQL>
```

This reveals that the file is in backup mode. But this, as was stated before, is just going to put the file in the backup mode but will not take the actual backup of the file. To do so, copy the file using the O/S command like below:

```
D:\ cp  D:\ORACLE\oradata\orcl\users01.dbf  d:\backup\
```

This prepares a copy of the file at the backup folder on the system. Now the checkpoint information of the whole datafile ends the backup as well.

```
SQL>
select
 checkpoint_change#
from
 V$datafile;

CHECKPOINT_CHANGE#
------------------
            936881
            936881
            936881
            937142
            936881

SQL>
alter
tablespace users
end
 backup;

Tablespace altered.

SQL>
select
 checkpoint_change#
from
 V$datafile;
```

```
CHECKPOINT_CHANGE#
------------------
          936881
          936881
          936881
          937142
          936881
SQL>
```

This shows that the *end backup* command does not do anything special for the datafile. Once the command is finished, the file's header is known to be out of the backup. The checkpoint is matched with the rest of the database at the next full checkpoint.

In case getting the file out of the backup mode was overlooked and the instance crashes, Oracle will not let the database be opened since there is an inconsistency between this file and the rest of the database. At that moment, if it is observed that the user-managed backup is a practice in the database, make sure to check the *v$backup* view to ensure that there are no active backups going on. If it is discovered that there is one, run the command:

```
SQL>
alter
 database datafile <backup file number>
end
 backup;
```

Since this is at the mount stage, use the *alter database* command only. If there are multiple files in the backup mode, there is no need to issue for an individual file with the *end backup* command since the following can be used:

```
SQL>
alter
 database
end
 backup;
```

Note: Though not recommended because of the heavy amount of redo generation, by using the same *alter database* command, the whole database can be put in the backup mode as well.

```
alter database begin backup;
```

Use OS utility to back up all database-related files.

```
alter database end backup;
```

The *alter database begin backup* command skips the read only and offline status tablespaces from hot backup mode. There is no *alter database datafile .. begin backup* command. The *begin backup* must be issued at the tablespace or database level. The ... *datafile ... end backup* command is made available specifically for the purpose of instance recovery following an instance failure while one or more tablespaces were in backup mode.

In case checking the backup status of the file from the *v$backup* view was skipped and the *end backup* command cannot be recalled, the recovery for the database can be mimiced and the database can still be opened. Oracle attempts to bring the file(s) which are in the backup to the latest checkpoint and after that, this is able to be done. Though the command works perfectly, still the preferred way should be to end the backup mode. See it all in action starting with putting a tablespace in the backup mode:

```
SQL>
alter
 tablespace users
begin
 backup;

Tablespace altered.
```

It is time to create an error, so crash the database instance.

```
SQL>
shut
 abort
Oracle instance shut down.
SQL>
startup

<.....output trimmed .....>
Database mounted.
ORA-10873: file 4 needs end backup before opening a database
ORA-01110: data file 4: 'D:\ORACLE\oradata\orcl\users01.dbf'
```

NOTE: In previous versions, Oracle would only say that the datafile needed recovery. The *ORA-10873* message has been added in 10g.

Oracle assumes that the file is restored from a previous backup and asks for it to be recovered. Though the file's backup status can be checked to see if it is active, do not do that. Instead, try to recover the file with the *recover* command:

```
SQL>
select
 checkpoint_change#
from
 V$datafile;

CHECKPOINT_CHANGE#
------------------
           978902
           978902
           978902
           979188
           978902

SQL>
recover
 database;

Media recovery complete.

SQL>
select
 checkpoint_change#
from
 V$datafile;

CHECKPOINT_CHANGE#
------------------
           979193
           979193
           979193
           979193
           979193

SQL>
alter
 database open;

Database altered.
```

The file is recovered and the database is also consistent. Do a sanity check for the backup mode of the files:

```
SQL>
select  * from
 V$backup;

FILE# STATUS              CHANGE# TIME
--------- ------------------ ---------- ---------
        1 NOT ACTIVE               0
        2 NOT ACTIVE               0
        3 NOT ACTIVE               0
        4 NOT ACTIVE          979188 22-FEB-10
        5 NOT ACTIVE               0
```

So none of the files are in the backup and when the file number 4 was put into the backup can be seen.

Since this is about the whole database backup, there must be a question about what if the database is huge, having many datafiles and tablespaces? Can the speed of the backup be increased; can the backup be done in parallel mode just like it is done with RMAN? Well, unfortunately, the answer of this is no.

Actually, it is a partial no since there is no support for parallelism in the case of the OS *copy* command. The *copy* command can only be run one time in one session. The command may do the copy of multiple files, but there is only one underlying process that is doing this. Also, there is no way that multiple tablespaces can be simultaneously put in the backup mode without using the *alter database begin backup* command. If it is not the case that the whole database needs to be put in the backup mode and multiple tablespaces also need to be put into the backup mode, the following can be done:

```
SQL>
alter
 tablespace users
begin
 backup;
SQL>
Alter
 tablespace example
begin
 backup;
```

Now, if that does not sound like a true parallel command or putting the files into the backup mode, that is correct. But this is what comes with the user-managed backup as well!

The *alter system archive log current* is recommended to specify before and after the online backup commands. The purpose of running the command is to archive the current online redo log so that the redo required to recover the tablespace backups will be available for later media recovery.
Example:

```
alter system archive log current;
alter tablespace data begin backup;
```

Use the OS utility *copy/cp/dd* to copy datafiles:

```
alter tablespace data end backup;
alter system archive log current;
```

Next to be examined is what happens when the database is running in noarchivelog mode and needs to be recovered without redo log files.

Restore/Recover the Database Running in Noarchivelog Mode

Oracle strongly recommends running the database in archivelog mode. If the database is run in noarchivelog mode, the database cannot be recovered and redo change cannot be applied because there are no archived redo log files generated. Oracle will write the redo log files in circular fashion and will not archive them.

To restore/recover the database running in noarchivelog mode since the redo log files are not backed up, simulate a cancel-based recovery and open the database with the *resetlogs* option. See the following scenario:

```
SQL>
startup

<.....output trimmed.....>
<.....output trimmed.....>
Database mounted.
ORA-00313: open failed for members of log group 1 of thread 1
ORA-00312: online log 1 thread 1:
'/u01/oracle/product/10.2.0/db_1/oradata/new/redo01.log'

SQL>
recover
 database until cancel;

Media recovery complete.

SQL>
alter
 database open resetlogs;

Database altered.
SQL>
```

If the datafiles are restored to the different location, use the *alter database rename file* command to rename the datafile before performing the cancel-based recovery as follows:

```
SQL>
alter
 database rename file
'/u01/oracle/product/10.2.0/db_1/oradata/new/users01.dbf' TO
'/u01/oracle/product/10.2.0/db_1/oradata/new/backup/users01.dbf ';
```

Oracle Backup and Recovery

```
Database altered.
SQL>
```

User-managed Backup of Control File

Control file backup is among the most crucial backups that must be there when the database is a working database. Any structural change that has happened to the database, the control file of it must be backed up right away. From the user-managed prospective, there are two methods used to do the backup of the control file; making a copy of the binary control file and creating a text file containing commands to recreate the control file. Both options are adequate enough to recover from a control file loss.

Backing Up Control File in Binary Format

The control file cannot be put in the backup mode like datafiles. This means it is not possible to copy the control file when the database is running using the simple *copy* command of the OS since it is ever changing! For this reason, another method is provided by Oracle which is basically from itself. This method uses an Oracle command which creates a backup copy of the control file at the user-specified location. Doing so does not tamper with the active or in-use control file. Make the binary copy of the control file using the following command:

```
SQL>
alter
 database backup controlfile to 'd:\backup\controlfilebkup.ctl';
```

If the said file is already present at the chosen location, this command would fail. At that time, the *reuse* switch can be used at the end of the file mentioning that the file which is already available at the specific location should be overwritten.

Text Backup of Control File

In case taking the backup of the control file was forgotten, there is still the option to recover from its loss by recreating it. For this purpose, Oracle offers the *create controlfile* command which can be used to create the control file again. This command can also be manually written by looking at the Oracle SQL Reference Documentation Guide or an easy way can be done with the *alter database backup controlfile to trace* command. The resultant trace file is available at the version-specific location.

For versions prior to 11.1, it is under the location of *user_dump_dest* which normally is available under the *admin* folder in the *$ORACLE_BASE* location. If a version greater than 11.1 is being used, this is in the *diag* folder which is in the *$ORACLE_BASE* location. Also, an entry is maintained in the alert log to reflect the command and the path of the trace file. For example, here is an excerpt taken from an 11.1 database's *alert log* file.

```
alter database backup controlfile to trace
Backup controlfile written to trace file
d:\oracle\diag\rdbms\orcl\orcl\trace\orcl_ora_3104_control.trc
Completed: alter database backup controlfile to trace
```

So both the command and the trace file location are shown in the alert log.

The file contains two sections which are usable depending on the availability of the online logs. If all the online logs are available, then the control file can be recreated and the database can be opened without using the *resetlogs* option. If the online logs are missing, then the *resetlogs* option must be used to recreate them after creating the control file.

While recreating the control file, care should be taken for any tablespaces which were either offline or read only at the time of the crash. It would be best to remove the reference of those tablespaces from the creation script and let the controlfile be created without them. Once the control file is created, there are entries in the database with the name *missing* representing the files which were not included. These files should be manually renamed to reflect the correct file names of those tablespaces which were omitted while creating the control file.

Backing Up Archive Files

As has been covered concerning the other files, the backup for the archived files is also done using the *copy* command only. The only difference would be that, unlike the control files and datafiles which are getting changed almost every instant, archive files are sitting quietly since they are just the replicas of the online redo logs. It is normally a good practice to have more than one copy of archive files available, but for their backup, any one site's archive files are good enough.

Take the backup of the archive files as follows:

```
$ cp /u01/app/oracle/arch/** /u01/app/oracle/backup/**
```

Backing Up Spfile, Password File and Network Files

All the other files except datafiles, control files and redo log files are optional files. So their presence or absence will not impact the availability of the database. Imagine losing the password file? What is the worst that can happen? Only this: that a connection cannot be made from a remote terminal to the database, that is all! But the running database will not come to a screeching halt. Moreover, the new password file should be created in seconds using the *orapwd* utility.

So looking at it from this prospective, it is not a real requirement that the miscellaneous files like the server parameter network be backed up; for example, *tnsnames.ora* and *listener.ora*, *password* and other files of the same nature. Still, as a good practice, it is better to back up these files also whenever any changes are made to them. For example, whenever any parameter is changed/modified from the server parameter file, a copy should be made of it.

There should be at least two copies of it maintained, one which has the current parameter changes and the second, the old one which is changed. The same is true for any other files as well which are used by the Oracle database but are not required for it being up. Make sure that there is at least one copy of these files somewhere safe!

To find out the configuration (*.ora*) files in Oracle Home (Unix/Linux):

```
$ -> find $ORACLE_HOME -name "*.ora" -print
```

Note: In the above command result, *init<SID>.ora/spfile<SID>.ora*, *orapw<SID>*, *tnsnames.ora*, *listener.ora* and *sqlnet.ora* files are important.

To backup the configuration files, use:

```
$ cp $ORACLE_HOME/dbs/spfile<SID>.ora /u01/bkups/spfile<SID>_<date>.ora
$ cp $ORACLE_HOME/dbs/orapw<SID> /u01/bkups/orapw<SID>_<date>
$ cp $ORACLE_HOME/network/admin/tnsnames.ora /u01/bkups/tnsnames_<date>.ora
$ cp $ORACLE_HOME/network/admin/listener.ora /u01/bkups/listener_<date>.ora
```

```
$ cp $ORACLE_HOME/network/admin/sqlnet.ora /u01/bkups/sqlnet_<date>.ora
```

Although the password file and network files can be recreated, some backups of the *ORACLE_HOME* (weekly, monthly or quarterly) might still be sufficient to include the password and network files. Nevertheless, make additional backups when these files are updated by configuration changes as the *ORACLE_HOME* is backed up before and after a patch.

Backing Up Offline and Read Only Datafiles

While backing up the offline and read only datafiles/tablespace, there is no need to put them in backup mode because the datafiles are prevented from being changed. What is needed is to just copy the datafiles to the backup directory.

Verifying User-managed Backups

Since user-managed backups are done through the operating system commands, it is not possible to validate the backups like RMAN's *validate backup* command. Still, not all hope is lost because Oracle offers a utility called *DB Verify* (*DBV*) which checks the source files for any sort of corruption. The files that are checked via *DBV* must be offline files. This command is used most of the time over the backed up files which are checked to ensure that they are free from any kind of corruptions which if present, may not let the recovery happen.

DBV is a command line tool which is shipped with the standard database binaries. There is no need to do anything special to use this tool except to run it from a proper Oracle home. If this tool is run without any options, this is the output that is seen:

```
Keyword      Description                      (Default)
----------------------------------------------------------
FILE         File to Verify                   (NONE)
START        Start Block                      (First Block of File)
END          End Block                        (Last Block of File)
BLOCKSIZE    Logical Block Size               (8192)
LOGFILE      Output Log                       (NONE)
FEEDBACK     Display Progress                 (0)
PARFILE      Parameter File                   (NONE)
USERID       Username/Password                (NONE)
SEGMENT_ID   Segment ID (tsn.relfile.block)   (NONE)
HIGH_SCN     Highest Block SCN To Verify      (NONE)
             (scn_wrap.scn_base OR scn)
```

Oracle Backup and Recovery

At a minimum, the datafile name needs to be supplied to run *DBV* like the following:

```
dbv file=users01.dbf

DBVERIFY - Verification starting : FILE = users01.dbf
DBVERIFY - Verification complete

Total Pages Examined         : 640
Total Pages Processed (Data) : 91
Total Pages Failing    (Data) : 0
Total Pages Processed (Index): 33
Total Pages Failing    (Index): 0
Total Pages Processed (Other): 497
Total Pages Processed (Seg)  : 0
Total Pages Failing    (Seg)  : 0
Total Pages Empty            : 19
Total Pages Marked Corrupt   : 0
Total Pages Influx           : 0
Total Pages Encrypted        : 0
Highest block SCN            : 916549 (0.916549)
```

DBV mentions data file blocks as pages. So the page count mentioned in the final output is the number of blocks which took part in the verification process.

It is advisable to run *DBV* over offline datafiles. The reason for that is that if the file is online, Oracle processes would be reading and writing into the datafile at the same time when it is being verified by *DBV*. *DBV* is not able to read those blocks which are in this kind of mode, so it waits for the blocks to become consistent before it can read them. The blocks which are being read and written at the same time are called influx blocks. Those blocks, which due to being in flux did not take part in the verification process, are shown in the output of the *DBV*.

NOTE: *DBV* may not be used against archivelogs, online redo logs and control files.

User-managed Recovery Scenarios

In the next part of this chapter, possible situations and user-managed recovery scenarios that may be faced in a DBA's career will be shown. The recovery of the control files, datafiles and redo log files will be seen. Instead of showing only the solutions, how the corruption environment can be corrupted and prepared will be covered. After that, step-by-step solutions and explanations of the recovery scenario will be given.

Recovering from the Loss of Control Files

As shown in the previous chapters, the loss of the control file of the running database brings the database down. This subchapter will show different scenarios where all control files of the database are lost and there is only a backup control file. The following list describes the scenarios and their solutions.

What is lost	Which backup is present	The additional case
all control files	backup of control file	No additional case
all control files	backup of control file	read only tablespace is present
all control files	backup of controlfile	a new datafile is created after backup of control file
all control files and a datafile with no backup	only backup of controlf ile	a datafile is lost with no backup

Table 9.1: *Loss of Control File Scenarios*

Recovering from Loss of All Control Files Using Backup Control File

Scenario 1

Bob took a binary backup of the control file. The next day he loses all control files of the database due to the media failure. As he has only the binary copy of the control file, he restores it and recovers the database.

1. Take a binary backup of the control file and delete all control files. Then shut down and start up the database:

```
SQL>
alter
 database backup controlfile to '/tmp/control_backup.ctl';

Database altered.

SQL>
```

```
select
 name
from
 v$controlfile;

NAME
----------------------------------------------------------
/u01/oracle/product/10.2.0/db_1/oradata/test/control01.ctl
/u01/oracle/product/10.2.0/db_1/oradata/test/control02.ctl
/u01/oracle/product/10.2.0/db_1/oradata/test/control03.ctl

SQL>
host
 rm -rf /u01/oracle/product/10.2.0/db_1/oradata/test/*.ctl

SQL>
startup
 force

<.....output trimmed .....>
ORA-00205: error in identifying control file, check alert log for more info

SQL>
select
 status
from
 v$instance;

STATUS
------------
STARTED

SQL>
alter
 database mount;
alter database mount
*

ERROR at line 1:
ORA-00205: error in identifying control file, check alert log for more info
SQL>
```

2. Copy the binary backup of control file to the original control file's destination and mount the database:

```
SQL>
host
[oracle@localhost ~]$ cp /tmp/control_backup.ctl
/u01/oracle/product/10.2.0/db_1/oradata/test/control01.ctl
[oracle@localhost ~]$ cp /tmp/control_backup.ctl
/u01/oracle/product/10.2.0/db_1/oradata/test/control02.ctl
[oracle@localhost ~]$ cp /tmp/control_backup.ctl
/u01/oracle/product/10.2.0/db_1/oradata/test/control03.ctl
[oracle@localhost ~]$ exit

exit

SQL>
```

User-managed Recovery Scenarios

379

```
alter
 database mount;

Database altered.
SQL>
```

3. If an attempt is made to open the database, the message that the *resetlogs* option must be used appears. If the *resetlogs* option is used, a request is made to perform a recovery. If an effort to recover the database is done, a request to use the USING BACKUP CONTROL FILE clause shows up. So use the *recover database using backup control file* command to tell Oracle that an attempt to recover the database from the binary copy of the control file is being made:

```
SQL>
alter
 database open;
alter database open
*

ERROR at line 1:
ORA-01589: must use RESETLOGS or NORESETLOGS option for database open

SQL>
alter
 database open resetlogs;
alter database open resetlogs
*

ERROR at line 1:
ORA-01194: file 1 needs more recovery to be consistent
ORA-01110: data file 1:
'/u01/oracle/product/10.2.0/db_1/oradata/test/system01.dbf'

SQL>
recover
 database;

ORA-00283: recovery session canceled due to errors
ORA-01610: recovery using the BACKUP CONTROLFILE option must be done

SQL>
recover
 database using backup controlfile;

ORA-00279: change 470859 generated at 04/22/2010 07:30:27 needed for thread
1
ORA-00289: suggestion :
/u01/oracle/product/10.2.0/db_1/flash_recovery_area/TEST/archivelog/2010_04_
22/o1_mf_1_2_%u_.arc
ORA-00280: change 470859 for thread 1 is in sequence #2

Specify log: {<RET>=suggested | filename | AUTO | CANCEL}
CANCEL
Media recovery cancelled.
SQL>
```

By using this command, Oracle asks the changes made after the backup of the control file was taken to be provided. In this scenario, a prompt to provide the redo log file name that contains the changes of the SCN value 470859 is seen. To get the correct file which contains the changes made after the specified *scn*, query both archived redo logs and online redo log files. In this scenario, since no archived redo log files are generated, query the *v$log* view:

```
SQL>
select
 group#, status, first_change# FROM v$log;

    GROUP# STATUS             FIRST_CHANGE#
---------- ---------------- --------------
         1 CURRENT                  470872
         3 ACTIVE                   470861
         2 ACTIVE                   470859
SQL>
```

From the above result, it can be seen that the redo log file of the groups 2, 3 and 1 need to be applied respectively because redo log file 2 contains the changes of the SCN value 470859 and the redo log members of groups 3 and 1 contain SCN values greater than specified above.

```
SQL>
recover
 database using backup controlfile;

ORA-00279: change 470859 generated at 04/22/2010 07:30:27 needed for thread
1
ORA-00289: suggestion :
/u01/oracle/product/10.2.0/db_1/flash_recovery_area/TEST/archivelog/2010_04_
22/o1_mf_1_2_%u_.arc
ORA-00280: change 470859 for thread 1 is in sequence #2

Specify log: {<RET>=suggested | filename | AUTO | CANCEL}
/u01/oracle/product/10.2.0/db_1/oradata/test/redo02.log
```

This shows that the */u01/oracle/product/10.2.0/db_1/oradata/test/ redo02.log* file has been passed for the recovery process. Oracle accepts and applies it, then asks for the next redo log file. The next two redo log files are provided and the following message comes up:

```
Specify log: {<RET>=suggested | filename | AUTO | CANCEL}
/u01/oracle/product/10.2.0/db_1/oradata/test/redo01.log
Log applied.
Media recovery complete.
SQL>
```

Now it is time to open the database with the *resetlogs* option:

```
SQL>
```

User-managed Recovery Scenarios

381

```
alter
 database open resetlogs;

Database altered.
SQL>
```

The database successfully opened!

If the creation script for the control file is available, i.e. a trace backup of the control file, and all redo log files are available, then the database can be recovered and opened without the *resetlogs* option. Take a backup of the control file to trace:

```
SQL>
alter
 database backup controlfile to trace as '/tmp/test.dat';

Database altered.
SQL>
```

Delete all control files:

```
[oracle@localhost ~]$ rm -rf
/u01/oracle/product/10.2.0/db_1/oradata/new/control0*
```

Create a new control file using the command that was generated in the trace file. Make sure that the *create control file* command contains the *noresetlogs* option:

Note: Confirm that all database files and online redo log files are correctly listed in the *create controlfile* command.

```
create controlfile reuse database "new" noresetlogs  archivelog
```

Shutdown the database and mount it. Then recover it and open without using the *resetlogs* option.

```
SQL>
Shutdown
 immediate
SQL>
Startup
 mount
SQL>
Recover
 database;

Media recovery complete.

SQL>
Alter
```

```
database open;

Database altered.
SQL>
```

Recovering From Loss of a Member of Multiplexed Control File

Oracle strongly recommends multiplexing control files and online redo log files to different hard drives. There might be some circumstances where only one member of the multiplexed control file can be lost. In this situation, there is no need to create a new control file. Instead, only shut down the database and copy the available control file to the directory of the missed one. In the following scenario, see how this happens:

1. Get the list of all control files, delete one of them and reboot the database:

```
SQL>
select
 name
from v$controlfile;

NAME
----------------------------------------------------------------
/u01/oracle/product/10.2.0/db_1/oradata/new/control01.ctl
/u01/oracle/product/10.2.0/db_1/oradata/new/control02.ctl
/u01/oracle/product/10.2.0/db_1/oradata/new/control03.ctl

SQL>
Host
 rm -rf /u01/oracle/product/10.2.0/db_1/oradata/new/control01.ctl

SQL>
startup
 force

ORACLE instance started.
ORA-00205: error in identifying control file, check alert log for more info
SQL>
```

2. Copy the available control file to the directory of the missed one and open the database. Do this when the database instance is down.

```
SQL>
Host
 cp /u01/oracle/product/10.2.0/db_1/oradata/new/control02.ctl
/u01/oracle/product/10.2.0/db_1/oradata/new/control01.ctl

SQL>
startup
 force;
```

```
Database mounted.
Database opened.
SQL>
```

Recovering Read Only Tablespace From Loss of Control Files

Scenario 2

Bob lost all control files of the database. While checking backups, he realized that he has the creation script of the control file and one of his tablespaces is read only. In this situation, he decides to perform the following steps to successfully open the database.

1. Create a corruption environment to test the solution. Create a tablespace, make it read only, take a backup of the control file and delete all available control files. Then create the control file using the *controlfile* script and try to open the database.

```
SQL>
create
 tablespace tbs_readonly datafile
'/u01/oracle/product/10.2.0/db_1/oradata/test/tbs_readonly.dbf' size 1m;

Tablespace created.

SQL>
alter
 tablespace tbs_readonly read only;

Tablespace altered.

SQL>
alter
 database backup controlfile to trace as '/tmp/control.dat';

Database altered.

SQL>
host
[oracle@localhost ~]$ rm -rf
/u01/oracle/product/10.2.0/db_1/oradata/test/*.ctl
[oracle@localhost ~]$ exit

exit

SQL>
startup
 force

ORACLE instance started.
```

```
ORA-00205: error in identifying control file, check alert log for more info

SQL>
create
 controlfile reuse database "test" resetlogs archivelog
    maxlogfiles 16
    maxlogmembers 3
    maxdatafiles 100
    maxinstances 8
    maxloghistory 292
logfile
  group 1 '/u01/oracle/product/10.2.0/db_1/oradata/test/redo01.log'  size
50m,
  group 2 '/u01/oracle/product/10.2.0/db_1/oradata/test/redo02.log'  size
50m,
  group 3 '/u01/oracle/product/10.2.0/db_1/oradata/test/redo03.log'  size
50m
-- standby logfile
datafile
  '/u01/oracle/product/10.2.0/db_1/oradata/test/system01.dbf',
  '/u01/oracle/product/10.2.0/db_1/oradata/test/undotbs01.dbf',
  '/u01/oracle/product/10.2.0/db_1/oradata/test/sysaux01.dbf',
  '/u01/oracle/product/10.2.0/db_1/oradata/test/users01.dbf'
character set we8iso8859p1;

Control file created.
```

There is no information about the read only datafile:

```
SQL>
startup
 force

ORACLE instance started.
Database mounted.
ORA-01589: must use resetlogs or noresetlogs option for database open

SQL>
alter
 database open resetlogs;
alter database open resetlogs
*

ERROR at line 1:
ORA-01194: file 1 needs more recovery to be consistent
ORA-01110: data file 1:
'/u01/oracle/product/10.2.0/db_1/oradata/test/system01.dbf'

SQL>
select
 name from v$datafile;

NAME
----------------------------------------------------------------
/u01/oracle/product/10.2.0/db_1/oradata/test/system01.dbf
/u01/oracle/product/10.2.0/db_1/oradata/test/undotbs01.dbf
/u01/oracle/product/10.2.0/db_1/oradata/test/sysaux01.dbf
/u01/oracle/product/10.2.0/db_1/oradata/test/users01.dbf
```

There is still no information about the datafile with read only status.

2. Try to recover the database and provide the *redo01.log* file to applying redo entries:

```
SQL>
recover
 database using backup controlfile;

ORA-00279: change 478702 generated at 04/22/2010 10:48:50 needed for thread
1
ORA-00289: suggestion:
/u01/oracle/product/10.2.0/db_1/flash_recovery_area/TEST/archivelog/2010_04_
22/o
1_mf_1_1_%u_.arc
ORA-00280: change 478702 for thread 1 is in sequence #1

Specify log: {<RET>=suggested | filename | AUTO | CANCEL}
/u01/oracle/product/10.2.0/db_1/oradata/test/redo01.log
ORA-00283: recovery session canceled due to errors
ORA-01244: unnamed datafile(s) added to control file by media recovery
ORA-01110: data file 5:
'/u01/oracle/product/10.2.0/db_1/oradata/test/tbs_readonly.dbf'

ORA-01112: media recovery not started
SQL>
```

Recovery stopped because it applied the information about the read only datafile which is missing since Oracle accepts it as *unnamed00005*. Query all datafiles using the *v$datafile* view:

```
SQL>
select
 name
from v$datafile;

NAME
----------------------------------------------------------------
/u01/oracle/product/10.2.0/db_1/oradata/test/system01.dbf
/u01/oracle/product/10.2.0/db_1/oradata/test/undotbs01.dbf
/u01/oracle/product/10.2.0/db_1/oradata/test/sysaux01.dbf
/u01/oracle/product/10.2.0/db_1/oradata/test/users01.dbf
/u01/oracle/product/10.2.0/db_1/dbs/unnamed00005
```

Now there is the *unnamed00005* file which is the read only datafile.

3. Rename the datafile as follows:

```
SQL>
alter
 database rename file '/u01/oracle/product/10.2.0/db_1/dbs/UNNAMED00005' TO
'/u01/oracle/product/10.2.0/db_1/oradata/test/tbs_readonly.dbf';

Database altered.
```

```
SQL>
```

As the recovery process was stopped on the creation of the read only datafile, the recovery will continue because the datafile has been renamed to its correct name:

```
SQL>
recover
 database using backup controlfile;

ORA-00279: change 479118 generated at 04/22/2010 10:53:27 needed for thread
1
ORA-00289: suggestion :
/u01/oracle/product/10.2.0/db_1/flash_recovery_area/TEST/archivelog/2010_04_
22/o
1_mf_1_1_%u_.arc
ORA-00280: change 479118 for thread 1 is in sequence #1

Specify log: {<RET>=suggested | filename | AUTO | CANCEL}
/u01/oracle/product/10.2.0/db_1/oradata/test/redo01.log

Log applied.
Media recovery complete.
SQL>
```

4.   Open the database and query the *v$datafile* view:

```
SQL>
alter
 database open resetlogs;

Database altered.

SQL>
select
 name
from
 v$datafile;

NAME
----------------------------------------------------------------
/u01/ORACLE/product/10.2.0/db_1/oradata/test/system01.dbf
/u01/ORACLE/product/10.2.0/db_1/oradata/test/undotbs01.dbf
/u01/ORACLE/product/10.2.0/db_1/oradata/test/sysaux01.dbf
/u01/ORACLE/product/10.2.0/db_1/oradata/test/users01.dbf
/u01/ORACLE/product/10.2.0/db_1/oradata/test/tbs_readonly.dbf
```

Recovering Database From Loss of All Control Files With Binary Backup

Imagine that all control files of the database have been lost and there is only a binary backup of the control file. Moreover, a new datafile has been added after the backup was taken. This situation is the same as the previous scenario. This scenario will show:

- Restore backup of the control file

- Recover the database using backup of the control file

- Rename the unnamed file with the original one

- Recover the database again using the backup control file. Open the database with the *resetlogs* option

Recovering Database From Loss of All Control Files and No Backup

Imagine that all control files and a datafile with no backup which was created after the backup of the control file have been lost. See the following timeline:

- 10.00: Take backup of the control file (binary backup)

- 10.10: Create a new tablespace with one datafile

- 10.20: All control files are lost

For this, do the following:

- Recover the database until creation of the tablespace

- Use the *alter database add datafile* command to create an empty datafile

- Recover the database using archived redo log files

Look at the following scenario:

1. To create a corruption environment, backup a control file, create a new tablespace, delete all control files and start the database with the *force* option:

```
SQL>
alter
 database backup controlfile to '/tmp/control.ctl';

Database altered.

SQL>
create
 tablespace tbs_test datafile
'/u01/oracle/product/10.2.0/db_1/oradata/rc/tbs_test.dbf' SIZE 1M;

Tablespace created.
```

Oracle Backup and Recovery

```
SQL>
select
 name
from
 v$controlfile;

NAME
----------------------------------------------------------------
/u01/oracle/product/10.2.0/db_1/oradata/rc/control01.ctl
/u01/oracle/product/10.2.0/db_1/oradata/rc/control02.ctl
/u01/oracle/product/10.2.0/db_1/oradata/rc/control03.ctl

SQL> host
[oracle@localhost ~]$ rm -rf
/u01/oracle/product/10.2.0/db_1/oradata/rc/*.ctl
[oracle@localhost ~]$ exit

exit

SQL>
startup
 force

ORACLE instance started.
<.....output trimmed .....>
ORA-00205: error in identifying control file, check alert log for more info
SQL>
```

2. Restore the backup control file, mount the database and perform a recovery by providing necessary redo log file:

```
SQL>
host
[oracle@localhost ~]$ cp /tmp/control.ctl
/u01/oracle/product/10.2.0/db_1/oradata/rc/control01.ctl
[oracle@localhost ~]$ cp /tmp/control.ctl
/u01/oracle/product/10.2.0/db_1/oradata/rc/control02.ctl
[oracle@localhost ~]$ cp /tmp/control.ctl
/u01/oracle/product/10.2.0/db_1/oradata/rc/control03.ctl
[oracle@localhost ~]$ exit

exit

SQL>
startup
 force

<.....output trimmed .....>
Database mounted.
ORA-01589: must use resetlogs or noresetlogs option for database open

SQL>
alter
 database open resetlogs;
alter database open resetlogs
*

ERROR at line 1:
```

```
ORA-01194: file 1 needs more recovery to be consistent
ORA-01110: data file 1:
'/u01/oracle/product/10.2.0/db_1/oradata/rc/system01.dbf'

SQL>
recover
 database using backup controlfile

ORA-00279: change 476745 generated at 04/23/2010 04:01:31 needed for thread
1
ORA-00289: suggestion :
/u01/oracle/product/10.2.0/db_1/flash_recovery_area/RC/archivelog/2010_04_23
/o1_
mf_1_3_%u_.arc
ORA-00280: change 476745 for thread 1 is in sequence #3

Specify log: {<RET>=suggested | filename | AUTO | CANCEL}
/u01/oracle/product/10.2.0/db_1/oradata/rc/redo02.log

ORA-00283: recovery session canceled due to errors
ORA-01244: unnamed datafile(s) added to control file by media recovery
ORA-01110: data file 5:
'/u01/oracle/product/10.2.0/db_1/oradata/rc/tbs_test.dbf'

ORA-01112: media recovery not started
SQL>
```

3. Query the *v$datafile* view and create a new datafile based on the unnamed
    one. Then recover the database once again:

```
SQL>
select
 name
from v$datafile;

NAME
-------------------------------------------------------------
/u01/ORACLE/product/10.2.0/db_1/oradata/rc/system01.dbf
/u01/ORACLE/product/10.2.0/db_1/oradata/rc/undotbs01.dbf
/u01/ORACLE/product/10.2.0/db_1/oradata/rc/sysaux01.dbf
/u01/ORACLE/product/10.2.0/db_1/oradata/rc/users01.dbf
/u01/ORACLE/product/10.2.0/db_1/dbs/UNNAMED00005

SQL>
alter
 database create datafile '/u01/oracle/product/10.2.0/db_1/dbs/UNNAMED00005'
as '/u01/oracle/product/10.2.0/db_1/oradata/rc/tbs_test.dbf';

Database altered.

SQL>
recover
 database using backup controlfile;

ORA-00279: change 481351 generated at 04/23/2010 04:04:28 needed for thread
1
ORA-00289: suggestion :
```

```
/u01/oracle/product/10.2.0/db_1/flash_recovery_area/RC/archivelog/2010_04_23
/o1_mf_1_3_%u_.arc
ORA-00280: change 481351 for thread 1 is in sequence #3

Specify log: {<RET>=suggested | filename | AUTO | CANCEL}
/u01/oracle/product/10.2.0/db_1/oradata/rc/redo02.log

Log applied.
Media recovery complete.

SQL> alter database open resetlogs;

Database altered.

SQL>
select
 name
from v$datafile;

NAME
----------------------------------------------------------------
/u01/ORACLE/product/10.2.0/db_1/oradata/rc/system01.dbf
/u01/ORACLE/product/10.2.0/db_1/oradata/rc/undotbs01.dbf
/u01/ORACLE/product/10.2.0/db_1/oradata/rc/sysaux01.dbf
/u01/ORACLE/product/10.2.0/db_1/oradata/rc/users01.dbf
/u01/ORACLE/product/10.2.0/db_1/oradata/rc/tbs_test.dbf
SQL>
```

A control file backup older than the creation of the new datafile is used and recovery halted because of the mismatch. This is one of the reasons why Oracle has introduced *configure controlfile autobackup on.* Control file autobackups when a change to the database physical structure is executed, e.g. adding a new tablespace/datafile, irrespective of the method used for database backups whether user-managed or Oracle-managed (RMAN). Therefore, it is good practice to configure control file autobackups.

Recovery of Datafiles and Tablespaces

To recover a corrupted or missed datafile, copy the backup of the datafile to the original location and use the *recover datafile* command to start applying all redo changes made after the backup of the datafile.

Before starting the recovery, query the *v$recover_file* view and get information about the file which needs to be recovered. Moreover, to get information about archived redo log files that are needed to be applied to the restored datafile, query the *v$recovery_log* view. In the following query, it has seen that recovering two datafiles is needed. The first datafile is made offline and the second database could not be found:

```
SQL>
select * from
v$recover_file;

    FILE# ONLINE  ONLINE_ ERROR                   CHANGE# TIME
---------- ------- ------- --------------------- ---------- -------
        4 OFFLINE OFFLINE OFFLINE NORMAL                0
        5 ONLINE  ONLINE  FILE NOT FOUND                0
```

Now start recovering a missing datafile using the *recover datafile* command.

1. To create a recovery environment, add a new datafile to the users tablespace, take the tablespace to the backup mode and take backup of the newly added datafile. Then delete the original datafile and reboot the database:

```
SQL>
alter
 tablespace users
begin
 backup;

Tablespace altered.

SQL>
host
[oracle@localhost ~]$ cd /u01/oracle/product/10.2.0/db_1/oradata/new/
[oracle@localhost new]$ cp users01.dbf users01.dbf_backup

SQL>
alter
 tablespace users
end
 backup;

Tablespace altered.

SQL>
alter
 system switch logfile;

System altered.

# Run the same command 4-5 times

<.....output trimmed ......>
<.....output trimmed ......>

SQL>
host
[oracle@localhost ~]$ rm -rf
/u01/oracle/product/10.2.0/db_1/oradata/new/users01.dbf
[oracle@localhost ~]$ exit

exit
```

```
SQL>
startup
 force

<.....output trimmed ......>
Database mounted.
ORA-01157: cannot identify/lock data file 4 - see DBWR trace file
ORA-01110: data file 4:
'/u01/oracle/product/10.2.0/db_1/oradata/new/users01.dbf'
SQL>
```

2. Now copy the backup file to the original file's destination, query the *v$recovery_log* view and recover the datafile:

```
[oracle@localhost ~]$ cd /u01/oracle/product/10.2.0/db_1/oradata/new/
[oracle@localhost new]$ cp users01.dbf_backup users01.dbf

SQL>
select * from
 v$recovery_log;

THREAD#   SEQUENCE# TIME           ARCHIVE_NAME
--------- --------- ---------      -------------------------
        1         7 29-APR-10      .../o1_mf_1_7_5xlks83z_.arc
        1         8 29-APR-10      .../o1_mf_1_8_5xlks94q_.arc
        1         9 29-APR-10      .../o1_mf_1_10_5xlksr8m_.arc
<.....output trimmed .....>

SQL>
recover
 datafile 4;

ORA-00279: change 489794 generated at 04/29/2010 04:44:57 needed for thread
1
ORA-00289: suggestion :
.../o1_mf_1_7_%u_.arc
ORA-00280: change 489794 for thread 1 is in sequence #7

Specify log: {<RET>=suggested | filename | AUTO | CANCEL}
AUTO

<.....output trimmed .....>
Log applied.
Media recovery complete.

SQL>
alter
 database open;

Database altered.
SQL>
```

When there is a requirement to provide the name of archived redo log files, just provide the *auto* command to let Oracle search for required archived redo log files in the archivelog destination. Oracle starts applying all archived redo log files to the restored datafile and performs a media recovery. The same steps are used to recover the tablespace using the *recover tabelspace* command.

If the tablespace is put to offline mode using the IMMEDIATE clause, the recovery will be required to take it back. See the following scenario:

```
SQL>
alter
 tablespace users
offline
 immediate;

Tablespace altered.

SQL>
alter
 tablespace users online;
alter
 tablespace users online
*

ERROR at line 1:
ORA-01113: file 4 needs media recovery
ORA-01110: data file 4:
'/u01/oracle/product/10.2.0/db_1/oradata/lindb/users01.dbf'

SQL>
recover
 tablespace users;

Media recovery complete.

SQL>
alter
 tablespace users online;

Tablespace altered.
SQL>
```

Here is the entry of the *alert.log* file. This shows that Oracle applied redo changes from the current redo log file to recovered datafiles:

```
Completed: alter database open
Fri Apr 16 16:13:16 2010
alter tablespace users offline immediate
Completed: alter tablespace users offline immediate
Fri Apr 16 16:13:21 2010
alter tablespace users online
Fri Apr 16 16:13:21 2010
ORA-1113 signalled during: alter tablespace users online...
Fri Apr 16 16:13:28 2010
alter database recover  tablespace users
Media Recovery Start
Fri Apr 16 16:13:28 2010
Recovery of Online Redo Log: Thread 1 Group 2 Seq 30 Reading mem 0
  Mem# 0 errs 0: /u01/oracle/product/10.2.0/db_1/oradata/lindb/redo02.log
```

```
Fri Apr 16 16:13:28 2010
Media Recovery Complete (lindb)
Completed: alter database recover tablespace users
Fri Apr 16 16:13:34 2010
alter tablespace users online
Completed: alter tablespace users online
```

Check the status of the file of group 2:

```
SQL>
select
 group#, status
from v$log;

    GROUP# STATUS
---------- ----------------
         1 INACTIVE
         2 CURRENT
         3 INACTIVE
SQL>
```

> 🔔 To make Oracle apply all archived redo log files automatically based on *log_archive_dest_n* and *log_archive_format* parameters, use either the *set autorecovery on* command before the *recover database* command or use the *recover automatic database* command.

If the archived redo log files are located in a different location than the value of the *log_archive_dest_n* parameter, there are three options:

1. Use the *alter system set log_archive_dest_1* command to change the location of the archived redo log files.

2. Use the *set logsource* command to specify the location of archived redo log files that will be used in the recovery.

3. Use the *recover automatic tablespace tbl_test from '/u01/archived_logs'* command to tell Oracle to use the archived redo log files that are located in the specified location for tablespace recovery.

Recovering Offline and Read Only Datafiles

If the datafile is backed up after it was made offline, there will be no need to recover it. See the following example:

```
SQL>
alter
 tablespace users offline normal;

Tablespace altered.

SQL>
host
[oracle@localhost ~]$ cp
/u01/oracle/product/10.2.0/db_1/oradata/lindb/users01.dbf /tmp/users01.dbf
[oracle@localhost ~]$ exit

exit

SQL>
host
[oracle@localhost ~]$ rm -rf
/u01/oracle/product/10.2.0/db_1/oradata/lindb/users01.dbf
[oracle@localhost ~]$ exit

exit

SQL>
shutdown
 immediate
SQL>
startup

SQL>
select
 name, checkpoint_change#
from
 v$datafile;
```

NAME	CHECKPOINT_CHANGE#
/u01/oracle/product/10.2.0/db_1/oradata/lindb/system01.dbf	933311
/u01/oracle/product/10.2.0/db_1/oradata/lindb/undotbs01.dbf	933311
/u01/oracle/product/10.2.0/db_1/oradata/lindb/sysaux01.dbf	933311
/u01/oracle/product/10.2.0/db_1/oradata/lindb/users01.dbf	932857

```
SQL>
alter
 tablespace users online;
alter tablespace users online
*

ERROR at line 1:
ORA-01157: cannot identify/lock data file 4 - see DBWR trace file
```

```
ORA-01110: data file 4:
'/u01/oracle/product/10.2.0/db_1/oradata/lindb/users01.dbf'

SQL>
host
[oracle@localhost ~]$ cp /tmp/users01.dbf
/u01/oracle/product/10.2.0/db_1/oradata/lindb/users01.dbf
[oracle@localhost ~]$ exit

exit

SQL>
alter
 tablespace users online;

Tablespace altered.
SQL>
```

Also, there is no need to place the tablespace to backup mode if the read only tablespace is being backed up. The above code is the same for read only tablespaces.

Recovering a Datafile Which Has No Backup

If a new tablespace has been created or a new datafile added to the existed tablespace and its backup was not made, it can still be recovered in case it is lost using all available archived redo log files that were created after the datafile itself was created. For this, use the *alter database create datafile* command to create the datafile and the *recover datafile* command to add redo changes from all available archived redo log files. In the following example, this will be demonstrated.

Create a tablespace, a new user and an object. Then remove the datafile from the OS and try to recover it without restoring it from anywhere.

```
SQL>
create
 user usr
identified by
 usr;

User created.

SQL>
grant
 dba
to
 usr;

Grant succeeded.
```

```
SQL>
create
 tablespace tbs datafile '/tmp/tbs01.dbf' size 1m;

Tablespace created.

SQL>
conn
 usr/usr

Connected.

SQL>
create
 table t (id number) tablespace tbs;

Table created.

SQL>
insert into
 t values(1);

1 row created.

SQL>
commit;

Commit complete.

SQL>
select * from
 t;


       ID
----------
        1
```

Remove the datafile:

```
SQL>
host
 rm -rf /tmp/tbs01.dbf
```

Flush the buffer and query the object again:

```
SQL>
alter
 system flush buffer_cache;

System altered.

SQL>
select * from
 t;
select * from
```

```
  t
  *
ERROR at line 1:
ORA-01116: error in opening database file 5
ORA-01110: data file 5: '/tmp/tbs01.dbf'
ORA-27041: unable to open file
Linux Error: 2: No such file or directory
Additional information: 3
```

Query the status column of the *v$datafile* view:

```
SQL>
select
 file#, status, name FROM v$datafile;

FILE# STATUS  NAME
---- ------- --------------------------------------------------
   1 SYSTEM  /u01/ORACLE/product/10.2.0/db_1/oradata/db/system01.dbf
   2 ONLINE  /u01/ORACLE/product/10.2.0/db_1/oradata/db/undotbs01.dbf
   3 ONLINE  /u01/ORACLE/product/10.2.0/db_1/oradata/db/sysaux01.dbf
   4 ONLINE  /u01/ORACLE/product/10.2.0/db_1/oradata/db/users01.dbf
   5 RECOVER /tmp/tbs01.dbf
```

As the necessary backup of this file is not available, create a new datafile with the same name and issue the *recover datafile* command to tell Oracle to apply redo changes from archived redo log files to the newly created datafile:

```
SQL>
alter
 database create datafile '/tmp/tbs01.dbf';

Database altered.

SQL>
recover
 datafile 5;

ORA-00279: change 446875 generated at 07/11/2010 20:51:23 needed for thread
1
ORA-00289: suggestion :
/u01/ORACLE/product/10.2.0/db_1/flash_recovery_area/DB/archivelog/2010_07_11
/o1_mf_1_1_%u_.arc
ORA-00280: change 446875 for thread 1 is in sequence #1

Specify log: {<RET>=suggested | filename | AUTO | CANCEL}
AUTO

ORA-00279: change 446992 generated at 07/11/2010 20:55:28 needed for thread
1
ORA-00289: suggestion :
/u01/ORACLE/product/10.2.0/db_1/flash_recovery_area/DB/archivelog/2010_07_11
/o1_mf_1_2_%u_.arc
ORA-00280: change 446992 for thread 1 is in sequence #2
ORA-00278: log file
```

```
'/u01/ORACLE/product/10.2.0/db_1/flash_recovery_area/DB/archivelog/2010_07_1
1/o1_mf_1_1_63nt008c_.arc' no longer needed for this recovery

Log applied.
Media recovery complete.
```

Now check the status of the datafile again. As a recovery has been performed, it must be offline. Bring it to online and query the table:

```
SQL>
select
 file#, status, name
from
 v$datafile;

FILE# STATUS  NAME
---- ------- ------------------------------------------------------------
1 SYSTEM  /u01/oracle/product/10.2.0/db_1/oradata/db/system01.dbf
2 ONLINE  /u01/oracle/product/10.2.0/db_1/oradata/db/undotbs01.dbf
3 ONLINE  /u01/oracle/product/10.2.0/db_1/oradata/db/sysaux01.dbf
4 ONLINE  /u01/oracle/product/10.2.0/db_1/oradata/db/users01.dbf
5 OFFLINE /tmp/tbs01.dbf

SQL>
alter
 database datafile 5 online;

Database altered.

SQL>
select * from
 t;

        ID
----------
         1
SQL>
```

Recovering *Undo* Datafile

The *undo* datafile contains previous images of changed blocks. For example, if an *update* command was performed, *undo* keeps previous images of all changed data blocks so that the transaction can be rolled back and all data retrieved before the transaction was committed.

First of all, note that the *undo* datafile must be backed up together with the rest of the datafiles of the database. Even in some circumstances, the database cannot be used because of loss of the *undo* datafile. Before talking about undo recovery, it must be mentioned that there are two conditions that should be considered before starting the recovery.

1. Is the database running or is it down?

2. Was the database closed cleanly or not?

According to the above mentioned conditions, three scenarios will be shown:

1. *Undo* datafile is missing and the database was closed cleanly

2. *Undo* datafile is missing and the database was not closed cleanly

3. *Undo* datafile is missing and the database is running

Scenario 1: Undo Datafile Missing and Database Closed Cleanly

In this scenario, the database has been closed cleanly using the *shutdown immediate* command and then it is realized that the *undo* datafile is missing. To create this scenario, perform the following:

1. Query the *v$datafile*, close the database and delete the *undo* datafile. Then open the database:

```
SQL>
select
 name
from v$datafile;

NAME
------------------------------------------------------------
C:\ORACLE\product\10.2.0\oradata\db1\system01.dbf
C:\ORACLE\product\10.2.0\oradata\db1\undotbs01.dbf
C:\ORACLE\product\10.2.0\oradata\db1\sysaux01.dbf
C:\ORACLE\product\10.2.0\oradata\db1\users01.dbf

SQL>
shutdown
 immediate
C:\>del C:\ORACLE\product\10.2.0\oradata\db1\undotbs01.dbf

SQL>
startup

<...output trimmed ... >
<...output trimmed ... >
Database mounted.
ORA-01157: cannot identify/lock data file 2 - see DBWR trace file
ORA-01110: data file 2: 'C:\ORACLE\product\10.2.0\oradata\db1\undotbs01.dbf'
```

To solve this problem:

- Change the *undo_management* parameter to manual

- Drop the missing file

- Open the database
- Drop the undo tablespace
- Create a new undo tablespace
- change *undo_tablespace* parameter to the new undo tablespace name and the *undo_management* parameter to auto
- Open the database

Here are the steps:

1. Change the *undo_management* parameter to manual and restart the database:

```
SQL>
show
 parameter undo_management


NAME                           TYPE         VALUE
------------------------       -----------  --------------------------
undo_management                string       AUTO

SQL>
alter
 system set undo_management=manual scope=spfile;

System altered.

SQL>
startup
 force

Database mounted.
ORA-01157: cannot identify/lock data file 2 - see DBWR trace file
ORA-01110: data file 2: 'C:\ORACLE\product\10.2.0\oradata\db1\undotbs01.dbf'

SQL>
show
 parameter undo_management

NAME                                TYPE         VALUE
----------------------------------  -----------  -------------------
undo_management                     string       MANUAL
```

2. Drop the datafile and open the database:

```
SQL>
alter
 database datafile 'C:\ORACLE\product\10.2.0\oradata\db1\undotbs01.dbf'
offline drop;

Database altered.

SQL>
```

```
alter
 database open;

Database altered.

SQL>
select
 file#, status, name
from
 v$datafile;

     FILE# STATUS  NAME
---------- -------  -------------------------------------------------
         1 SYSTEM   C:\ORACLE\product\10.2.0\oradata\db1\system01.dbf
         2 offline  C:\ORACLE\product\10.2.0\oradata\db1\undotbs01.dbf
         3 ONLINE   C:\ORACLE\product\10.2.0\oradata\db1\sysaux01.dbf
         4 ONLINE   C:\ORACLE\product\10.2.0\oradata\db1\users01.dbf
```

3. Drop the undo tablespace and create new one:

```
SQL>
drop
 tablespace undotbs1 including contents;

Tablespace dropped.

SQL>
create
 undo tablespace undotbs2 datafile
'C:\ORACLE\product\10.2.0\oradata\db1\undotbs02.dbf' size 100m;

Tablespace created.
SQL>
```

4. Change the *undo_tablespace* parameter to the new undo tablespace name, the *undo_management* parameter to auto and reboot the database:

```
SQL>
alter
 system set undo_management=auto scope=spfile;

System altered.

SQL>
alter
 system set undo_tablespace=undotbs2 scope=spfile;

System altered.

SQL>
startup
 force

Database mounted.
Database opened.
SQL>
```

Recovering Undo Datafile

Scenario 2: Undo Datafile Missing and Database Not Closed Cleanly

In this scenario, the database was not closed cleanly due to a power outage and the hard drive where the *undo* datafiles reside was lost. To create this scenario, perform the following steps:

1. In order to fill the *undo* datafile with some data, create a table from *dba_objects* and update any column by not committing the transaction:

```
SQL>
create
 table t as
 select * from dba_objects;

Table created.

SQL>
update t
 set owner=null;

49814 rows updated.
SQL>
```

2. Now close the database using the *shutdown abort* command and move the *undo* datafile to another location:

```
SQL>
shutdown
 abort

ORACLE instance shut down.

[oracle@locahost db2]$ mv undotbs01.dbf undotbs01.dbf_backup

SQL>
startup

ORACLE instance started.
Database mounted.
ORA-01157: cannot identify/lock data file 2 - see DBWR trace file
ORA-01110: data file 2:
'/u01/oracle/product/10.2.0/db_1/oradata/db2/undotbs01.dbf'
```

If the above error appears, shut down the instance and get the *undo* datafile from backup. Then mount the database and recover it.

```
SQL>
shutdown
 immediate

ORA-01109: database not open
Database dismounted.
ORACLE instance shut down.
```

```
SQL>
host
[oracle@locahost oradata]$ cp db2_backup/undotbs01.dbf db_2/undotbs01.dbf

SQL>
startup
 mount

Database mounted.

SQL>
recover
 datafile 2;

ORA-00279: change 447670 generated at 07/12/2010 00:51:24 needed for thread
1
ORA-00289: suggestion :
/u01/oracle/product/10.2.0/db_1/flash_recovery_area/DB2/archivelog/2010_07_1
2/o1
_mf_1_1_%u_.arc
ORA-00280: change 447670 for thread 1 is in sequence #1

Specify log: {<RET>=suggested | filename | AUTO | CANCEL}
AUTO

Log applied.
Media recovery complete.
```

Now open the database and query the table. Updates will not be seen in the table as they were not committed:

```
SQL>
alter
 database open;

Database altered.

SQL>
select
 count(*)
from t
where owner is null;

COUNT(*)
----------
         0
SQL>
```

Scenario 3: Undo Datafile Missing and Database is Running

Imagine that the database is running and suddenly it is realized that the *undo* datafile is missing because of hard disk failure. If there are no active transactions in that datafile and there are no queries doing consistent reads from *undo* in that datafile, do not close the database. Try to solve the problem while the database is running. This might be much easier.

In this case, there are two solutions:

- Create a new undo tablespace and drop the missing one
- Get the missing *undo* datafile from backup and recover it

It would be good if the problem can be solved using the first method. If it is a success, then it is ok. If not, then use the second method. To create this environment, update a table and delete the *undo* datafile. Then flush the buffer cache and query the table again.

```
SQL>
create
 table t
as
select * from all_objects where rownum<10;

Table created.

SQL>
select
 count(1)
from t;

  COUNT(1)
----------
         9

SQL>
update
 t set owner='test';

9 rows updated.

#Delete undo datafile

SQL>
alter
 system flush buffer_cache;

System altered.

SQL>
select
count(1)
from
 t
where owner='test';

  COUNT(1)
```

Oracle Backup and Recovery

```
----------
         9

SQL> exit
ERROR:
ORA-00603: ORACLE server session terminated by fatal error
```

There is an error, so check the *alert.log* file:

```
Errors in file
/u01/oracle/product/10.2.0/db_1/admin/db3/bdump/db3_pmon_5039.trc:
ORA-00376: file 2 cannot be read at this time
ORA-01110: data file 2:
'/u01/oracle/product/10.2.0/db_1/oradata/db3/undotbs01.dbf'
[oracle@locahost bdump]$
```

Login to SQL*Plus and try to query the table again:

```
SQL>
conn
 usr/usr

Connected.

SQL>
select
 count(1)
from
 t
where owner='test';
select count(1) from t where owner='test'
*

ERROR at line 1:
ORA-00376: file 2 cannot be read at this time
ORA-01110: data file 2:
'/u01/oracle/product/10.2.0/db_1/oradata/db3/undotbs01.dbf'
```

Oracle tries to get the data from the *undo* datafile and fails. Try the first method by creating a new undo tablespace.

```
SQL>
create
 undo tablespace undotbs2 datafile
'/u01/oracle/product/10.2.0/db_1/oradata/db3/undotbs02.dbf' size 100m;
create undo tablespace undotbs2 datafile
'/u01/oracle/product/10.2.0/db_1/oradata/db3/undotbs02.dbf' size 100m
*

ERROR at line 1:
ORA-00604: error occurred at recursive SQL level 1
ORA-00376: file 2 cannot be read at this time
ORA-01110: data file 2:
'/u01/oracle/product/10.2.0/db_1/oradata/db3/undotbs01.dbf'
```

Recovering Undo Datafile

Unfortunately, it was not possible. So there is only one option: to restore the datafile from backup and perform a recovery,

```
[oracle@locahost db3]$ mv undotbs01.dbf_backup undotbs01.dbf

SQL>
conn
/ as sysdba

Connected.

SQL>
recover
datafile 2;

ORA-00279: change 466951 generated at 07/12/2010 02:46:31 needed for thread
1
ORA-00289: suggestion :
/u01/ORACLE/product/10.2.0/db_1/flash_recovery_area/DB3/archivelog/2010_07_1
2/o1
_mf_1_2_%u_.arc
ORA-00280: change 466951 for thread 1 is in sequence #2

Specify log: {<RET>=suggested | filename | AUTO | CANCEL}
AUTO

ORA-00279: change 467217 generated at 07/12/2010 02:52:29 needed for thread
1
ORA-00289: suggestion :
/u01/ORACLE/product/10.2.0/db_1/flash_recovery_area/DB3/archivelog/2010_07_1
2/o1
_mf_1_3_%u_.arc
ORA-00280: change 467217 for thread 1 is in sequence #3
ORA-00278: log file
'/u01/ORACLE/product/10.2.0/db_1/flash_recovery_area/DB3/archivelog/2010_07_
12/o
1_mf_1_2_63ogxf8f_.arc' no longer needed for this recovery

ORA-00603: ORACLE server session terminated by fatal error
ERROR:
ORA-03114: not connected to ORACLE
```

The server session terminates because the subsequent redo is not in an archivelog but in the online redo log file. The *alter database datafile online* command can resynchronize the datafile.

```
SQL>
conn
/ as sysdba

Connected.

SQL>
alter
database datafile 2 online;
```

```
Database altered.

SQL>
select
 count(1)
from
 usr.t
where
 owner='test';

  COUNT(1)
----------
         0
SQL>
```

Performing User-managed Recovery from Loss of Redo Log Files

In some cases, losing redo log files may be a tragedy. As the redo log files contain changes made to the database, it means that by losing redo log files, those changes can be lost forever. Look at the redo log loss scenarios and learn how to act accordingly.

Here is the list of possible redo log failures and their solutions with step-by-step demonstrations and explanations.

- Scenario 1: Recovering from loss of multiplexed redo log file

- Scenario 2: Recovering from loss of the redo log member of the Inactive group

- Scenario 3: Recovering from loss of the redo log member of the Current group

- Scenario 4: Recovering from loss of the redo log member of the Active group

Now test all the above scenarios step-by–step.

Scenario 1: Recovering from Loss of Multiplexed Redo Log File

When one of the multiplexed members of any group is corrupted or accidently dropped, the LGWR process ignores it and writes the information to the only available member. The following scenario gives a little demonstration to easily understand the main concept:

1. Add one member to each redo log group. Query all redo log members and their status:

```
SQL>
select
 b.group#, a.status, b.status, b.member
from
 v$log a, v$logfile b
 where
 a.group#=b.group#
 order by
 1,2;

GROUP#     STATUS           STATUS  MEMBER
---------- ---------------- ------- --------------------------------
         1 CURRENT                  /u01/oracle/product/10.2.0/db_1/ora
                                    data/testdb/redo01.log
         2 INACTIVE                 /u01/oracle/product/10.2.0/db_1/ora
                                    data/testdb/redo02.log
         3 ACTIVE                   /u01/oracle/product/10.2.0/db_1/ora
                                    data/testdb/redo03.log
```

2. Add one member per group:

```
SQL>
alter
 database add logfile member '/u02/oradata/testdb/redo01.log'
to
 group 1;

Database altered.

SQL>
alter
 database add logfile member '/u02/oradata/testdb/redo02.log'
to
 group 2;

Database altered.

SQL>
alter
 database add logfile member '/u02/oradata/testdb/redo03.log'
to
 group 3;

Database altered.
```

3. Query both views again. The *invalid* status is seen for each member because they are newly created.

```
SQL>
select
 b.group#, a.status, b.status, b.member
from
 v$log a, v$logfile b
where
 a.group#=b.group#
order by
 1,2;
```

```
GROUP#    STATUS          STATUS  MEMBER
--------- --------------- ------- -------------------------------
        1 CURRENT                 /u01/oracle/product/10.2.0/db_1/ora
                                  data/testdb/redo01.log

        1 CURRENT         INVALID /u02/oradata/testdb/redo01.log
        2 INACTIVE        INVALID /u02/oradata/testdb/redo02.log
        2 INACTIVE                /u01/oracle/product/10.2.0/db_1/ora
                                  data/testdb/redo02.log

        3 ACTIVE          INVALID /u02/oradata/testdb/redo03.log
        3 ACTIVE                  /u01/oracle/product/10.2.0/db_1/ora
                                  data/testdb/redo03.log
6 rows selected.
```

4. Perform a manual redo log switch to make those members available and query the views again:

```
SQL>
alter
 system switch logfile;

System altered.

SQL>
/

System altered.

SQL>
/

System altered.

SQL>
select
 b.group#, a.status, b.status, b.member
from
 v$log a, v$logfile b
where
 a.group#=b.group#
order by
 1,2;

GROUP# STATUS          STATUS  MEMBER
--------- --------------- ------- -----------------------------------
        1 CURRENT                 /u01/oracle/product/10.2.0/db_1/ora
                                  data/testdb/redo01.log
        1 CURRENT                 /u02/oradata/testdb/redo01.log
        2 INACTIVE                /u02/oradata/testdb/redo02.log
<.....output trimmed ......>
<.....output trimmed ......>
6 rows selected.
```

5. Delete one of the redo log files from OS, shut down the database, start it, switch the redo log file and query the views again:

```
SQL>
host rm -rf /u02/oradata/testdb/redo01.log
SQL>
shut
 abort
SQL>
```

```
startup
SQL>
alter
 system switch logfile;

System altered.

SQL>
select
 b.group#, a.archived, a.status, b.status, b.member
from
 v$log a, v$logfile b
where
 a.group#=b.group#
order by
 1,2;
```

```
    GROUP# ARC STATUS           STATUS  MEMBER
---------- --- ---------------- ------- ----------------------------
         1 NO  CURRENT           /u01/oracle/product/10.2.0/db_1/ora
                                 data/testdb/redo01.log
         1 NO  CURRENT          INVALID /u02/oradata/testdb/redo01.log
         2 NO  INACTIVE          /u02/oradata/testdb/redo02.log
<......output trimmed ......>
<......output trimmed ......>
6 rows selected.
```

6. Recreate the member by dropping and creating it again. As the redo log member is in the currently used redo log group, it cannot be dropped. Thus, switch the redo log file and try again:

```
SQL>
alter
 database drop logfile member '/u02/oradata/testdb/redo01.log';
alter
 database drop logfile member '/u02/oradata/testdb/redo01.log'
*

ERROR at line 1:
ORA-01609: log 1 is the current log for thread 1 - cannot drop members
ORA-00312: online log 1 thread 1:
'/u01/ORACLE/product/10.2.0/db_1/oradata/testdb/redo01.log'
ORA-00312: online log 1 thread 1: '/u02/oradata/testdb/redo01.log'

SQL>
alter
 system switch logfile;

System altered.


SQL>
alter
 database drop logfile member '/u02/oradata/testdb/redo01.log';

Database altered.
SQL>
```

7. Add the new redo log file to the same group:

```
SQL>
```

```
alter
 database add logfile member '/u02/oradata/testdb/redo01.log'
to
 group 1;

Database altered.

SQL>
select
 b.group#, a.archived, a.status, b.status, b.member
from
 v$log a, v$logfile b
where
 a.group#=b.group#
order by
 1,2;

    GROUP# ARC STATUS          STATUS  MEMBER
---------- --- --------------- ------- ----------------------------
         1 NO  INACTIVE         /u01/oracle/product/10.2.0/db_1/ora
                                data/testdb/redo01.log
         1 NO  INACTIVE        INVALID /u02/oradata/testdb/redo01.log
<......output trimmed ......>
<......output trimmed ......>
6 rows selected.
```

8. Perform a manual redo log switch to make active the redo log file:

```
SQL>
alter
 system switch logfile;

System altered.

SQL>
 /

System altered.

SQL>
select
 b.group#, a.archived, a.status, b.status, b.member
from
 v$log a, v$logfile b
where a.group#=b.group#
order by 1,2;



    GROUP# ARC STATUS          STATUS  MEMBER
---------- --- --------------- ------- ----------------------------
         1 NO  CURRENT          /u01/oracle/product/10.2.0/db_1/ora
                                data/testdb/redo01.log
         1 NO  CURRENT          /u02/oradata/testdb/redo01.log
6 rows selected.
```

Recovering Undo Datafile

Scenario 2: Recovering From Loss of Members of Inactive Group

Here the loss of a nonmultiplexed redo log member of the Inactive redo log group will be recovered. To test this scenario, follow these steps:

1. Get the list of all redo log files:

```
SQL>
select
 b.group#, a.archived, a.status, b.status, b.member
from
 v$log a, v$logfile b
where a.group#=b.group#
order by 1,2;

    GROUP# ARC STATUS          STATUS  MEMBER
---------- --- ---------------- ------- ----------------------------
         1 YES INACTIVE         /u01/oracle/product/10.2.0/db_1/ora
                                data/testdb/redo01.log
         2 YES ACTIVE           /u01/oracle/product/10.2.0/db_1/ora
                                data/testdb/redo02.log
         3 NO  CURRENT          u01/oracle/product/10.2.0/db_1/ora
                                data/testdb/redo03.log
```

2. Delete the first redo log file:

```
SQL>
host
[oracle@localhost ~]$ rm -rf
/u01/oracle/product/10.2.0/db_1/oradata/testdb/redo01.log
[oracle@localhost ~]$ exit
```

3. Do two manual log switches. In the second log switch, the session will hang because Oracle will not be able to find the redo log file that should be archived.

```
SQL>
alter
 system switch logfile;

System altered.

SQL>
alter
 system switch logfile;

<...Session suspends, we decide to check the alert.log file ...>
```

Here is the entry of the *alert.log* file:

```
Errors in file
/u01/ORACLE/product/10.2.0/db_1/admin/testdb/bdump/testdb_arc1_6755.trc:
ORA-00313: open failed for members of log group 1 of thread 1
ORA-00312: online log 1 thread 1:
'/u01/ORACLE/product/10.2.0/db_1/oradata/testdb/redo01.log'
ORA-27037: unable to obtain file status
Linux Error: 2: No such file or directory
Additional information: 3
```

```
Sat Apr 17 15:26:09 2010
ARC1: Failed to archive thread 1 sequence 47 (0)
```

4. If the database is shut down, it will not be opened:

```
SQL>
shut
 abort
SQL>
startup

<.....output trimmed ......>
<.....output trimmed ......>
Database mounted.
ORA-00313: open failed for members of log group 1 of thread 1
ORA-00312: online log 1 thread 1:
'/u01/ORACLE/product/10.2.0/db_1/oradata/testdb/redo01.log'
```

5. Check again the *alert.log* file:

```
Errors in file
/u01/ORACLE/product/10.2.0/db_1/admin/testdb/bdump/testdb_lgwr_8587.trc:
ORA-00313: open failed for members of log group 1 of thread 1
ORA-00312: online log 1 thread 1:
'/u01/ORACLE/product/10.2.0/db_1/oradata/testdb/redo01.log'
ORA-27037: unable to obtain file status
Linux Error: 2: No such file or directory
Additional information: 3
```

6. So decide to clear this unarchived and unavailable redo log file:

```
SQL>
alter
 database clear unarchived logfile group 1;

Database altered.

SQL>
```

7. Try to open the database and check for the redo log file:

```
SQL>
alter
 database open;

Database altered.

SQL>
host
 ls /u01/oracle/product/10.2.0/db_1/oradata/testdb/redo01.log
/u01/oracle/product/10.2.0/db_1/oradata/testdb/redo01.log
```

8. The database opened successfully and the missed redo log file was created.
    Now check the *alert.log* file again:

```
alter database clear unarchived logfile group 1
WARNING! CLEARING REDO LOG WHICH HAS NOT BEEN ARCHIVED. BACKUPS TAKEN BEFORE
04/17/2010 15:20:14 (CHANGE 511006) CANNOT BE USED FOR RECOVERY.
```

```
Clearing online log 1 of thread 1 sequence number 47
Sat Apr 17 15:27:09 2010
Errors in file
/u01/ORACLE/product/10.2.0/db_1/admin/testdb/udump/testdb_ora_8618.trc:
ORA-00313: open failed for members of log group 1 of thread 1
ORA-00312: online log 1 thread 1:
'/u01/ORACLE/product/10.2.0/db_1/oradata/testdb/redo01.log'
ORA-27037: unable to obtain file status
Linux Error: 2: No such file or directory
Additional information: 3
Completed: alter database clear unarchived logfile group 1
Sat Apr 17 15:27:22 2010
alter database open
Sat Apr 17 15:27:22 2010
Thread 1 advanced to log sequence 50
Thread 1 opened at log sequence 50
  Current log# 1 seq# 50 mem# 0:
/u01/ORACLE/product/10.2.0/db_1/oradata/testdb/redo01.log
Successful open of redo thread 1
```

> **NOTE:** As the warning makes clear, a redo log file is now missing. Rolling forward through redo cannot happen from prior backups. The advice is to make a fresh backup of the database and archivelogs as soon as possible.

Scenario 3: Recovering From Loss of Redo Log Member of Current Group

The following scenario will demonstrate the recovery steps from the loss of the redo log member of the Current redo log group. This is the most dangerous situation where the DBA will lose everything that is written to the redo log file which is not multiplexed.

1. First of all, take a backup of the database (shutdown the database and copy all *.dbf* and *.ctl* files to another directory). Then get the member name of the current redo log group and delete it. Then restart the database:

```
SQL>
shutdown
 immediate;

[oracle@localhost ~]$ cd $ORACLE_HOME/oradata/new/
[oracle@localhost new]$ mkdir backup
[oracle@localhost new]$ cp *.dbf backup/
[oracle@localhost new]$ cp *.ctl backup/
[oracle@localhost new]$ exit

SQL>
startup
```

```
<.....output trimmed .....>
Database opened.

SQL>
select
 a.group#, a.status, b.member
from
 v$log a, v$logfile b
where
 a.group#=b.group# and a.status='current';

    GROUP# STATUS          MEMBER
---------- --------------- ----------------------------------------
3 CURRENT         /u01/ORACLE/product/10.2.0/db_1/oradata/new/redo03.log

SQL>
host
[oracle@localhost ~]$ rm -rf
/u01/oracle/product/10.2.0/db_1/oradata/new/redo03.log
[oracle@localhost ~]$ exit

exit

SQL>
startup
 force

<.....output trimmed .....>
Database mounted.
ORA-00313: open failed for members of log group 3 of thread 1
ORA-00312: online log 3 thread 1:
'/u01/ORACLE/product/10.2.0/db_1/oradata/new/redo03.log'
ORA-27037: unable to obtain file status
Linux Error: 2: No such file or directory
Additional information: 3
SQL>
```

2. It is not possible to clear the *current* redo log file as has been done for the loss of the inactive redo log member. It is also not possible to drop and add a nonmultiplexed current redo log member as has been done for the loss of the multiplexed member of any group. If this is tried, there will be failure:

```
SQL>
alter
 database clear unarchived logfile
'/u01/ORACLE/product/10.2.0/db_1/oradata/new/redo03.log';
alter
 database clear unarchived logfile
'/u01/ORACLE/product/10.2.0/db_1/oradata/new/redo03.loq'
*

ERROR at line 1:
ORA-01624: log 3 needed for crash recovery of instance new (thread 1)
ORA-00312: online log 3 thread 1:
'/u01/ORACLE/product/10.2.0/db_1/oradata/new/redo03.log'
```

Recovering Undo Datafile   **417**

```
SQL>
alter
 database drop logfile
'/u01/ORACLE/product/10.2.0/db_1/oradata/new/redo03.log';
alter
 database drop logfile
'/u01/ORACLE/product/10.2.0/db_1/oradata/new/redo03.log'
*

ERROR at line 1:
ORA-01623: log 3 is current log for instance new (thread 1) - cannot drop
ORA-00312: online log 3 thread 1:
'/u01/ORACLE/product/10.2.0/db_1/oradata/new/redo03.log'
SQL>
```

3. In this situation, recover the database to the lost redo log's first sequence number. To get this *SCN value*, use the following query:

```
SQL>
select
 a.first_change#, a.status, b.member
from
 v$log a, v$logfile b
where
 a.group#=b.group# and a.status='current';

FIRST_CHANGE# STATUS           MEMBER
------------- ---------------- -------------------------------------
446985 CURRENT   /u01/oracle/product/10.2.0/db_1/oradata/new/redo03.log
```

4. Shut down the database, restore all files from the backup directory and bring the database to mount mode. Then use the *recover database until change* command to recover the database until the *first_change#* value of the missing redo log file and open the database with the *resetlogs* option:

```
SQL>
shutdown
 immediate;

[oracle@localhost ~]$ cd $ORACLE_HOME/oradata/new
[oracle@localhost new]$ rm -rf *.dbf
[oracle@localhost new]$ rm -rf *.ctl
[oracle@localhost new]$ cd ./backup
[oracle@localhost new]$ mv ./backup/* .
[oracle@localhost new]$ exit

SQL>
startup
 mount

<.....output trimmed .....>
Database mounted.

SQL>
recover
 database until change 446985;
```

```
Media recovery complete.

SQL>
alter
 database open resetlogs;

Database altered.
SQL>
```

Scenario 4: Recovering From Loss of Redo Log Member of Active Group

The active group member is needed for instance recovery, so an incomplete recovery may need to be performed if its members were lost as has been done for the group members with *current* status. Remember, the first action which should be performed when the active member of the redo log file is lost is running the *alter system checkpoint* command. If it does not fail, then go on and clear the redo log file as has been done in the inactive member loss.

If it fails, then there is only one option which is performing an incomplete recovery. All steps are the same as in the current group loss scenario.

Performing Incomplete Recovery

Sometimes there is a need to perform an incomplete recovery to recover the database to a specific point in time. Imagine that an archived redo log file was lost and cannot continue the recovery process. Or a critical table was dropped accidently and it was also purged from the recycle bin as there are only user-managed backups. In such situations, perform an incomplete recovery and apply only a limited count of archived redo log files such as redo entries.

There are three main types of an incomplete recovery:

1. Time-based

2. Change-based

3. Cancel-based

After performing an incomplete recovery, open the database with the *resetlogs* option. By opening the database with this, all datafiles' headers are changed and updated with new *resetlogs scn* and *timestamp* values. These values are stored in the *resetlogs_change#* and *resetlogs_time* columns in the *v$datafile_header* view.

The next generated archived redo log files' headers are also updated with new *resetlogs* information of both *scn* and *timestamp*. Doing this, Oracle guarantees that it will not apply archived redo log files that belong to the previous incarnation of the database.

In the following scenario, it is shown that Oracle will not use the archived redo log files with the required SCN value because the headers of datafiles and archived redo log files are not consistent. Instead, it will use the previous archived redo log files.

Get the list of archived redo log files:

```
SQL>
select
 sequence#, first_change#, resetlogs_change#, resetlogs_time, name from
 v$archived_log;

SEQUENCE# FIRST_CHANGE# RESETLOGS_CHANGE# RESETLOGS_TIME    NAME
--------- ------------- ----------------------------------  -----
1    440636    440636    01-MAY-10 ../2010_05_01/o1_mf_1_1_5xqvyxbz_.arc
2    446878    440636    01-MAY-10 ../2010_05_01/o1_mf_1_2_5xqw4g79_.arc
```

Shut down the database and take a backup of all datafiles. Then switch some log files:

```
SQL>
shutdown
 immediate
#Take backup of the database

SQL>
startup
#Switch some log files and query the V$ARCHIVED_LOG view
SQL>
select
 sequence#, first_change#, resetlogs_change#, resetlogs_time, name from
 v$archived_log;

SEQUENCE# FIRST_CHANGE# RESETLOGS_CHANGE# RESETLOGS_TIME    NAME
--------- ------------- ----------------------------------  -----
1    440636    440636 01-MAY-10 ../2010_05_01/o1_mf_1_1_5xqvyxbz_.arc
2    446878    440636 01-MAY-10 ../2010_05_01/o1_mf_1_2_5xqw4g79_.arc
3    448433    440636 01-MAY-10 ../2010_05_01/o1_mf_1_3_5xqw83n7_.arc
4    454114    440636 01-MAY-10 ../2010_05_01/o1_mf_1_4_5xqw86ht_.arc
5    459265    440636 01-MAY-10 ../2010_05_01/o1_mf_1_5_5xqwb034_.arc
```

Close the database, delete all datafiles, thereby simulating media crash, start the database in mount mode and recover the database until the fourth archived redo log and open the database with the *resetlogs* option:

```
SQL>
shutdown
 immediate
```

```
# Delete all datafiles and restore the backup to the original location
SQL>
startup
 mount
#We have 5 archived redo logs generated. Now we recover until the fourth
archived redo log file and open the database with resetlogs option (It's
MUST, as we've performed incomplete recovery)

SQL>
recover
 database until change 454000;

ORA-00279: change 448776 generated at 05/01/2010 05:13:07 needed for thread
1
ORA-00289: suggestion : ../2010_05_01/o1_mf_1_3_%u_.arc
ORA-00280: change 448776 for thread 1 is in sequence #3

Specify log: {<RET>=suggested | filename | AUTO | CANCEL}
AUTO

Log applied.
Media recovery complete.

SQL>
alter
 database open resetlogs;

Database altered.
SQL>
```

Issue some DMLs and *commit* the transaction, then switch the redo log file.
New archived redo log files appear with a *new resetlogs_change* value. As the
database has been opened with the *resetlogs* option, the header of datafiles and
the archived redo log files that are generated afterwards contain the new SCN
value, the same as the *resetlogs_change#* value of the database.

```
SQL>
select
 sequence#, first_change#, resetlogs_change#, resetlogs_time, name
from
 v$archived_log;

SEQUENCE# FIRST_CHANGE# RESETLOGS_CHANGE# RESETLOGS_TIME      NAME
---------- ------------- ----------------- ----------------- -----
1      440636      440636 01-MAY-10 ../2010_05_01/o1_mf_1_1_5xqvyxbz_.arc
2      446878      440636 01-MAY-10 ../2010_05_01/o1_mf_1_2_5xqw4g79_.arc
3      448433      440636 01-MAY-10 ../2010_05_01/o1_mf_1_3_5xqw83n7_.arc
4      454114      440636 01-MAY-10 ../2010_05_01/o1_mf_1_4_5xqw86ht_.arc
5      459265      440636 01-MAY-10 ../2010_05_01/o1_mf_1_5_5xqwb034_.arc
6      470689      440636 01-MAY-10 ../2010_05_01/o1_mf_1_6_5xqwhjxx_.arc
1      454001      454001 01-MAY-10 ../2010_05_01/o1_mf_1_1_5xqwj716_.arc
2      454871      454001 01-MAY-10 ../2010_05_01/o1_mf_1_2_5xqwjrwq_.arc
8 rows selected.
```

Imagine that the database has been crashed and there is a backup of the
previous incarnation which was made before *resetlogs* done. Restore all datafiles
and perform an incomplete recovery till the SCN value 454700.

Oracle will not apply the last archived redo log files of what is generated, even though the second archived redo log file contains changes made before the SCN value 454700. As the backup was restored from the previous incarnation and contains the SCN value 440636 in the header of its datafiles, it will look for the archived redo log files for the same information. The recovery process will look to the header of the archived redo log files and check the SCN value.

```
SQL>
shutdown
 immediate
SQL>
startup
 mount
SQL>
recover
 database until change 454700;

ORA-00279: change 448776 generated at 05/01/2010 05:13:07 needed for thread
1
ORA-00289: suggestion : ../2010_05_01/o1_mf_1_3_%u_.arc
ORA-00280: change 448776 for thread 1 is in sequence #3

Specify log: {<RET>=suggested | filename | AUTO | CANCEL}
AUTO

Log applied.
Media recovery complete.

SQL>
alter
 database open resetlogs;

Database altered.
SQL>
```

If the archived redo log files are checked, Oracle has applied the third archived redo log file from the first incarnation:

```
alter database recover    continue default
Sat May  1 05:21:57 2010
Media Recovery Log ../2010_05_01/o1_mf_1_3_5xqw83n7_.arc
Sat May  1 05:21:58 2010
Recovery of Online Redo Log: Thread 1 Group 2 Seq 1 Reading mem 0
  Mem# 0 errs 0: /u01/ORACLE/product/10.2.0/db_1/oradata/new/redo02.log
Sat May  1 05:21:58 2010
Incomplete Recovery applied until change 454837
Sat May  1 05:21:58 2010
Media Recovery Complete (new)
Completed: alter database recover    continue default
```

Time-based Incomplete Recovery

This type of incomplete recovery means that the database can be recovered up to a specific time. Imagine that a critical table has been dropped and there are only user-managed backups. For the approximate time of the *drop table* command, use the UNTIL TIME clause. For this, create a table, take a current time and drop the table. Then restore all datafiles and recover the database until the taken time as follows:

```
SQL>
shutdown
 immediate
SQL>
host
# Take backup of all datafiles to the backup/ folder

[oracle@localhost new]$ cp *.dbf backup/

SQL>
startup

SQL>
create
 table test
as select * from
 dba_objects;

Table created.

SQL>
select
 count(1)
from test;

  COUNT(1)
----------
     49814

SQL>
select
 to_char(sysdate,'dd-mm-yyyy hh24:mi:ss') ddate
from
 dual;
DDATE
------------------
29-04-2010 10:25:51

SQL>
alter
 system switch logfile;

System altered.

SQL>
```

```
drop
 table test;

Table dropped.

SQL>
alter
 system switch logfile;

System altered.

SQL>
shutdown
 immediate

SQL>
host
# Delete all datafiles and restore the backup of the datafiles from the
backup/ directory

[oracle@localhost new]$ rm -rf *.dbf
[oracle@localhost new]$ mv backup/*.dbf .

SQL>
startup
 mount

SQL>
recover
 database until time '2010-04-29:10:25:51';

Media recovery complete.

SQL>
alter
 database open resetlogs;
Database altered.

SQL>
select
 count(1)
from
 test;

  COUNT(1)
----------
     49814
SQL>
```

Change-based Incomplete Recovery

If there is a specific SCN value, the database can be recovered to the specific SCN value using the *recover database until the change* ... command. As the procedure is the same with the previous scenario, switch to the next and last incomplete recovery type, cancel-based incomplete recovery.

Cancel-based Incomplete Recovery

If an archived redo log file which should be added to the restored datafiles has been missed, the recovery cannot go on and therefore, there is a need to process before Oracle asks for the missing archived redo log file. Oracle Support can also be called to help with some hidden initialization parameters like _allow_resetlogs_corruption_.

In the following scenario, a backup of all datafiles is restored and media recovery is performed using the _until cancel_ option and the recovery process is stopped when the missing archived redo log file is asked for:

```
SQL>
recover
 database until cancel;

ORA-00279: change 447754 generated at 04/29/2010 09:43:30 needed for thread
1
ORA-00289: suggestion :
/u01/ORACLE/product/10.2.0/db_1/flash_recovery_area/NEW/archivelog/2010_04_2
9/o1_mf_1_1_%u_.arc
ORA-00280: change 447754 for thread 1 is in sequence #1

Specify log: {<RET>=suggested | filename | AUTO | CANCEL}
/u01/ORACLE/product/10.2.0/db_1/flash_recovery_area/NEW/archivelog/2010_04_2
9/o1_mf_1_1_5xm3qfvb_.arc

ORA-00279: change 448599 generated at 04/29/2010 09:51:36 needed for thread
1
ORA-00289: suggestion :
/u01/ORACLE/product/10.2.0/db_1/flash_recovery_area/NEW/archivelog/2010_04_2
9/o1_mf_1_2_%u_.arc
ORA-00280: change 448599 for thread 1 is in sequence #2
ORA-00278: log file
'/u01/ORACLE/product/10.2.0/db_1/flash_recovery_area/NEW/archivelog/2010_04_
29/o1_mf_1_1_5xm3qfvb_.arc' no longer needed for this recovery

Specify log: {<RET>=suggested | filename | AUTO | CANCEL}
CANCEL

Media recovery cancelled.

SQL>
alter
 database open resetlogs;

Database altered.
SQL>
```

Remember that the recovery procedure needs to be cancelled after making sure that all datafiles are recovered to the consistent *scn* number; otherwise, an *ORA-01113: file # needs media recovery* error will occur.

Conclusion

Oracle strongly recommends using RMAN for backup and recovery operations. However, there might be some circumstances where there might be a need to take a backup using user-managed techniques or perform recovery without using RMAN. In this chapter, detailed information was provided on user-managed backup and recovery techniques and a step–by–step instruction was shown for each scenario.

In the beginning of the chapter, information on user-managed backup techniques was given and the backup methods of control files, datafiles, archived redo log files, parameter and network files and more were shown.

Next was a demonstration of the recovery techniques of control files, redo log files, datafiles and such. Along with demonstrating the solution, the steps of corrupting the specific physical file and getting the real error were shown. This should help in practicing the scenarios individually and learning the practical solutions before facing the error on the production database.

At the end of the chapter, after covering much information on redo log recovery, the methods of performing an incomplete recovery were explained. The next chapter will explore the Oracle flashback technologies and show all its features in practical scenarios.

Using the Media Management Layer

Introduction

To store the backup of the database on external tape drives, install the media manager software of the third-part vendor and use Media Management Layer (MML) APIs that are available in RMAN. While backing up the database, the RMAN client connects to the media manager using specific allocated channels via the target database instance. To install the third part media manager, refer to the vendor's software documentation for instructions.

To establish the connection, allocate a channel for RMAN by specifying the *sbt_library* parameter with the path to the library of the media manager. The general syntax is:

```
RMAN>configure channel device type sbt parms 'sbt_library=pathname';
```

To test the media manager connection, allocate a channel and examine the RMAN output. In order to test the backup and restore, perform backup of spfile and its restoration.

The *sbttest* Utility

Using this diagnostic tool, RMAN checks whether it can connect to the third part tape drive incorporating the current media manager configuration settings. This tool checks whether the MML is installed correctly and reading and writing to tape can be done through SBT API. Just call the executable by passing a filename as a parameter and check the result. If the following lines come up as a result, then the test was successful:

```
-bash-3.2$ sbttest test_file
The sbt function pointers are loaded from libobk.so library.
-- sbtinit succeeded
-- sbtinit (2nd time) succeeded
```

To get the list of all parameters that the *sbttest* tool supports, run it without any parameters:

```
Error: backup file name must be specified
Usage: sbttest backup_file_name # this is the only required parameter
<-dbname database_name>
<-trace trace_file_name>
<-remove_before>
<-no_remove_after>
<-read_only>
<-no_regular_backup_restore>
<-no_proxy_backup>
<-no_proxy_restore>
<-file_type n>
<-copy_number n>
<-media_pool n>
<-os_res_size n>
<-pl_res_size n>
<-block_size block_size>
<-block_count block_count>
<-proxy_file os_file_name bk_file_name
[os_res_size pl_res_size block_size block_count]>
<-libname sbt_library_name>
```

Simulating SBT Channel

If there are no tape drives but a tape backup needs to be simulated, use an API named *disksbt* while allocating a channel. The channel will be allocated as a tape channel allocation. Look at the following example:

```
RMAN> run {
allocate channel ch1 device type 'sbt_tape'
parms="sbt_library=oracle.disksbt, env=(backup_dir=/tmp/backup)";
backup datafile 1 format='%u';
}

using target database control file instead of recovery catalog
allocated channel: ch1
channel ch1: SID=31 device type=sbt_tape
channel ch1: WARNING: Oracle Test Disk API
```

As this shows, RMAN reacts as it is connecting to the tape drive and the warning "Oracle Test Disk API" appears in the output. To make it a default channel, change the RMAN configuration as follows:

```
RMAN> configure channel device type 'sbt_tape'
parms="sbt_library=oracle.disksbt, env=(backup_dir=/tmp/backup)";
```

Now make the default device type as tape:

```
configure default device type to sbt_tape;
```

After making the above configuration, take backup of any file and RMAN uses a tape backup instead of disk backup.

Introduction to Oracle Secure Backup

When backups are examined, there are only two options that are reviewed. One is the physical hard drive. This is the default place where the backups go if no settings are mentioned. This sounds like a reasonable place where backups can be maintained, but unfortunately it is not. The reason for this is that available disk space is finite and the database that is being backed up just keeps on growing, thereby leaving not enough available space on the drive. So what happens when the backup cannot be kept at the default place, i.e. disk? Where else can it be kept?

Enter the second option, the tape drives! The tape drives are the most popular and viable place where backups are kept. There are many companies which produce tape drives that are available to the industry and for almost all the platforms as well that are used in the production systems. RMAN has been made capable by the Oracle Corporation to work with these tape drives and is able to take backup over them. But the issue with this great story is that RMAN does not have the built-in support of all the possible software drivers and other pieces of code which are required for it to talk to the tape drive. Since there are far too many vendors of tape drives, it is really a mammoth task in itself to make it work.

The software stack which is needed for RMAN to work with the tape drives is called the Media Management Library (MML). The MML drivers come from the vendors of the tape drives and to be honest, it is a tough task to make them all work with RMAN in a seamless manner! This, unfortunately, makes RMAN a not-so-popular choice when being considered as an efficient and usable backup solution. This, in turn, inspired the origin of the Oracle Secure Backup, a centralized backup management system which works seamlessly with almost all the major tape drives and with environments like SAN, Gigabit Ethernet and more. In addition to being an excellent solution for the backups of Oracle databases, this also can work as a protection for the file system and can be used for the file system-based recoveries as well.

A Closer Look at Oracle Secure Backup (OSB)

As mentioned already, OSB is a centralized tape management system. With its built-in support of MML, integrating it with RMAN makes the tape backups effortless. With its Symmetric Binary Tape interact (SBT), both backup and restore of the files can be done to and from the tape. Being fully compatible with all the SAN and SCSI environments, it can use the tape storage available anywhere in the network that is accessible.

Also, there is no need for workarounds like Network File System (NFS) and such. OSB is fully compatible with the RAC environments and offers the backup and restore from the RAC's OCFS as well. Using this, both full and incremental backups are possible and backups can also be secured while creating multiplexed backups across various destinations over the network. OSB's access can be completely controlled by its administrator so that any backup-related operations are not misused.

Here is a pictorial representation of how OSB works with both an Oracle database and a file system that takes their backup to the tape drives.

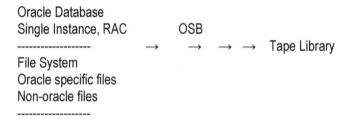

Figure 10.1: *Oracle Secure Backup Diagram*

Oracle Application Servers

OSB also offers security for the backup taken by using SSL implementation and Oracle wallets. With its GUI interface available from the OEM and also from the command line, the manageability and administration becomes a breeze. Now, with the assumption that the information about OSB is understood, the following introduces its architectural components.

OSB server can be categorized into three different streams. These are the administrative server, media server and client. The administrative server is the machine which, as the name suggests, controls the entire operations of backup and recovery via OSB. The configuration files and catalog and related metadata are both stored over it only. There is also an administrator created that handles the administrative tasks like managing devices or libraries. It also runs the scheduler which spawns and maintains the backup jobs. To configure a machine as the administrative server, pick the same type of installation while installing OSB.

The media server is the machine to which the tape media is connected. There can be several media servers which can have several storage media attached to them. At least one media server must be there before the backup operations are started. The administrative server, if attached to the storage, can also be configured as the media server.

The client machines are the machines for which OSB is working and doing the tasks of backup and recovery. These clients have the respective files stored locally over them which are backed up by OSB.
When OSB is configured, an administrative domain also needs to be designated. Administrative domain is the group of all those machines which are used to do the backup and recovery tasks. Each administrative domain must include one administrative server and there can be only one administrative server under one domain but there can be several media and clients which can be a part of the administrative domain.

Administrative domain contains the information related to the configuration of the OSB in a catalog. The secure backup-related information is maintained with classes which are a collection of privileges a user of OSB can enjoy. There are several categories of classes available. Each class comes with its set of privileges which can be used by the user who is a part of the class. Below is a list of the classes available and the related actions which a user can perform.

ADMIN Class

As the name says, this is for the administrator of OSB. Anything which deals with the OSB's administrative options like doing backup or restores are available through this class only. This class's user has the permissions to do the maintenance and management of all kinds of servers including the administrative domain.

Operator Class

This class has the option to view the information related to the devices attached.

Oracle Class

This class is the required class for maintaining and manipulating Oracle database-related backup and recovery settings. The permissions to do backups and restore are also granted to the users of this class.

User Class

The users of this class can only do restore operations. Backups and other related actions are not permissible for the users of this class.

Reader Class

As the name says, this class allows only the reading of the metadata related to OSB catalog. No administrative actions, including backup and restore, are allowed to users of this class.

The available classes can be viewed or their properties changed using the obtool. Below is a list of the classes derived from obtool's *lsclass* command:

```
ob> lsclass

admin
monitor
operator
oracle
reader
user
```

On the OS side, information about classes is maintained under the Class folder stored within the Config folder. Below is the output of Oracle class:

```
[root@localhost class]# pwd
/usr/local/oracle/backup/admin/config/class
[root@localhost class]# ls
admin  monitor  operator  oracle  reader  user
[root@localhost class]# more oracle
name:           oracle
uuid:           fc80cb3c-7f5a-102d-9aac-000c2926d8cd
rights:         0x13CEB
browse rights:  permitted
```

Oracle Backup and Recovery

```
oracle rights:  owner
file system rights:  owner
```

OSB offers two kinds of users that are created and maintained to work with it. One is a privileged user who has root rights and can do any work using OSB. The other one is a non-privileged user who has limited powers, like oracle user of the Oracle database. The user must be configured over the administrative domain before he can do any sort of work. The rights are based on the nature of the job assigned to the user.

The configuration data is maintained on OSB, and if not changed, is under the */usr/local/oracle/backup* folder. The backup folder must be backed up almost all the time. The folder contains the information in the form of the objects where object is anything whose configuration is maintained within OSB like the user, class, tape, or library. All the object-related configurations are stored within the */admin/config* folder with sub-folders named as per the objects.

The administrative domain also contains backup-related information in the catalog which is information maintained by OSB of the backups managed via OSB. This also contains the information about the hosts which are configured within OSB. This information is maintained within the */admin/config/host*. As was stated before, all of this information is required to be backed up. This is done by OSB automatically with a pre-configured backup job which gets created at the time of the installation of OSB itself. This job is managed by OSB scheduler which is maintained by the obsscheduled daemon that schedules all the jobs and runs them as per the schedule to the tape. The most recent backup over the tape can be restored if the data of the catalog is lost.

Daemons Related to OSB

There are seven types of daemons which run on OSB and are responsible for various operations within OSB. Here is a brief introduction to these daemons.

ObServiced

This is the daemon which can be considered as the service running OSB for both Unix, Linux and Windows environments. There surely is a difference in the way it is maintained on both the platforms. On Unix and Linux, it is maintained from the init.d daemon and is controlled from */etc/init.d* which has scripts to control it. On Windows, it runs as a service like the services of any other software running over it.

This daemon is available on three kinds of hosts of the OSB and is responsible for maintaining the jobs which are scheduled from the OSB like mentioned above as the backup job for doing the auto backup of the catalog data.

ObScheduled

The backup is supposed to go over a file system or SBT from either OSB's command line interface *obtool* or the web interface called the OSB web tool. The backups are maintained by the backup schedule which is maintained by the DBA. This is going to be a regularly scheduled backup. This daemon runs on the administrative server. The complete management of scheduling the backups, maintaining that on which tape, which backup goes and so on are maintained by this daemon.

Obixd

This is referred as the index daemon and is responsible for managing the backup catalogs for all the clients connected. As soon as the backup gets finished, this daemon gets invoked and updates the data related to the backup over the catalog available on the administrative server.

Obhttpd

OSB's apache daemon is responsible for running the web tool of the OSB and is running all the time over the administrative server.

Odndmpd

As OSB supports both host-based and NDMP-based hosts, this daemon maintains the NDMP protocol on the client and host machines. This daemon is active at each backup and restore operation.

Obrobotd

This daemon is used by OSB to maintain the tape drives within the tape library and is started by the osbserviced daemon when a request to interact with the tape library is made by any operation.

Obproxyd

The user authorization is done by this daemon.

The access to the OSB with the hosts is maintained in two ways, native and NDMP-based. The native mode is the mode which is used when the host has the OSB running over itself and using the above-mentioned daemons to communicate either with the attached tape drives or with the other media servers where the tapes are attached. This also is referred to as primary access mode or ob access mode depending on whether OSB is used from the web tool or from the command line *obtool*.

The NDMP is used to communicate with all the servers which are not having the OSB natively installed over them and they communicate with the devices using the NDMP protocol. Since the OSB is meant for maintaining the tape drives, it is essential to give a reference about the tape and its related components. RMAN stores the backup over a volume which is used to store the actual physical pieces of the backup. A volume is also considered a physical tape device. A volume or tape is available to RMAN within a tape library. The volume is linked with a storage element.

The management of OSB can be done through three ways. Oracle Enterprise Manager comes with an interface which can be used to work with OSB. Also, there are options available in the Backup section of OEM to configure OSB. In addition to OEM, OSB also comes up with its own GUI interface which can be used to configure and manage OSB backups. If GUIs are not used often, then a complete command line interface called *obtool* is the ticket. This contains a lot of commands which can be used to work with different areas of OSB.

Installing OSB on Linux

The software for the OSB is available as a download from the Oracle's OTN website. OSB's versioning is different from the rest of the database and does not include special characters like *g* or *i*. The current version at the time of this writing is 10.3. When doing the installation of OSB over the Linux environments, the recommended path is the */usr/local/oracle/backup* folder. This folder is made by the root user and from here, there must be an access to any sort of unzipping software. The unzipping needs to be done over the secure backup software downloaded from OTN. Along with accessing the unzipping software, the machines must be running over TCP/IP and also have a static IP.

In addition to the above, before doing the installation, it is a must to make sure that there exists attach points for the devices which are used with OSB over the media server. An attach point is a logical name that is assigned to the physical device. The physical devices are mapped under the /dev folder as a file. An attach point is the naming convention through the device that is used by OSB. Oracle recommends using the /dev/sg interface for the devices. The sg is the interface that is used for SCSI devices. It may also be referred to as a sg driver for SCSI devices.

To find the attach points over a Linux box, use the Linux command sg_map –i –x, finding the right mapping of the device with the interface at the lower level. Using this sg_map command, listings of the devices with their maps in the disk becomes evident. Once done, using the mkdev command, these attach points can be mapped. For example, here is one sample command from Oracle OSB docs which shows how an attach point can be mapped.

```
Mkdev -t library -O -a machine1:/dev/sg4 vliba2
```

The software for the installation of OSB, as stated before, can be downloaded from OSB's home page, http://www.oracle.com/us/ products/database/secure-backup-066578.html. This page, besides having the download link, hosts many of the white papers related to it as well as lots of technical information about the same. The installation should be started from the folder which contains the downloaded and unzipped software of OSB.

Once the software is downloaded and unzipped, start the installation from the folder where the installation files are extracted. As mentioned above, the installation should be done in the recommended location. The installation of OSB is done by the root user and is a command line installation. Below is the output of the installation summary which appears once the installation is finished after supplying the answers to the questions asked by the installer:

```
[root@localhost backup]# /home/oracle/osb-10.3.0.2.0_linux32/setup
Welcome to Oracle's setup program for Oracle Secure Backup.  This
program loads Oracle Secure Backup software from the CD-ROM to a
filesystem directory of our choosing.

This CD-ROM contains Oracle Secure Backup version 10.3.0.2.0_LINUX32.
```

```
Please wait a moment while I learn about this host... done.

- - - - - - - - - - - - - - - - - - - - - - - - - - - - -
1. linux32
administrative server, media server, client

- - - - - - - - - - - - - - - - - - - - - - - - - - - - -
Loading Oracle Secure Backup installation tools... done.
Loading linux32 administrative server, media server, client... done.

- - - - - - - - - - - - - - - - - - - - - - - - - - - - -
Loading of Oracle Secure Backup software from CD-ROM is complete.
We may unmount and remove the CD-ROM.


Would we like to continue Oracle Secure Backup installation with
'installob' now?  (The Oracle Secure Backup Installation Guide
contains complete information about installob.)
Please answer 'yes' or 'no' [yes]:

- - - - - - - - - - - - - - - - - - - - - - - - - - - - -

Welcome to installob, Oracle Secure Backup's installation program.
For most questions, a default answer appears enclosed in square brackets.
Press Enter to select this answer.
Please wait a few seconds while I learn about this machine... done.

Have we already reviewed and customized install/obparameters for wer Oracle
Secure Backup installation [yes]?

- - - - - - - - - - - - - - - - - - - - - - - - - - - - -


Oracle Secure Backup is not yet installed on this machine.
Oracle Secure Backup's Web server has been loaded, but is not yet
configured.

Choose from one of the following options. The option we choose defines the
software components to be installed.

Configuration of this host is required after installation completes.

We can install the software on this host in one of the following ways:
(a) administrative server, media server and client

(b) media server and client

(c) client

If we are not sure which option to choose, please refer to the Oracle Secure
Backup Installation Guide. (a,b or c) [a]?

Beginning the installation.  This will take just a minute and will produce
several lines of informational output.

Installing Oracle Secure Backup on localhost (Linux version 2.6.18-128.el5)

We must now enter a password for the Oracle Secure Backup encryption key
store.  Oracle suggests we choose a password of at least 8 characters in
length, containing a mixture of alphabetic and numeric characters.
```

Installing OSB on Linux

```
Please enter the key store password:
Re-type password for verification:

We must now enter a password for the Oracle Secure Backup 'admin' user.
Oracle suggests we choose a password of at least 8 characters in length,
containing a mixture of alphabetic and numeric characters.

Please enter the admin password:
Re-type password for verification:

We should now enter an email address for the Oracle Secure Backup 'admin'
user. Oracle Secure Backup uses this email address to send job summary
reports and to notify the user when a job requires input. If we leave this
blank, we can set it later using the obtool's 'chuser' command.

Please enter the admin email address:
generating links for admin installation with Web server
updating /etc/ld.so.conf
checking Oracle Secure Backup's configuration file (/etc/obconfig)
setting Oracle Secure Backup directory to /usr/local/oracle/backup in
/etc/obconfig
setting local database directory to /usr/etc/ob in /etc/obconfig
setting temp directory to /usr/tmp in /etc/obconfig
setting administrative directory to /usr/local/oracle/backup/admin in
/etc/obconfig
protecting the Oracle Secure Backup directory
creating /etc/rc.d/init.d/observiced
activating observiced via chkconfig
initializing the administrative domain

***************************** N O T E ******************************
On Linux systems Oracle recommends that we answer no to the next two
questions. The preferred mode of operation on Linux systems is to use the
/dev/sg devices for attach points as described in the 'ReadMe' and in the
'Installation and Configuration Guide'.


Is localhost connected to any tape libraries that we'd like to use with
Oracle Secure Backup [no]?

Is localhost connected to any tape drives that we'd like to use with Oracle
Secure Backup [no]?

Installation summary:

Installation  Host              OS          Driver      OS Move    Reboot
Mode          Name              Name        Installed?  Required?  Required?

admin         localhost         Linux       no          no         no

Oracle Secure Backup is now ready for wer use.
```

The installation that has been done is over a box with the machine name
localhost. This is the name that must be used whenever OSB is configured; for
example, in the database console! The information about the host that is
chosen for the installation as the administrative domain is maintained within

the *config/host* folder in a file named the same as the name of the machine. For the box, here are the contents of the *localhost* file:

```
[root@localhost host]# pwd
/usr/local/oracle/backup/admin/config/host
[root@localhost host]# more localhost
name:            localhost
uuid:            fc557e32-7f5a-102d-9aac-000c2926d8cd
roles:           ADMIN MEDIASERVER CLIENT
cert key size:   1024
flags:           0x3
in service:      yes
ostype:          LINUX_OS
access mode:     OB
ip name:         192.168.0.103
algorithm:       aes192
encryption:      allowed
keytype:         transparent
rekeyfrequency:  1 month
[root@localhost host]#
```

This information can also be seen using the obtool's command *lshost*.

```
ob> lshost

localhost        admin,mediaserver,client          (via OB)   in service
```

The *config* folder not only contains the information of the host, it also contains all the configuration records which are created by either the web tool or the command line *obtool*. Once installed, the information of the OSB can be viewed by either CLI or GUI mode.

This shows that logging in as admin user has been done which is like the sys user of OSB. It is actually the root interface set via OSB. The information about this user and any other one configured can be retrieved from the already mentioned config/user object where each user created is maintained via a file named after his name.

The password token for the admin is required at the time of the installation and this must be remembered since it is needed to do any administrative work in OSB like creating a data selector which will be covered later. If the admin user password has been forgotten, there is no way to retrieve it. Then a reinstall needs to be done, but do not worry about losing all the configuration settings that may have been done while installing it earlier. Oracle keeps the configuration details but asks the user for the new password.

Installing OSB on Linux

Configuring OSB

Just installing the OSB is not enough since it is important for it to be used from the database console as well as being able to handle the backup and restore operations related to Oracle database. It is also important to mention that an Oracle database does not need to be installed to make OSB work since it works in a standalone manner. That is the reason that there is a file system-based backup and restore.

Before tweaking OEM of the Oracle database begins, make sure that except for the default admin user, there is an additional person there who is responsible for all Oracle related tasks. For this purpose, it is better to fire up the GUI mode of OSB. In general, the login page is found at https://localhost.localdomain/index.jsp. From there, go to Configure>> Users where the following figure should show up as the initial output:

Figure 10.2: *OSB Gui Mode Screen – Configure Users*

To configure the user oracle here, click on Add and enter user credentials like name as oracle, password of the user, the group that it belongs to and also choose the media family since RMAN mentions that it can be used to do the backup via OSB from the RMAN. The user class must be Oracle only! Once this is done, the final screen has an additional entry in the above screen for the user oracle.

For the Oracle user who is doing the backup and recovery related tasks, there is a pre-authorization process that must be completed. The pre-authorization means that the authorized user is able to use a binary like RMAN to do these operations. Any backup job that needs SBT to be used succeeds only when it is made through a user which is going to be pre-authorized within OSB. The access can be assigned to the user either for all the hosts or a few selected ones as required. If OSB is used from a Windows-based machine and that machine is a part of the Windows domain, the details of the domain can also be put right in the configuration process.

To assign the authorization to the user, click, once again, to Configure>>Users and from here, enter that user's name whom should be assigned this privilege. In addition to this, a mention about the host(s) needs to be made to state where he can use which kind of interface. There are two interfaces supported, *cmdline*, which makes the user eligible to do the work through the command like *obtool*. The other option is RMAN which, in general, is recommended though one can choose both as well. Here is how the screen looks where all of this detail is being entered:

Figure 10.3: *OSB Pre-authorized Access*

Once done with all this, the final result in the next figure shows that the user oracle is authorized to work on all hosts, with any OS user name, on any domain of Windows and can use RMAN.

Figure 10.4: *Result of Pre-authorized Access*

RMAN Configuration with OSB

Though RMAN can work standalone as well as from its CLI interface and can do the backup over the tape drives using OSB, the preferred way would be to use it from the GUI, i.e. OEM interface. Before RMAN's web interface can be used from OEM, there are some configurations which must be done beforehand.

The very first thing is to add the administrative machine in OEM and this can be done by going to the Availability section and then from there, the Backup Settings page. Normally, the administrative server's name should be reflected on this page but if not, manually enter the host name and credentials of the users. These credentials are used in almost all the operations like backup and restore, so this must be correct. Below is what this page looks like:

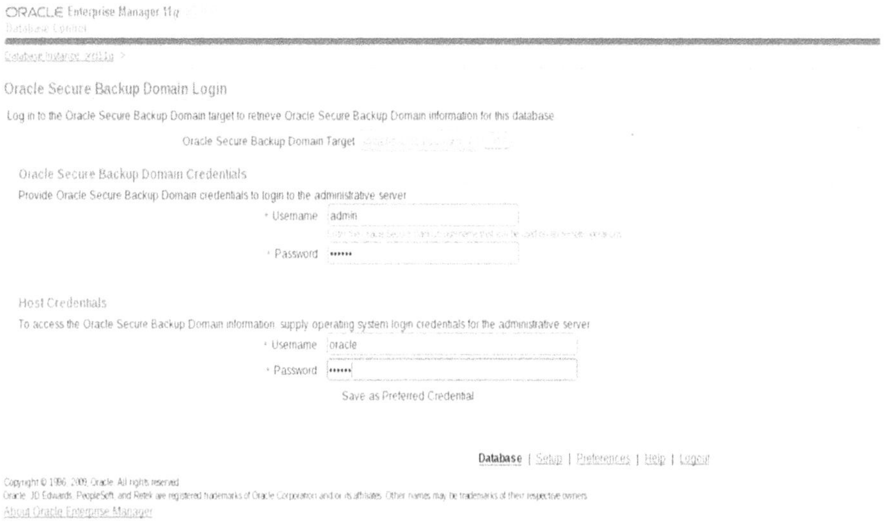

Figure 10.5: *OSB Login and Credentials Page*

Once done, the next step is to further configure for storage selectors and such. So for this, click on the Configure button that brings up the page where OS and admin users' credential information is requested. Here is how the page looks:

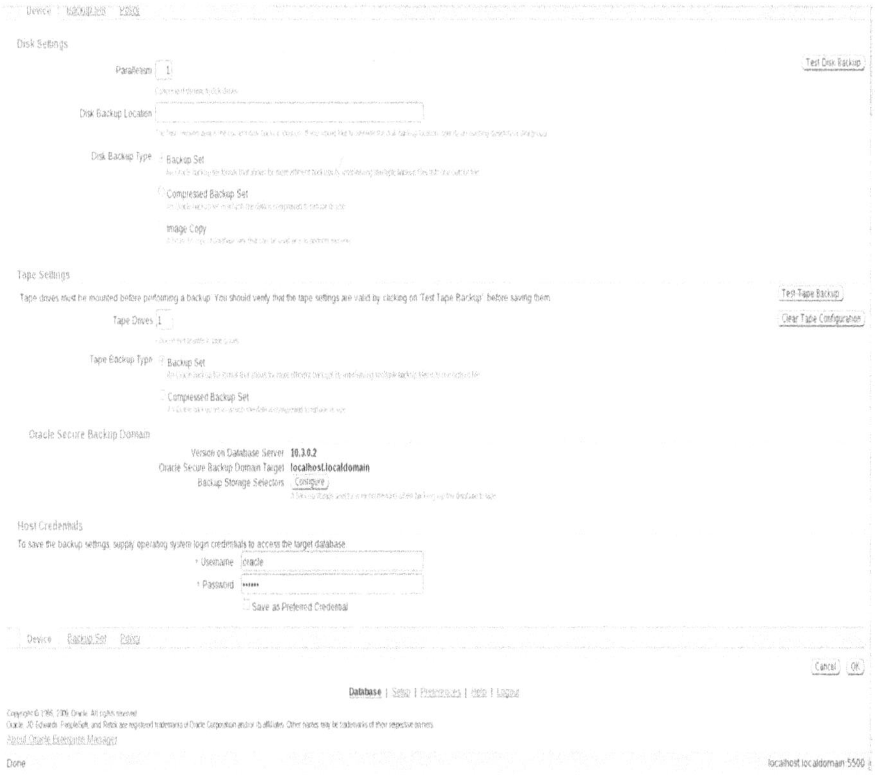

Figure 10.6: *Configuration Settings Screen*

Before proceeding further, a little information about storage selector is a must. Storage selector's definition from the official Oracle document (11.2) is "an Oracle Secure Backup configuration object that specifies characteristics of Recovery Manager (RMAN) SBT backups. The storage selector acts as a layer between RMAN, which accesses the database, and the Oracle Secure Backup software, which manages the backup media."

More simply, it is the way in which RMAN tells OSB what kind of files are eligible to be backed up using Amazon. Also, whether it is done using full backup or even incremental backup can be decided here only. By default, there is no storage selector(s) defined in the first place as shown in the following figure.

Figure 10.7: *Backup Storage Selectors Screen – Default*

Therefore, a new one needs to be created and after selecting the options, this is how the screen looks:

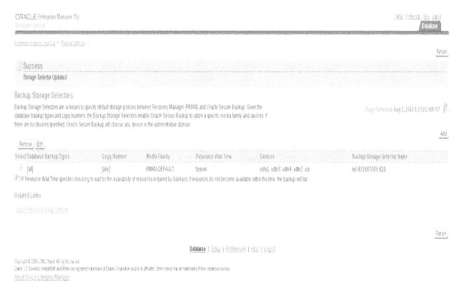

Figure 10.8: *Storage Selector Updated*

Once done, choose the number of tape drives and also ask for a test for the tape backup. All of this can be done using the Backup Settings page of the database console.

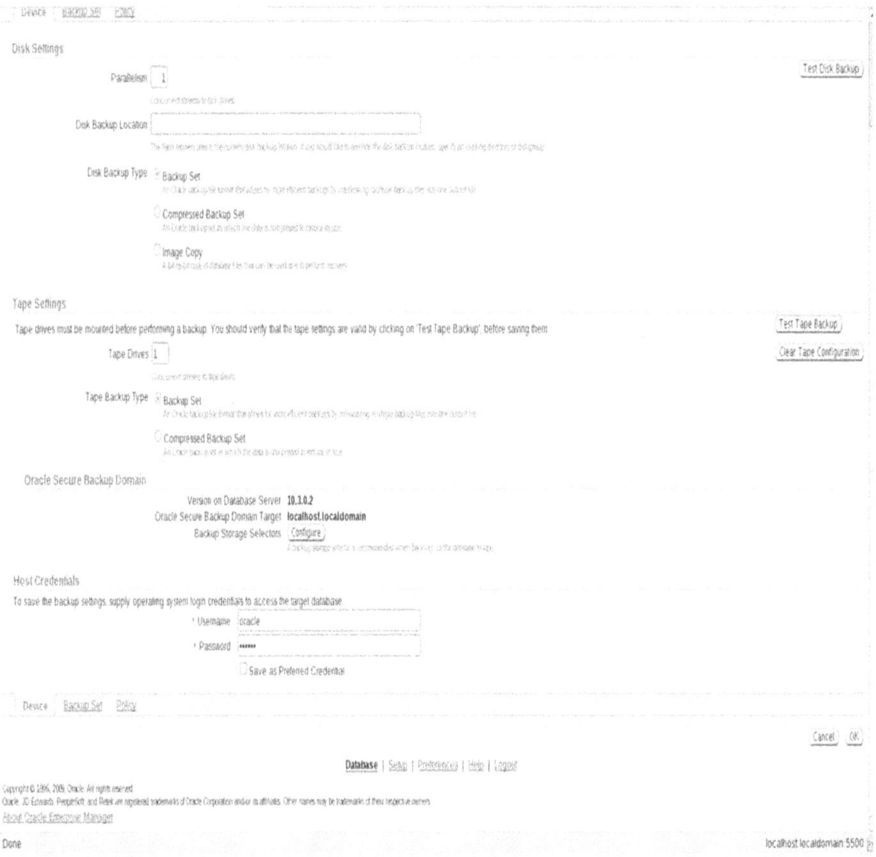

Figure 10.9: *Backup Settings for Database*

Once the test is complete, a success message appears like the next figure:

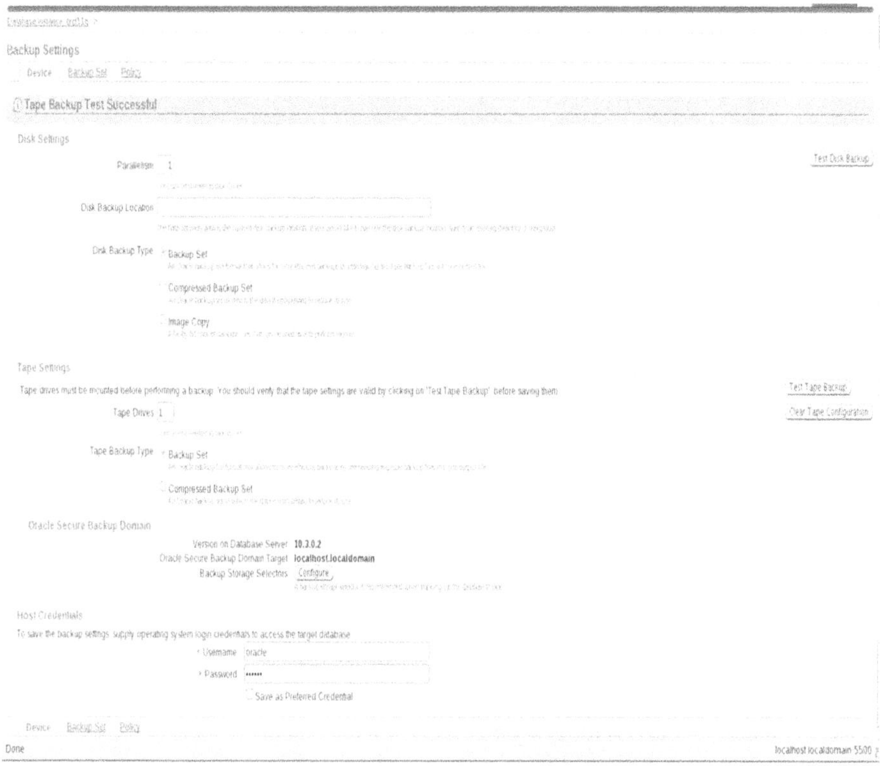

Backup Settings

Device   Backup Set   Policy

ⓘ Tape Backup Test Successful

Disk Settings

Parallelism   1   Test Disk Backup

Disk Backup Location

Disk Backup Type   • Backup Set

Compressed Backup Set

Image Copy

Tape Settings

Tape drives must be mounted before performing a backup. You should verify that the tape settings are valid by clicking on 'Test Tape Backup' before saving them.   Test Tape Backup

Tape Drives   1   Clear Tape Configuration

Tape Backup Type   • Backup Set

Compressed Backup Set

Oracle Secure Backup Domain

Version on Database Server   **10.3.0.2**
Oracle Secure Backup Domain Target   **localhost.localdomain**
Backup Storage Selectors   Configure

Host Credentials

To save the backup settings, supply operating system login credentials to access the target database

* Username   oracle
* Password   ••••••

Save as Preferred Credential

Device   Backup Set   Policy

Done   localhost.localdomain 5500

Figure 10.10: *Tape Backup Test Successful*

Now it is time to perform the backups of Oracle database and the file system using OSB. Do a test for the backup and recovery of a datafile using OSB's tape.

Database Backup and Recovery Using OSB

The backup of RMAN is not much different from the disk-based backup. The extra layer is OSB which takes the command to push the backup. While configuring the backup job either from OEM or from the command line, configure the SBT channel(s) for the backup. Next is the output of one such backup done for a tablespace.

RMAN>

RMAN Configuration with OSB   **447**

```
connected to target database: ORCL11G (DBID=832687005)
using target database control file instead of recovery catalog

RMAN>
echo set on
RMAN> set command id to 'BACKUP_ORCL11G_000_073110022318';

executing command: SET COMMAND ID

RMAN> backup device type sbt tag 'BACKUP_ORCL11G_000_073110022318'
tablespace 'USERS';

Starting backup at 31-JUL-10
allocated channel: ORA_SBT_TAPE_1
channel ORA_SBT_TAPE_1: SID=53 device type=SBT_TAPE
channel ORA_SBT_TAPE_1: Oracle Secure Backup
channel ORA_SBT_TAPE_1: starting full datafile backup set
channel ORA_SBT_TAPE_1: specifying datafile(s) in backup set
input datafile file number=00004
name=/u01/app/oracle/oradata/orcl11g/users01.dbf
channel ORA_SBT_TAPE_1: starting piece 1 at 31-JUL-10
channel ORA_SBT_TAPE_1: finished piece 1 at 31-JUL-10
piece handle=02lk60jf_1_1 tag=BACKUP_ORCL11G_000_073110022318 comment=API
Version 2.0,MMS Version 10.3.0.2
channel ORA_SBT_TAPE_1: backup set complete, elapsed time: 00:00:45
Finished backup at 31-JUL-10

RMAN> run {
2> allocate channel oem_backup_sbt1 type 'SBT_TAPE' format '%U' maxpiecesize
1000 G;
3> backup tag 'BACKUP_ORCL11G_000_073110022318' current controlfile;
4> release channel oem_backup_sbt1;
5> }

released channel: ORA_SBT_TAPE_1
allocated channel: oem_backup_sbt1
channel oem_backup_sbt1: SID=53 device type=SBT_TAPE
channel oem_backup_sbt1: Oracle Secure Backup

Starting backup at 31-JUL-10
channel oem_backup_sbt1: starting full datafile backup set
channel oem_backup_sbt1: specifying datafile(s) in backup set
including current control file in backup set
channel oem_backup_sbt1: starting piece 1 at 31-JUL-10
channel oem_backup_sbt1: finished piece 1 at 31-JUL-10
piece handle=03lk60ku_1_1 tag=BACKUP_ORCL11G_000_073110022318 comment=API
Version 2.0,MMS Version 10.3.0.2
channel oem_backup_sbt1: backup set complete, elapsed time: 00:00:35
Finished backup at 31-JUL-10

released channel: oem_backup_sbt1

RMAN> exit;

Recovery Manager complete.
```

A similar job can also be scheduled from OEM as well. Following is a walkthrough for doing the same using OEM's Schedule Backup. The very first thing that is required is to choose the component that needs to be backed up like database, tablespace and so on. In this case, it is a tablespace, so select that.

Figure 10.11: *Schedule Backup of Selected Component*

The next step is to pick the desired tablespace out of the many available. For this, select the users tablespace.

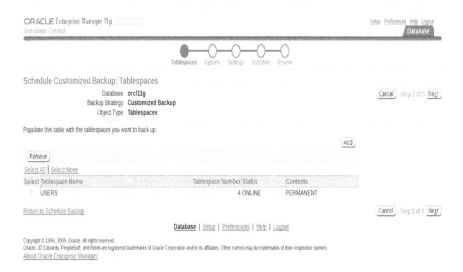

Tablespaces   Options   Settings   Schedule   Review

Schedule Customized Backup: Tablespaces

Database **orcl11g**
Backup Strategy **Customized Backup**
Object Type **Tablespaces**

Cancel   Step 1 of 5   Next

Populate this table with the tablespaces you want to back up.

Add

Remove

Select All | Select None

Select	Tablespace Name	Tablespace Number	Status	Contents
☐	USERS	4	ONLINE	PERMANENT

Return to Schedule Backup

Cancel   Step 1 of 5   Next

Database | Setup | Preferences | Help | Logout

Figure 10.12: *Specific Component Chosen for Scheduling Backup*

Once the tablespace has been selected, next is to configure the backup-related options such as is it going to be a full backup or incremental backup and should the backup of archivelogs be taken as well with this tablespace backup. These options can be specified at the next screen.

Schedule Customized Backup: Options

Database **orcl11g**
Backup Strategy **Customized Backup**
Object Type **Tablespaces**

Cancel   Back   Step 2 of 5   Next

Backup Type

- Full Backup

   Use as the base of an incremental backup strategy
- Incremental Backup
   A level 1 cumulative incremental backup includes all blocks changed since the most recent level 0 backup

   Refresh the latest datafile copy on disk to the current time using the incremental backup

Advanced

- Also back up all archived logs on disk

   Delete all archived logs from disk after they are successfully backed up
- Delete obsolete backups
   Delete backups that are no longer required to satisfy the retention policy

- Use proxy copy supported by media management software to perform a backup
   If proxy copy of the specified files is not supported, a conventional backup will be performed

Maximum Files per Backup Set

Section Size   KB ÷
Backup high-high files in parallel using sections of the specified size. This parameter overrides Maximum Backup Piece size in Backup Settings.

▼ Encryption

Encrypt the backup using the Oracle Encryption Wallet, a user-supplied password, or both, to protect sensitive data

- Use Recovery Manager encryption

   Encryption Algorithm AES128 ÷

   Encryption Mode   Backups will be encrypted using the Oracle Encryption Wallet

                  Backups will be encrypted using the following password

   TIP Checking both encryption modes will provide the flexibility of restoring a backup using either the Oracle Encryption Wallet or a password.

Figure 10.13: *Backup Options Screen*

The next screen allows choosing the destination where the backup should be done, whether it is on disk or tape drive. Since OEM has already been configured with the OSB, there is no need to do any configurations here and Tape is selected as a destination before proceeding.

Figure 10.14: *Choosing Backup Destination Screen*

If desired, the tape settings can be reconfirmed by clicking on the View Default Settings button which goes back to the Backup Settings page. If any setting needs to be changed, this can be done by clicking on the Override Default Settings button.

The next two screens show the summary of the options that have been chosen and the RMAN script is presented, which can be further modified manually; otherwise, the backup job can be submitted with the assigned options.

Figure 10.15: *Backup Schedule Screen*

RMAN Configuration with OSB

Figure 10.16: *Scheduled Backup Review Screen w/ RMAN*

Once submitted, based on how big the size of the tablespace is, time is taken by Oracle to finish the request. Once done, the summary presents the status of each step.

Figure 10.17: *Summary of Backup from Oracle*

The backup of the tablespace users has now been successfully completed and the same can be confirmed from the *rman's list backup* command.

```
RMAN> list backup of tablespace users;

using target database control file instead of recovery catalog
List of Backup Sets
===================

BS Key  Type LV Size       Device Type Elapsed Time Completion Time
------- ---- -- ---------- ----------- ------------ ---------------
2       Full    1.38M       SBT_TAPE    00:00:38     02-AUG-10

BP Key: 2   Status: AVAILABLE   Compressed: NO   Tag:
DACKUP_ORCL11G_000_000210021045
Handle: 02lkb8k2_1_1   Media: RMAN-DEFAULT-000002
List of Datafiles in backup set 2
File LV Type Ckp SCN    Ckp Time  Name
---- -- ---- ---------- --------- ----
```

RMAN Configuration with OSB

```
4       Full 897288     02-AUG-10
/u01/app/oracle/oradata/orcl11g/users01.dbf
```

There is now a backup. This backup can be tested for restore through attempting to restore it over the current datafile by removing the file from the file system to perform the restore. Here is the output of the restore operation done from the RMAN in CLI mode.

```
RMAN> restore datafile 4;

Starting restore at 02-AUG-10
using target database control file instead of recovery catalog
allocated channel: ORA_SBT_TAPE_1
channel ORA_SBT_TAPE_1: SID=49 device type=SBT_TAPE
channel ORA_SBT_TAPE_1: Oracle Secure Backup
allocated channel: ORA_DISK_1
channel ORA_DISK_1: SID=50 device type=DISK

channel ORA_SBT_TAPE_1: starting datafile backup set restore
channel ORA_SBT_TAPE_1: specifying datafile(s) to restore from backup set
channel ORA_SBT_TAPE_1: restoring datafile 00004 to
/u01/app/oracle/oradata/orcl11g/users01.dbf
channel ORA_SBT_TAPE_1: reading from backup piece 02lkb8k2_1_1
channel ORA_SBT_TAPE_1: piece handle=02lkb8k2_1_1
tag=BACKUP_ORCL11G_000_080210021045
channel ORA_SBT_TAPE_1: restored backup piece 1
channel ORA_SBT_TAPE_1: restore complete, elapsed time: 00:00:45
Finished restore at 02-AUG-10
```

This shows that RMAN has chosen the backup from the tape and has restored the file. Once restored, the recovery of the file and bringing it online can be accomplished.

```
RMAN> recover datafile 4;

Starting recover at 02-AUG-10
using channel ORA_SBT_TAPE_1
using channel ORA_DISK_1

starting media recovery
media recovery complete, elapsed time: 00:00:01

Finished recover at 02-AUG-10

RMAN> sql "alter database datafile 4 online";

sql statement: alter database datafile 4 online
```
The same process is applicable to any other datafile or even the entire database as well. There is no difference in RMAN's commands or behavior or in the steps that are chosen for doing the restore or recovery of the database

components. The difference, if any, would be only in the destination to and from RMAN.

Doing File System Backup and Restore Using OSB

OSB can be used to do the backup of the files that are on the file system. Since OSB chooses its own catalog and schedule to maintain the information of the backup, the database being connected or brought up is not needed. However, OSB does need to be told which folder(s) and at what path the backup is able to be taken. This is done through the creation of data selectors.

The data selectors are instructions which contain the information about the path, folders and the host of whose file system need to be backed up. The dataset can be configured from the OSB's web tool. Each of the datasets created are stored in a file format in the OSB's home with an extension of *ds* (dataset) and can be managed through the CLI mode of OSB as well. As an example, list the available datasets by using the command *lsds*.

```
ob> lsds
Top level dataset directory:

new_clients/
OSB-catalog-ds
oh_dataset
```

There are three datasets created here where the *oh_dataset* is made and represents the Oracle Home's backup-related dataset. The content of this dataset can be viewed from the *obtool* itself and also checked for any mistakes:

```
ob> chkds oh_dataset
```

There is no error reported, so this means that the dataset is free from any error. The content of this can be seen as well:

```
ob> catds oh_dataset
include host localhost
{
include path /u01/app/oracle/oraInventory
}
```

The dataset can be created from the Configure tab of the web tool, thereby proceeding to the New Dataset link. A default template shows up here which can be used as a source to create a specific dataset. Once done, the dataset should appear like below:

Figure 10.18: *OSB Backup Dataset*

When a backupset is ready, this can be used to back up the file system content that was mentioned in it. This can be done using the Backup tab of the web tool with the option Backup Now. Once done, the summary of the backup can be seen with the confirmation that the backup is complete or not as shown from the Manage tab.

Figure 10.19: *OSB Manage Tab Results*

There is an option to see both the job's properties as well as the transcript. The properties show the attributes of the job whereas the transcripts show the details of the job. Either the transcript can be seen from the web interface or by using the command *catxcr*. Looking at the transacript can be helpful in debugging the failed jobs. Following is the transcript of the job that was scheduled for the file system's backup.

Volume set owner: root
Volume set created: Sun Aug 01 17:38:58 2010
Original UUID: 65ce6c7a-7f65-102d-942b-000c2926d8cd
Archive label:
File number: 1
File section: 1
Owner: root
Client host: localhost
Backup level: 0
S/w compression: no
Archive created: Sun Aug 01 17:38:58 2010
Encryption: off
Dumping all files in /u01/app/oracle/oraInventory
Backup complete on Sun Aug 01 2010 at 17:39:16
Backup statistics:
status 0
devices vdrive2
devices 1
volumes VOL000001
voltags d90a0bf27f62102a0c3000c2926d8cd
file 1
host localhost
encryption off
start_time Sun Aug 01 2010 at 17:38:58 (1280664538)
end_time Sun Aug 01 2010 at 17:39:16 (1280664556)
backup_time Sun Aug 01 2010 at 17:38:58 (1280664538)
entries_scanned 13
kbytes_scanned 3556
entries_excluded 0
entries_skipped 0
mount_points_skipped 0
files 9
directories 4
hardlinks 0
symlinks 0
sparse_files 0
filesys_errors 0
unknown_type 0
file_kbytes 3540
dev_kbytes 3591
dev_iosecs 18
dev_iorate 204.3 KB/S
wrt_iosecs 13
wrt_iorate 282.9 KB/S
physical_blks_written 7168
write_errors 0

Figure 10.20: *Transcript of Sample OSB Job*

Once done with the backup, this can be used to do the restoration of the content over the host using the Restore tab.

Oracle Secure Backup Cloud Module

With the inception of Cloud Computing, Amazon has started a service called Amazon Simple Storage Service, aka Amazon S3. This is maintained by Amazon to assist in the needs of the storage. OSB can also take use of this service offered by Amazon with its Cloud Computing module which can be downloaded, installed and configured to work with Amazon S3.

The backups maintained over Cloud are faster to access compared to tape drives and are almost always available, thus making it a better choice compared to tapes. The access to the data stored on disks is also faster compared to tape drives, so there is a performance boost as well. Oracle's OSB can be used for storing the backup over Cloud for database releases starting from 9iR2 to the current one. Amazon S3 is a paid service and to use it, an account is required at Amazon with the pricing chosen based on specific needs. Check Amazon S3 at http://aws.amazon.com/s3/ and see which pricing model works the best for the circumstances. OSB's Cloud module can be downloaded from http://www.oracle.com/technology/software/tech/cloud/ index.html.

Conclusion

Oracle Secure Backup is the best tool to maintain RMAN backups over tape drives. With its ability to go beyond Oracle database backups and its ability to be a part of Cloud Computing, it is an essential asset to be deployed when designing a backup strategy.

The next chapter will explain Oracle flashback technology, its features and examples of their use.

Performing Flashback Recovery

Introduction

Being human, it is inevitable to make a mistake in daily life. A DBA that administers hundreds of databases should be able to go back and solve any human errors made to a database. Therefore, the database needs to be configured and Oracle's features used to successfully solve the errors made by users incorrectly. This chapter shows how to configure the database and learn from Bob how he successfully recovers the data from different situations by not performing a full database incomplete recovery at all.

There should be different situations to recover the data or part of data that changed, deleted or dropped incorrectly. Oracle provides different complex solutions for each kind of human error and lets the DBA go back to a specific time in a minute and even seconds!

Imagine that:

- There is a developer who forgot to put the WHERE clause in the end of the statement, changed the salary of each employee in the company and committed the transaction.

- Or by mistake, a critical table named *emp_salary* is dropped instead of dropping the *emp_salary_backup*.

- A night script is run that changes the number of tables and get a call from the manager who says that there were bugs in the scripts. Therefore, there is a need to go back to the previous state of the database without any downtime by not performing incomplete recovery.

- A call is received from a user who changed some data erroneously and wants to recover only that table by not performing incomplete recovery of the whole database.

- The transaction or list of transactions that was committed by a user three hours ago needs to be undone.

In each release, Oracle comes with different new features and solutions to increase availability of the database. So if the necessary configurations are done correctly, any recovery operation can be performed by not impacting the users that connect to the database.

This chapter will help with ways to face human errors and solve them using Oracle flashback technology. This technology consists of some features that help to not perform incomplete recovery due to human error. Also, the following features with different scenarios and detailed explanations will be examined:

- Flashback query

- Flashback version query

- Flashback transaction query

- Flashback transaction backout

- Flashback table

- Flashback drop

- Flashback database

- Flashback data archive

As an overview, here is a brief explanation of each of these features:

- Oracle flashback query feature allows viewing the committed data of the table as it was at some time in the past.

- Oracle flashback versions query feature allows viewing all committed versions of the rows that existed at a specific time interval in the past.

- Oracle flashback transaction query feature lets the DBA view the changes made to a particular table in a transaction level and perform transactional recovery.

- Oracle flashback transaction backout feature allows rolling back the transactions with all its dependent transactions.

- Oracle flashback table feature allows for recovering a table or set of tables to a specific point in time.

- Oracle flashback drop feature lets the DBA recover the dropped table in a second if it is still in the recycle bin.

Introduction   **463**

- Oracle flashback database feature enables returning the database back to a particular point in time without performing any restore/recovery operation.

- Oracle flashback data archive feature allows storing all transactional changes of any table from its creation.

Some of these features use undo information, some of them use the recycle bin and flashback logs to retrieve the data to the point in time. In the following table, the source of data that is retrieved during flashback recovery process can be seen.

Flashback Technology	The Source of the Data Retrieved
Flashback query	undo tablespace
Flashback version query	undo tablespace
Flashback transaction query	undo tablespace
Flashback transaction backout	undo tablespace
Flashback drop	recycle bin
Flashback table	undo tablespace
Flashback data archive	flashback data archive
Flashback database	flashback logs

Table 11.1: *Source of Data Retrieved During Flashback Recovery Processes*

Before covering each technology in detail, begin to understand the mechanism of how some of these features use undo information to retrieve the data back. When a user changes data, the before image of that data is written to the undo tablespace. This is a consistent image of the data for that time. In case the user wants to revert back the change using the *rollback* command, Oracle uses the information written to the undo tablespace to undo the change. If there is not enough data in the undo tablespace, then these features cannot be used because Oracle overwrites the undo tablespace in case it cannot find enough free space for new changes. To keep committed data in the undo tablespace for a specific time, set the *undo_retention* initialization parameter which is specified in seconds. Moreover, the RETENTION GUARANTEE clause should be specified for the undo tablespace to guarantee that the expired undo data will not be overwritten.

Now that there is the basic information on flashback technology features, their usage will be demonstrated in detailed explanation and different scenarios.

 All flashback technologies are available only in Oracle Enterprise Edition except flashback query which is available on the Standard Edition, too.

Oracle Flashback Query

Using Oracle flashback query, the committed data can be retrieved as it was at a past point in time. As most other flashback technologies, this feature retrieves data from the undo tablespace. It is possible to get undo data based on a specific time or *scn* number. Using the *select ... as of* statement with both OF TIMESTAMP and OF SCN clauses, this feature can be used easily. It can even be performed by any application developer without any DBA intervention. Developers can use the *dbms_flashback* package to perform flashback query directly from their applications, but the *execute* privilege should be granted on the *dbms_flashback* package. Now see it in action through the following scenario:

Scenario 1

At 12:00, Bob got a call from an application developer who told him that somebody deleted all the rows from one of the tables by omitting the WHERE clause and committing the transaction. He wanted to know which rows were deleted from the table. Bob decided to use flashback query to get the before image of the deleted rows. To test a case similar to Bob's situation, perform the following steps:

1. Create a table as it was created by the application developer and query it as follows:

```
SQL>
create
 table tbl_seg_tbs as
  2  select
 segment_name, tablespace_name
from
```

```
 dba_segments
   3  where
 rownum<7
order by
 bytes desc;

Table created.

SQL>
select
 count(*)
from
 tbl_seg_tbs;

  COUNT(*)
----------
         6
SQL>
```

2. In order to return back to this state of the table anytime, get the current *scn* number and timestamp:

```
SQL>
select
 to_char(sysdate,'dd-mm-yyyy  hh24:mi:ss') ddate,
dbms_flashback.get_system_change_number() scn from dual;

DDATE                       SCN
--------------------    ----------
07-02-2010   15:14:21      460141
```

This step was not performed by Bob or by the application developer. The developer knows the time when the table was in a correct state and told that time to Bob. Here the date and current SCN number are obtained just for testing purposes.

3. Now run the *delete* command to clear the table and *commit* the transaction:

```
SQL>
delete from
 tbl_seg_tbs;

6 rows deleted.

SQL>
commit;

Commit complete.

SQL>
SELECT * from
 tbl_seg_tbs;

no rows selected
```

4. As Bob knows the exact time of the correct state of the table, he uses flashback query and retrieves the before state of deleted rows from the undo tablespace as follows:

```
SQL>
select
count(*)
from tbl_seg_tbs
  2  as of
 timestamp to_timestamp('07-02-2010 15:14:21','dd-mm-yyyy hh24:mi:ss');

  COUNT(*)
----------
         6
SQL>
```

In case he knows the SCN number, he uses the OF SCN clause to view the data of the table at the specified SCN as follows:

```
SQL>
select * from
 tbl_seg_tbs
  2  as of scn 460135;



  COUNT(*)
----------
         6
SQL>
```

To view the data of the table as it was 15 minutes ago, use the following query:

```
SQL>
 select
 count(*)
from tbl_seg_tbs
2        as of timestamp (systimestamp -interval '15' minute);

COUNT(*)
----------
         6
SQL>
```

It is possible to convert *scn* to *timestamp* and *timestamp* to *scn* using *scn_to_timestamp* and *timestamp_to_scn* functions:

```
SQL>
select
 scn_to_timestamp(460141) ddate,  timestamp_to_scn(to_timestamp('07-02-2010
15:14:21','dd-mm-yyyy hh24:mi:ss')) scn from dual;

DDATE                                      SCN
```

```
--------------------------------------          ----------
07-FEB-10 03.14.21.000000000 PM          460141
SQL>
```

Viewing/Retrieving the Dropped PL/SQL Object Codes Using Flashback Query

Any dropped PL/SQL object can be retrieved using flashback query. How? It is very easy. The source of these objects is stored in an internal table: *sys.source$*. It means that when a trigger is created, the line that contains its source is added to that table. The same works for dropping the procedure. Please note that recreating the objects relies on the dependencies being valid; thus, any tables/views referenced in the procedure must be present or recreated before recreating the procedure. So see how it works:

1. Create a simple trigger and get the current SCN value of the database:

```
SQL>
create or replace
 trigger trg_logon
  2  after logon on database
  3  begin
  4  insert into tbl_logons values(sysdate, user);
  5  end;
  6  /

Trigger created.

SQL>
select
 current_scn
from
 v$database;

CURRENT_SCN
-----------
     528857
SQL>
```

2. Now drop the trigger.

```
SQL>
drop
 trigger trg_logon;

Trigger dropped.
SQL>
```

3. Using the SCN value that has been noted before dropping the trigger, query the *dba_source* view as follows:

```
SQL>
select
```

```
 text
from dba_source
as of
 scn 528857
  2  where name='trg_logon';

TEXT
--------------------------------------------------
trigger trg_logon
after logon on database
begin

insert into tbl_logons values(sysdate, user);
end;
SQL>
```

Using the about result text code, the trigger can be created or replaced again.

Using Flashback Query on Dropped Table

It is even possible to retrieve the data of the dropped table as it was at some time in the past. Starting from Oracle 10g, when a table is dropped, the recycle bin stores the table so that it can be recovered later. See the following example on using flashback query on dropped tables.

1. Create a new table and insert two rows in it:

```
SQL>
create
 table tbl_test (id number, type varchar2(20));

Table created.

SQL>
insert into
 tbl_test values(1,'flashback query');

1 row created.

SQL>
insert into
 tbl_test values(2,'Flashback Drop');

1 row created.

SQL>
commit;

Commit complete.
```

2. Query the current SCN number of the database and insert one more row. Then take the current SCN number of the database again and delete the table:

```
SQL>
select
 current_scn
from
 v$database;

CURRENT_SCN
-----------
     529570

SQL>
insert into
 tbl_test values(3,'flashback table');

1 row created.
SQL>
commit;

Commit complete.

SQL>
select
 current_scn
from
 v$database;

CURRENT_SCN
-----------
     529575

SQL>
drop
 TABLE tbl_test;

Table dropped.
```

3. Next, get the table name from the recycle bin and use flashback query over it :

```
SQL>
select
 object_name, original_name, type
from
 recyclebin;

OBJECT_NAME                       ORIGINAL_NAME                    TYPE
--------------------------------- -------------------------------- ------
BIN$fwmLSapkfIDgQAB/AQATyQ==$0 TBL_TEST                            TABLE

SQL>
select * from
 "bin$fwmlsapkfidgqab/aqatyq==$0";

        ID TYPE
---------- --------------------
         1 Flashback Query
         2 Flashback Drop
         3 Flashback Table
```

```
SQL>
select * from
 "bin$fwmlsapkfidgqab/AQATyQ==$0" as of scn 529570;

        ID TYPE
---------- --------------------
         1 Flashback Query
         2 Flashback Drop

SQL>
```

Oracle Flashback Versions Query

Using the flashback versions query feature of Oracle, the history of all changes made to the table are found by getting committed data directly from the undo tablespace. See the following scenario to understand the main issue of this feature.

Scenario 2

Bob got a call from an end user which claims that somebody modified the table that he owns. The data of a row was changed many times by different users. The user asked Bob whether he can get the list of all changes made to that row between specific time ranges.

Facing this situation, Bob decides to use the flashback versions query feature. To be in Bob's situation, create a new table, insert one row and change it by committing transactions each time. Do not forget to get begin and end SCN values.

```
SQL>
create
 table tbl_fl_versions (id number, name varchar2(25));

table created.

SQL>
alter
 table tbl_fl_versions enable row movement;

table altered.

SQL>
insert into
 tbl_fl_versions values (1,'flashback versions query');

1 row created.
```

```
SQL>
commit;

Commit complete.

SQL>
update
 tbl_fl_versions set name='' where id=1;

1 row updated.
SQL>
commit;

Commit complete.

SQL>
update
 tbl_fl_versions set name='test ...' where id=1;

1 row updated.

SQL>
commit;

Commit complete.

SQL>
update
 tbl_fl_versions set name='flashback ..' where id=1;

1 row updated.

SQL>
commit;

Commit complete.

SQL>
update
 tbl_fl_versions set name='flashback drop' where id=1;

1 row updated.

SQL> commit;

Commit complete.
SQL>
```

To get all committed versions of that row, use the VERSIONS BETWEEN SCN [TIMESTAMP] clause. But before the query is run, it is important to mention about pseudo-columns that are used with flashback versions query. The following columns are used to get more information about each version of that row:

- *versions_start(scn)_time*: The start timestamp (SCN value) when the version of the row was firstly created

- *versions_end(scn)_time*: End timestamp (SCN value) when the version of the row expired

- *versions_xid*: The column that identifies the transaction that created the version of the row

- *versions_operation*: Operation performed by the transaction. (D – for delete, I – for insert and U – for update)

Run the following query to get all that is needed about each version of that row:

```
SQL>
select
 to_char(versions_starttime,'hh24:mi:ss')                        start_time,
to_char(versions_endtime,'hh24:mi:ss')          end_time,          versions_xid,
versions_operation,  versions_startscn  start_scn,  versions_endscn  end_scn,
id, name from tbl_fl_versions versions between scn 461133 and 461185;

START_TI END_TIME VERSIONS_XID      V  START_SCN   END_SCN  ID   NAME
-----    --------  -------------    -   ------     -------- ---   -----
07:28:00          0A001A00C4000000 U  461156                1
Flashback Drop

07:27:54 07:28:00 02000A00F9000000 U   461152    461156     1
Flashback ..

07:27:48 07:27:54 09001A0020010000 U   461146    461152     1
test ...

07:27:39 07:27:48 06001E00F9000000 U   461141    461146     1

         07:27:39                       461141     1
Flashback Versions Query
```

From the above result, enough information about each committed version of that row. Use the value of the *versions_xid* column to get detailed information about the specific transaction.

To use this feature, there needs to be *select* and *flashback table* (or *flashback any table*) privileges on the base table. Using flashback versions query, what has been changed cannot be exactly seen. Instead, the already changed data is seen. Moreover, flashback versions query cannot be used after the database has been restarted.

Oracle Flashback Transaction Query

To get information about each version of the row in a transaction level, use flashback transaction query. If there is enough space in the undo tablespace to keep committed data for a long time and not let them expire, then there is no need to use the Log Miner utility to get information about the changes made to the database in a past point in time. Just using the *flashback_transaction_query* view, enough information can be revealed about the transaction. From the following table, the name of the columns of this view and its description are seen:

Name of Column	Description
xid	Identifies the transaction. It is mainly used in flashback version query by joining its pseudo column *versions_xid.*
start_scn	System change number (*scn*) when transaction started
start_timestamp	Timestamp when transaction started
commit_scn	System change number (*scn*) when transaction committed
commit_timestamp	Timestamp when transaction committed
logon_user	Name of user that performed the transaction
undo_change#	Undo system change number
operation	DML operation that performed on the row
table_name	Name of the table that DML operation performed on
table_owner	Owner of the table that transaction belongs to
row_id	ROWID of the row that was modified by the DML
undo_sql	SQL command that reverts back the specified transaction that was performed with DML command indicated by the *operation* column

Table 11.2: *Flashback_transistion_query Views and Descriptions*

To query this view, the *select any transaction* privilege should be granted. It is possible to get very detailed information in each transaction from the above query. To test this technique, create a table and perform *insert*, *update* and *delete* commands over it. Then query the view as follows:

```
SQL>
create
```

```
 user usr
identified by
 usr;

user created.

SQL>
grant
 connect, resource, select any transaction to usr;
Grant succeeded.

SQL>
conn
 usr/usr

Connected.

SQL>
create
 table tbl_fl_tr (id number, name varchar2(10));

Table created.

SQL>
insert into
 tbl_fl_tr values(1,'Test row');

1 row created.

SQL>
update
 tbl_fl_tr SET name='Updated..';

1 row updated.

SQL>
delete from
 tbl_fl_tr;

1 row deleted.

SQL>
commit;

Commit complete.

SQL>
select
 start_scn, start_timestamp, logon_user, operation, table_name, table_owner,
undo_sql FROM flashback_transaction_query
where
 table_name='TBL_FL_TR';
```

START_SCN	START_TIM	LOGON_USER	OPERATION	TABLE_NAME	TABLE_OWNER	UNDO_SQL
538844	20-FEB-10	USR	INSERT	TBL_FL_TR	USR	delete from

`"USR"."TBL_FL_TR" where ROWID ='AAAMjYAAEAAAABMAAA';`

| 538844 | 20-FEB-10 | USR | UPDATE | TBL_FL_TR | USR | update |

`"USR"."TBL_FL_TR" set "NAME" = 'Test row' where ROWID = 'AAAMjYAAEAAAABMAAA';`

Oracle Flashback Transaction Query

```
538844      20-FEB-10    USR           DELETE    TBL_FL_TR              USR              insert into
"USR"."TBL_FL_TR"("ID","NAME") values ('1','Updated..');
SQL>
```

By running the code which is in the *undo_sql* column, the data can be reclaimed and therefore, a rollback of committed data can be performed.

Flashback Transaction Backout

Starting from Oracle 11g, it is possible to undo a transaction and all its dependencies using a new procedure: *dbms_flashback.transaction_backout*. In Oracle 10g, the committed transactions were rolled back with two steps; the first one being querying the transaction ids with flashback versions query and the second, getting *undo_sql* using flashback transaction queries. But in Oracle 11g, this is able to be performed with only one step by executing flashback transaction backout where the dependent transactions are able to be rolled back.

Imagine that there are two tables joined with a primary/foreign key and there is an *after insert* trigger on the second table which inserts the same value of the first table to the second one. After performing a wrong insertion, rolling back the transactions of the first table needs to be done as well as all dependent transactions of the second table. For this, the transaction ID needs to be obtained and is passed to the *transaction_backout* procedure with the *cascade* option. This is demonstrated in the following scenario:

1. To use the flashback transaction backout feature, the database must be in archivelog mode and the supplemental logging must be enabled as well.

```
SQL>
alter
 database add supplemental log data;

Database altered.
SQL>
```

2. Create two tables, *test* and *test_two*, and join them with a primary/foreign key relation. Then create the *after insert* trigger on the second table to insert the first table's value:

```
SQL>
create
 table test (id number primary key);

Table created.

SQL>
```

```
create
 table test_two (id number constraint fk_test_two references test_t(ID));

Table created.

SQL>
create or replace
 trigger trg_test_two
  2   after insert on test
  3   for each row
  4   begin
  5   insert into test_two values(:new.id);
  6   end;
  7   /

Trigger created.
```

3. Insert one row to the first table, commit the transaction and switch the log file.

```
SQL>
insert into
 test values(1);

1 row created.

SQL>
commit;

Commit complete.

SQL>
alter
 system switch logfile;

System altered.
SQL>
```

4. Query *flashback_transaction_query* to get the transaction ID and the list of all transactional changes from the undo data.

```
SQL>
select
 xid, table_name, operation, undo_sql
from
 flashback_transaction_query
where
 table_name IN ('test','test_two');

XID           TABLE_NAME OPERATION  UNDO_SQL
-----------   ---------- ---------- -----------------------------------
0800130091020000 test_two insert     delete from "test"."test_two"
where rowid = 'aaarvkaaeaaaalwaaa';

0800130091020000 test     insert     delete from "test"."test" where rowid=
'aaarviaaeaaaaigaaa';
```

5. Now use the *transaction_backout* procedure with the *cascade* option to get back all dependent transactions to keep the data consistency. The list of all transactions can be passed to the variable which was declared with default data type: *xid_array*. In this example, use only one transaction:

```
SQL>
declare
  2   v_txid xid_array;
  3
begin
  4   v_txid:=sys.xid_array('0800130091020000');
  5   dbms_flashback.transaction_backout(1,v_txid,dbms_flashback.cascade);
  6   end;
  7   /

PL/SQL procedure successfully completed.
```

Do not forget to commit:

```
SQL>
commit;

Commit complete.
SQL>
```

6. Now query the *flashback_transaction_query* view to see which transactions run to roll back the changes. Do not forget to query the two tables:

```
SQL>
select
 xid, table_name, operation, undo_sql
from
 flashback_transaction_query
where
 table_name IN ('test','test_two');

XID              TABLE_NAME OPERATION  UNDO_SQL
---------------- ---------- ---------- -------------------------------
030003009C020000 test       DELETE     insert into "TEST"."test"("ID") values ('1');

030003009C020000 test_TWO   DELETE     insert into "TEST"."test_TWO"("ID") values ('1');

0800130091020000 test_TWO   INSERT     delete from "TEST"."test_TWO" where ROWID =
'AAARVkAAEAAAAIWAAA';

0800130091020000 test       INSERT     delete from "TEST"."test" where ROWID= 'AAARViAAEAAAAIGAAA';

SQL>
select * from
 test;

no rows selected

SQL>
select *from
 test_two;

no rows selected
SQL>
```

Oracle Backup and Recovery

Oracle Flashback Table

Use flashback table to revert back the table to any *scn* state or *timestamp* to any restore point. Look at the following scenario and the solution made by Bob to understand the concept easily.

Scenario 3

Bob got a call from a user: "Hi Bob. I've changed some data in my table by running a batch job, but unfortunately it stopped in the middle due to the space issue. As I issue a *commit* after every hundredth *insert* statement, the first part of the job changed the table, whereas the second part didn't run. So the table is now inconsistent. Please revert back my table to its past point in time version."

Getting such a call, Bob decides to use the flashback table feature instead of performing an incomplete recovery and reverts back the table to its past point in time state. To test Bob's solution, do the following steps:

1. Create a table, add some rows and change the data by performing *update* and *delete* statements:

```
SQL>
create table
 tbl_fl_table (id number, name varchar2(25));

Table created.

SQL>
insert into
 tbl_fl_table values(1,'flashback Table');

1 row created.

SQL>
insert into
 tbl_fl_table values(2,'Flashback Query');

1 row created.

SQL>
insert into
 tbl_fl_table values(3,'Flashback Drop');

1 row created.

SQL>
commit;
```

```
Commit complete.

SQL>
select * from
 tbl_fl_table;

        ID NAME
---------- ------------------------
         1 Flashback Table
         2 Flashback Query
         3 Flashback Drop

SQL>
select
 systimestamp
 from dual;

systimestamp
------------------------------------------
09-FEB-10 10.41.25.016568 AM -05:00

SQL>
update
 tbl_fl_table set name=null
where
 id=2;

1 row updated.

SQL>
delete from
 tbl_fl_table
where
 id in (2,3);

2 rows deleted.

SQL>
commit;

Commit complete.

SQL>
select * from
 tbl_fl_table;


        ID NAME
---------- ------------------------
         1 Flashback Table
```

2. Now use the *flashback table to timestamp* command to take the table back to its specified past time:

```
SQL>
flashback table
 tbl_fl_table
```

```
to
 timestamp to_timestamp('09-feb-10 10.41.25','dd-mon-yyyy hh24.mi.ss');
flashback    table    tbl_fl_table    to    timestamp    to_timestamp('09-FEB-10
10.41.25','dd-mon-yyyy hh24.mi.ss')
                    *

ERROR at line 1:
ORA-08189: cannot flashback the table because row movement is not enabled
```

If row movement of the table has not been enabled, the *flashback table* command cannot be used against it. The reason is that *flashback table* can change ROWID of the table rows. So enable row movement for that table and run the above command again:

```
SQL>
alter table
 tbl_fl_table
enable
 row movement;

Table altered.

SQL>
flashback table
 tbl_fl_table
to
 timestamp to_timestamp('09-02-2010 10:41:25','dd-mm-yyyy hh24:mi:ss');

Flashback complete.

SQL>
select * from
 tbl_fl_table;

        ID NAME
---------- ------------------------
         1 Flashback Table
         2 Flashback Query
         3 Flashback Drop
SQL>
```

The table was taken to the past when its rows were all consistent. Please note that it is not possible to use *flashback drop* with SYS user. If this is tried, the following error occurs:

```
ERROR at line 1:
ORA-08185: Flashback not supported for user SYS
```

Furthermore, a definition of whether the table that should be flashbacked has any dependencies with other tables needs to happen. If there are any dependencies, those tables need to be flashed back as well, or it will fail due to constraint violation. The *flashback table* command enables reverting back more than one table in one command, thereby helping to flashback dependent objects as well.

When the table is flashed back, Oracle automatically disables and enables all triggers that the table has. In order to enable triggers during the flashback table operation, use the ENABLE TRIGGERS clause at the end of the command. To flashback the table, there needs to be either the *flashback table* or *flashback any table* privilege with *select*, *insert*, *update* and *alter* privileges on the table that is used. Moreover, as shown above, row movement needs to be enabled for that table.

The *ddl* statement that changes the structure of the table or truncates the table prevents the usage of the *flashback table* command. In case the structure of the table is changed by modifying or dropping the column or a constraint is added to the table or is truncated, there is no change to go back to the SCN that is before the above mentioned operations. The following example shows how it is not possible to get the table back to its previous state due to the *truncate table* command:

```
SQL>
create
 table tbl_fl_table (id number);
Table created.

SQL>
alter table
 tbl_fl_table
enable
 row movement;

Table altered.

SQL>
insert into
 tbl_fl_table values(1);

1 row created.

SQL>
commit;

Commit complete.

SQL>
select
 current_scn
from v$database;

CURRENT_SCN
-----------
```

Oracle Backup and Recovery

```
        724235

SQL>
truncate
 table tbl_fl_table;

Table truncated.

SQL>
flashback
 table tbl_fl_table to scn 724235;
flashback table tbl_fl_table to scn 724235
            *

ERROR at line 1:
ORA-01466: unable to read data - table definition has changed
```

In this example, it is not possible to use the *flashback table* command if any column is dropped from the table:

```
SQL>
alter
 table tbl_fl_table add (id2 number);

Table altered.

SQL>
select
 current_scn
from
 v$database;

CURRENT_SCN
-----------
     724387

SQL>
alter
 table tbl_fl_table
drop
 column id2;

Table altered.

SQL>
flashback
 table tbl_fl_table to scn 724387;
flashback table tbl_fl_table to scn 724387
            *

ERROR at line 1:
ORA-01466: unable to read data - table definition has changed
```

Oracle Flashback Drop

It takes only some seconds to restore the dropped table. Starting from Oracle 10g, the recycle bin is used to keep dropped objects until there is enough free space for new objects. When a table is dropped, it does not actually drop it, it just renames it and moves it to the recycle bin.

Scenario 4

Bob got a call from a user: "Bob! I have accidently dropped the most critical table of our project! Could it be restored somehow without any downtime and data loss?"

In this situation, Bob decides to restore the table using the flashback drop feature. To show how Bob has restored the table, perform the following steps.

1. Create a table based on another table and query its row count. Then drop it using *drop table*.

```
SQL>
create
 table tbl_fl_drop as
  2  select * from
 dba_segments;

Table created.

SQL>
select
 count(1)
from tbl_fl_drop;


COUNT(1)
----------
      4133

SQL>
drop
 table tbl_fl_drop;

Table dropped.

SQL>
select
 count(1)
from
 tbl_fl_drop;
select count(1) from tbl_fl_drop
                     *
```

```
ERROR at line 1:
ORA-00942: table or view does not exist
```

2. The table is dropped. Now look to the recycle bin:

```
SQL>
show
 recyclebin;

ORIGINAL NAME    RECYCLEBIN NAME               OBJECT TYPE  DROP TIME
---------------  ----------------------------  -----------  ----------
TBL_FL_DROP      BIN$fy2Ztc1m6bfgQAB/AQAUjw==$0 TABLE       2010-02-09:11:42:15
```

The table is renamed *BIN$fy2Ztc1m6bfgQAB/AQAUjw==$0* and moved to the recycle bin.

3. The dropped table can also be queried using its recycle bin name:

```
SQL>
select
 count(1)
from
 "bin$fy2ztc1m6bfgqab/aqaujw==$0";

  COUNT(1)
----------
      4133
```

4. Now it is time to get the table back. Use the *flashback table … to before drop* command as follows:

```
SQL>
flashback
 table tbl_fl_
drop
 to before drop;

Flashback complete.
SQL>
select
 count(*)
from
 tbl_fl_drop;

  COUNT(*)
----------
      4133
SQL>
```

The table has been restored. Now by querying the recycle bin, it is found to be empty:

```
SQL>
show
 recyclebin;

SQL>
```

It is also possible to rename the table during the flashback drop operation. If the table has dropped and another table was created instead, then rename the table when restoring it from the recycle bin using the RENAME TO clause at the end of the command. To test it, create a new table, drop it and create another one with the same name:

```
SQL>
create
 table tbl_fl_drop2 (id number);

Table created.

SQL>
drop
 table tbl_fl_drop2;

Table dropped.

SQL> create
 table tbl_fl_drop2 (id number);

Table created.
```

Now try to get the table back from the recycle bin without renaming it. As the table has been created with the same name, an error occurs:

```
SQL>
flashback
 table tbl_fl_drop2 to before drop;
flashback table tbl_fl_drop2 to before drop
*

ERROR at line 1:
ORA-38312: original name is used by an existing object
```

So rename the table as follows:

```
SQL>
flashback
 table tbl_fl_drop2 to before drop rename to tbl_fl_drop2_old;

Flashback complete.
SQL>
```

Retrieving Table From Recycle Bin

It is possible to restore the table that was dropped more than one time. It is even possible to restore any version of that table from the recycle bin if it is not purged yet. When there are multiple tables with the same original name in the recycle bin, the latest dropped one is restored. See the following example.

Create a table and delete it two times:

```
SQL>
create
 table tbl_fl_drop (id number);

Table created.

SQL>
insert
 into tbl_fl_drop values(1);

1 row created.

SQL>
commit;

Commit complete.

SQL>
drop
 table tbl_fl_drop;

Table dropped.

SQL>
create
 table tbl_fl_drop (id number);

Table created.

SQL>
insert
 into tbl_fl_drop values(2);

1 row created.

SQL>
commit;

Commit complete.

SQL>
drop
 table tbl_fl_drop;

Table dropped.
```

Query the recycle bin and try to restore the table using its original name. The latest dropped one should be restored:

```
SQL>
show
 recyclebin;

ORIGINAL NAME     RECYCLEBIN NAME          OBJECT TYPE  DROP TIME
------------      -------------------      ------  -------------------
```

```
TBL_FL_DROP    BIN$gBQVXSYM0bXgQAB/AQAQ0w==$0 TABLE    2010-02-20:21:29:31
TBL_FL_DROP    BIN$gBQVXSYL0bXgQAB/AQAQ0w==$0 TABLE    2010-02-20:21:29:17
SQL> FLASHBACK TABLE tbl_fl_drop TO BEFORE DROP ;
Flashback complete.

SQL>
show
 recyclebin;
ORIGINAL NAME    RECYCLEBIN NAME              OBJECT TYPE DROP TIME
------------     --------------------         ------ -------------------
TBL_FL_DROP      BIN$gBQVXSYL0bXgQAB/AQAQ0w==$0 TABLE  2010-02-20:21:29:17
SQL> SELECT * FROM tbl_fl_drop;

       ID
----------
        2
```

If what was dropped earlier needs to be restored, use the recycle bin name of the table. But if there is already a restored table with the same name, either drop it or use the RENAME clause:

```
SQL>
flashback
 table "bin$gbqvxsyl0bxgqab/aqaq0w==$0" to before drop;
flashback table "bin$gbqvxsyl0bxgqab/aqaq0w==$0" to before drop
*

ERROR at line 1:
ORA-38312: original name is used by an existing object

SQL>
drop
 table tbl_fl_drop;

table dropped.

SQL>
flashback
 table "bin$gbqvxsyl0bxgqab/aqaq0w==$0" to before drop;

Flashback complete.

SQL>
select * from
 tbl_fl_drop;


       ID
----------
        1

SQL>
```

Or use the RENAME TO clause instead of dropping the table:

```
SQL>
flashback
 table "bin$gbqvxsyo0bxgqab/aqaq0w==$0" to before drop rename to
tbl_fl_dropped;
```

```
Flashback complete.
SQL>
```

Limitations of the Flashback Drop

There are also some limitations that should be taken into account when using flashback drop. When a table is dropped, all indexes are also dropped. And when the table is flashed back, indexes are also flashed back instead of domain and bitmap join indexes. They are not saved in the recycle bin. However, if there is not enough space, the indexes may not come back, so the indexes need to be created again.

In case there is not enough free space, Oracle first starts to free the recycle bin. So there is no guarantee that all tables that have been dropped are now in the recycle bin. It may be that they are purged automatically from the recycle bin due to the space pressure. It is not possible to run any DML or DDL statement against the objects that are in the recycle bin.

 Note: A truncated table cannot be flashed back.

Managing the Recycle Bin

The recycle bin is a new feature in Oracle 10g which keeps dropped objects. When an object is dropped, no space is released and the object is moved to the logical container called the recycle bin. In case getting the table back is desired, issue the *flashback drop* command as it was explained in the previous scenarios. Each user has a view called *recycle_bin* which he can use to get the list of dropped objects.

Query the dropped object by not restoring it from the recycle bin. This is done by using the special name that was given to the dropped object by Oracle, i.e. the object name starting with *bin$*. To get the name of all dropped objects, use the *show recycle_bin* command. More detailed information can be found by querying the *user recyclebin* view. To understand the concept, see the following example:

```
SQL>
create
 table tbl_rc_bin (id number);
```

```
Table created.

SQL>
drop
 table tbl_rc_bin;

Table dropped.

SQL>
show
 recyclebin;

ORIGINAL NAME    RECYCLEBIN NAME         OBJECTTYPE  DROP TIME
-------------    --------------------    ----------- -------
TBL_RC_BIN    BIN$fzdTKcxkrMDgQAB/AQAUbA==$0 TABLE  2010-02-09:22:06:47
SQL>
select
 object_name, original_name, operation, type, droptime
from
 user_recyclebin;

OBJECT_NAME                ORIGINAL_NAME   OPERATION  TYPE  DROPTIME
-----------                -------------   ---------- ----  -------
BIN$fzdTKcxkrMDgQAB/AQAUbA==$0 TBL_RC_BIN   DROP TABLE        2010-02-09:22:06:47
SQL>
```

Note: When running queries for used space and free space in a tablespace, segments that have moved to the *recyclebin* are not listed as normal table/index segments consuming used space, but do reduce the free space. So be aware of the size of the *recyclebin* when generating space usage reports for the database.

Recycle bin objects, i.e. dropped objects, are not included during the Oracle export. Only the real objects can be exported. So after importing, there is no need to panic when it is found that the total number of objects count is different from source to target.

Purging Objects From the Recycle Bin

To remote the tables and indexes from the recycle bin and free the space that they consume, use the PURGE clause.

To purge the specific table or index, use:

```
SQL>
purge
 table tbl_rc_bin;

Table purged.

SQL>
purge user_recyclebin;
```

```
Recyclebin purged.
```

To purge the objects in the user's recycle bin, use:

```
SQL>
purge
 recyclebin;

Recyclebin purged.
```

To purge all objects from the recycle bin, use:

```
SQL>
conn / as
 sysdba

Connected.

SQL>
purgE
 dba_recyclebin;

DBA Recyclebin purged.
SQL>
```

To purge all objects of the specific tablespace, use:

```
SQL>
purge
 tablespace users;

Tablespace purged.
SQL>
```

Disabling the Recycle Bin Functionality

There is a *recyclebin* parameter in the parameter file whose default is ON.

```
SQL>
show
 parameter recyclebin;

NAME                       TYPE        VALUE
------------------------   ----------  ------------------------------
recyclebin                 string      ON
SQL>
```

To keep it from functioning, use:

```
alter system set recyclebin=off;
```

To disable it in the session level, use:

```
alter session set recyclebin=off;
```

To delete the table without putting it in the recycle bin, use the *purge* command at the end of the DROP TABLE clause as follows:

```
SQL>
create
 table tbl_rc (id number);

Table created.

SQL>
drop
 table tbl_rc purge;

Table dropped.

SQL>
show
 recyclebin;

SQL>
```

Although this is enabled by default, if the parameter *recyclebin* is set to OFF at the instance level, dropped tables are not retained in the recycle bin. Similarly, if the tablespace has low free space, older dropped tables are silently purged from the recycle bin. So it is advisable to query the recycle bin immediately after the problem is identified. Take care to ensure that a recycle bin is available before running tests for *flashback query* on a dropped table or *flashback table to before drop*.

Oracle Flashback Database

Starting from Oracle 10g, it becomes possible to revert the whole database back to any time without performing any incomplete recovery. This is done by the new feature called flashback database which comes with new a background process called Recovery Writer (RVWR) that copies changed blocks from the database buffer cache to the newly introduced buffer. These are called *flashback buffer* and from there it copies the changes to *flashback logs*.

When enabling flashback database, the performance overhead may be 2% or less. Check with Oracle Support for information on potential performance degradation when using flashback logs in a high transaction (particularly insert) environment.

As mentioned previously, performing flashback database is faster than incomplete recovery because the recovery needs to restore datafiles first. By using flashback database, nothing is restored, thus it consumes less time. This technology is used to reverse user errors, so it cannot be used to recover from media corruption.

Look at the following scenario and its solution to understand the concept more clearly:

Scenario 5

Bob got a call from the head of the application developer team, "Hi Bob. We were testing a batch job on the test database, but unfortunately the job was interrupted erroneously due to the incorrect SQL statement. We need the database to be reverted back one hour. Please take it back to its one-hour before state."

Being an experienced DBA, Bob does not decide to perform an incomplete recovery and uses the flashback database feature. He can flashback the database if he had already enabled flashback logs before the error situation arose. The following example shows Bob's implementation that can be tested now.

Enable the flash recovery area by setting the following initialization parameters:

```
SQL>
alter
 system set db_recovery_file_dest_size=1g scope=both;

System altered.

SQL>
alter
 system set db_recovery_file_dest=
'/u01/oracle/product/10.2.0/db_1/flash_recovery_area';

System altered.
SQL>
```

For more information on the flash recovery area, please refer to the section in Chapter 2, "Configuring and Using the Flashback Recovery Area".
In order to disable the flash recovery area in the future, run:

```
SQL>
```

```
alter
 system set db_recovery_file_dest= '';

System altered.
SQL>
```

The next step should be the checking of the archive mode of the database. In order to enable flashback database, the database should be in archivelog mode:

```
SQL>
archive
 log list;

Database log mode              Archive Mode
Automatic archival             Enabled
Archive destination            use_db_recovery_file_dest
Oldest online log sequence     66
Next log sequence to archive   68
Current log sequence           68
SQL>
```

Or by querying the *v$database* view:

```
SQL>
select
 log_mode
from
 v$database;

LOG_MODE
------------
ARCHIVELOG
SQL>
```

If the database is running in noarchivelog mode, then go to the "Switching to Archivelog Mode" section of Chapter 2.

Now, specify the *db_flashback_retention_target* parameter which is specified in minutes (default is 1440 minutes – 1 day) and defines how far back in time the database may be flashed back. Make it for five days:

Note: The flashback database cannot be turned on if the database is running in noarchivelog mode since the minimum requirement to enable the flashback is to keep the database in archivelog mode. Moreover, once the flashback is turned on at the database level, until and unless it is turned off, the archivelog mode cannot be changed.

```
SQL>
alter
 system set db_flashback_retention_target=7200;

System altered.
SQL>
```

It is time to enable the flashback option. For this, bring the database to the mount mode:

```
SQL>
shutdown
 immediate
SQL>
startup
 mount
SQL>
alter
 database flashback on;

database altered.

SQL>
alter
 database open;

Database altered.

SQL>
```

To check whether the flashback database has been enabled, use:

```
SQL>
select
 flashback_on
from
 v$database;



FLASHBACK_ON
-----------------
```

```
YES
SQL>
```

Moreover, as has been shown above, the new background process (RVWR) starts when the flashback database is enabled.

```
[oracle@localhost ~]$ ps -ef | grep rvwr
oracle    10930    1   0 04:50 ?        00:00:00 ora_rvwr_FB
[oracle@localhost ~]$
```

The following lines are written to the *alert.log* file when flashback database is enabled:

```
ALTER DATABASE FLASHBACK ON
Sat Mar 13 11:53:25 2010
db_recovery_file_dest_size of 5120 MB is 31.08% used. This is a
user-specified limit on the amount of space that will be used by this
database for recovery-related files, and does not reflect the amount of
space available in the underlying filesystem or ASM diskgroup.
Allocated 3981120 bytes in shared pool for flashback generation buffer
Starting background process RVWR
RVWR started with pid=16, OS id=274508
Sat Mar 13 11:53:26 2010
Flashback Database Enabled
Turn database flashback on at SCN 3212381
DB_RECOVERY_FILE_DEST/<db_name>/flashback
Completed: ALTER DATABASE FLASHBACK ON
Sat Mar 13 11:54:07 2010
```

> 🔔 Note: Flashback log files with the *.flb* extension are generated under the following location:

Create a table and insert a row in it. Then get the current time:

```
SQL>
create
 table tbl_fl_db (id number);

Table created.

SQL>
insert
 into tbl_fl_db values(1);

1 row created.

SQL>
```

```
commit;

Commit complete.

SQL>
select
 dbms_flashback.get_system_change_number() scn, to_char(sysdate,'ddmmyyyy
hh24:mi:ss') ddate
from
 dual;

       SCN DDATE
---------- -----------------
    817520 14022010 04:59:58
SQL>
```

Now delete the row and drop the table by getting *scn* and *sysdate* after each operation:

```
SQL>
delete from
 tbl_fl_db;

1 row deleted.

SQL>
commit;

commit complete.

SQL>
select
 dbms_flashback.get_system_change_number() scn, to_char(sysdate,'ddmmyyyy
hh24:mi:ss') ddate
from
 dual;

       SCN DDATE
---------- -----------------
    817527 14022010 05:00:13

SQL>
drop
 table tbl_fl_db;

Table dropped.


SQL>
select
 dbms_flashback.get_system_change_number() scn, to_char(sysdate,'ddmmyyyy
hh24:mi:ss') ddate
from
 dual;
```

```
      SCN DDATE
---------- -----------------
    817629 14022010 05:00:37
SQL>
```

Revert the database back to each *scn* that is taken above using the *flashback database to* command. For this, shutdown the database, bring it to mount mode and use the last SCN value that was used to revert the database back. As this SCN value is taken after the *drop table* command has been run, the table cannot be queried:

```
SQL>
shutdown
 immediate
SQL>
startup
 mount
SQL>
flashback
 database to scn 817629;

Flashback complete.

SQL>
alter
 database open read only;

Database altered.

SQL>
select * from
 tbl_fl_db;
select * from tbl_fl_db
              *

ERROR at line 1:
ORA-00942: table or view does not exist
SQL>
```

Here, the decision is made to take the database to another *scn* where the table was not dropped or rows deleted, so shut down the database, bring it in mount mode and issue the command again with a different SCN value:

```
SQL>
shutdown
 abort

ORACLE instance shut down.

SQL>
startup
 mount
SQL>
flashback
```

```
 database to scn 817520;

Flashback complete.

SQL>
alter
 database open read only;

Database altered.

SQL>
select * from
 tbl_fl_db;

        ID
----------
         1
SQL>
```

It is possible to test it repeatedly until it is certain that this is the point to which the database should be reverted back. Then the database should be shut down and opened with the *resetlogs* option, or the following error occurs:

```
SQL>
alter
 database open;
alter database open
*

error at line 1:
ORA-01589: must use resetlogs or noresetlogs option for database open

SQL>
shutdown
 abort
SQL>
startup
 mount
SQL>
alter
 database open resetlogs;

Database altered.
SQL>
```

Excluding Tablespace from Flashback

Initially, when the *flashback database* option is set to ON at the database level, all the tablespaces are under flashback mode, but still any tablespace can be excluded from flashback using the *alter tablespace … flashback off* command:

```
SQL>
select
```

```
 name, flashback_on
from
 v$tablespace
where
 name='TBS';

NAME                                FLA
----------------------------        ---
TBS                                 YES

SQL>
alter
 tablespace tbs flashback off;

Tablespace altered.

SQL>
select
 name, flashback_on
from
 v$tablespace
where
 name='TBS';

NAME                                FLA
----------------------------        ---
TBS                                 NO
SQL>
```

Performing Flashback Database When There is Tablespace Excluded From Flashback

There should be some circumstances when a tablespace is excluded from flashback and then flashback database needs to be performed to take the database back to the specific SCN value. In this situation:

- Take the excluded tablespace to offline mode

- Perform flashback database up to the specific SCN value

- Drop offline datafile or restore it from a backup (as of before the flashback *scn*)

- Recover the offline datafile up to the same SCN value

- Open database with *resetlogs* option

Now perform the above plan in step-by-step manner:

1. Create a new tablespace and new table. Insert one row to the table and commit the transaction:

```
SQL>
```

```
create
 tablespace tbs datafile '/tmp/tbs.dbf' size 1M;

Tablespace created.

SQL>
create
 table tbl_tbs (id number) tablespace tbs;

Table created.

SQL>
insert
 into tbl_tbs values(1);

1 row created.

SQL>
commit;

Commit complete.
```

2. Exclude the newly created tablespace from flashback and get the current SCN value of the database:

```
SQL>
alter
 tablespace tbs flashback off;

Tablespace altered.

SQL>
select
 current_scn
from
 v$database;

CURRENT_SCN
-----------
    521651
```

3. Take a full RMAN backup of the database:

```
RMAN> backup database;
```

4. Bring the database to the mount stage to flash the database back:

```
SQL>
shutdown
 abort
SQL>
startup
 mount
```

5. Before the flashback operation, make offline all excluded tablespaces. So bring its datafile to offline mode and perform flashback database to the SCN value that was taken in the previous step:

```
SQL>
alter
 database datafile '/tmp/tbs.dbf' offline;

Database altered.

SQL>
flashback
 database to scn 521651;
flashback database to scn 521651
*

ERROR at line 1:
ORA-38795: warning: flashback succeeded but open resetlogs would get error
below
ORA-01245: offline file 5 will be lost if resetlogs is done
ORA-01110: data file 5: '/tmp/tbs.dbf'
SQL>
```

It is seen from the message that the flashback operation succeeded. But a message is received that the offline file will be lost if the database is opened with the *resetlogs* option.

6. Before the database is opened with the *resetlogs* option, restore the datafile from backup and recover it up to the *SCN value* that the database flashed back.

```
[oracle@localhost ~]$ rman target /
RMAN> restore datafile 5;
RMAN> recover database until scn 521651;
<.....output trimmed ...........>
<.....output trimmed ...........>
ORA-01547: warning: RECOVER succeeded but OPEN RESETLOGS would get error
below
ORA-01245: offline file 5 will be lost if RESETLOGS is done
ORA-01110: data file 5: '/tmp/tbs.dbf'
RMAN>
```

7. From the SQL*Plus session, bring the datafile to online mode and open the database with the *resetlogs* option. Then check the data that was inserted into the table:

```
SQL>
alter
 database datafile '/tmp/tbs.dbf' online;

Database altered.

SQL>
alter
 database open resetlogs;

Database altered.

SQL>
```

```
select * from
 tbl_tbs;

        ID
----------
         1
SQL>
```

There should be additional steps performed in case any tablespace is excluded from the flashback operation.

Recover Dropped Schema with Flashback Database

Using the flashback database feature, a dropped user can be recovered with its schemas. Look at the following scenario:

- Scenario 6: Bob got a call from a Junior DBA, "Hi Bob. I'm so sorry, but I accidently dropped the user with all its objects. After that, I created another object under the SYS schema. We need to recover the dropped schema without implementing incomplete recovery. I know we're going to implement the *flashback database* option. But we need to keep the objects that were created after the schema dropped. Please help me! It's very urgent!"

Bob decides to use the *flashback database* option using a little trick. In this scenario, there is:

1. A user called test which is dropped and should be recovered

2. A table (*tbl_test*) the test user owns that should be recovered

3. A table (*tbl_sys*) that was created after the schema drop which should be kept during recovery process

To implement this scenario, first create a user and tables as follows:

```
SQL>
create
 user test
identified by
 test;

User created.

SQL>
grant
 dba to test;

Grant succeeded.
```

```
SQL>
conn
 test/test

Connected.

SQL>
create
 table tbl_test (id number);

Table created.

SQL>
insert
 into tbl_test values(1);

1 row created.

SQL>
commit;

Commit complete.
```

Now get the current SCN number. This is for testing purposes. In real time, there will be no the SCN number. Use the timestamp of the action that was performed by a user and create the second table under the schema *sys*:

```
SQL>
select
 current_scn
from v$database;

CURRENT_SCN
-----------
     481640

SQL>
conn / as
 sysdba

Connected.

SQL>
create
 table tbl_sys (id number);

Table created.

SQL>
insert
 into tbl_sys values(1);

1 row created.

SQL>
commit;
```

```
Commit complete.
```

Now delete the schema *test*:

```
SQL>
drop
 user test cascade;

User dropped.
SQL>
```

Being in this situation, Bob decides to use the flashback database technique to get the user back. But in case he finishes the process and opens the database with the *resetlogs* option, he will lose the *tbl_sys* table as it was created after the specified action. So he decides to open the database in read only mode, export the metadata of the user, and recover the database by applying redo changes from redo log files or archived redo log files. After opening the database without the *resetlogs* option, Bob imports the dump file to the database and gets all data for the test user. Here are the steps:

1. Shut down the database and open it in mount mode. Perform the *flashback database* command and open the database in read only mode to check the data:

```
SQL>
shutdown
 immediate
SQL>
startup
 mount
SQL>
flashback
 database to scn 481640;

Flashback complete.

SQL>
alter
 database open read only;

Database altered.

SQL>
select * from
 test.tbl_test;

        ID
----------
         1

SQL>
```

```
select * from
 tbl_sys;
select * from tbl_sys
              *

ERROR at line 1:
ORA-00942: table or view does not exist
SQL>
```

Although the test user was recovered, the *tbl_sys* table cannot be queried.

2. Take export of the user test:

```
SQL>
host
 exp owner=test file=/tmp/test_user.dmp

Username: / AS SYSDBA
Connected to: Oracle Database 10g Enterprise Edition Release 10.2.0.1.0 -
Production
With the Partitioning, OLAP and Data Mining options
Export done in US7ASCII character set and AL16UTF16 NCHAR character set
server uses WE8ISO8859P1 character set (possible charset conversion)

About to export specified users ...
. exporting pre-schema procedural objects and actions
. exporting foreign function library names for user TEST
. exporting PUBLIC type synonyms
. exporting private type synonyms
. exporting object type definitions for user TEST
About to export TEST's objects ...
<....output trimmed ......>

. . exporting table                      TBL_TEST          1 rows exported

<....output trimmed ......>
Export terminated successfully without warnings.
```

3. Shut down the database, open it in mount mode and do not open it with *resetlogs*. Perform a recovery and open it:

```
SQL>
shutdown
 immediate
SQL>
startup
 mount
SQL>
recover
 database;

Media recovery complete.

SQL>
alter
 database open;

Database altered.
```

```
SQL>
```

4. Create the user test and import the dump file that was exported above:

```
SQL>
create
 user test
identified by test;

User created.

SQL>
grant
 dba to test;

Grant succeeded.

SQL>
host
 imp file=/tmp/test_user.dmp full=y
Username: / as sysdba

<....output trimmed ......>
. importing TEST's objects into TEST
. . importing table                "TBL_TEST"            1 rows imported
<....output trimmed ......>

Import terminated successfully without warnings.
SQL>
```

Now, query both tables:

```
SQL>
select * from
 test.tbl_test;

        ID
----------
         1

SQL>
select * from
 tbl_sys;

        ID
----------
         1
SQL>
```

The first table (*tbl_test*) is able to be queried because the dropped schema was recovered, and the second table because the database was not opened with the *resetlogs* option, but instead a recovery was performed to apply redo changes.

Restoring Dropped Tablespace Using Flashback Database

Using flashback database, the dropped tablespace and all objects that were created on it can be retrieved. It gets back the database to the time when the tablespace existed. Follow the next steps to restore the dropped tablespace.

1. Before starting, have a tablespace which will be dropped and restored. So create the tablespace and a table with one row:

```
SQL>
create
 tablespace tbs datafile '/tmp/tbs.dbf' size 1M;

Tablespace created.

SQL>
create
 user tbs
identified by
 tbs;

User created.

SQL>
grant
 dba
to
 tbs;

Grant succeeded.

SQL>
alter
 user tbs default tablespace tbs;

User altered.

SQL>
conn
 tbs/tbs

Connected.

SQL>
create
 table tbs (id number);

Table created.

SQL>
insert
 into tbs values(1);

1 row created.

SQL>
```

```
commit;

Commit complete.
```

2. For testing purposes, create an index on the column of the newly created table and place it in the different tablespace. Then get the current *scn* number:

```
SQL>
create
 index idx_tbs
ON
 tbs(id) tablespace users;

Index created.

SQL>
select
 current_scn
from
 v$database;

CURRENT_SCN
-----------
    460217
```

3. Drop the tablespace and try to perform flashback database to the previously taken SCN value:

```
SQL>
conn / as
 sysdba

Connected.

SQL>
drop
 tablespace tbs including contents and datafiles;

Tablespace dropped.

SQL>
shutdown
 immediate
SQL>
startup
 mount
SQL>
flashback
 database to scn 460217;
flashback database to scn 460217
*

ERROR at line 1:
ORA-38795: warning: flashback succeeded but open resetlogs would get error
below
ORA-01245: offline file 5 will be lost if resetlogs is done
ORA-01111: name for data file 5 is unknown - rename to correct file
```

```
ORA-01110: data file 5: '/u01/oracle/product/10.2.0/db_1/dbs/UNNAMED00005'
```

Recreate the datafile using the *alter database create datafile* command as follows:

```
SQL>
alter
 database create datafile '/u01/oracle/product/10.2.0/db_1/dbs/UNNAMED00005'
AS '/tmp/tbs.dbf';

Database altered.
```

4. Perform the *flashback database* again:

```
SQL>
flashback
 database to scn 460217;

Flashback complete.
SQL>
```

As it succeeded, open the database with the *resetlogs* option and query the table. Then query the index and the name of the tablespace:

```
SQL>
alter
 database open resetlogs;

Database altered.

SQL>
select * from
 tbs.tbs;

        ID
----------
         1

SQL>
select
 index_name
from
 dba_indexes
where
 table_name='TBS';

INDEX_NAME
------------------------------
IDX_TBS

SQL>
select
 tablespace_name
from
 dba_data_files
where
 file_name='/tmp/tbs.dbf';
```

```
TABLESPACE_NAME
------------------------------
TBS
SQL>
```

It should be noted that flashback database takes the whole database back in time and all changes made to the database after the specified SCN were lost.

During this process, detailed information was added to the *alert.log* file. Here is the source of the *alert.log* file:

```
Flashback Restore Start
Flashback: created tablespace #6: 'TBS' in the controlfile.
Flashback: created OFFLINE file 'UNNAMED00005' for tablespace #6 in the
controlfile.
Filename was:
'/tmp/tbs.dbf' when dropped.
File will have to be restored from a backup and recovered.
Flashback: deleted datafile #5 in tablespace #6 from control file.
Flashback: dropped tablespace #6: 'TBS' from the control file.
Flashback Restore Complete
Flashback Media Recovery Start
Mon Mar 15 06:37:43 2010
Recovery of Online Redo Log: Thread 1 Group 2 Seq 1 Reading mem 0
  Mem# 0 errs 0: /u01/oracle/product/10.2.0/db_1/oradata/testrc/redo02.log
Flashback recovery: Added file #5 to control file as OFFLINE and
'UNNAMED00005'
because it was dropped during the flashback interval
or it was added during flashback media recovery.
File was originally created as:
'/tmp/tbs.dbf'
File will have to be restored from a backup or
recreated using alter database create datafile command,
and the file has to be onlined and recovered.
Mon Mar 15 06:37:44 2010
Incomplete Recovery applied until change 460213
Flashback Media Recovery Complete
ORA-38795 signalled during: flashback database to scn 460211...
```

Oracle created an *offline* file *unnamed00005* and used the redo log file to recover it. Then as the *alter database create datafile* command was issued and the flashback performed for the second time, the following information was added to the *alert.log* file:

```
alter database create datafile
'/u01/oracle/product/10.2.0/db_1/dbs/UNNAMED00005' as '/tmp/tbs.dbf'
Mon Mar 15 06:45:08 2010
Completed: alter database create datafile
'/u01/oracle/product/10.2.0/db_1/dbs/UNNAMED00005' as '/tmp/tbs.dbf'
Mon Mar 15 06:45:31 2010
flashback database to scn 490829
Mon Mar 15 06:45:32 2010
ORA-38743 signalled during: flashback database to scn 490829...
Mon Mar 15 06:45:55 2010
```

```
flashback database to scn 460217
Mon Mar 15 06:45:55 2010
Flashback Restore Start
Deleted file /tmp/tbs.dbf
Flashback: deleted datafile #5 in tablespace #6 from control file.
Flashback: dropped tablespace #6: 'TBS' from the control file.
Flashback Restore Complete
Flashback Media Recovery Start
Mon Mar 15 06:45:56 2010
Recovery of Online Redo Log: Thread 1 Group 2 Seq 1 Reading mem 0
  Mem# 0 errs 0: /u01/oracle/product/10.2.0/db_1/oradata/testrc/redo02.log
Recovery created file /tmp/tbs.dbf
Successfully added datafile 5 to media recovery
Datafile #5: '/tmp/tbs.dbf'
Mon Mar 15 06:45:56 2010
Incomplete Recovery applied until change 460235
Flashback Media Recovery Complete
Completed: flashback database to scn 460217
```

Disabling Flashback Database

```
SQL>
alter database flashback off;

Database altered.
SQL>
```

It is possible to disable flashback when the database is open and running. By disabling flashback database, Oracle stops the RVWR process, deletes all flashback logs and information is written to the *alert.log* file as follows:

```
Wed Feb 17 17:20:30 2010
alter database flashback off
Wed Feb 17 17:20:30 2010
Stopping background process RVWR
Deleted Oracle managed file
/u01/oracle/product/10.2.0/db_1/flash_recovery_area/BK/flashback/o1_mf_5qrts
ofs_.flb
Deleted Oracle managed file
/u01/oracle/product/10.2.0/db_1/flash_recovery_area/BK/flashback/o1_mf_5qrtv
sov_.flb
Flashback Database Disabled
Completed: alter database flashback off
```

In case the flashback log files are removed manually, the subsequent startup of the database will fail. Therefore, all that is needed is to shut down the database, start up mount, flashback off, flashback on, and finally open the database. It is better not to remove the flashback log files manually; rather, let Oracle delete them automatically by turning the flashback off.

Oracle Backup and Recovery

As Oracle performs flashback database using flashback logs, if it cannot find any log, it throws the following error:

```
SQL>
flashback
 database to scn 479111;
flashback database to scn 479111
*

ERROR at line 1:
ORA-38701: Flashback database log 2 seq 2 thread 1:
"/u01/oracle/product/10.2.0/db_1/flash_recovery_area/BK/flashback/o1_mf_5qrv
5513_.flb"
ORA-27037: unable to obtain file status
Linux Error: 2: No such file or directory
Additional information: 3
SQL>
```

To determine how far back it went, it is possible to revert the database using flashback logs by running the following query:

```
SQL>
select
 oldest_flashback_scn,
to_char
(oldest_flashback_time,'dd-mm-yyyy hh24:mi:ss')oldest_flashback_time from
 v$flashback_database_log;

OLDEST_FLASHBACK_SCN             ODLEST_FLASHBACK_TIME
--------------------             --------------------
            544000               20-02-2010 21:46:37
SQL>
```

Revert Database Back to Before *resetlogs* Operation

The database is able to be taken back to the prior *resetlogs* option using flashback database. Imagine that an incomplete recovery was performed to the specific *scn* and after opening the database with the *resetlogs* option, there is a request to take the database back using the *flashback database* option to the *scn* that was before *resetlogs* was done. To do this, there needs to be a value of *resetlogs_change#* column in the *v$database* view greater than the value of the *oldest_flashback_scn* column of the *v$flashback_database_log* view. If the first value is greater than the second, then perform the *flashback database to before resetlogs* command to take the database back to the prior *resetlogs* option.

In the following example, create a new table, then perform incomplete recovery and open the database with the *resetlogs* option. After that, drop the table, bring the database to its prior *resetlogs* state and get the table back.

First of all, enable the flashback feature for the database:

```
SQL>
startup
 mount
SQL>
alter
 database flashback on;
SQL>
alter
 database open;
```

Then create a table and insert one row in it:

```
SQL>
create
 table test (id number);

Table created.

SQL>
insert
 into test values(1);

1 row created.

SQL>
commit;

Commit complete.
SQL>
```

Now take a backup of the database using RMAN:

```
RMAN> backup database plus archivelog;
```

Get the current SCN number to go back and perform an incomplete recovery, delete the *system01.dbf* file to make manual media corruption, shut down the database and try to open it:

```
SQL>
select
 current_scn
from v$database;

CURRENT_SCN
-----------
    454695

SQL>
host
[oracle@localhost ~]$ rm -rf
/u01/oracle/product/10.2.0/db_1/oradata/test/system01.dbf
SQL>
```

Oracle Backup and Recovery

```
startup
 force

Database mounted.

ORA-01157: cannot identify/lock data file 1 - see DBWR trace file
ORA-01110: data file 1:
'/u01/oracle/product/10.2.0/db_1/oradata/test/system01.dbf'
SQL>
```

Now restore the database and recover it until the *SCN value* that was taken in the prior step. Then open the database with the *resetlogs* option:

```
RMAN> restore database;
RMAN> recover database until scn 454695;
RMAN> alter database open resetlogs;

database opened
RMAN>
```

Now choose to take the database back to the prior *resetlogs* state using flashback database. To make sure that the database has gone back to the prior *resetlogs* state, drop the table. Moreover, check both the *oldest_flashback_SCN* value of the *v$flashback_database_log* view and the *resetlogs_change#* value of the *v$database* view in order to make sure that the database is taken back and the *resetlogs* is undone. Drop the table and get those values as follows:

```
SQL>
select
 oldest_flashback_scn
from
 v$flashback_database_log;

OLDEST_FLASHBACK_SCN
-------------------
            454372

SQL>
select
 resetlogs_change#
from
 v$database;

RESETLOGS_CHANGE#
----------------
            454622

SQL>

SQL>
 drop
 table test;

Table dropped.
```

```
SQL>
```

The result 454622>454372 shows that it is possible to go back and undo the *resetlogs* option. Bring the database to the mount state and revert the database back:

```
SQL>
shutdown
 immediate
SQL>
startup
 mount
SQL>
flashback
 database to before resetlogs;

Flashback complete.
SQL>
```

Open the database with the *resetlogs* option and query the table that was created before and dropped after *restelogs*:

```
SQL>
alter
 database open resetlogs;

Database altered.

SQL>
select * from
 test;

        ID
----------
         1
SQL>
```

Calculating Flashback Log Generation

According to the Metalink note: 761126.1, to calculate the volume for the flashback logs, multiply the size of daily redo log generation to the value of the parameter *db_flashback_retention_target* which determines how far back in time flashback logs can be used to recover the database. If 20 days of flashback logs needs to be held and the daily redo log generation volume is 4.5 GB, then there should be approximately 90 GB - 100 GB of space for flashback logs.

Monitoring Changes in Flashback Database

There are two main views which help to monitor the flashback database: the *v$flashback_database_log* and *v$flashback_database_stat* views. Using the first view, it is possible to get information about the lowest *scn* number and its time, retention information in minutes which was defined to keep flashback logs inside the flash recovery area, size of all flashback logs and the size that is needed to fulfill the requirement of the retention target:

```
SQL>
select * from
 v$flashback_database_log;

OLDEST_FLASHBACK_SCN OLDEST_FL RETENTION_TARGET FLASHBACK_SIZE  ESTIMATED_FLASHBACK SIZE
-------------------- --------- ---------------- --------------  ------------------------
467751                24-FEB-10 1440             16269312        164044800
SQL>
```

The second view is *v$flashback_database_stat* which displays the historical rate of disk I/O redo logs, datafiles and flashback logs. Moreover, using this view the flashback space needed should be estimated:

```
SQL>
select * from
 v$flashback_database_stat;

BEGIN_TIM END_TIME  FLASHBACK_DATA    DB_DATA   REDO_DATA  ESTIMATED_FLASHBACK_SIZE
--------- --------- --------------  ---------- ----------  ------------------------
24-FEB-10 24-FEB-10       6389760     9232384    4923392                          0

SQL>
```

Oracle Flashback Data Archive (Total Recall)

Most of the previously explained flashback technologies rely on *undo* data. This means that if *undo* data is overwritten, the before image of any table cannot be obtained and flashback performed.

Starting from the Oracle 11g version, every transaction made to the table can be kept as long as needed. Before 11g, in order to get the before image of any row, either it was coming from archived redo log files (if they are kept) using Log Miner, or a trigger was written to save the data in another log table. But now by using the flashback data archive feature, there is no need to use Log Miner or a trigger to track changes made to the table.

The new background process, FBDA (Flashback Data Archive), tracks all changes made to the table and stores it in a file in a compressed and partitioned format. However, this feature cannot be used with clustered, temporary, nested, remote or external tables and long or nested columns. It tracks all transactional changes made to specific tables for the specific time interval. In the following scenario, the configuration and usage of this feature will be shown in detailed examples.

Scenario 7

Bob got a call from the manager: "Hi Bob. We know we are currently working on a new project and we need to keep all changes made to all tables for one year. We do not want to use trigger and auditing because of performance degradation. We cannot use Log Miner because we do not keep archived redo log files for a long time. Please find another solution!"

As Bob's company uses Oracle 11g, Bob automatically decides to use Oracle's flashback data archive technology to implement this task. Now see the steps of creation of the transactional history of the table using flashback data archive. For this, the user should have the flashback archive administer system privilege to create a new flashback data archive. Moreover, the flashback archive object privilege should be granted to the user to enable historical data tracking.

Create a new user and grant him the required privileges:

```
SQL>
create
 user usr
identified by
 usr;

User created.

SQL>
grant
 connect, resource, flashback archive administer to usr;

Grant succeeded.
SQL>
```

Create a new separate tablespace for data archive:

```
SQL>
create
 tablespace tbs_arch datafile 'c:\flashback_archive.dbf' size 10m;
```

```
Tablespace created.
SQL>
```

Create flashback archive on this tablespace using the *create flashback archive* command as follows:

```
SQL>
create
 flashback archive fl_arch
  2  tablespace tbs_arch retention 1 year;

Flashback archive created.
SQL>
```

With the above command, a flashback archive named *fl_arch* is created which resides in the tablespace tbs_arch and holds information for one year. It means that any flashback query which contains one year of historical information can be used regarding the table that is assigned to this flashback archive.

Now, create a table, insert one row and assign it to the flashback archive:

```
SQL>
create
 table tbl_fl_archive (id number, name varchar2(20));

Table created.

SQL>
insert into
 tbl_fl_archive values(1,'Flashback Archive');

1 row created.

SQL>
commit;

Commit complete.

SQL>
select * from
 tbl_fl_archive;

       ID NAME
---------- --------------------
        1 Flashback Archive

SQL>
alter
 table tbl_fl_archive flashback archive fl_archive,

Table altered.
SQL>
```

The historical change on the table *tbl_fl_archive* is now written to the flashback archive named *fl_archive*. To test it, delete all rows from the table and use flashback query on that table. Remember, it does not look for the *undo* data; it looks to the flashback archive file for the changes:

```
SQL>
select
 to_char(sysdate,'ddmmyyyy hh24:mi:ss') ddate
from
 dual;



DDATE
-----------------
13022010 12:46:49

SQL>
delete
 from tbl_fl_archive;

1 row deleted.

SQL>
commit;

Commit complete.

SQL>
select * from
 tbl_fl_archive;

no rows selected

SQL>
select * from
 tbl_fl_archive as of timestamp to_timestamp('13022010 12:46:49','ddmmyyyy
hh24:mi:ss');

        ID NAME
---------- --------------------
         1 Flashback Archive
SQL>
```

In order to show and prove that it does not look to the undo tablespace for the historical information on the rows for the specific time, create a new undo tablespace and make it default by dropping the old one. Then use flashback query on that table:

```
SQL>
conn / as sysdba

Connected.
```

```
SQL>
show
 parameter undo_tablespace;

NAME                                     TYPE        VALUE
---------------------- -----------       ---------   ------------
undo_tablespace                          string      UNDOTBS1

SQL>
select
 a.name
from
 v$datafile a, v$tablespace b
where
 a.ts#=b.ts# AND b.name='UNDOTBS1';

NAME
------------------------------------------------
C:\app\administrator\oradata\db2\undotbs01.dbf

SQL>
create
 undo tablespace undotbs2 datafile
'c:\app\administrator\oradata\db2\undotbs02.dbf' size 10m;

Tablespace created.

SQL>
alter
 system set undo_tablespace='undotbs2';

System altered.

SQL>
startup
 force

ORACLE instance started.

Total System Global Area   431038464 bytes
Fixed Size                   1333676 bytes
Variable Size              251659860 bytes
Database Buffers           171966464 bytes
Redo Buffers                 6078464 bytes
Database mounted.
Database opened.

SQL>
show
 parameter undo_tablespace;

NAME                                     TYPE        VALUE
-------------------------                -----------  ------------
undo_tablespace                          string      UNDOTBS2
```

Oracle Flashback Data Archive (Total Recall)   **521**

The different undo tablespace that is currently being used does not have any information about before images of data blocks of the *tbl_fl_archive*. Now use flashback query against that table:

```
SQL>
conn
 us1/us1

Connected.

SQL>
select * from
 tbl_fl_archive as of timestamp to_timestamp('13022010 12:45:30','ddmmyyyy
hh24:mi:ss');

        ID NAME
---------- --------------------
         1 Flashback Archive
SQL>
```

This query gets the data from flashback data archive.

Modify the Flashback Data Archive

Use the *alter flashback archive* command to change the retention time, purge data or add or remove the tablespace. For this, the *flashback archive administer* privilege needs to be granted. To change the retention time, use:

```
SQL>
alter
 flashback archive fl_archive modify retention 6 month;

Flashback archive altered.
SQL>
```

To change the tablespace quota of the tablespace that is used by a flashback data archive, use:

```
SQL>
alter
 flashback archive fl_archive
add
 tablespace tbs_arch quota 50M;

Flashback archive altered.
SQL>
```

To add another tablespace for flashback data archive, use:

```
SQL>
create
```

```
       tablespace tbs_arch2 datafile 'c:\flashback_archive2.dbf' size 10M;

Tablespace created.

SQL>
alter
 flashback archive fl_archive
add
 tablespace tbs_arch2 quota 10M;

Flashback archive altered.
SQL>
```

To remove the tablespace from use by flashback data archive, use:

```
SQL>
alter
 flashback archive fl_archive
remove
 tablespace tbs_arch2;

Flashback archive altered.
SQL>
```

To purge the data from flashback data archive, use *purge before scn (timestamp)* or *purge all* as follows:

```
SQL>
alter
 flashback archive fl_archive purge all;

Flashback archive altered.

SQL>
alter
 flashback archive fl_archive purge before timestamp to_timestamp('13022010
12:49:30','ddmmyyyy hh24:mi:ss');

Flashback archive altered.

SQL>
alter
 flashback archive fl_archive purge before scn 988827;

Flashback archive altered.
SQL>
```

Dropping Flashback Data Archive

To drop flashback data archive use:

```
SQL>
drop
 flashback archive fl_archive;
```

```
Flashback archive dropped.
SQL>
```

Using Default Flashback Data Archive for the System

As default, Oracle does not use any flashback data archive. To set the default flashback data archive, use the following command by connecting as sys user:

```
SQL>
conn / as
 sysdba

Connected.

SQL>
alter
 flashback archive fl_arc set default;

Flashback archive altered.
SQL>
```

By setting the default flashback data archive, there is no need to specify it manually on each table where changes should be kept.

To disable flashback archive for a table, use:

```
SQL>
alter
 table tbl_fl_archive no flashback archive;

Table altered.
SQL>
```

Query Flashback Data Archive

There are mainly three views that are used to query the information regarding flashback data archive. The first view is *dba_flashback_archive* which gives information about flashback data archive files.

```
SQL>
select * from
 dba_flashback_archive;

FLASHBACK_ARCHIVE_NAME FLASHBACK_ARCHIVE# RETENTION_IN_DAYS  CREATE_TIME  LAST_PURGE_TIME
---------------------------------------- ------------------ ------------------------------------------------
FL_ARCH                2                  365                13-FEB-10  08.05.14.000000000 PM
            13-FEB-10 08.05.14.000000000 PM
```

The second view is *dba_flashback_archive_ts* which gives information about tablespace that contains flashback data archives:

```
SQL>
select * from
 dba_flashback_archive_ts;

FLASHBACK_ARCHIVE_NAME     FLASHBACK_ARCHIVE#  TABLESPACE_NAME QUOTA_IN_MB
------------------         ------------------  --------------- -----------
FL_ARCH                          2                TBS_ARCH       FL_ARC
```

The third view is *flashback_archive_tables* which displays the information of the tables that use flashback data archive:

```
SQL>
select * from
 dba_flashback_archive_tables;

TABLE_NAME     OWNER_NAME    FLASHBACK_ARCHIVE_NAME    ARCHIVE_TABLE_NAME
----------     ----------    ----------------------    ------------------
TBL_FL_ARCHIVE US1           FL_ARC                    SYS_FBA_HIST_69845
```

As shown above, flashback data archive stores data in compressed and partitioned format. It should be checked easily. Get the name of the main table that is used to store the data and query the *user_tab_partitions* view as follows:

```
SQL>
select
 table_name,tablespace_name
from
 user_tables;

TABLE_NAME                     TABLESPACE_NAME
------------------------------ ------------------------------
sys_fba_hist_69845
sys_fba_tcrv_69845             tbs_arch
sys_fba_ddl_colmap_69845       tbs_arch
tbl_fl_archive                 users

SQL>
select
 table_name, partition_name, compression, compress_for
from
 user_tab_partitions
where
 table_name='sys_fba_hist_69845';

TABLE_NAME                PARTITION_NAME          COMPRESS
----------------          --------------          ---------
sys_fba_hist_69845        high_part               enabled
SQL>
```

Using Flashback Versions Query and Flashback Table with Enterprise Manager

To use OEM to perform flashback versions query, go to the Maintenance tab and select the perform recovery link:

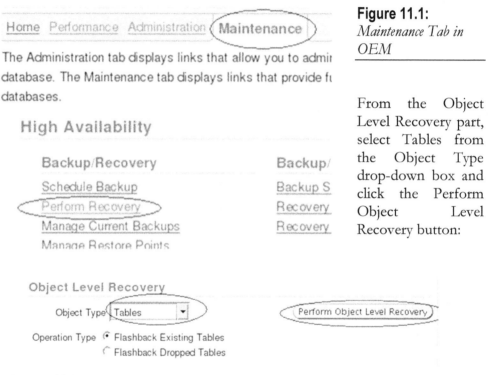

Figure 11.1:
Maintenance Tab in OEM

From the Object Level Recovery part, select Tables from the Object Type drop-down box and click the Perform Object Level Recovery button:

Figure 11.2: *Choices Under Object Level Recovery*

To query all versions of rows of the specific table, select the table from the list or type *schema.table_name* and Click the Next button. Please note that as an example, the scenario that was performed in the "Oracle Flashback Versions Query" subchapter will be shown.

Figure 11.3: *Peform Object Level Recovery Screen*

Now move column names that are to be viewed, write the WHERE clause that is desired and either select the *timestamp/scn* or leave it as default to get all history for the specific row, then click the Next button.

Figure 11.4: *Specifying Column and Row History Request*

In the following page, the list of transactions appears.

Figure 11.5: *Flashback Versions Query Result*

To get any information about a specific transaction, just click on it and there will be detailed information about the transaction as well as the *undo_sql* column which should be used to rollback the committed transaction.

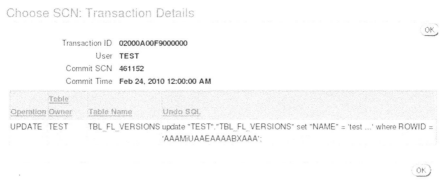

Figure 11.6: *Detailed Transaction Information*

From the previous list of transactions, select the second transaction which has a SCN value equal to 461151 and click the Next button. Doing so, all transactions are rolled back up to that SCN value. The following page appears:

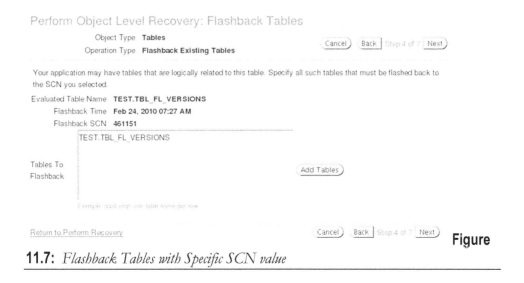

Figure 11.7: *Flashback Tables with Specific SCN value*

It informs that the table is goind to be flashed back up to the specific *scn*. Click
the Next button and the last page comes up as follows:

Figure 11.8: *Flashing Back Specific Table*

It is easy to click on the Show SQL button to get the SQL code which is going
to be performed.

Figure 11.9: *SQL Code*

Also click on the Show Row Changes button to get the result of this
operation:

Table TEST.TBL_FL_VERSIONS ▾

The following table displays the rows that will be
difference in the contents between the content r

# Time	ID NAME
1 after flashback	1 test ...
before flashback	1 Flashback Drop

Figure 11.10: *Show Row Changes Result*

Next, go back and Click on the Submit button. As a confirmation, the
following message comes up:

 Confirmation

The selected tables, TEST.TBL_FL_VERSIONS, have been flashed back.

Figure 11.11: *Table Flashback Confirmation*

Now, go back to SQL*Plus and query the table:

```
SQL>
select * from
 tbl_fl_versions;

        ID NAME
---------- ------------------------
         1 test ...
SQL>
```

The list of transactional changes that were made over the table is found as well as flashback the table to any transaction using OEM.

Using Flashback Drop from OEM

To perform flashback drop from OEM, first drop the table:

```
SQL>
drop table tbl_fl_versions;

Table dropped.
SQL>
```

Go to the Maintenance tab and click the Perform Recovery link. Select Tables from Object Type and select the Flashback Dropped Table option, then click the Perform Object Level Recovery button.

Figure 11.12: *Perform Object Level Recovery*

Select Schema Name and click the Go button:

Figure 11.13: *Schema Name Screen with Results*

It is possible to see the entire table by clicking on the View Content button as follows:

Figure 11.14: *View Content Screen*

Go back, select the checkbox that is before the name of the table and click the Next button.

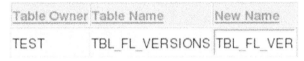

Figure 11.15: *Specifying New Name for Dropped Tables*

Here any name for the table can be defined that is going to be restored. Type any name desired and click the Next and then Submit buttons. At last, recovering the dropped table will be confirmed:

 Confirmation

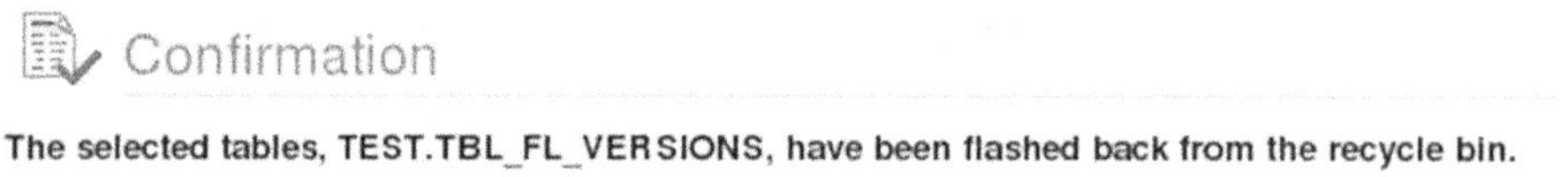

The selected tables, TEST.TBL_FL_VERSIONS, have been flashed back from the recycle bin.

Figure 11.16: *Confirmation Screen*

Conclusion

As noted at the beginning of this chapter, starting with 9i and going forward in 10g and 11g Oracle has been adding features that allow the DBA to revert data and/or view previous versions of data. However, the DBA must know how these features can be enabled up front, e.g setting appropriate *undo_retention*, not disabling the *recyclebin*, configuring flashback logs and such before/when the database goes live. More important is to have practiced these scenarios, preferably with different volumes of data like many more rows/transactions being undone in a flashback operation.

The next chapter will explain in more detail the benefits of the Data Pump utility.

Backing Up Database Using Data Pump Utility

Introduction

Oracle database has many entities that contain tables, indexes, procedures and such objects that are dealt with as an end user. Many times, these objects need to be moved from one environment to another; for example, from the production box to the development box or to the test box. Also, often the similar object is needed in some other project with slight changes.

For these kinds of object movements between Oracle databases, Oracle offers a very handy mechanism, Data Pump, which can do both the export of the object and also import it to the target database. In addition to this, the resultant dump files, which are created through Data Pump Export, are also independent of the underlying hardware and operating system which makes it an excellent tool for the movement of objects. Other than moving objects, this also is used as one of the options to upgrade the database.

Data Pump allows for the selective copying of a schema or a set of tables from one database to another. It also allows for the selective copying of rows with the *query* option. Data Pump exports can be used to backup schema definitions so that empty schemas can be recreated in test/development environments.

Data Pump Overview

The solution to the above problem is the logical backup and recovery tool and technique offered by Oracle which was traditionally called Export/Import and now is called Data Pump. This tool was first introduced in Oracle 10g and this chapter will examine the suggested way by Oracle on how to use it. Please refer to Oracle documentation about the traditional export and import utilities and also the comparison of both with newer utilities.

Data Pump Architecture

There are various components in Data Pump which act together to make it work. These are listed below:

- Client process
- Shadow process
- Master control process (MCP)
- Worker process

The client process is the process which is started over the client terminal that initiates a Data Pump export or import job. This is the process which calls up the Data Pump API. This could be running from anywhere, either a terminal prompt, OEM or from some API as well. Once the job is kicked in, the client process itself is not needed.

The shadow process is started when the client process initiates a session with the Oracle database. This is the process which creates the master table that stores the information of the Data Pump job for restarting it and creates the table used by the AQ service. It also maintains the status of the underlying job.

The master control process is the process which controls the entire execution of Data Pump jobs. The job state and its progress are maintained by this process only. The naming convention of this process is DMnn. When the job request is received by the MCP process, it spawns many worker processes which eventually do the job of import or export. The number of worker processes depends on the PARALLEL clause supplied with the initiation of the job. The worker processes are the actual processes which eventually do the work and are named as DWnn.

The Data Pump supports four ways to perform the loading and unloading of the data:

- Direct path
- External tables
- Data file copy
- Network link

Direct path method is the default method and fastest one after data file copy method on data load/unload operation. If the objects do not contain any encrypted columns, *long* data types as a last column, *bfile* datatype or queue table, then the direct path method is used. External table method is used where direct path method cannot be used due to the above-mentioned reasons.

Data file copy method is the fastest method because the data is not interpreted during the process. Data Pump just exports metadata of the objects and the data is moved with datafiles. This method is used while transporting tablespaces and explained in more detail in Chapter 6.

Network link method is used while transferring the data between two databases using database link. As it uses the *insert select* command via the database link to move the data, it is the slowest method of moving the data.

Data Pump Dumpfile

Unlike the traditional export binary, the Data Pump's dumpfile is not created at the local client side from where the export job is initiated. In the same manner, for the import job, the dump file cannot be kept on the client side and used. The file is created and used from the server side only and also is not available from the absolute path specification.

The Data Pump takes the directory object which maps the path of the OS directory within it and makes it available for Data Pump's use. The directory object is owned by the SYS user irrespective of who has created it, so it is important that whoever is supposed to use the Data Pump must have proper privileges set over the directory object, either reading or writing or both! For the ease of the users, Oracle offers a default directory object *data_pump_dir* which is used in case there is no other object specified.

Data Pump Modes

Data Pump can be called in various modes depending on the requirement. The modes in which the Data Pump works are:

- Full database export
- Schema mode

- Table mode
- Tablespace mode
- Transport tablespace mode

Each of the modes is needed in a specific requirement. Next to be covered is what each mode has to offer.

Full Database Export

This is used to export the whole database. The full database export can be done by the user who has been granted the *exp_full_database* role. This role is there by default with the SYSDBA role.

It is worth mentioning that many people believe that the full database export can be used for the physical database failure's recovery as well which is far from being true. Though it looks like an easy option, it is certainly not the right one! Physical database recovery is only possible through the physical backup with the archivelog mode enabled.

Schema Mode

The schema mode is used when the objects of one user are being moved to another database or to another user in the same database. In Data Pump, this is the default mode as well if no other option is mentioned. To use this option to export a schema other than the connected user, either the DBA role or the *exp_full_database* role must be explicitly granted. If neither of these two roles is available, the only schema that can be exported is the user's own. Please note that the SYS schema cannot be used as a source schema for export jobs. The SYS schema cannot be exported or imported.

Table Mode

This mode enables exporting the structure and data of a table which, in the case of said table being dropped, it can be recovered through the import option. Though this is the easiest option to get the table back, this will not be a complete recovery and the recovered table's data is limited to the data captured in the dump file. Cloning a single table or set of tables to another schema/database is the most frequent use for the table export.

Tablespace Mode

This mode is used to designate the objects mentioned in the specific tablespace only.

Transport Tablespace Mode

This is the mode which is used to move the tablespace(s) across the Oracle databases. This mode does not, in fact, export the tablespace as such but exports just the metadata of the tablespace in the export dump file. The actual physical file(s) of the tablespace must be manually moved across the servers to get them attached to the target database. The said tablespace(s) must be self-contained in order for the export to be completed.

Using Data Pump Export Utility (*expdp*)

To use the Data Pump export and/or import job, run its binary executable which would be, for export, *expdp* and for import, *impdp*. If just the *expdp* command is typed in with the switch *help=Y*, all the options of said binary are shown with a brief description of each.

```
The Data Pump export utility provides a mechanism for transferring data
objects between Oracle databases. The utility is invoked with the following
command:
   Example: expdp scott/tiger directory=dmpdir dumpfile=scott.dmp

Keyword                 Description (Default)
-------------------------------------------------------------------
attach                  Attach to existing job, e.g. attach [=job
            name].
compression             Reduce size of dumpfile contents where valid
                        keyword values are: (metadata_only) and none.
content                 Specifies data to unload where the valid keywords are:
                        (all), data_only, and metadata_only.
directory               Directory object to be used for dumpfiles and
            logfiles.
<....output trimmed ....>
<....output trimmed ....>
```

Before starting the Data Pump export utility, at least the following parameters should be known:

- *directory*: The name of the database directory object that is used to store the dump file

- *dumpfile*: The name of the exported dumpfile

- *logfile*: The name of the directory object that is used to store the log file of the export operation, i.e. the name of the log file

- *parfile*:   The name of the parameter file which contains the list of parameters that are used in the export. This is optional as most parameters can be specified on the expdp command-line.

If none of the options are going to be specified, Data Pump would go into the schema mode for default. To use the Data Pump utility, create a directory object and grant READ and WRITE privileges to the user who will use it.

In the following scenario, a user and a directory are created. Now create some database objects such as table, procedure, function, sequence and such, and create the logical backup of the whole schema using the *expdp* utility. Here are the steps of the above scenario:

```
SQL>
create
 user test
identified by
 test;
User created.

SQL>
grant
 connect, resource, exp_full_database
to
 test;

Grant succeeded.

SQL>
create
 directory dir_test
as '/tmp';

Directory created.

#In case we want to create the directory on ASM, then
SQL>
create
 or
replace
 directory dpump_dir as '+data/dpdump';

SQL>
grant
 read, write on directory dir_test
to
 test;

Grant succeeded.
SQL> exit
```

To view the owner, directory name and path, use the *dba_directories* view. Now use the *expdp* utility to get the dumpfile of the schema *test*:

```
[oracle@localhost ~]$ expdp test/test directory=dir_test dumpfile=test.dmp
Starting "test"."sys_export_schema_01":  test/******** directory=dir_test
dumpfile=test.dmp
estimate in progress using blocks method...

processing object type schema_export/table/table_data
total estimation using blocks method: 64 kb
processing object type schema_export/user
processing object type schema_export/system_grant
processing object type schema_export/role_grant
processing object type schema_export/default_role
processing object type schema_export/pre_schema/procact_schema
processing object type schema_export/sequence/sequence
processing object type schema_export/table/table
processing object type schema_export/table/index/index
processing object type schema_export/table/constraint/constraint
processing object type schema_export/table/index/statistics/index_statistics
processing object type schema_export/table/comment
Processing object type schema_export/function/function
processing object type schema_export/procedure/procedure
processing object type schema_export/function/alter_function
processing object type schema_export/procedure/alter_procedure
. . exported "test"."tbl_one"                       4.914 kb       1
rows
master table "test"."sys_export_schema_01" successfully loaded/unloaded
************************************************************************
dump file set for test.sys_export_schema_01 is:
  /tmp/test.dmp
job "test"."sys_export_schema_01" successfully completed at 11:30:20
```

In this example, logical backup of the test schema was taken to the *test.dmp* file.

There is a table which is created over here with the name of *sys_schema_mode_type_nn*. Since a schema level export is being done, the table's name is *sys_export_schema_01*. This table is the master table that was mentioned before which holds the metadata of the job. Once the job is successfully over, the table is dropped automatically and is added to the dumpfile. With the import, this is the first object that is imported, again to maintain the metadata of the import job.

Data and Metadata Filtering Using Data Pump

In order to export only a specific type of object, use the *include* parameter. To get the list of all valid objects which might be used with the *include* parameter, query the following views:

- *database_export_objects*

- *schema_export_objects*

- *table_export_objects*

In the following example, use the *include=table* parameter to export logical backup of tables only:

```
[oracle@localhost ~]$ expdp test/test DIRECTORY=dir_test
dumpfile=test_tables.dmp logfile=test_tables.log  include=table
```

To export only the specific table, use the following syntax:

```
expdp test/test directory=dir_test dumpfile=test_tables.dmp
logfile=test_tables.log  include=table:\"=\'tbl_one\'\"
```

To export more than one table, use the following syntax:

```
expdp test/test directory=dir_test dumpfile=test_tables.dmp
logfile=test_tables.log  include=table:\"in \(\'tbl_one\',\'tbl_two\'\)\"
```

Using the *include* and *exclude* parameters in the parameter file is the preferred method because, in this case, there is no need to use double quotes. Create a text file and define all parameters inside it. Then use the *parfile* parameter to use the parameter file as follows:

```
[oracle@localhost tmp]$ cat test.par
directory=dir_test
dumpfile=test_tables.dmp
logfile=test_tables.log
include=table:" in ('tbl_one','tbl_two')"

[oracle@localhost tmp]$ expdp test/test parfile=/tmp/test.par
```

Use the *like* syntax to get the list of exported objects:

```
[oracle@localhost tmp]$ cat test.par
directory=dir_test
dumpfile=test_tables.dmp
logfile=test_tables.log
include=table:"like 'tbl%' "

[oracle@localhost tmp]$ expdp test/test parfile=/tmp/test.par
. . exported "test"."tbl_one"                  4.914 KB       1 rows
. . exported "test"."tbl_two"                     0 KB        0 rows
```

Data Pump exports only the *tbl_one* and *tbl_two* tables.

Use the SQL statement to get the list of the objects as well. In the following example, query *all_objects* and get those objects which start with *tbl*:

```
[oracle@localhost tmp]$ cat test.par
directory=dir_test
dumpfile=test_tables.dmp
logfile=test_tables.log
include=table:" in (select object_name from all_objects where
object_type='table' and object_name like 'tbl%')"
```

Using the *exclude* Parameter to Exclude Objects From Export/Import

In case specific objects should not be imported, use the *exclude* parameter. The following parameter file will export all tables instead of *tbl_one*:

```
[oracle@localhost tmp]$ cat test.par
directory=dir_test
dumpfile=test_tables.dmp
logfile=test_tables.log
exclude=table:"='tbl_one'"
```

Using the *query* Parameter to Employ WHERE Clause During Export

To export part of the data of a specific object, use the *query* parameter. In the following example, use the *query* parameter to get only one row from the *tbl_two* table and exclude table *tbl_one*:

```
directory=dir_test
dumpfile=test_tables.dmp
logfile=test_tables.log
exclude=table:"='tbl_one'"
query=test.tbl_two:"where id=1"

[oracle@localhost tmp]$ expdp test/test parfile=/tmp/test.par
. . exported "test"."tbl_two"              4.914 KB      1 rows
```

To use different restrictions, apply more than one *query* parameter in the same parameter file.

Using Undocumented Parameter *access_method*

To enforce using specific loading/unloading data, incorporate the undocumented parameter *access_method*. This parameter accepts two values: *direct_path* and *external_table*.

Data and Metadata Filtering Using Data Pump   **543**

The *access_method* parameter must be used only by contacting Oracle Support.

Using the *sample* Parameter

To export a specific percentage of the object, use the *sample* parameter. In the following example, export 50% of the data of the object *tbl_two*:

```
directory=dir_test
dumpfile=test_tables.dmp
logfile=test_tables.log
sample=tbl_two:50

[oracle@localhost tmp]$ expdp test/test parfile=/tmp/test.par
. . exported "test"."tbl_two"                    4.914 KB        1 rows
```

The table has two rows and 50% of the data (one row) was exported. To export 80% of the schema data, use *sample=80* syntax.

Using the *reuse_dumpfiles* Parameter

One of the new parameters that was added to Oracle 11g Data Pump is the *reuse_dumpfiles* parameter. Prior to Oracle 11g, Data Pump was throwing an error if there were any dumpfiles that were already created.

```
C:\>expdp usr1/usr1 directory=dp_dir dumpfile=test.dmp tables=tbl_test

ORA-39001: invalid argument value
ORA-39000: bad dump file specification
ORA-31641: unable to create dump file "c:\test1.dmp"
ORA-27038: created file already exists
OSD-04010: <create> option specified, file already exists
```

However, in Oracle 11g there is a new parameter, *reuse_dumpfiles*, which overwrites any created dumpfile in a specified folder. This parameter accepts two values: Y and N. Default is N. If the parameter was set to Y, then Data Pump overwrites the files that already exist.

```
C:\>expdp usr1/usr1 directory=dp_dir dumpfile=test1.dmp

tables=tbl_test reuse_dumpfiles=y
```

```
<....output trimmed …>
<....output trimmed …>
dump file set for usr1.sys_export_table_03 is:
  c:\test1.dmp
job "usr1"."sys_export_table_03" successfully completed at 16:00:44
```

Using *filesize* Parameter

The size of the dump file might be divided into specific sized pieces if there is a large file which is not supported by the OS. For this, use the *filesize* parameter. If the dumpfile is divided into pieces, then specify a substitution variable to have the necessary generated dumpfiles. In the following example, define *filesize* to 20m to have logical backup of the table *tbl_test* in files per 20m size:

```
C:\>expdp usr1/usr1 TABLES=tbl_test directory=dp_dir
dumpfile=test_dump%u.dmp filesize=20m

dump file set for usr1.sys_export_table_02 is:

  c:\test_dump01.dmp
  c:\test_dump02.dmp
  c:\test_dump03.dmp
C:\>
```

> 🔔 Note: If there is a space issue, generate the multiple dump files on multiple disks/drives.

```
expdp usr1/usr1 tables=tbl_test dumpfile=dump_dir1:test_dump01.dmp,
dump_dir1.test_dump02.dmp, dump_dir3.test_dump03.dmp filesize=20m
```

If the substitution variable is omitted and not enough file names for Data Pump export are given, the following error appears:

```
C:\>expdp usr1/usr1 tables=tbl_test directory=dp_dir
dumpfile=test_dump01.dmp filesize=20m

ora-39095: dump file space has been exhausted: unable to allocate 4096 bytes
job "usr1"."sys_export_table_02" stopped due to fatal error at 12:06:28
```

After creating the first dumpfile, the job tries to create a new one according to the *dumpfile* parameter, but it cannot find the file name and throws an error.

Moreover, if it is known how many dumpfiles will show up as a result, file names can be passed as a value to the *dumpfile* parameter:

```
C:\>expdp usr1/usr1 tables=tbl_test directory=dp_dir
dumpfile=test_dump01.dmp, test_dump02.dmp, test_dump03.dmp filesize=20m
```

```
c:\test_dump01.dmp
c:\test_dump02.dmp
c:\test_dump03.dmp
```

Using the *content* Parameter

The *content* parameter is very useful when there is a need to load or unload data or metadata of the object. It has three values:

1. *all* which is used to load/unload both data and metadata

2. *data_only* which is used to load/unload only data of the object

3. *metadata_only* is used to load/unload only metadata of the object

The following example will get only data of the table *tbl_test*. The dumpfile can be easily imported to the same schema which adds the exported row to the already existing table and does not throw the error because it does not create the object:

```
C:\>expdp usr1/usr1 directory=dp_dir dumpfile=test.dmp tables=tbl_test
content=data_only
```

```
c:\>impdp usr1/usr1 directory=dp_dir dumpfile=test.dmp tables=tbl_test
content=data_only
```

Exporting Remote Database Schema Objects

To export remote database schema objects, use the *network_link* parameter. For this, a database link needs to be created. Just create a database link from the first database to the second one, change the parameter file and add the *network_link=db_link_name* parameter. Thus, objects will be exported from the second database to the dumpfile that is created on the first server.

Exporting Objects Consistent with Specified *scn* or *time*

Using Data Pump, the logical backup of any object can be found that is consistent with the given SCN value or time. For this, use the *flashback_scn* parameter. In the following example, create a table and add two rows. After adding the first row, get the current SCN value and note it. Then add the second row and take logical backup of the table with and without specifying the SCN value.

```
SQL>
create
 table tbl_three (ID number);

Table created.

SQL>
insert into
 tbl_three values(1);

1 row created.

SQL> commit;

Commit complete.

SQL>
select
 current_scn
from
 v$database;

CURRENT_SCN
-----------
     728886

SQL>
insert into
 tbl_three values(2);

1 row created.

SQL>
commit;

Commit complete.
SQL>
```

Create the following parameter file without the *flashback_scn* parameter:

```
directory=dir_test
dumpfile=test_tables.dmp
logfile=test_tables.log
include=table:"='tbl_three'"
```

The result of the export dump will be as follows:

```
[oracle@localhost tmp]$ expdp test/test parfile=test.par
. . exported "test"."tbl_three"                 4.929 KB     2 rows
```

Now change the parameter file, add the *flashback_scn* parameter and take logical backup of the table:

```
directory=dir_test
dumpfile=test_tables6.dmp
logfile=test_tables6.log
include=table:"='tbl_three'"
```

```
flashback_scn=728886

[oracle@localhost tmp]$ expdp test/test parfile=test.par
. . exported "test"."tbl_three"                    4.921 KB     1 rows
```

As the table has only one row on the specified *scn*, Data Pump has taken a backup of only one row.

Estimating the Size of the Dump File

The Data Pump export allows checking what will be the expected dumpfile size by its estimate switch. This option can use either the total number of blocks of a table or the statistics of the table. The following shows how it can be done.

```
E:\>expdp test/test estimate=blocks directory=dp tables=scott.emp
dumpfile=test1.dmp

processing object type table_export/table/table_data
.  estimated "scott"."emp"
  64 KB   ←-----
Total estimation using blocks method: 64 KB
```

This option actually does an export of the said object in addition to calculating the estimation. If an export does not actually need to be done, it may be best to use the *estimate_only* switch where just the estimation is reported, but the actual export is done. It looks like this:

```
E:\>expdp test/test estimate_only=y directory=dp tables=scott.emp
starting "test"."sys_export_table_01":  test/******** estimate_only=y
directory=dp tables=scott.emp
estimate in progress using blocks method...
processing object type table_export/table/table_data
.  estimated "scott"."emp"                                   64 KB
Total estimation using blocks method: 64 KB
Job "test"."sys_export_table_01" successfully completed at 23:24:10
```

In this option, even if the dumpfile is explicitly mentioned, Oracle will not accept it and will throw an error.

```
E:\>expdp test/test estimate_only=y directory=dp tables=scott.emp
dumpfile=test.dmp
ORA-39002: invalid operation
ORA-39201: Dump files are not supported for estimate only jobs.
```

There are two modes available for the estimation, blocks and statistics. The blocks method is used by multiplying the blocks the object uses by the block size chosen by the database. The other method relies on the statistics of the object. Obviously, to make it as accurate as possible, it is better that to make sure the statistics are refreshed when this option is used.

Parallelizing Export Process

To improve Data Pump performance, the process can be divided into different parallel executions. The *parallel* parameter is valid only in the Enterprise Edition. Each allocated server process writes to one file at a time in a parallel mode. To enable the parallelism, use the *parallel* parameter. As Data Pump requires dumpfile for each process, use the *%U* wildcard to automate the creation of multiple dumpfiles. Here is the parameter file:

```
directory=dir_test
dumpfile=test_tables%u.dmp
logfile=test_tables.log
parallel=3
```

Now call the parameter file and see the result:

```
[oracle@localhost tmp]$ expdp test/test PARFILE=/tmp/test.par
```
And the following dumpfiles are as follows:

```
Dump file set for test.sys_export_schema_02 is:

  /tmp/test_tables01.dmp
  /tmp/test_tables02.dmp
  /tmp/test_tables03.dmp
job "test"."sys_export_schema_02" successfully completed at 10:23:23
```

Compressing the Data While Exporting

11g onwards, Data Pump offers compression of the data before pushing it to the dumpfile. This option works for data, metadata (which is the default value), both and none. Also, it is worth mentioning that this option demands that the compatible parameter value be set to at least 11.0.0 (metadata option can be used with 10.2 as well) and the Advanced Compression License option must be enabled which is an extra cost.

The *compression* parameter has four values:

- *all*
- *data_only*

- *metadata_only*

- *none*

Try to check this option by looking at the size of the dumpfile with and without this option. Exports can be done as one without compression and the other with compression enabled for both data and metadata.

```
E:\>expdp test/test directory=dp dumpfile=woutcomp.dmp
e:\>expdp test/test compression=all directory=dp dumpfile=wcomp.dmp
```

Now check the dumpfile sizes given by both the exports.

```
05/30/2010  02:45 AM              94,208 wcomp.dmp
05/30/2010  02:34 AM             237,568 woutcomp.dmp
```

A huge difference can be clearly seen in the resultant dumpfiles. With compression, the file size is much smaller compared to the normal dumpfile. Please note that the time taken to do the export with compression enabled would be much longer without this option. Also, this option only makes the resultant dumpfile smaller in size. The target table and its data remain intact.

Exporting a Tablespace

Export can also be used to do the transport of the tablespace from one database to another. The most common use is to move the data across the databases without doing much effort. All that is needed is to ship the files and the metadata of the tablespace stored in the dump file and push it. Other than that, this is a really good way to archive the historical data. For example, there may be a tablespace which contains some objects which are not needed right now, but that does not mean that they must be deleted. The reporting may be asked for at a later time.

An example of this can be a table storing the data of quarters in a year. The data of each quarter may be pushed in a separate segment and then in a tablespace. Once the quarter ends, that data is not needed but it cannot be deleted. So what can be done is get that segment's tablespace exported and stored somewhere in the repository. After this, the segment can be dropped assuming that its copy is available somewhere safe. If needed, it can always be attached again either to the same database or to some reporting database. Transport tablespace also makes it possible to do the tablespace point-in-time recovery. Exporting tablespaces is widely explained in Chapter 6.

Export of the Whole Database

Data Pump export is used to take an export of the whole database. This option can be used with the PARALLEL clause to make it faster. Following is an example on how it can be done.

```
expdp hr full=y dumpfile=dpump_dir1:full1%u.dmp, dpump_dir2:full2%u.dmp
filesize=2g parallel=3 logfile=dpump_dir1:expfull.log job_name=expfull
```

Here, three parallel slaves are being used to do the export and the dumpfile size is limited to 2 GB. The dump files are created in a round robin fashion in the directories *dpdump_dir1* and *dpdump_dir2*.

Encrypted Export

Data Pump allows the export to be done in encrypted mode. This mode allows having the encrypted columns maintained in the dumpfile. There are different modes of the encryption available, i.e. dual, transparent and password. Also, it can be decided where the encryption mode should be applied; for example, to the entire data and metadata (*all*), just the metadata (*metadata_only*) or *none*. The encryption modes of dual and transparent require the Oracle Wallet to be open and available and need the compatible mode of the database to be set to 11.0.0. The simplest mode is the password mode which needs the password to be supplied at the time of the export and the same password is needed with the import. Failing would lead to the import's failure. Encryption requires the Advanced Security license option.

Data Pump has the following encryption parameters:

- *encryption*: Is used to encrypt data before writing it to the dump file and accepts five values
- *all*: Enables encryption for both data and metadata of the exported objects
- *data_only*: Enables encryption for only data that is exported
- *encrypted_columns_only*: Enables encryption only for encrypted columns
- *metadata_only*: Enables encryption of the metadata of the exported objects
- *none*: Disables encryption of the data and metadata of the exported objects
- *encryption algorithm*: Specifies the algorithm for the encryption and accepts three algorithms:

- AES128: The default value

- AES192

- AES256

- *encryption_mode*: Specifies the type of security and accepts the following values:

  - *password*: Required to provide a password to encrypt the dump file

  - *transperent*: Requires a wallet to use

  - *dual*: Creates a dump file which might be imported using both the above mentioned modes

- *encryption_password*: Is used to provide a password for the dump file and differs between Oracle 10g and 11g. If this parameter is used, then the *encryption* parameter's default value becomes ALL. If both parameters are omitted, then the *encryption* parameter is set to NONE.

In the following example, use all parameters to export data that is encrypted and password provided using the AES256 algorithm mode:

```
expdp usr1/usr1 dumpfile=dp_dir:test.dmp logfile=dp_dir:test.log
encryption=all encryption_mode=password encryption_password=test
encryption_algorithm=aes256 tables='tbl_test';
```

When an attempt is made to import the dumpfile without providing any password, the following error appears:

```
impdp usr2/usr2 remap_schema=usr1:usr2 dumpfile=dp_dir:test.dmp
logfile=dp_dir:log.dmp

ORA-39002: invalid operation
ORA-39174: Encryption password must be supplied.
```

However, by supplying the correct password, the object is able to be imported:

```
impdp usr2/usr2 remap_schema=usr1:usr2 dumpfile=dp_dir:test.dmp
logfile=dp_dir:log.log encryption_password=test
```

Using Data Pump to Export/Import Tables

As default, Data Pump creates a dump file of the encrypted column with clear text. The following example shows the usage of Oracle Wallet and exporting/importing the table with an encrypted column.

First of all, create a wallet using the following command:

```
SQL>
alter
 system set encryption key identified by "wallet_key";

System altered.
```

> 🔔 If the error *ORA-28368* shows up and a wallet cannot be auto-created, then create a wallet folder in the *$ORACLE_BASE/admin/$ORACLE_SID* folder.

Create a table with an encrypted column and insert two rows:

```
SQL>
conn
 usr1/usr1

Connected.

SQL>
create
 table test (id number, ddate date encrypt
identified by
 "table_key");

Table created.

SQL>
insert into
 test values(1,sysdate);

1 row created.

SQL>
insert into
 test values(2,sysdate);

1 row created.
SQL>
commit;

Commit complete.

SQL>
select * from
 test;

        ID DDATE
---------- ---------
```

```
         1 22-JUN-10
         2 22-JUN-10
SQL>
```

Now, export the dumpfile of the table:

```
C:\>expdp usr1/usr1 dumpfile=dp_dir:test01.dmp logfile=dp_dir:test01.log
tables=test

. . exported "usr1"."test"
            5.429 KB        2 rows
ORA-39173: Encrypted data has been stored unencrypted in dump file set.
Job "USR1"."sys_export_table_03" completed with 1 error(s) at 18:39:00
```

By not providing a password, the dumpfile is created in unencrypted format. So provide a password using the *encryption_password* parameter:

```
C:\>expdp usr1/usr1 dumpfile=dp_dir:test02.dmp logfile=dp_dir:test01.log
tables=test encryption_password=exp_pass

. . exported "usr1"."test"
                5.437 KB        2 rows
Job "usr1"."sys_export_table_03" successfully completed at 18:40:20
```

If there is an attempt to import the dumpfile without passing the correct password, the following error appears:

```
C:\>impdp usr2/usr2 remap_schema=usr1:usr2 dumpfile=dp_dir:test02.dmp
logfile=dp_dir:log2.dmp encryption_password=exp_passw

ORA-39002: invalid operation
ORA-39176: Encryption password is incorrect.
```

So provide a password and import the table:

```
C:\>impdp usr2/usr2 remap_schema=usr1:usr2 dumpfile=dp_dir:test02.dmp
logfile=dp_dir:log2.dmp encryption_password=exp_pass
. . imported "usr2"."test"                      5.437 KB        2 rows
Job "usr2"."sys_import_full_01" successfully completed at 18:41:48
```

If the table is described, it can be seen that the date column is encrypted:

```
SQL>
desc
 test;

 Name                                     Null?    Type
 -------------------------------------- -------- -------------------------
  ID                                                number
  DDATE                                             date encrypt
SQL>
```

Using Data Pump Import Utility (*impdp*)

As the name suggests, *import* (*impdp*) is the reverse of *export* and is used to move the data back into the Oracle database from the dumpfile. *import* needs a mandatory dumpfile to be passed to it. All the options that are there with the *expdp* are there in the import as well and it also runs in the same modes as *export*. In addition to *export*, there are some specific options to *import* which will be covered in this section. For the complete listing of all the import options and their syntax, please refer to the Utilities Guide in the Oracle documentation.

This part mainly examines and demonstrates the remapping function of the Data Pump import.

Remapping Through Data Pump

At times, there is a requirement to remap or assign different owners and move the objects to different tablespaces. To do so, Data Pump offers a couple of facilities which help in completing these tasks very easily. The following remapping options are available in Data Pump:

- *remap_data*
- *remap_datafile*
- *remap_schema*
- *remap_table*
- *remap_tablespace*

Using *remap_data* Parameter

There are many times when a DBA has to make a data transformation before he has to send the data to someone. This is needed for many reasons; for example, a transformation may be needed to obscure the data so that the important data remains invisible or maybe some kind of formatting is needed on the data before it can be moved. These transformations are possible using the *remap_data* switch of the export Data Pump that was first introduced in Oracle 11g. This switch lets the transformation be done on the table when an export is finished and also allows for reverting it back when the import is done.

In the following scenario, export a converted format of the table which contains credit card information for the subscribers using a special function. Create two users with default privileges, then create a table in the first schema and insert three rows:

```
SQL>
create
 user usr1
identified by
 usr1;

User created.

SQL>
grant
 connect,
resource to
 usr1;

Grant succeeded.

SQL>
create
 user usr2
identified by
 usr2;

User created.

SQL>
grant
 connect,
resource to
 usr2;

Grant succeeded.

SQL> conn
 usr1/usr1

Connected.

SQL>
create
 table tbl_test (id number, credit_card number);

Table created.

SQL>
insert into
 tbl_test values(1,3432654);
```

```
1 row created.

SQL>
insert into
 tbl_test values(2,6345324);

1 row created.

SQL>
insert into
 tbl_test values(3,7998347);

1 row created.

SQL>
commit;

Commit complete.
```

Create a package and a function which will be used to change the values of the table before export:

```
SQL>
create or replace
 package pkg_test
as
  2   function f_test (credit_card in number) return number;
  3   end;
  4   /

Package created.

SQL>
create or replace
 package body pkg_test as
  2   function f_test (credit_card in number) return number
  3   as
  4   changed_value number;
  5   begin
  6   changed_value:=round(credit_card*2/3);
  7   return changed_value;
  8   end;
  9   end;
 10   /
```

Export the first table using the *remap* function as follows:

```
expdp usr1/usr1 directory=dp_dir dumpfile=test.dmp logfile=test.log
tables=usr1.tbl_test
remap_data=usr1.tbl_test.credit_card:usr1.pkg_test.f_test
```

Running the above command, the *f_test* function is called against each row of the table *tbl_test* and a dumpfile is created with the changed new value.

Using Data Pump Import Utility (impdp)

Now import the dumpfile to the second schema and see the difference:

```
impdp usr2/usr2 directory=dp_dir dumpfile=test.dmp logfile=imp.log
remap_schema=usr1:usr2
```

Connect to SQL*Plus with SYS user and query both tables:

```
SQL>
select * from
 usr1.tbl_test;

        ID CREDIT_CARD
---------- -----------
         1     3432654
         2     6345324
         3     7998347

SQL>
select * from
 usr2.tbl_test;

        ID CREDIT_CARD
---------- -----------
         1     2288436
         2     4230216
         3     5332231
```

As this shows, the values are different. The first table shows original value, while the second table created the dumpfile which remapped the first table's data using a special function.

Using *remap_datafile*

If the data is moved between two databases which have different directory structures, Data Pump throws an error while creating the tablespace of the datafile with a different directory. For this, the *remap_datafile* parameter can be used which helps to change the datafile name during import. Now see how it works. In the following example, move the database from Windows to Linux. First of all, take an export dump of the first database (Linux) using the following command:

```
expdp full=y dumpfile=dir_test:test.dmp logfile=test.log
```

Next, copy the dumpfile to the second machine (Windows), create a parameter file and get all the SQL commands of the dumpfile using the *sqlfile* parameter.

Parameter file:

```
dumpfile=dir_tmp:test.dmp
logfile=dir_tmp:test.log
sqlfile=dir_tmp:test.sql
full=y
```

Execute the following command:

```
C:\>impdp parfile=c:\tmp\test.par
```

For testing purposes, type Ctrl+C and use the *kill_job* command to terminate the job after 10 seconds. Check the SQL file. Here is the portion that is needed:

```
create tablespace "users" datafile

  '/u01/oracle/product/10.2.0/db_1/oradata/test/users01.dbf' SIZE
5242880
```

 Since the dumpfile is being imported to the Windows OS, change the datafile name. Use the *remap_datafile* parameter and check the SQL file again.
Add the following line to the parameter file:

```
remap_datafile=\"/tmp/test01.dbf\":\"c:\tmp\test01.dbf\"
```

Import the dump file:

```
C:\>impdp parfile=c:\tmp\test.par
```

Check the SQL file:

```
create tablespace "users" datafile

'c:\tmp\users01.dbf' SIZE 5242880
```

As can be seen, Data Pump automatically changed the datafile name for the specified file.

Using *remap_table* to Rename Table Names

One of the Oracle 11g new features is the new parameter *remap_table* which is used to rename the table during the import job. The syntax of this parameter is as follows:

```
remap_table=schema.table_name:new_table
```

Using *remap_schema* Parameter to Import Objects to Different Schema

Many times it is required to move a schema from one database to another. Most likely, this happens when there is a schema developed in a test box with all the required objects that need to be imported into the production environment. Also, sometimes objects within the same database need to be moved from one schema to another. At times like this, the option comes in really handy. The following example shows how to move a schema from 10r2 to 11r2.

 Please note that whenever an export and import are being done in two different versions, the binary of the export used should be from the lower version. Many times, this is a common mistake which is done and the export does not work.

The export of the schema can be done in the first sitting in 10g using 10g's *expdp* executable.

```
expdp test/test directory=dp dumpfile=exp10.dmp
```

The next task is to import it into 11g using the *remap_schema* option. Before doing so, create a user in the 11g release. Now see everything in action:

```
SQL>
create
 user test_expdp
identified by
 test;

User created.

SQL>
grant
 dba
to
 test_expdp;

Grant succeeded.

impdp system/oracle directory=dp dumpfile=exp10.dmp
remap_schema=test:test_expdp
```

```
<....output trimmed ....>
<....output trimmed ....>
job "system"."sys_import_full_01" completed with 1 error(s) at 15:45:17
```

This shows that even though the command was completed successfully, there
is still one error reported: that the target schema is already there. In 11.2, this
is an option given where when the target schema mentioned is not available at
the time of the import, it is created by Oracle automatically. If the same is
done in the previous versions, this throws an error and explicit creation of the
schema is required. So now, try the same with a completely new user which is
not yet available.

```
impdp system/oracle directory=dp dumpfile=exp10.dmp
remap_schema=test:test_expdp1

import: release 11.2.0.1.0 - production on fri may 28 15:47:34 2010
<....output trimmed ....>
<....output trimmed ....>
job "system"."sys_import_full_01" successfully completed at 15:47:48
```
This reveals that the job was completed successfully without any error this
time.

Using *remap_tablespace* to Import Objects to a Different Tablespace

Being a DBA, there are plenty of times when the objects have to be moved
around the tablespaces to get them reorganized. This can be done in many
ways; for example, using the *alter table move* command or the *dbms_redefinition*
package. One of the easy ways to do so is to the use the *remap_tablespace* switch.
As the name suggests, this option moves the object from the source tablespace
to the target tablespace. To see this in action, make a table and explicitly create
some fragmentation in it.

```
test@orcl112> create table t as select * from dba_objects;

table created.

test@orcl112> exec dbms_stats.gather_table_stats(user, 't');

PL/SQL procedure successfully completed.

test@orcl112> select sum(bytes) , sum(blocks) from dba_extents where
segment_name='t';

SUM(BYTES) SUM(BLOCKS)
---------- -----------
   9568256        1168
1 row selected.
```

```
test@orcl112> delete t;

72615 rows deleted.

test@orcl112> commit;

commit complete.

test@orcl112> exec dbms_stats.gather_table_stats(user, 't');

PL/SQL procedure successfully completed.

test@orcl112> select sum(bytes) , sum(blocks) from dba_extents where
segment_name='t';

SUM(BYTES) SUM(BLOCKS)
---------- -----------
   9568256        1168
1 row selected.
```

So this shows that even after the complete delete, the table does not release
the used space and it is reported again.

Check which tablespace the object belongs at the moment.

```
test@orcl112> select table_name, tablespace_name from dba_tables where
table_name='t' and owner='test';

TABLE_NAME                    TABLESPACE_NAME
----------------------------  ------------------------------
T                             USERS
1 row selected.
```

This shows that it is the users tablespace at the moment. Though not good but
for the sake of this demonstration, move the table to the system tablespace
using Data Pump. Export the table first:

```
E:\>expdp test/test directory=dp dumpfile=exptab.dmp tables=T
```

Now use the *import* command and the *remap_tablespace* switch to move the
object into a different tablespace. Also, since the table is already there in the
schema, the switch *table_exists_action* must be used with its value *replace*. Check
it out in action:

```
E:\>impdp test/test directory=dp dumpfile=exptab.dmp
table_exists_action=replace  remap_tablespace=users:system
```

Check the tablespace of the object to see whether it has changed or not:

```
SQL>
```

```
select
 tablespace_name, table_name
from
 dba_tables
where
 table_name='t' and owner='test';

TABLESPACE_NAME                TABLE_NAME
----------------------------   ----------------------------
SYSTEM                         T
```

Using *table_exists_action* Parameter

When importing a table, Data Pump skips the job if the object already exists in the imported schema. However, by using the *table_exists_action* parameter with its available values, it is possible to bypass skipping the table import. This parameter accepts the following values:

- *skip*: Is the default value and used to skip importing the table if it already exists

- *append*: Appends the data to an already existing table

- *truncate*: Truncates the already existing table and imports fresh data

- *replace*: Drops already an existing table and creates a new one with fresh data

The next example demonstrates the usage of the above values. For this, create a table with one row:

```
SQL>
create
 table tbl_test (id number);

Table created.

SQL>
insert into
 tbl_test values(1);

1 row created.

SQL>
commit;

Commit complete.
SQL>
```

Now export the table:

```
expdp usr1/usr1 directory=dp_dir dumpfile=test.dmp tables=tbl_test
```

Using the *skip* value:

skip is the default value and it will just abort the process by saying that the table already exists.

```
impdp usr1/usr1 directory=dp_dir dumpfile=test.dmp table_exists_action=skip

ora-39151: table "usr1"."tbl_test" exists. All dependent metadata and data
will be skipped due to table_exists_action of skip
```

Using the *append* value:

```
C:\>impdp usr1/usr1 directory=dp_dir dumpfile=test.dmp
table_exists_action=append

ORA-39152: Table "usr1"."tbl_test" exists. Data will be appended to existing
table but all dependent metadata will be skipped due to table_exists_action
of append
```

Now check the table. Since import used the *append* value for the *table_exists_action* parameter, there should be two rows:

```
SQL>
select * from
 tbl_test;

       ID
----------
        1
        1
```
Using *truncate* and *replace* values:

Both values give the same result; however, the first just truncates the table, where the second value drops and recreates it. It is shown here in one example:

```
C:\>impdp usr1/usr1 directory=dp_dir dumpfile=test.dmp
table_exists_action=truncate

ora-39153: table "usr1"."tbl_test" exists and has been truncated. Data will
be loaded but all dependent metadata will be skipped due to
table_exists_action of truncate

C:\>impdp usr1/usr1 directory=dp_dir dumpfile=test.dmp
table_exists_action=replace
```

The *replace* value will not give an informative message and just drops and recreates the table with new values.

Using the *sqlfile* Parameter to Get the Content of the Dump File

Many times there is a need to get the DDL (Data Definition Language) of the objects in the schema. This is the required thing to do before creating the object in some other schema or database, and there are some modifications which are needed in the definition. In the traditional import, this was done through the help of the *indexfile* option which did not do the actual import of the dump file and lets the DBA have a peek at it.

Data Pump does this in a more elegant way with the *sqlfile* switch. With the *sqlfile*, there is a text file created which has the complete DDL of the schema objects. This can be run right away or can be modified as per the requirement. It is worth mentioning that the *sqlfile* option will not do an actual import of the object and just results in a text file.

```
impdp scott/tiger directory=data pump_test dumpfile=scott.dmp
sqlfile=scottsql.sql

<....output trimmed ....>
<....output trimmed ....>
Starting "SCOTT"."SYS_SQL_FILE_TABLE_01":  scott/******** directory=dptest
tables=scott.emp dumpfile=new.dmp encryption_password=***
***** sqlfile= scottsql.sql
Processing object type TABLE_EXPORT/TABLE/TABLE
<....output trimmed ....>
<....output trimmed ....>
```

The job name clearly states what mode the import ran in and this time, it is a sqlfile mode with the name *test.sql*. Open the file and see its contents.

```
-- new object type path: table_export/table/table
create table "scott"."emp"
   (    "empno" number(4,0),
        "ename" varchar2(10 byte),
        "job" varchar2(9 byte),
        "mgr" number(4,0),
        "hiredate" date,
        "sal" number(7,2),
        "comm" number(7,2),
        "deptno" number(2,0)
   ) segment creation immediate
  pctfree 10 pctused 40 initrans 1 maxtrans 255 nocompress logging
  storage(initial 65536 next 1048576 minextents 1 maxextents 2147483645
  pctincrease 0 freelists 1 freelist groups 1 buffer_pool default
flash_cache default cell_flash_cache default)
  tablespace "users";
```

The output is trimmed to fit here but the relevant section is completely displayed. The complete DDL of the object EMP is shown including its storage and segment properties. This can now be modified by a DBA and he can pass the resulting, modified SQL to the end user or developer for his use. But wait a minute, if this SQL command is passed as it is to the end user, will this not be really scary for the end user when he notices some really big keywords like *pctincrease* and such? For this, using the *transform* switch of *impdp* is required which can create extra things to do.

It comes with the options to remove either the storage attributes or segment attributes from the SQL file. An option's values cannot be changed using this, but the option can be made to be present or not in the file. For example, if segment attributes are not wanted, they can be removed like this:

```
>impdp test/test directory=dptest tables=scott.emp dumpfile=new.dmp
encryption_password=foo sqlfile=test.sql transform=storage:n
```

This is how the DDL of the *emp* table looks like now:

```
create table "scott"."emp"
    (    "empno" number(4,0),
         "ename" varchar2(10 byte),
         "job" varchar2(9 byte),
         "mgr" number(4,0),
         "hiredate" date,
         "sal" number(7,2),
         "comm" number(7,2),
         "deptno" number(2,0)
    ) segment creation immediate
  pctfree 10 pctused 40 initrans 1 maxtrans 255 nocompress logging
  tablespace "users";
```

It is evident that all the storage level attributes are gone from the DDL. There are still segment level attributes which are shown and can be removed using the *segment_attribute=n* option.

Network Mode Import

Data Pump offers a target-only import mode which frees the DBA from the hassle of creating first the dumpfile and then importing it to the target database. This mode does not need anything to be done on the source database except to link to it via a target through a database link.

Here is a demonstration of that:

```
impdp scott/tiger directory=data pump1 tables=test_nw
logfile=network_imp.log network_link=testing_to_testing2
```

So a network database link is being used here to import a table in the database. Long columns or evolved columns are not supported by network mode.

If errors are expected to come in the import with the data being incorrect and not adhering to the constraints, apply the *data_options* switch of the import. This has the options of *disable_append_hint* and *skip_constraint_errors*. Where using the *disable_append_hint* is not a good choice if a huge chunk of the data is being loaded, the *skip_constraint_errors* only works for those constraints which are non-deferrable.

Using *dbms_data pump* Package to Move Data

All operations made by Data Pump tools (*expdp* and *impdp*) are able to be performed by the *dbms_data pump* package inside any PL/SQL procedure. This is the powerful advantage of Data Pump over the old export/import utilities. This package provides some base functions to perform data transformation using PL/SQL codes. Here is the list of the main functions that will be used and demonstrated in this chapter:

- *open* is used to declare a new job which returns a handle that is used in all procedures and functions.
- *add_file* is used to add files to the dumpfile set for an export or import job.
- *metadata_filter* is used to perform an item filtering during the job.
- *data_filter* is used to perform adding restrictions to the rows.
- *set_parallel* is used to define the parallelism mode of the job.
- *start_job* is used to begin or resume the execution of the job.
- *detach* is used to deallocate the handle that was opened by the *open* function.
- *get_dumpfile_info* is used to get information about the provided dump file.
- *set_parameter* is used to set some optional parameters.

Use some of these parameters to export a table using PL/SQL code. Look at the following code and the description of each command:

```
declare
#Declare a handle with number type
    v_handle number;

begin
```

```
#Use open function to declare a new job and return a handle which will be
used as a parameter in other dbms_data pump functions
v_handle := dbms_data pump.open (operation => 'export',job_mode  =>
'table');

#use add_file procedure to specify the type of the file (dumpfile), the file
name with substitution variable, the size of the file and the name of the
directory object

    dbms_data pump.add_file (handle => v_handle,
          filename => 'exp_test_%u.dmp',
          directory => 'dp_dir',
          filesize=>'500k',
          filetype => dbms_data pump.ku$_file_type_dump_file);

#the same procedure is used to specify the logfile name
    dbms_data pump.add_file (handle => v_handle,
          filename => 'exp_test.loh',
          directory => 'dp_dir',
          filetype => dbms_data pump.ku$_file_type_log_file);
#use metadata_filter procedure to specify the name of tables that we want to
export
    dbms_data pump.metadata_filter (handle => v_handle, name =>
'name_expr',value => 'in (''tbl_test'')');

#Use data_filter procedure to specify restriction on the rows. in this
situation data pump exports the rows of the table tbl_test that id column
equals to 1

    dbms_data pump.data_filter (handle => v_handle,
          name => 'subquery',
          value => 'where id=1',
          table_name => 'tbl_test',
          schema_name => 'usr1');

#use set_parallel procedure to specify degree of parallelism
    dbms_data pump.set_parallel(handle => v_handle, degree => 2);

#use set_parameter procedure to export the values that were consistent with
the given scn
    dbms_data pump.set_parameter(v_handle,'flashback_scn',1256742);

#use start_job procedure with handle parameter to start the job
    dbms_data pump.start_job (handle => v_handle);

#use detach procedure to free the resource which is associated with the job
    dbms_data pump.detach (handle => v_handle);
end;
/
```

Interactive Command Line Mode of Data Pump

To make some changes to the currently running Data Pump job, the
interactive command line mode is used. Here is a list of the commonly used
parameters and their explanations:

- *add_file* is used to add a new additional dumpfile to the currently running job.

- *continue_client* is used to exit the interactive mode and return back to the logging mode.

- *exit_client* is used to leave the running job; however, the job could be attached later. If the export session needs to be exited by leaving the job running, use this command.

- *filesize* is used to redefine the file size of the subsequently generated dumpfiles. If a new file size is set for the dump files, all subsequent dumpfiles will be generated according to the new value.

- *kill_job* is used to kill the currently running job and returns to the terminal prompt.

- *parallel* is used to change the parallelism (increase or decrease the degree) of the running job.

- *start_job* is used to restart the current job.

- *status* is used to view the status of the currently running job.

- *stop_job* is used to stop the running job.

Using *add_file* and *continue_client* Commands

Imagine that a dumpfile is exported with more than 220 MB size using the *filesize=100m* parameter. Suddenly, this is realized and the decision is made to add two more dumpfiles to the currently running export job. For this, click on Ctrl+C and enter to the interactive command mode. By using the *add_file* command, the dumpfiles are added and the *continue_client* command is used to get back to the job execution output. Look at the following demo:

```
C:\>expdp usr2/usr2 dumpfile=dp_dir:test.dmp logfile=dp_dir:test.log
tables='tbl_test' filesize=100m;

starting "usr2"."sys_export_table_02":  usr2/********
dumpfile=dp_dir:test.dmp logfile=dp_dir:test.log tables='tbl_test'
filesize=100m;

estimate in progress using blocks method...
processing object type table_export/table/table_data

#Press ctrl+c to enter to the interactive command mode
#Use add_file command to add two more dump files
export> add_file=dp_dir:test02.dmp, dp_dir:test03.dmp
```

Using dbms_data pump Package to Move Data

```
#Use continue_client command to go back to the logging mode
export> continue_client

total estimation using blocks method: 256 mb
processing object type table_export/table/table
. . exported "usr2"."tbl_test"                          218.3 mb 2188192
rows
master table "usr2"."sys_export_table_02" successfully loaded/unloaded
***********************************************************************
**
dump file set for usr2.sys_export_table_02 is:
  c:\test.dmp
  C:\test02.dmp
  C:\test03.dmp
Job "usr2"."sys_export_table_02" successfully completed at 14:56:58
```

Now list the files with .DMP extensions:

```
C:\>dir

06/23/2010  02:56 PM     104,857,600 test.DMP
06/23/2010  02:56 PM     104,857,600 test02.DMP
06/23/2010  02:56 PM      19,357,696 test03.DMP
```

Attaching to a Job

Oracle Data Pump allows a job to be suspended and then re-attached. Data Pump does not offer the traditional interactive interface to work with it but still it has the interactive, administrative interface which allows a DBA to work with Data Pump. One such option is *attach*. Now see it in action:

```
E:\dp>expdp test/test directory=dp dumpfile=schema.dmp

<....output trimmed ....>
<....output trimmed ....>
Processing object type schema_export/user
Processing object type schema_export/system_grant
Processing object type schema_export/role_grant
Processing object type schema_export/default_role

Export> stop_job

Are we sure we wish to stop this job ([yes]/no): y
```

The result is that the job has been explicitly suspended. Check the job status by reattaching to the same job by the job name given. In this case, it is *sys_export_schema_01*.

```
E:\dp>expdp test/test ATTACH=sys_export_schema_01

Job: sys_export_schema_01
  Owner: test
  Operation: export
```

```
Creator Privs: true
GUID: 2FD2638035DF4552B02E4C41E68DFD6D
Start Time: Saturday, 29 May, 2010 12:35:53
Mode: schema
Instance: orcl112
Max Parallelism: 1
EXPORT Job Parameters:
Parameter Name      Parameter Value:
 Client_command        test/******** directory=dp dumpfile=schema.dmp
State: IDLING
Bytes Processed: 0
Current Parallelism: 1
Job Error Count: 0
Dump File: e:\dp\schema.dmp
  bytes written: 24,576

Worker 1 Status:
  Process Name: DW00
  State: UNDEFINED

Export>
```

So the job is in the idle stage. Now it can be restarted.

```
Export> start_job

Export> status

Job: sys_export_schema_01
  Operation: export
  Mode: schema
  State: executing
  Bytes Processed: 0
  Current Parallelism: 1
  Job Error Count: 0
  Dump File: e:\dp\schema.dmp
    bytes written: 28,672

Worker 1 Status:
  Process Name: dw00
  State: executing
```

The job is now in the state of *executing*. Once done, this job will not be available to be used anymore.

Following are the views to find the details about Data Pump jobs.

VIEWS	DESCRIPTION
user_data pump_jobs	Data Pump jobs for current user
dba_data pump_jobs	Data Pump jobs
dba_data pump_sessions	Data Pump sessions attached to a job
v$data pump_job	Synonym for v_$data pump_job
v$data pump_session	Synonym for v_$data pump_session

Table 12.1: *Detailed Data Pump Job Views*

Using the *v$session_longops* dynamic performance view, the progress of executing jobs of Data Pump can be monitored.

Getting the Best Out of the Data Pump

Data Pump is optimized by Oracle and performs much better than the traditional export. Still, there are some points which, if remembered, can help in getting the best performance out of Data Pump.

Since Data Pump is a complete server side utility, while it runs it puts a huge impact on the server where it is running. This includes the creation of all the additions processes and the I/O calls needed for both export and import. If the machine on which Data Pump is running already has a hardware resource crunch, this would surely slow down the Data Pump operations as well.

Though Data Pump comes with the option of parallelism, this is not very helpful if there are not enough resources on the system to spawn additional resources. Also, care should be taken when the *parallel* option is used since it is most beneficial where there is more than one CPU on the box. Even on multiple CPUs, care should be taken as to how many slaves are going to be spawned. Ideally, this should not be more than two per CPU.

Also, using compression and encryption while running Data Pump severely impacts its performance with the additional CPU requirements. Any sort of block corruption checks should not be done while using Data Pump since although this would ensure the block's consistency, it also slows down the underlying Data Pump job.

Other than this, because the Data Pump frequently uses the Streams Pool, the *streams_pool_size* value should be set generously. Even better would be to leave it on the ASMM or AMM and let Oracle decide what is best suited for it. Also, Streams Pool memory comes from the data buffer cache, which means there is less memory allocated to the buffer cache from what has been specified originally and therefore, leads to errors when Data Pump is run. So it is better to set a properly sized buffer cache and not just to its minimum size when the plan is to use Data Pump.

Main Differences Between Data Pump and Original Export/Import Tools

Oracle strongly recommends using Data Pump export/import utilities instead of the original export/import tools. The following list describes the main differences between Data Pump and original exp/imp tools.

- Data Pump utilities are self-tuning. There are additional parameters in original export/import to tune the job (*recordlength*, *buffer*)

- While importing the data to the existing table with Data Pump, the job is terminated if any row violates an active constraint. The original export tool logs the violated row and continues loading the rest of data.

- Data Pump import automatically compresses the data if the main table is compressed. The original import tool does not compress the data upon import.

- Data Pump tools use parallel execution instead of single stream of execution.

- Data Pump tools access files on the server, thus improving the performance of the job.

- Data Pump supports character set conversion.

- Using interactive mode in Data Pump, the job can be stopped, started and killed and parameters changed while the job is running. Data Pump jobs can be restarted without loss of data.

- Using Data Pump, job time can be estimated without loading or unloading the data.

- New remapping parameters that were added to the Data Pump import makes it more powerful against the original import.

Conclusion

This chapter covered the many ways to move objects from one place to another using the Data Pump utility. The components in Data Pump were introduced along with its import and export utilities and how they are much better than the traditional import/export utilities. Data Pump's dumpfile was also examined in detail.

Book Conclusion

Oracle Backup and Recovery, Expert Secrets for Using RMAN and Data Pump is a book which is written keeping in mind the fact that a DBA must be well equipped to know about two of the most critical pieces of Oracle database administration, Backup and Recovery. Both of these go hand in hand. As important as it is to know the various techniques to recover from critical errors, it is equally important to know that it is inevitable without having a proper backup.

This book comes with tons of practical tips and how-tos which would empower anyone to learn these things very well in both conceptual and practical terms. We have tried to put as many practical demonstrations as possible along with detailed explanations to make it easier for DBAs to learn and replay on their own machines because there is nothing better than seeing things happening right before their eyes. Much care is taken in making sure that all that is needed to know that is practically usable in day-to-day DBA life is covered.

The secret to being a DBA who masters in recovery and backup techniques has much to do with a lot of practice and also knowing what is going on behind that command which has just been fired to recover from a crash.

Though practice is something which a DBA should be seeking, the other part is to know what to look for; therefore, we have written this book in hopes that it acts as a complete reference guide dealing with such situations.

Kamran Agayev Agamehdi & Aman Sharma

Index

Index

About the Authors

Kamran Agayev Agamehdi

 ***Kamran Agayev Agamehdi*** is an Oracle ACE and an Oracle Certified Professional DBA with many years of experience managing complex UNIX-based Oracle Databases. As a working IT professional, Kamran has experience in a wide range of mission critical technologies, specializing in database administration best practices for backup and recovery.

Kamran has hands-on experience with real-world Production environments and he has risen in the ranks from a developer to a managing DBA. Kamran possesses the rare combination of technical and managerial skills and his outstanding communication skills enhance his duties as liaison between functional business management and the technical DBA and SA professionals.

Currently Kamran is pursuing a PhD in Computer Science at the Azerbaijan Oil Academy and he serves as an adjunct professor teaching Oracle Database Administration in a Qafqaz University. Kamran also publishes a popular blog at http://kamranagayev.wordpress.com.

Oracle ACE

Aman Sharma

Aman Sharma is an Oracle database specialist, an Oracle Certified Professional (9i,10g,11g), an Oracle Certified Expert for Linux and SQL and an Oracle ACE. He is a Sun Certified System Admin with over six years of experience.

Mr. Sharma works as an instructor training professionals around Asia Pacific in Oracle related technologies. Prior to his work as an instructor, he worked as a DBA for a large software development company.

In his spare time, when he is not teaching or not traveling, he likes to spend his free time in various Oracle forums over the web. Mr. Sharma also writes about Oracle database over his blog at http://blog.aristadba.com.

Oracle ACE

www.ingramcontent.com/pod-product-compliance
Lightning Source LLC
Chambersburg PA
CBHW081449050326

40690CB00015B/2735